WHERE TO RETIRE America's Best and Most Affordable Places

JOHN HOWELLS
FIFTH EDITION

The Globe Pequot Press

GUILFORD, CONNECTICUT

Text design: Kevin Lynch

ISBN: 0-7627-2202-9
ISSN 1543-4095

Manufactured in the United States of America
Fifth Edition/First Printing

Table of Contents

Help Us Keep This Guide Up to Date

Every effort has been made by the author and editors to make this guide as accurate and useful as possible. However, many things can change after a guide is published—establishments close, phone numbers change, facilities come under new management, etc.

We would love to hear from you concerning your experiences with this guide and how you feel it could be made better and be kept up to date. While we may not be able to respond to all comments and suggestions, we'll take them to heart and we'll also make certain to share them with the author. Please send your comments and suggestions to the following address:

The Globe Pequot Press
Reader Response/Editorial Department
P.O. Box 480
Guilford, CT 06437

Or you may e-mail us at:

editorial@GlobePequot.com

Thanks for your input, and happy travels!

Introduction

AS THE TITLE SUGGESTS, this book focuses more on *where* to retire than *how* to retire. It's designed for those who are approaching retirement with a vague notion that they should move away from their hometowns after they retire but aren't sure where.

Further, we hope to help you decide what could be an equally important question: Why should I move after retirement? Maybe you shouldn't. Many people assume that relocating is an obligatory part of retirement. Actually, most *don't* move away when they retire. For some moving to a new town or a different state and starting over just doesn't make sense. But for others finding a new home can be exciting and can contribute to a longer, happier life. Those living in places where recreational and cultural opportunities abound, the weather is nice, and they have many friends see no reason to move from their neighborhoods when they retire.

People who live in large cities are more likely to relocate than those who live in small towns. Depending on the state, as many as 25 percent of those leaving the workforce will move to another town, and between 1 and 10 percent will move to another state. This book is for that 1 to 10 percent who want to make a major change.

The *why* of moving to a new town or state when you retire requires a good deal of self-examination. You need to evaluate your goals, motives, and present lifestyle to be sure just where you need to relocate. People often think of retirement as a "permanent vacation." Nothing wrong with that. But before you pack up the proverbial lock, stock, and barrel to move to that beach town or mountain village where you've enjoyed spending your regular two-week vacations, ask yourself these questions: Will I be happy living there year-round? Will I become bored with trout fishing after a couple of months? Will I enjoy the beach during the winter, when my summer-resident friends have left, the shops and restaurants are closed, and northern winds sweep in from a cold ocean?

After taking everything into consideration, you may find moving away is your best option. If you are like many people, your closest friends are those you work with. When you retire you'll be leaving your friends at the office; you won't be part of the "gang" any more. You'll have to make new friends anyway, so why not try it in a more agreeable environment? Have your children grown up and moved away? If so, you have even less reason to stick around.

One of the few things my wife and I completely agree on is that you can't find an ideal retirement place by studying statistics. A computer can't swallow a bunch of numbers and then spit out the "ideal" place for you to spend the rest of your lives! It isn't that simple. You must look beyond statistics. You must see your new home through your own eyes.

Even if statistics are interpreted rationally and accurately, there remains the common fallacy that there is a "best" place for retirement. What is ideal for you could be excruciatingly boring for me. What I might consider a wonderful climate could be far too warm for you. The choice of a retirement location is as personal as the choice of an automobile or a vacation resort. Just as there is no one best car or ideal vacation, there is no perfect retirement spot. You'll need to give this decision a lot of thought.

Research Methods

Because we feel that statistics tell only part of the story, my wife and I personally visit each community before evaluating it as a place for retirement. Of course it would be impossible for one couple to visit all potential retirement locations in the United States. Instead we travel to regions of the country where retirement is practical—places where people tend to retire—then we describe a few towns and communities typical of that region. Our research has been ongoing for almost twenty years. We visit neighborhoods, residential developments, and senior citizens' centers and look at shopping, entertainment, and medical care. We interview chambers of commerce, talk with managers and residents of retirement complexes, and chat with retired couples and singles.

In each location we visit at least one real estate office and interview salespeople. It turns out that many are retirees. They enjoy the sociability of their jobs, the chance to meet new people, and, of course, the opportunity to pick up a few commissions. They're especially helpful because they understand the problems involved in moving away for retirement.

We learn which neighborhoods retirees prefer, and we visit to see for ourselves. Sometimes we pose as buyers or renters looking for retirement property. This helps when looking at large retirement complexes, where potential customers tour in groups, because we find opportunities to talk with prospective buyers to find out what brings them to that particular place for retirement.

We use U.S. government publications, drawing statistics from the Bureau of the Census, Department of Labor, and National Oceanographic Administration weather charts. The FBI's crime statistics are carefully tabulated, and consultations are made with noted sociologists and police officials. The Consumer Price Index and the American Chamber of Commerce Research Association supply us with trends.

Over the years we've investigated hundreds of retirement areas and examined many different lifestyles before making the final selections for this book. However, because a town is *not* described here doesn't necessarily mean it wouldn't be a great place to retire.

CHAPTER 1

Finding Your Shangri-La

MAGAZINE ARTICLES AND GUIDEBOOKS commonly grade retirement communities, ranking the top places from one to ten, as if they were rating major league baseball teams. With a baseball team we can check the scores; can't argue with that. But cities and towns don't receive scores except in somebody's mind. The fact that a freelance writer likes a city and ranks it number one in his magazine article doesn't prove a thing. The writer's next article had better rank *another* city as number one, or the editor won't buy the article.

Favorable ratings are often awarded on the basis of conditions that don't affect retirees. For example, good schools, high employment, and a booming business climate will boost a town's popularity rating, whereas horrible weather and high taxes are often ignored. Quality grammar schools and juvenile recreational programs matter less to retirees than quality restaurants, continuing education programs, and safe neighborhoods. Full employment and thriving business conditions often spell high prices and expensive housing. Cultural amenities, such as museums and operas, receive high marks in retirement analysis. Yet how many times a month will you be going to the opera? Would you rather live in a town with ten golf courses and no museums, or ten museums and *no* golf courses? To find your ideal location, you're going to have to do your own ranking.

Ideally you'll start your retirement analysis early. A great way to do this is by combining research with your vacations. Instead of visiting the same old place each year, try different parts of the country. Check out each location as a possible place to live. Look at real estate, medical care, and recreation. What about libraries? (An appalling number are closing because of lack of funds.) Does this town offer the types of cultural events you enjoy? Cultural events can be anything from concerts and stage plays to square-dance lessons and quilting bees to bowling tournaments and chili cookoffs. The point is, will you be happy there?

The local chamber of commerce office can be an excellent source of information. Make sure to ask if the community has a "retiree attraction committee" or "retiree welcoming committee." This growing concept of welcoming retirees into a community is usually coordinated by the chamber of commerce. A welcoming committee can be a marvelous way to make new friends and to adjust to your new surroundings.

If you can't or don't care to travel, you can do research at your local library. Many libraries subscribe to a variety of out-of-town newspapers. You'll learn much about a community by the news. If drunk-driving arrests are top news stories, you have one picture of crime. If murders and mutilations are so common that they are reported on page twenty-seven, you get another picture.

Check real estate prices, rentals, and mobile home parks; compare them with your hometown newspaper and you'll begin to get a picture of relative costs. Contrast help-wanted ads with work-wanted ads. This tells you wage rates, should you consider working part-time, and clues you in on what kind of competition you will have for jobs. Even if you don't plan on working, you might be interested in local wages, so you'll know what you'll have to pay for help around your new home.

The Internet is an enormously valuable research tool. If you don't have Internet access at home, chances are your library will have computers at your service. Not only can you read local newspapers on-line, but you can access real estate pages and compare houses for sale. The town's chamber of commerce information Web site (they all have 'em) brings you up to date on what kinds of cultural events are going on in your new hometown. Most cities display "welcome" web pages that provide valuable information about the region, complete with pictures of the community, descriptions of neighborhoods, and recreational activities available. If you don't know how, ask your grandkids to show you how to browse the Internet. You'll love it!

What to Look For

Following is a list of requirements my wife and I personally consider essential for a successful retirement relocation. Your needs may be different; feel free to add or subtract from the list, and then use the list to measure communities against your standards.

1. Safety.   Can you walk through your neighborhood without fearful glances over your shoulder? Can you leave your home for a few weeks without dreading a break-in?

2. Climate.   Will temperatures and weather patterns match your lifestyle? Will you be tempted to go outdoors and exercise year-round, or will harsh winters and suffocating summers confine you to an easy chair in front of the television set?

3. Housing.   Is quality housing available at a price you're willing and able to pay? Is the area visually pleasing, free of pollution and traffic snarls? Will you feel proud to live in the neighborhood?

4. Nourishment for your interests.   Does your retirement choice offer facilities for your favorite pastimes, cultural events, and hobbies, be they hunting, fishing, adult education, art centers, or whatever?

5. Social compatibility.   Will you find common interests with your neighbors? Will you fit in and make friends easily? Will there be folks with your own cultural, social, and political background?

6. Affordability.   Are goods and services reasonably priced? Will you be able to afford to hire help from time to time when you need to? Will your income be high enough to be significantly affected by state income taxes? Will taxes on your pension make a big difference?

7. Medical care.   Are local physicians accepting new patients? Does the area have an adequate hospital? (You needn't live next door to the Mayo Clinic; you can always go there if your hospital can't handle your problem.) Do you have a medical problem that requires a specialist?

Most doctors accept at least a limited number of Medicare patients, but others refuse to deal with Medicare. Also some HMOs don't offer coverage in unprofitable communities (more often in low-density populations), and some HMOs have been known to discontinue their health-care programs without notice. If you'll be depending on Medicare, it pays to check out the situation before moving.

8. Distance from family and friends.   Are you going to be too far away or in a location where nobody wants to visit? Would you rather they *don't* visit? (In that case you'd do better even farther away.)

9. Transportation.   Does your new location enjoy intercity bus transportation? Many small towns have none, which makes you totally dependent on an automobile or taxis. How far is the nearest airport with airline connections? Can friends and family visit without driving?

10. Jobs and/or volunteer opportunities.   Will there be enough interesting volunteer jobs or paid jobs (if that's what you want) to satisfy your need for keeping busy? What about continuing education programs at the local college?

Adult Retirement Communities

Year by year retirement becomes more of a big business, prompting impressive corporate investment. Planned retirement communities, often of astounding size, are popping up all over the country. These complexes are usually centered on a lake, golf course, or some natural attraction. Often these are "gated" communities; that is, to enter the property you must be a member of that development or have good reason to be there. Wanting to price property is usually a good enough reason to visit, although a few developments permit you to purchase only by invitation of other residents. Round-the-clock guards often staff the gates, scrutinizing everyone who enters.

Occasionally private developments are "open" communities—without gates—yet are still age restricted. Some are enormous. Arizona's Sun City West, for example, has more than 15,000 homes on 7,100 acres. (At this point in time, these units are almost all sold and a new development, Sun City Grand, is under way.)

Many complexes restrict buyers to those age fifty-five and older. Youngsters may visit but may not live there. This affects the community in two ways. Obviously your lives will be more tranquil, without gangs of kids riding bikes, playing boom boxes, and knocking baseballs through your living room window. But more important than that, you'll enjoy a lower crime rate. Burglaries, vandalism, and theft usually occur in direct proportion to the number of teenagers in the neighborhood. The other side of the coin is that many retirees prefer living in mixed-age neighborhoods; they find young children and teenagers fun to be with.

Home buyers seem to be split into two groups when it comes to age restrictions. On the one hand we often hear, "I can't imagine a more dreary and stifling situation—living in a same-age community! We prefer to socialize with a mixed-age group, with young people as well as those our own age and older." However, you might find that mixed-generation communities tend to segregate into age groups anyway. When you want to play golf or go fishing, your younger neighbors have to go to work. When you have a barbecue and a few drinks in the backyard, they have a Cub Scout meeting scheduled. Instead of joining you for a concert or a play, your neighbors have to attend a PTA meeting or would rather relax in front of the television after a hard day's work.

The bottom line is that age-restricted developments are selling a lifestyle as much as real estate. With organized activities and social groups ready to welcome new residents, transition to retirement is made painless and swift.

Moving to the Country

You might picture living in a rural or backwoods community as being the ultimate in get-away-from-it-all living. It's nice to enjoy an incredibly low cost of living with housing at giveaway prices. I have mixed feelings about recommending retirement in some inexpensive areas—particularly rural, farming communities—to folks from big-city backgrounds.

When you share few common interests with your neighbors, it's easy to feel left out. When almost everyone in the community is in some way involved in agriculture, ordinary conversations tend to dwell on the price of soybeans or the best way to deworm hogs. When your agricultural experience is limited to watering houseplants, you find you have few words of wisdom others care to hear. When your accent sounds funny to your neighbors, when your tastes in movies, politics, and food are different (or when you don't even own a pickup!), you could feel like an alien.

Happily situations like this are changing as more and more retirees from all over the nation are moving into small-town U.S.A. Nonetheless it behooves you to look beyond the cost-of-living charts and real estate averages.

College Town Retirement

For more than fifteen years my wife and I have been researching cities, towns, and villages across the nation, evaluating communities as possible retirement destinations. We enjoy our work immensely. From time to time a magazine editor requests a freelance article on the "top twenty U.S. retirement towns" or something like that. Even though we resist the idea that there are "twenty best" towns out there, I must fulfill the request if I want to sell the article. So my wife and I sit down and compile a list of our favorites, emphasizing that these are simply *our personal* choices, not necessarily the best for *everybody.*

Gradually we began to notice something curious. Almost all our favorite towns happened to have a college or university as one of its features. At first we assumed this to be a coincidence. After all, we liked each of these towns for its own personality and individual characteristics, conditions that scarcely seem connected with the presence or absence of a school.

Then, when analyzing *why* we prefer some places over others, we realized that a desirable feature of a preferred community is a lively downtown business center. We like to see an old-fashioned town square or small park surrounded by small shops and boutiques, as well as some good restaurants with reasonable prices. Often there'll be a bookstore that offers entertainment or readings by authors, perhaps a movie theater, and, of course, neighborly people—in short a user-friendly town center.

But none of the above has anything to do with college or university. Or does it? Suddenly it dawned on us: Even though an attractive town center adds to a community's desirability, it's the presence of the college that creates this ambience! A classic chicken-or-egg quandary.

Look at it this way: Throughout the nation the business districts of many small cities and hometowns have been abandoned.

What's left are shabby civic centers filled with neglected buildings and boarded-up storefronts—nothing left but a few lonely second-hand stores. The streets are all but deserted. This came about with the advent of strip malls. Merchants and businesses fled downtown in a mass migration as they moved—lock, stock, and pizza parlor—to the outskirts of town, out on the Highway 161 bypass. Each strip mall is a mirror image of the last one: Wal-Mart, Home Depot, Burger King—the whole enchilada—sitting there in a predictable lineup, serving the town's consumers as the new business district. See one, you've seen 'em all.

For some very logical reasons, this doesn't usually happen to a college town. Students are not overly fond of hanging out at strip malls. They patronize local restaurants, nearby shopping, and entertainment, preferably within walking or biking distance of the dorms and campus. Therefore, with thousands of affluent students, faculty, and college support staff as customers—all with money in their pockets—you can bet that some merchants will stay put and enjoy this business. New enterprises move into the empty stores, thus keeping downtown alive. Because the old business center is still the focus of the community, local residents use it as an alternate place for shopping and entertainment. In this way the college keeps a town's historical central district from oblivion.

Strolling around a college town's square is like stepping back in time forty years. People smile at you as you pass, stores are open and welcoming your business, and you'll even find an old-fashioned movie theater—the Bijou or Rex—single screen, with the smell of buttered popcorn just as things were when we were kids. Remember? Maybe it's foreign or classic films nowadays, but the movie is still there. The town center is where you meet friends for lunch, browse the library, shop for birthday presents, or just stroll around the square, saying hello to neighbors. You don't often do this at the strip mall, now do you?

Of course there's more to college town retirement for those interested in college sporting events, concerts, lectures, drama, light opera, and lots more. Retirees take full advantage of this. In fact check out any college concert and notice that 80 percent of the audience is local residents older than fifty. (Not surprising. Think about it: When you were a student, which did you prefer—a Bach festival or a rock-and-roll band at the local pizza parlor?)

Most colleges and universities offer continuing education

classes for adults older than fifty at reduced or free tuition. Unless you wish to be graded, you'll not be bothered with tests, term papers, or grades. Just have fun attending lectures and field trips while sharpening the old brain. You'll have a choice of classes such as beginning computers, conversational French, Chinese cooking, tying fishing flies, or whatever appeals to other students your age. By taking fascinating adult education classes, you'll meet kindred spirits, the kind of people you'd like for friends. This is a marvelous way to become acquainted in your new hometown.

Another advantage to college town living is reasonable real estate. It isn't engraved in marble, but most college towns offer bargain real estate prices compared with similar quality towns elsewhere. With 25 percent of the population being students on limited budgets and another 20 percent working as beginning teachers or support staff, housing prices can't be bid up past peoples' ability to pay. Asking prices and rental rates have to compete for the available dollars in the community. That's not to say there aren't some beautiful and expensive neighborhoods for those who want to pay a little more for a higher quality of life.

Another benefit of college town living: low crime rates and high personal safety. For some reason most college towns report low incidences of crime on the FBI's Uniform Crime Report. Why this should be is puzzling to me, but that's the way the FBI reports it.

Besides the usual amenities such as climate, airline and intercity bus transportation, cost of living, housing, and proximity to large cities, you need to think about some additional points when considering a college town for retirement:

♦ The town should not be so large that the general population overwhelms the college and dilutes its influence on the community.

♦ Ideally the campus is not far from the town center. If the school is located away from the town itself, it could be isolated and have little impact on the town's cultural and entertainment life.

♦ Does the school actively reach out to the community? Some schools don't bother because they are basically technical or religious schools.

♦ Does the school invite the community to participate in continuing education classes with either free or reduced tuition for noncredit classes for senior citizens?

♦ Are school events such as sports, drama, music, and lecture forums open to the public?

• Do homes in the neighborhood where you'd like to live fit your pocketbook? Remember, bargain-priced homes are often found in neighborhoods where students live. Choose a quiet, quality neighborhood, away from continual frat house parties with round-the-clock stereo music so loud it peels the paint off your bedroom wall.

Cost of Living

The most comprehensive research on the cost of living in the United States is done by the American Chamber of Commerce Research Association (ACCRA). They tabulate the cost of groceries, real estate, utilities, and other everyday necessities and publish them quarterly. Although not all communities are indexed by ACCRA, it's possible to see regional patterns in the cost of living for various communities. Whenever statistics are available, they are mentioned at the end of each community description. You can be reasonably confident that nearby communities will have a similar price structure.

Local boosters too often place undue emphasis on low cost of living and cheap real estate as the prime attractions of their area. True, these items go hand in hand; that is, when you find low-cost housing, you'll also find economical living costs in general. In our travels we've encountered places where $39,000 will buy a three-bedroom home; where carpenters will remodel for $9.00 per hour, where haircuts are still $6.50, and permanent waves cost $20.00. However, *inexpensive* living isn't necessarily the same as *quality* living. Some low-cost areas are exceptional bargains, combining a high quality of life with welcoming neighbors and affordable living costs. Yet other low-cost areas are intensely dreary and boring, and sometimes dangerous.

Why is the cost of living and housing dramatically less in some localities? Basically you'll find two reasons for cheap real estate and low rents. The most common reason: an undesirable place to live. These towns steadily lose population because they have absolutely nothing going for them—no jobs, no charm. Homes sell for rock-bottom prices because eager sellers outnumber reluctant buyers. Unless you are sincerely dedicated to boredom, bad weather, and cable TV, these are not places you would seek out for retirement.

The second situation deals with an unforeseen, disastrous

business slump or trend that causes the job market to disintegrate. In this event people don't necessarily *want* to leave and seek work elsewhere—they *have* to. Homes go on the real estate market at give-away prices because sellers have no other choice.

Although situations like this are personal tragedies for displaced families, they open windows of opportunity for retired folks. Because jobs and regular weekly paychecks aren't essential for most retired couples, quality real estate is theirs for a fraction of what similar housing would cost elsewhere. As younger folks with growing children move away, older people move in and raise the ratio between retired and working people to impressive levels. Retirees become a majority and wield appreciable influence over local government and political processes.

We've visited a few of these towns and reported on them in earlier editions, places like the towns of Ajo and Bisbee in Arizona, where mines closed, and Colorado's Grand Junction, whose economy toppled when the shale oil industry collapsed. As you might imagine, opportunities like these don't last forever. As retirees move in and snap up the bargains, prices naturally rise. Yet they rarely rise to the level they were at before the problem occurred.

Our latest bargain discovery in quality retirement is a two-state section of Virginia and West Virginia, an area calling itself "Four Seasons Country." An unusual set of circumstances has made this a very desirable place of inexpensive housing and welcoming neighbors. You may read about it in Chapter 2.

Working During Retirement

A few years ago, the question of working seemed out of place in a book on retirement. Used to be most people eagerly looked forward to the day they no longer had to get up every morning, down a cup of coffee, and drag themselves off to work. The ideal was a house on the golf course or a home by a bass lake. If someone merely changed jobs or went into business for themselves, how could they be retired?

How things have changed! For one thing the average age of those leaving the workplace is rapidly decreasing. Instead of holding on until age sixty-five, the trend is toward early retirement. These baby boomers are now crossing the fifty-years-and-older bridge, and according to surveys, most have plans on working at least part-time.

Going into business is another popular goal for early retirees, whereas sitting in a rocking chair in front of television is not.

Another development that forces many to consider working during retirement is the corporate scandals of companies such as Enron and World.com that left innumerable employees not only without jobs but with worthless pension plans. Thought will have to be given to selecting communities where some kind of employment is available.

Even for those with good jobs and viable pensions, dropping out of the job market at age sixty, fifty-five, and even younger is a common goal. Vigorous and healthy, these early retirees eagerly seek the challenge of a part-time job or, if the pay is good enough and the work interesting, maybe a full-time job. Going into business is another favored option. These younger retirees don't consider themselves retired at all; they are simply working at tasks they want to do instead of what they have to do. They are not only more youthful, but in general more affluent and clearly not ready to kick back with a cane fishing pole or watch soap operas all day long. They seek places where they can enjoy vigorous outdoor recreation and actively participate in community activities.

Therefore, many like to consider themselves "relocating" rather than "retiring." They often relocate within striking distance of their former employer's business base, or similar enterprises, to keep their hand in the job market, if only on a consulting basis. This is why southern states are becoming so popular with those leaving jobs in the highly industrialized areas of New England and the Great Lakes states. That's where industry is relocating. Their former employers are moving south as well.

Many people just *think* they need part-time jobs. The real problem is that they've always worked and are horrified at the prospect of suddenly not having anything meaningful to do. The curse of the work ethic is all too real; after all those years of toil, folks tend to feel guilty and decadent when they no longer leap out of bed at 6:30 A.M. and scurry off to a job. Too often those who don't really need the income end up working just for the sake of working.

This work ethic is understandable, and it is difficult to shake. Our recommendation is to get into volunteer pursuits should you not find enough to do around the house. As a volunteer you will not only be doing meaningful work, but also you'll meet others in the community, widen your network of friends, and lay the groundwork for later years when *you* may need volunteers to help you. A special bonus is that your services will be sincerely appreciated and valued more highly than if you were to work in a fast-food restaurant or some other high-competition, low-paying job, trying to please an employer you don't like in the first place.

Let's take the case of Katharine, a retired librarian who lived in a tiny apartment in Monterey, California. Her rent was $900 a month. A part-time job in a bookstore paid a little more than minimum wage for working 20 hours a week ($500 a month after taxes). When she moved to a small town in coastal Oregon, she found a larger apartment for $400 a month. This one had a view of the Pacific Ocean. Part-time jobs in a place like this pay minimum wages, but part-time jobs were all filled. However, Katharine discovered that the $500 she saved in rent made up for the $500 she had been earning at her bookstore job. In other words she had been working half a day, five days a week just to pay higher rent. Now she devotes her time to art classes and satisfying volunteer work in the community.

Taxes

Property taxes vary from state to state and locality to locality, with states like Arkansas or Alabama taking less than Arizona or California. But choosing retirement in Alabama over Arizona simply to save a few dollars a year would be foolish unless Alabama has everything you want in the way of retirement and Arizona lacks something. Taxes are just one component of many. Just because a state has no individual income taxes or sales tax doesn't mean the total tax burden will necessarily be less. States have ways of making up the difference. No income tax? Don't rejoice so quickly—higher property taxes and sales taxes will make up the deficit. No sales tax? You can be sure the state will figure out a way to tax you one way or another.

If you are like most retirees, your income will be lower; a lot of it will come from tax-deductible pensions and Social Security, so state income taxes may not be all that serious. (Of course, some states tax Social Security and pensions.) On the other hand, if you're in a high tax bracket, elevated tax rates could be significant, so you might consider a state that taxes income lightly or not at all. Those states without individual income taxes are Alaska, Florida, Nevada, South Dakota, Texas, Washington, and Wyoming.

Sales taxes are creeping up around the country as states try to scrounge funds for keeping their ships afloat. Rates vary from 8.5 percent in some states to no tax at all in Delaware, Montana, New Hampshire, and Oregon. Example: A $20,000 automobile will cost $1,700 more in Texas than in Oregon. The balancing factor is that in Oregon you pay state income tax, and in Texas you do not. One couple we interviewed in Vancouver, Washington, reported that because they live in Washington, they pay no state income tax, and when they shop across the river in Oregon they pay no sales tax!

Relative Tax Burdens

According to the Advisory Commission of Intergovernmental Relations, the tax burdens of the states discussed in this book are ranked as follows (from lowest to highest):

1. Alabama	12. North Carolina
2. Arkansas	13. Florida
3. Utah	14. New Mexico
4. Washington	15. Missouri
5. Tennessee	16. Georgia
6. Oklahoma	17. Nevada
7. Kentucky	18. Virginia
8. Texas	19. Oregon
9. Mississippi	20. California
10. South Carolina	21. Colorado
11. Louisiana	22. Arizona

Real Estate Prices

Throughout this book you will find references to real estate prices somewhat vague, and deliberately so. When available, the consumer's price index (from the American Chamber of Commerce Research Association) is included with a town's description, providing readers a general idea of housing costs. The problem with quoting specific prices in a book is that they can, and will, be out of date long before the book is ready for its next revision. This is particularly relevant at this point in time: In some parts of the country, real estate markets are highly volatile, whereas prices hold steady in other places.

In addition to the expected price differentials between places like California and North Dakota, you'll find occasional regional anomalies that may make home asking prices surreal. For example, in California (where my wife and I live most of the year), the real estate market was blown out of reality by dot.com millionaires from the distant Silicon Valley who bought homes for use as occasional weekend retreats. Small, 900-square-foot cottages on narrow lots (that used to be overpriced at $150,000) began selling for $600,000! The same thing occurred in other parts of the nation where high-tech success stories were legendary.

But then the economy took a nose-dive in reaction to the disastrous collapse of high-tech stocks, corporate bankruptcy scandals, growing unemployment, and a loss of faith in the stock market. As a result, the real estate market has been undergoing some severe adjustments in some parts of the country. Although prices have been slowly falling in the more expensive and unique markets, they began at such a high plateau that it could be some time, if ever, before property could be considered "affordable." In the meantime, if you don't already own a house in one of those neighborhoods, you may never be able to afford one.

Choosing Your Climate

All your working life you've heroically put up with whatever inconveniences, insults, and misery your local weather dumped on you. The good news is when you retire, you no longer have to take it; you can look for a perfect climate and live happily ever after. The bad news is there is no perfect climate.

Folks in Maine love their summers but say it's too cold in the winter. Their friends in Miami love Florida winters but complain because summers are hot and muggy. Newcomers say they miss the change of seasons. Parts of California have what I consider the best overall climate—sunny, relatively bug-free and comfortable, with low humidity most of the year—yet folks here grumble when winter days drop below 50 degrees and winter rains keep them from walks along the beach or sunning beside the pool. (My friends in Michigan think we Californians are weather wimps!)

Even though you can't find the *perfect* climate, you certainly can find one that suits you best. And chances are that you will find one far superior to the weather you've had to put up with all those working years. This is one of the exciting features about retirement: For the first time in your life, work doesn't dictate where you must live. You now have a choice in the matter!

Another advantage of retirement: You needn't lock yourself into one weather pattern. You can choose any combination of climates that fits your new lifestyle. Many people keep their hometowns as base camps, enjoying wonderful springs and summers there, and then head south to Florida, Texas, or Arizona and enjoy another summer. Some retirees choose Mexico or Costa Rica as an escape from the coldest winter months. It takes a little gumption to get started "following the sun," but thousands upon thousands do just that, and they love it!

Why Not My State?

Occasionally we receive letters from readers demanding to know why we didn't include their home states: Iowa or Indiana, for example. "What do you have against my state?" they inquire. "It's a wonderful place to retire." Other readers complain that we don't cover places in Idaho, Montana, or Maine that often receive retirement writers' praise.

Aside from the obvious explanation that it would be impossible to cover all communities in one book, there are two reasons for limiting coverage. Let's take Montana as an example. We've been there in the summer and can vouch for the fact that it's a delightful place in an exceptionally beautiful part of the country. Places like Glacier National Park make the Big Sky country a wonderful place to visit. Most folks who were born and raised in Montana will surely retire there when they leave their jobs, just as most retirees in Pittsburgh, Omaha, and Milwaukee probably will never move away from their hometowns.

However, I feel that it is irresponsible to encourage someone from Pittsburgh, Omaha, or Milwaukee to leave one cold climate to move to an even colder, bitterly frigid environment just for the sake of a few glorious summer months. If you're going to move, why not choose someplace comfortable? For those who love snow, surely the

40 to 45 total inches per season in Pittsburgh or Omaha should suffice. But in places like Montana or Idaho, winter effectively begins in October, often with an average 3-foot snowpack that remains until April. From my point of view, it's far better to retire in your hometown or move to a pleasantly warm winter climate and then make *summer* visits to glorious parts of the north.

Weather aside, our retirement selections are mostly popular communities where most people actually do retire, places that retirees consider most appropriate for a new beginning. To take book space away from well-liked retirement destinations and dedicate it to places where few retirees have any interest would be counterproductive. Of course there is nothing wrong with the idea of retiring in Illinois, Minnesota, or Massachusetts. Uncounted millions of people who live in these states do retire there, never even thinking about moving away. However, not many future retirees from Illinois, Minnesota, or Massachusetts harbor a burning passion to move to Iowa, Michigan, or Vermont. Granted, these states are pleasant places for working, living, and retiring. But statistics clearly show that for every thousand retirees who move out of New England, for example, to retire somewhere else, only a tiny handful move into New England for full-time retirement. Even then, most moves are for a specific reason, such as returning to the old hometown, where family lives, or to a college town where weather and location aren't all important.

Personal Safety

Many people agree that crime is one of the major problems in the United States. It's true that crime rates are dropping dramatically in most parts of the country, but there are still some neighborhoods where people are virtual prisoners in their own homes. Instead of criminals being behind bars, some law-abiding citizens find themselves hiding behind barred windows and chained doors.

There is little we, as private citizens, can do about any of this. The only solution is to look for safe places to live. Curiously, in neighborhoods not so very far away from high-crime areas, people can leave their doors unlocked and can walk home from a late movie without anxiety. There are still places where things are almost as calm as they used to be when we were children. Remember when kids used to play outside long after dark? Remember when nobody locked doors? In our research we've come across many locations with almost that same safe feeling of those good old days. (I say *almost* because conditions have changed, even in the best of places.)

A few years ago my wife and I bought a summer home in a small Oregon town (population less than 100). When we inquired about safety there, we discovered some residents never lock their cars and some even leave their keys in the ignition so they won't lose them! On the other hand residents in a nearby, much larger city also didn't lock their cars—but for another reason. Automobile break-ins were so common in their neighborhood that locking the car doors was an invitation for a thief to break the windows to see if something valuable might be inside. Yet in the better neighborhoods of that same city, things are safe.

Finding a Safe Place to Live

Unfortunately there is no such thing as a crime-free area. As long as people live in social groups, there will always be individuals who can't seem to distinguish between their belongings and those of their neighbors. It just stands to reason that the larger the social group, the more deviant individuals it produces. Thus, you find much higher crime rates in Washington, D.C., than in Walla Walla, Washington, and more crime in New Orleans than in New Madrid, Missouri. On the other hand, just because a town is peaceful doesn't make it a great place to live. It could also be so boring that burglars and robbers can't stand working there, or perhaps it's so cold in the wintertime that car thieves can't get the cars started.

Generally speaking the larger the city, the higher the crime rate. Yet many big cities have neighborhoods as safe as nearby suburbs and smaller towns. These are usually middle-class, low-turnover neighborhoods, places where residents know each other and where most people are older than the age of fifty. For example, Hermosa Beach, an affluent suburb in the Los Angeles metropolitan area, ranks exceptionally high in safety—often at the top of the list—yet it is just twenty minutes away from one of the most crime-ridden areas in the country.

You can learn a great deal about a neighborhood by simply driving around and observing. Are the homes neat, with trimmed shrubbery and mowed lawns? Or are they shabby, obviously owned by absentee landlords? Are there old junkers parked around the neighborhood, with teenagers trying to get them started? Or do you see folks your own age working in the yard, walking the dog, or polishing the car? The best way to ascertain a neighborhood's safety is to simply ask. If folks feel safe living there, they're happy to tell you all about it. If they offer to lend you a weapon to protect yourself, it's probably not a safe neighborhood.

In this book I've used the latest version of the FBI's publication *Crime in the United States* to discuss personal safety in a community. Although FBI statistics are quite detailed, they sometimes do not provide a solid basis for comparing crime rates among communities. For one thing not all police departments send reports to the FBI. For example, every police department in New Jersey, some 225 towns, reports every conceivable crime to the FBI. Yet only four cities in the entire state of Illinois report! Furthermore, the FBI has to rely on whatever statistics local police departments *choose* to report. Some departments report thefts of lawn statuary and tricycles; others report only major crimes. Some don't even bother to report rapes. The FBI admits that some police departments hedge their crime reports to make their town look good. Others might exaggerate the crime situation in order to embarrass the city council into increasing police department budgets.

Therefore, our analysis of personal safety for a community is based partly on the FBI reports, but influenced by our personal observations and interviews with folks living in the community.

The Southeast Coast States

FOR THOSE WHO LIVE in the Midwest or on the East Coast, the idea of a West Coast retirement is a pleasant thought, but it often seems too far away from friends and family. Florida, too, may be out of the question for any number of reasons. The search is then narrowed to an affordable location with a mild, four-season climate that isn't too far to return "home" periodically and where friends and family can reasonably be expected to visit from time to time. Of course your retirement home should be in an attractive setting where friends and family will look upon visits with joyful anticipation rather than with dread. The southeastern part of the United States—Georgia, the Carolinas, and Virginia—fulfills all these requirements for a growing number of retired families.

From earliest times Southern colonists who owned plantations in the warm coastal regions enjoyed the cool highlands as summer retreats. Mountain sections of Georgia, the Carolinas, and Virginia are noted for a growing population of "part-time" retirees from Florida who come here to cool off in the summer. After spending a couple of seasons in the upland hill country, many visitors become *ex*-Florida retirees, choosing to settle here permanently. One North Carolina native said, "Northerners are discovering our part of the country by going to Florida first and then making a second retirement move here. We call that 'making a J turn.' "

The coastal Atlantic states offer a rich variety of retirement settings: sandy beaches, rolling green hills, and forested mountains brightened with azaleas, mountain laurel, and myrtle trees. From fertile agricultural lands with neat farms and white fences to rugged mountains where bears and herds of deer roam unmolested by humans, the Atlantic Coast region has it all. The ocean yields harvests of fish, crab, and oysters; inland streams offer superb sport opportunities for trout, bass, and other game fish. Modern cities with full conveniences and cultural attractions are but short distances from rural villages that are steeped in nineteenth-century atmosphere and country friendliness.

Any of these ecological worlds are within a few easy driving hours from almost anywhere in this area you might select as a home base. Florida is just next door and accessible for visits any time. Some Southeasterners take advantage of Florida's merciful winters by spending the coldest months there and returning to their mountain homes for the rest of the year.

Southern Hospitality

"Southern hospitality" is an oft-tossed-about phrase, but one with more than a kernel of truth. It's interesting to note how Southerners interact with one another as well as with strangers. You'll notice an open friendliness and sharing that differs from the general custom in other parts of the country. For example, when visiting friends or relatives in the South, I am always surprised how often people drop in unannounced for a visit. Sometimes it's a steady procession of acquaintances coming and going all day long. Close friends sometimes don't bother to knock. They'll just open the door and call out, "Anybody home?" They know they're always welcome for a chat. "Just passin' by," they'll explain, "Thought I'd stop in to say hello." An extra cup of coffee is usually on the kitchen table before they can pull out a chair.

In other parts of the country this would be unheard of. In my California neighborhood, before you visit someone other than a close friend, you telephone first and see if it's okay to come over. In still other parts of the country, you either wait for an invitation or you suggest meeting for lunch at a nearby restaurant. For some folks Southern-style hospitality would take some getting used to. Some feel abused if casual acquaintances drop in and expect them to interrupt whatever they're doing to entertain them. Other folks love it.

Nonetheless don't expect to move into a Southern neighborhood and immediately become friends with all the other kids on the block. It doesn't work that way in Southern communities any more than it does in your hometown. Although small-town Southerners are inclined to be more courteous and considerate than people from other parts of the country, you have to work at making friends just as you did back home. When asked whether residents of a small North Carolina town were friendly to outsider retirees, the local chamber of commerce representative thought for a moment and then replied, "Well, we tend to be friendly to everyone. But it's the *outsiders* who are most friendly to other outsiders." She added, "Outsiders have to learn to accept mountain people for who we are: sincere, hard-working folks who enjoy a simple life. We hate it when outsiders try to change things." They have a saying here, "You don't push mountain folks; you have to try and lead them."

Churches in the South

In some sections of the country, churches play a minor role in most people's lives. They'll attend sporadically, maybe on Christmas Eve or Easter, and every time someone gets married or buried. According to estimates 28 million people in the United States almost never go to church. They aren't all atheists; they're too just busy catching up on weekend chores or going fishing. Such is not the case in the South, and this is important to understand. In the typical Southern town, churches are an integral part of people's social lives. Church on Sunday is as much a part of the weekly routine as mowing the lawn. Close friends almost always belong to the same church.

Something Northerners aren't used to is that churches in the South can be politically active. When a congregation decides to pressure local politicians, the message gets across and the church musters votes. This is why so many parts of the South are "dry" and why the local bootlegger is an esteemed Southern institution. "Vote dry, drink wet" is the motto. (By the way, bootleggers always support the local preachers as enthusiastic campaigners for prohibition.)

On the other hand, churches can make relocation easy by welcoming and introducing newcomers to a community. The moment strangers show up, churchgoers begin shaking hands, inquiring where they are from, and welcoming the newcomers to their new hometown. We've interviewed numerous retirees who seldom, if ever, attended church where they came from but are now resolute members of a congregation. A church can be the doorway to the community.

A Geography Lesson

The Southeast Coast states are divided into three distinct regions. The first is a broad coastal plain that rises from the Atlantic, often in low, marshy ground studded with palmettos and scrub oak. Several hundred miles of beautiful white sand beaches are convenient for retirees who need to include the seashore in their retirement schemes. Farther inland fertile fields and comfortable small towns offer a quieter, more introspective lifestyle.

These flat lowlands end at the fall line, where the foothills of the Blue Ridge and Great Smoky Mountains begin. Rivers, creeks, and streams flowing down from the mountains suddenly change into rapids and low waterfalls at this point, hence the name "fall line." This is the Piedmont or foothill region, a country of rolling hills covered with hardwood forests and dotted with more than 400,000 acres of lakes. Peach orchards, horse farms, neighborly small-town squares, and country lanes characterize the Piedmont country.

Finally we come to the Blue Ridge and Great Smoky highlands, where the Appalachians lift to an elevation of nearly 3,000 feet. This mountain chain runs in a northeast-southwest direction from near the Canadian border to just north of Atlanta. Ancient, eroded mountains, sometimes scarcely touched by civilization, are richly cloaked with hardwoods and flowering trees, pines, beeches, poplars, and birch. Crystal-clear rivers and streams cascade through canyons and tumble over waterfalls into deep pools. This is a nature lover's treat. More than 250 miles of trout streams run through South Carolina, and there are probably at least that many in North Carolina. Northern Georgia also shares in this bounty.

Yet the mountain country isn't so high that it catches harsh winters. Snow is a regular winter visitor, but it seldom sticks around more than a day or two (except for a few higher elevations and skiing areas). Compared with Cleveland or Chicago weather, even the worst days of winter here seem gentle. The mountains have other functions besides being picturesque. They deflect or delay cold air masses approaching from the north and west and thus protect coastal areas from arctic blasts.

North Carolina

Many changes have taken place across the nation over the last half of the twentieth century, and North Carolina is the state that has changed most of all. Until the

middle of the twentieth century, North Carolina was a backward, underdeveloped place whose main industry, other than agriculture, seemed to be military bases: places such as Fort Bragg, Camp Lejeune, and others. The state's social and economic doldrums lasted so long that in addition to North Carolina's nickname, the "Tarheel State," it was dubbed the "Rip Van Winkle State."

This began to change as northern manufacturers relocated their facilities to North Carolina to take advantage of cheap labor. New high-tech industry stimulated local economies and started a chain reaction of northerners moving into North Carolina to follow their jobs, which in turn attracted more industry because of the abundant skilled-labor pool.

The turning point came in the 1960s with the success of the huge Research Triangle Park in the Raleigh–Durham area, which quickly developed into the nation's largest governmental and industrial research laboratories. The facility required an army of laboratory scientists, technicians, business experts, and academics of all descriptions. New manufacturing processes were introduced to the state: electronics plants, rubber and plastic factories, and fabrication of light machinery. High-tech jobs brought more northerners into the state as North Carolina's top universities turned out highly qualified graduates.

North Carolina has clearly shed its Rip Van Winkle image, ranking as the South's most highly industrialized state and one of the nation's leaders in technology. Many of today's "early-bird retirees" are relocating here as a place for

NORTH CAROLINA TAX PROFILE

Sales tax: 4% to 6%, drugs exempt
State income tax: graduated, 6% to 7.75% greater than $60,000; can't deduct federal income tax
Property taxes: about 1.2%
Intangibles tax: 0.25%
Social security taxed: no
Pensions taxed: excludes $4,000 government, $2,000 private pensions
Gasoline tax: 22.3¢ per gallon

part-time or consulting work within a short distance of their retirement homes.

The good news is that progress has had little impact on the beauty of the state. Actually the increased population has opened previously isolated communities in the Blue Ridge and Great Smoky Mountains and has turned them into ideal places for retirement.

Blue Ridge and Great Smoky Mountains

We're conyinced that some of the most beautiful and scenic places in the world are found in the Blue Ridge and Great Smoky Mountains. October, when leaves are turning, is a marvelous time for a visit. Hardwood trees display a full explosion of color, with brilliant reds, yellows, purples, lavenders, and all colors in between to dazzle the eye, while evergreens provide a conservative background of green. We've also made the rounds in the spring, when the dogwoods, azaleas, and mountain laurel trees are in full bloom. The sight and smell of spring make one forget winter.

Driving the Blue Ridge Parkway is an experience not soon forgotten. The parkway starts at the small town of Front Royal in northern Virginia and wends its way southwest until it ends at Great Smoky Mountains National Park, which is partly in Tennessee and partly in North Carolina. The scenic highway winds through beautiful mountain terrain, past wild rivers and thick forests. Hikers and river rafters love this country. Golf is a top sport here, with more than twenty first-quality courses throughout the Great Smoky Mountains area alone.

Unless you are country bred and raised, you'll probably prefer to settle within striking distance of a city. Once in a while you'll get a hankering for a genuine supermarket or a department store. Even the bigger mountain towns—Asheville (pop. 85,000), Greenville (pop. 59,000), and Hendersonville (pop. 10,000) in the southern parts; Bristol (pop. 24,000) and Johnson City (pop. 41,000) up around the Tennessee border—aren't all that large. Each of these cities is large enough, however, for adequate medical care, heavy shopping, and services you might need from time to time.

Asheville   Three North Carolina towns in this region form a triangle, with Asheville as the apex and Hendersonville and Brevard forming the triangle's base. All three towns consistently receive praise as retirement locations in magazines, newspapers, and retirement guides. Because there's only about 20 miles or so between one city and the next, it would seem they could be treated as one subject, but we feel they are different enough to deserve separate consideration. We are starting with Asheville, the best known of the three.

Asheville is the queen city of North Carolina's western region, residing in the fingerlike projection of the state that forces its way between Tennessee and Georgia. Nestled where the Great Smoky and Blue Ridge Mountains meet, Asheville sits 2,340 feet above sea level. This elevation accounts for the city's pleasant summer weather as well as its brisk, but not harsh, winters.

As the largest city in western North Carolina, Asheville (pop. 85,000) is the region's cultural and commercial center. The region is characterized by prosperous farms and forest-covered foothills, rounded and green, growing steeper toward the north. Its natural setting, surrounded by a million acres of national forest, combines with the convenience of city living to make Asheville and its environs one of North Carolina's most desirable retirement destinations. Not surprisingly Asheville was famous as a resort town, attracting tourists and retirees—long before Thomas Wolfe described his hometown in his novel *Look Homeward, Angel* and even before George Vanderbilt thought about creating America's largest home here, the 255-room Biltmore House. Since the turn of the twentieth century, famous Americans such as Henry Ford, his friend Thomas Edison, F. Scott Fitzgerald, and William Jennings Bryan enjoyed summers here. Many came for the summer and stayed on for retirement. They now come in ever-increasing numbers, with a surprising number of "second-chance retirees" moving here after having tried Florida, California, or Arizona.

Because of its distance from a truly large metropolitan center, Asheville enjoys many services and amenities normally absent in a small city. No fewer than sixteen shopping centers—four of them indoor malls—ensure wide selections of merchandise. Two interstate highways (I-40 and I-26) intersect in Asheville, as well as the Blue Ridge Parkway and ten other U.S. and state highways. This maze of freeways, plus an airport with daily flights and connections to several major cities, makes Asheville a transportation hub for this area.

The University of North Carolina at Asheville sponsors a unique resource for seniors living in the region. It's called the North Carolina Center for Creative Retirement. The center consists of several programs designed to introduce retirement-age people to a wide

ASHEVILLE AREA WEATHER						
In degrees Fahrenheit						
	Jan.	April	July	Oct.	Rain	Snow
Daily highs	48	69	84	69	48"	17"
Daily lows	26	43	62	43		

ASHEVILLE AREA COST OF LIVING					
	Overall	Housing	Medical	Groceries	Utilities
Percentage of national average	101	111	96	97	92

variety of learning experiences as it integrates them into the community. The center should be one of the first stops on your pre-retirement tour of Asheville, and, should you decide to move here, the center should become part of your retirement scenario for continuing education.

One of the center's programs is called College for Seniors. Drawing on retirees' professional expertise and life experiences, curricula and classes are designed and taught by students as well as university faculty. Classes range from Chaucer to computers, from foreign affairs to opera. Another is the Senior Academy for Intergenerational Learning, which matches retired professionals with university students to work as research partners, tutors, and career mentors. The Leadership Asheville Seniors program brings seniors together to explore ways to link their talents and expertise with community needs. They work with civic leaders, social scientists, political activists, and other experts to learn about the community's past and present and confront future challenges. Lastly, the Seniors in the Schools program matches talented senior volunteers with public school students, where they tutor, present enrichment programs, and organize special projects.

A concentration of hospitals and related facilities firmly establishes the city as a medical center for the entire region. The claim is that Asheville has more doctors per capita than anywhere else in the world. Whether or not this is accurate, the fact remains that health care here is outstanding. Eight hospitals ensure excellent medical care for the Asheville triangle. Among them is a veterans' hospital. Asheville's Saint Joseph's medical facility and heart center ranks very high among the nation's community hospitals.

Outdoor recreation here is enhanced by Asheville's nearness to some of the prettiest Appalachian country imaginable. Always within view, the Blue Ridge and Great Smoky Mountains soar to heights greater than 5,000 feet. Hiking, fishing, camping, and winter skiing make for year-round outdoor recreation within walking or driving distance. Several public and private golf courses challenge players with good weather in all but the two coldest months of the year.

A few years ago Asheville was known for its low-cost, high-quality real estate market. But Asheville's popularity as a retirement destination has boosted prices until they are probably the highest in the state, at about 15 percent above the national average.

Hendersonville   Not far from Asheville, at a slightly lower altitude, Hendersonville is a small-town alternative to Asheville's city retirement. The region's mild mountain climate is created by the Great Smoky Mountain barrier that shields Asheville, Henderson, and Brevard from winter storms. Even in the coldest months, temperatures almost always rise above freezing in the afternoon. Summers, in turn, are cooled by the 2,200-foot altitude and breezes flowing down from the mountain peaks. Well-balanced and adequate rainfall supports bountiful flowers in spring, healthy crops in summer, brilliant rainbows of fall colors, and relative greenery in the winter.

Like Asheville, Hendersonville has reaped benefits from a growing trend of relocation in Southeast over the past decade. Its population has increased by one-third, with much of the growth attributed to the new generation of retirees enjoying the amenities of Blue Ridge Mountain retirement. Hendersonville's population today is approximately 10,500 (within the town limits), although the city appears to be much larger because it's the shopping center for an area of about 80,000 people. More than 30 percent of the population is sixty years old or older—the majority retired, of course.

The town center of Henderson has undergone a very successful rehabilitation program that includes new businesses and face-lifts for existing buildings. By making the main street one way and adding lots of new parking spaces, they've slowed the pace and given the town center a pleasant, mall-like atmosphere. This makes the downtown an important part of the community, a place to meet friends and shop away from the hustle of the strip malls. Also important is the wide variety of cultural attractions the community presents for tourists and residents alike. You'll find everything from apple festivals to live performances of off-Broadway shows, as well as original theater productions, bluegrass, and classical concerts.

Residential neighborhoods throughout the city and county offer quiet, traffic-free living with the advantage of being only minutes from shopping. Like Asheville, property prices have been on the increase over the past ten years, although asking prices are still below those in Asheville. A surprising number of upscale developments are under way and in place, complete with golf courses and lakes that compete with lovely, more conventional neighborhoods with modestly priced homes.

The local community college boasts a Center for Lifelong Learning that reaches out to the fifty-plus population, featuring seminars and lectures as well as popular classes. The program is member directed and responsive to the needs of retirees. This is a great place for newcomers to make new friends in the community.

Although Asheville's excellent medical facilities are just 25 miles by interstate from Hendersonville, the town has two hospitals with 360 beds. The hospitals have advanced diagnostic equipment, a cancer treatment center, and surgical and intensive care services.

Seven miles from downtown Hendersonville, the village of Flat Rock is a delightful residential community with an artistic flair—a place of art shows, concerts, and theater. Carl Sandberg maintained a home here for many years; the house, dating from 1838, is now a popular tourist attraction. Flat Rock received its name from a vast outcropping of granite rock, which is said to have been the site of Cherokee gatherings. The town's nickname is "Little Charleston of the Mountains" because it was first settled by wealthy Charlestonians escaping the harsh coastal summers. Today the entire area is becoming an attraction for those who once retired to Florida but have been captivated by the cooler, mountain climate of this region.

Brevard   The nearby towns of Hendersonville and Brevard are known for well-groomed residential districts and more than adequate shopping. Both towns routinely receive top recommendations as retirement destinations by retirement writers. Brevard (pop. 6,800) is about 22 miles southwest of Hendersonville, situated in a picturesque wooded setting in Transylvania County. The region is nicknamed the "Land of Waterfalls" because of more than 250 falls throughout the forest. The cascades have colorful names such as

Looking Glass, Slippery Witch, Horsepasture, Rainbow, and Turtle-back. The highest is Whitewater Falls, with a beautiful 411-foot plume of water crashing into the valley below. Brevard is a some-what upscale residential community, with no industry or high-tech to lure retirees who plan on working in the community. Asheville, however, is within easy commuting distance.

Golf is a favorite sport around here, with a dozen golf courses ready for play—although only two or three are public, the others being private country clubs. Trout fishing is also said to be premiere, with mountain streams stocked by one of the largest hatcheries in the Southeast.

Real estate costs in Brevard range from above average to high, with one nearby private community on the extremely expensive side—many homes are priced at more than $500,000. Homes in Bre-vard enjoy a natural setting of trees and mature shrubs, with 33 per-cent of the county in the Pisgah National Forest. Because much of the remaining land cannot be developed, land is expensive in com-parison with surrounding counties.

North Carolina's High Country

The rugged mountain country to the north of Asheville is appro-priate for those demanding the best in Appalachian settings. This was Daniel Boone country. The famous pioneer was supposedly born and raised in Boone, one of the major towns in this area.

For more than a century, wealthy families from all over the na-tion have traditionally used these mountains as summer hideaways, secluded places where they could slip away for quiet vacations. In-dustrialists from Chicago and Pittsburgh, socialites from New York and Boston, and southern aristocracy from Charleston, Charlotte, and other affluent cities maintained summer retreats deep in the mountains. Places like Linville, Banner Elk, and Blowing Rock are places unknown to most of the country, but quite familiar to the wealthy.

The first resorts and retirement homes appeared on the scene in the 1890s, but it wasn't until the advent of the automobile and good roads that retirement began in earnest. Then anyone who could afford a Chevy could visit and settle in these formerly exclu-sive areas. And they did. This turned out to be a natural retirement haven, with inexpensive property, a mild climate, and gorgeous sur-roundings.

NORTH CAROLINA'S HIGH COUNTRY WEATHER					
In degrees Fahrenheit					
	Jan.	April	July	Oct.	Rain	Snow
Daily highs	45	68	84	68	49"	18"
Daily lows	25	41	62	44		

NORTH CAROLINA'S HIGH COUNTRY COST OF LIVING					
Percentage of	Overall	Housing	Medical	Groceries	Utilities
national average	96	83	93	103	98

Today's latest retirement wave began around twenty or thirty years ago when a few developers bought small valleys of wooded land and built golf courses. Golf was the irresistible bait to entice Northern buyers to these parts. The ones with money built posh homes, at first for summer getaways, eventually for retirement.

Hound Ears   Despite its down-home name, Hound Ears is an example of an expensive development, one of the area's earliest. A developer visualized a golf course there, spreading over a valley floor. After laying out beautiful greens and fairways and an attractive clubhouse, he quickly sold the lots he had developed around the golf course. Buyers demanded more lots for retirement homes. He began cutting roads through the woods and into the hills that overlooked his valley golf course. As fast as he could lay out a new section of lots, it sold out. Each new house seemed to be more luxurious than the previous, with some homes valued well into six figures. We were told that one couple put $500,000 into construction, but before they could finish, someone offered them a million dollars for the house, as is.

Obviously these places aren't for folks with ordinary pocketbooks. Security guards staff the entrances twenty-four hours a day, keeping out us riffraff. In fact one development (Linville Ridge) is said to be so exclusive that one can buy into the development only by invitation! So far the developers haven't invited me, so I suppose I won't buy. They probably wouldn't let me put it on my credit card, anyway.

However, all isn't for the rich. Enjoying the North Carolina mountains is practical because there are many affordable properties available. Although these dwellings may not be as costly, the view, the fresh air, and the delightful weather do not depend on our bank accounts. There are many small towns (and some not so small) where you can blend into the daily routine and live among friendly neighbors. The local folk, who proudly refer to themselves as "mountain people," are famous for their hospitality to "flatlanders." The number of such outsiders from various parts of the country is growing larger every day.

Boone   Nestled in a scenic valley, amidst some of the oldest mountains in the world, Boone is the region's largest town, with a population of 13,500 inhabitants. Boone likes to be referred to as the "Heart of the High Country." The town has a surprisingly large downtown business district and an expansive strip mall that belies its population figures. This is partly because Boone serves as the major commercial center for surrounding towns but also because of Appalachian State University's 12,000 students, who almost double the town's population. Not all of them live in town, of course; about 25 percent commute daily from surrounding communities. The full-time resident population has increased by at least 30 percent since the last census and university students by even more.

We've enjoyed watching Boone grow from a small town into a small city over the years that we've been visiting there. It boasts an historic downtown with turn-of-the-twentieth-century brick buildings that fit in perfectly with the Blue Ridge Mountain setting. The city center is bustling and in a healthy condition, as most college towns are.

Nearby you'll find numerous small towns and villages where you can blend into the daily routine among friendly neighbors. The local folk, who proudly refer to themselves as mountain people, are famous for their hospitality to "flatlanders." However, the large number of outsiders moving in from various parts of the country is growing larger every day. Before long flatlanders will probably outnumber the mountain people. We flatlanders must remember to be hospitable to mountain people at that point.

The city of Boone is the health-care center for the region. A recently expanded 127-bed hospital has a critical care unit and a new outpatient surgical facility, resulting in more than adequate medical care.

Blowing Rock   Picturesque Blowing Rock is the second-largest town in the High Country, although its population of 1,200 actually makes it best described as a large village. Perched atop the Eastern Continental Divide, Blowing Rock is an elegant place for all seasons: cool in the summer, dazzling in the fall, a Currier and Ives portrait in the winter, and a festival of wild-flowers in the spring. The town features historic heirloom homes in the style of the nineteenth century, exquisite yet rustic in design and construction.

Blowing Rock is a very popular tourist destination for those visiting the region and is famous for quaint shops, fabulous dining, and charming accommodations. In short it's become a tourist-oriented artists' colony. Visitors come by the droves—so many that you'll have trouble finding a parking spot during the season. This extra traffic is the only downside we could find here.

Even though the region is somewhat isolated from Asheville (a long hour's drive away), a surprising array of cultural activities are available to residents. Mayland College, located in Spruce Pine, sponsors extension-class programs in many surrounding communities. This program, called Lifelong Learning, is associated with the Elderhostel Institute, which has as its purpose the fostering of continuing education among older people, regardless of their previous academic pursuits. Classes offered are pottery, studio glass, traditional weaving, jewelry and iron working, and sculpture/bronze casting.

Newland   The roads in this area are not for high-speed driving; they meander lazily around hill and dale. Every few miles turns up another surprise, another lovely town for retirement-home seekers. Each has its own personality and charm. The little town of Newland, for example, is a quiet, country town, unpretentious and economical. A house set back from the road on several acres can sometimes be found for less than a tract home in most areas of the country, and cozy little homes in a friendly in-town neighborhood can be exceptionally affordable. The most popular restaurant has an old-fashioned soda fountain and sells a lunch special for less than $4.00. A public golf course—just as beautiful as the exclusive, private ones—provides sport for the duffers in the crowd.

When you ask people why they chose this part of the Blue Ridge Mountains to retire, a major reason (right after the area's beauty) is the mountain weather. Residents delight in contrasting seasons: Mild summers, beautiful springs, honest-to-goodness autumns, and winters with soft blankets of snow create a wonderland of beauty. Skiing draws visitors from Florida and other parts of the South. Although Floridians visit here in the winter to enjoy winter sports, many mountain retirees head for Florida to *escape* the snow. We interviewed several retired residents who regularly go to Florida from December through March. Some take RVs; others rent condos or houses on the beach. The wealthier folks own a second home in Florida, with Vero Beach a popular destination for a winter reunion with their warm-weather neighbors.

Jefferson/West Jefferson   We discovered Ashe County more or less by accident. The twin towns of Jefferson and West Jefferson are slightly off the beaten track for relocation—almost a best-kept secret. During a recent research trip through the Blue Ridge Mountains, we decided to make a short detour and check the possibilities here. Jefferson sits a few miles off the Blue Ridge Parkway near the Virginia state line. Previously we had heard little about Jefferson as a potential place for Appalachian retirement, even though it's not far from some popular places like Boone and Banner Elk. We were pleasantly surprised to find Jefferson a good retirement possibility.

The town was established in 1803, the first in America named for Thomas Jefferson. For more than one hundred years, Jefferson remained the sole incorporated town in Ashe County. Of all the Blue Ridge country, Jefferson has probably changed the least since the Blue Ridge country was "discovered" by the outside world. The population boom hasn't struck as it has in other parts of the High Country. Since 1900 the populations of Jefferson and West Jefferson have risen and fallen but changed little overall. Combined, the twin towns muster a population of only 1,500, but this figure is misleading, because most retirees choose to live outside the town limits. Only about 10 percent of the county's residents live in town. The rest live on farms, in small crossroad communities, or in one of two newly developed golf-course subdivisions. Hardly a metropolis, the quaint downtown serves as the shopping center for the entire county of about 22,000 inhabitants, so all the facilities are in place, more so than in some other towns of this size. Jefferson's downtown, turn-of-the-twentieth-century courthouse is a marvel of Victorian construction.

Local people say Jefferson reminds them of Boone, before Appalachian State University expanded and tourism took over to create traffic jams in the Appalachians. This northernmost region isn't quite as hilly, forested, or picturesque as some of the more popular places, but that's a matter of degree; it's still a beautiful place. One nice thing about Jefferson is that real estate prices haven't sky-rocketed as they have in the Boone–Blowing Rock area. One couple told us, "When we retired from New Jersey, we wanted to live in North Carolina, in the mountains. But we realized we couldn't afford to buy property in Watauga County, where everybody wants to live. Then we discovered Ashe County and Jefferson." A home costing $130,000 near Boone might sell for $90,000 here.

Like all of North Carolina's Blue Ridge country, outdoor recreation is convenient and varied. Many miles of trout streams flow through the region, and the abundance of game such as wild turkey, squirrel, and deer can satisfy a hunter's dream. (One of the area's most famous hunters was the legendary Daniel Boone. In fact Boone's descendants were among the first landowners in Ashe County.)

The University Triangle

Between the flat coastal region of the Atlantic and the Appalachian foothills, a stretch of gently rolling countryside, strewn with farms and hardwood forests, is interspersed by crossroad villages, small towns, and sophisticated cities. The region is known as the *Midlands*. The terrain is too rolling to be considered plains yet not hilly enough to be foothills. The Midlands present a unique combination of cultural choices: from Beethoven to bluegrass and from stock-car racing to scholarly research. Just about any kind of intellectual and recreational pursuit imaginable can be found here.

Because three of North Carolina's top universities are clustered in the Midlands in three of the state's best-known cities, the region around Chapel Hill, Durham, and Raleigh is rightly labeled the University Triangle. Chapel Hill is home of the University of North Carolina, Duke University is located in Durham, and North Carolina State in Raleigh. Besides these three major universities, five four-year colleges plus eight two-year colleges are grouped within a few miles of the others. The University Triangle has more than 64,000 students in attendance, deeply influencing the region's culture, social structure, and worldviews.

Unlike some sections of the South, where outsiders are rare curiosities, outsiders are pretty much in the majority here. The Triangle's famous universities—plus numerous research labs, think tanks, and other academic institutions—draw new residents from all over North America from all walks of life. All races and religions are represented. It's claimed that per capita, more academics, Ph.D.s, and scientists live in the University Triangle than in any other part of the country. This is arguably the "least Southern" place in the Carolinas, maybe in the entire South. Finding neighbors from your old hometown is highly possible.

Universities and colleges profoundly influence lifestyles here, with a large percentage of the community either working for or with educational institutions and others benefiting from the many stimulating events connected with academic life. Dramatic performances, lectures, sports, and a host of other presentations are open to the public as well as those involved with the schools.

Research Triangle Park   High technology and research is big business here in the Carolina Midlands with Research Triangle Park. One of the nation's major centers for industrial and governmental research, this enormous facility is located on a 6,800-acre wooded tract of land located between the three cities. It employs more than 30,000 people, including some of the nation's top scientists.

Within easy driving distance from any of the Triangle cities, employees, support personnel, and associates can live just about anywhere. This recession-proof industry has beneficial impact on the economics as well as the social makeup of the community. Because of the vast number of employment opportunities in the high-tech field, this area is a popular retirement destination for engineers, electronic technicians, and computer experts. Part-time work and consulting jobs are readily available for those who do not view retirement as a career in itself.

Raleigh   The state capital, Raleigh has 286,000 inhabitants, making it the largest city in the Triangle. The combined population is fast approaching the one-million mark; however, because this is

RALEIGH–DURHAM–CHAPEL HILL WEATHER

In degrees Fahrenheit

	Jan.	April	July	Oct.	Rain	Snow
Daily highs	50	72	88	72	42"	2"
Daily lows	30	47	67	48		

RALEIGH–DURHAM–CHAPEL HILL COST OF LIVING

	Overall	Housing	Medical	Groceries	Utilities
Percentage of national average	101	106	101	99	108

spread over three cities, the density appears to be much lower than you would expect.

Home prices are predictably higher than in most other North Carolina cities, but neighborhood quality is also considerably upscale. You'll find fewer low-priced neighborhoods than elsewhere and for good reason. Wages are higher and employment steady, not varying with economic recessions.

Homes in the $250,000-plus price range have no trouble finding buyers. We visited a couple who moved to Raleigh from New York City, from a small apartment into a spacious five-bedroom home on two acres of wooded grounds. "Our entire apartment could fit into our new dining room, living room, and kitchen," they said. "And never in our wildest dreams could we have afforded to buy an apartment there." Because they bought when interest rates bottomed out, the monthly mortgage payments are one-third what they paid in rent for a tiny Manhattan apartment.

Chapel Hill   Chartered in 1789 as the nation's first state university, the University of North Carolina has helped Chapel Hill to retain the essence of what a true college town should look like. Because the population of Chapel Hill is only around 48,000, the university—with 23,000 students, 1,800 professors, and many support personnel—exerts an enormous influence on the cultural and recreational lives of the town's inhabitants. The school and the city's residents have acquired a reputation as an island of a somewhat liberal shape, conflicting with North Carolina's moderately conservative political currents.

Chapel Hill's downtown setting is user-friendly, with the casual, laid-back pace one would expect from a community that hosts a world-class university. The school is set on a 687-acre campus that is as beautiful as the institution is prestigious. The city's residential neighborhoods seem to compete with the school's famous landscaping in beautifying Chapel Hill. Nonstudent residents are encouraged to participate in the university's agenda via interesting, noncredit adult classes.

Durham   Needless to say, medical care in the Triangle is as good as it gets. All three cities and universities are loaded with hospitals, clinics, and medical schools, but Durham leads the way. It's adopted the motto "the City of Medicine." (It used to be nicknamed "Tobacco Town" because tobacco money founded Duke University—but that name seems to be politically incorrect today.) Five excellent hospitals serve the area, and Durham is famous for the university's teaching hospital. In fact, this is a larger city, with a population of about 136,000.

Duke University's two impressive campuses also influence the community, not only financially but culturally. Whether it's black-tie or blue jeans, ballet or beach music, the entire area has something for everyone. The school's cultural programs amount to an astounding 500 presentations a year.

Pinehurst/Southern Pines/Aberdeen   The villages of Pinehurst, Southern Pines, and Aberdeen, in the central part of the state, have long enjoyed the distinction of being premier golf destinations. Located within minutes of each other, this triangle of towns contains thirty-five superb championship courses within a 16-mile radius, some of which are among the most highly rated in the world.

Before they considered retirement here, many people simply thought of Pinehurst and Southern Pines as convenient stopover places on their way to Florida vacations. This was the logical place to break up the trip—about halfway for many Easterners. Why not stay over a day or two and get in a few rounds of golf? As retirement time drew nearer, some folks naturally began thinking more about Pinehurst and less about Florida.

Of course membership in Pinehurst Club was mandatory for those who bought lots in the many subdivisions ringing the golf-tennis complex. So today new buyers automatically inherit their memberships as part of the purchase price of their lots or homes.

PINEHURST–SOUTHERN PINES–ABERDEEN WEATHER

In degrees Fahrenheit

	Jan.	April	July	Oct.	Rain	Snow
Daily highs	55	68	91	71	41"	2"
Daily lows	34	51	67	58		

(They inherit the monthly fees as well.) This is an important feature, because some golf-club developments have a waiting list for membership.

Southern Pines is an offshoot development, separate from Pinehurst. Southern Pines is larger, with a population of 9,700 and a downtown area somewhat less touristy than Pinehurst's Village Center. Southern Pines is basically a residential community, liberally endowed with golf facilities and shopping malls and a quaint town center. The homes we looked at were superbly designed to fit into the Carolina Sandhills' pine and oak ambience.

Aberdeen, with 3,400 inhabitants, is the third village in this grouping. In its early days Aberdeen was a bustling center of trade and commerce. Then came quieter years as the downtown saw businesses moving out. But Aberdeen has emerged from its slump, and Main Street is lively once more, with its fine antiques shops, boutiques, and other shopping. Our impression of Aberdeen is that it's a place for relatively more affordable housing, but it's still in the golf-club circuit.

Because the elevation here is higher than most of Florida, summers aren't quite as warm or humid. Furthermore, the 55-degree January days permit plenty of outdoor activities. "Any day it's not raining, I can golf, hike, or ride horseback," said a retiree here. "When I lived in Florida, it was too damned muggy in the summer!"

More than adequate health care is covered by a 397-bed regional hospital with a medical staff of 112 physicians and 1,400 employees, assisted by 500 volunteers. A twenty-four-hour mobile intensive care unit provides up-to-date life support treatments.

The small-town atmosphere lends itself to a feeling of security, with an exceptionally low crime rate. Yet because of the large percentage of out-of-state retirees, newcomers don't feel that they stand out as they might in some other small Southern towns.

Pinehurst and Southern Pines communities are clearly upscale residential communities with a focus on golf courses and quality homes, yet they are not gated as are many country club–type developments. The neighborhoods are open; anyone can cruise through the streets without having to be a resident. This is not much of a problem, because crime levels in the Pinehurst–Southern Pines region are very low anyway.

Carolina Trace   About 25 miles north of Southern Pines, the Carolina Trace Country Club is an example of a gated development with restricted entry and twenty-four-hour security. A lake for boating and fishing plus a golf course are the central features. An interesting feature of this kind of private club community is that its isolation brings residents together. They have dinner at the clubhouse, play golf together, and make decisions about how the joint-venture should function.

When asked how they felt about being "locked in" and guarded by roving patrols, most felt good about this arrangement. It turns out that many residents retired here from high-crime places like New York, Chicago, or Detroit, so they enjoy their newfound feeling of being safe.

The centerpiece of the development is a sparkling lake that covers 300 acres with 7 miles of shoreline. This means just about everyone has either a view of the lake or a place on the water with a boat dock. In all there are seventeen small sections, or clusters, of homes. Each section has its own swimming pool and tennis courts, creating a series of neighborhoods within the development. Medical care, shopping, and other services are to be found in nearby Sanford, a town of 23,000 residents.

South Carolina

The Carolinas have much in common. They share 500 miles of scenic Atlantic coastline on one side and the spectacular Appalachian Blue Ridge Mountains on the other. Like North Carolina, the South Carolina ocean coast and Blue Ridge foothills are separated by sandhill formations, rich farmlands, and forested acreage. Aristocratic low-country cities,

SOUTH CAROLINA

Cheraw
Myrtle Beach
Columbia
Aiken   Summerville
Georgetown
Charleston
Hilton Head

SOUTH CAROLINA TAX PROFILE

Sales tax: 5% to 7%, food, drugs exempt
State income tax: graduated, 2.5% to 7%
   greater than $10,600; can't deduct
   federal income tax
Property taxes: approximately 2.5%, resi-
   dents older than 65 receive exemptions
Intangibles tax: no
Social security taxed: no
Pensions taxed: $3,000 exclusion
Gasoline tax: 16¢ per gallon

based on the plantation culture dating from the colonial plantation days, invite retirement. South Carolina is much less industrialized and high-tech than its northern neighbor and is perhaps a bit more laid-back. The coastline here is more accessible than farther north, with ocean and freshwater recreation readily available.

Like the other Atlantic coastal states, South Carolina can be divided into three regions. The first is the Coastal Plain, bordered by South Carolina's many miles of tidal shoreline, barrier islands, and colonial cities. Next is the Piedmont region, whose rolling hills, rich farmlands, and foothills comprise about two-thirds of the state's land. The third division is the Appalachians, with the highest elevation in the Blue Ridge Mountains in the northwestern part of the state.

Columbia   Here in the heart of the South, on Columbia's coastal plain, there's a city that combines all the graces of a rich past with the vibrancy of the emerging sunbelt. Columbia, South Carolina, is a center for military, academic, government, and business life. With a population of 118,000, Columbia is a city, yet small enough to feel like a small town. A surprising number of Northerners have found this to be a great place for retirement. By the way, Columbia claims to have a higher percentage of retirees living here than anywhere else in the state.

Columbia is situated at the point where the coastal plain meets the beginning of the Piedmont. At the western edge of the city, rolling foothills begin, and at the opposite edge, the country is flat all the way to the ocean. This is a comfortable city, with the vast majority of the housing owner occupied. The streets are shaded with large trees, and there's a quiet charm that comes with ordinary people living in ordinary neighborhoods. Yet Columbia has its sophisticated side as well, with a cosmopolitan feeling that goes with being a university town.

Most Old South cities grew haphazardly, with roads and streets going in random directions, without planning of any sort. But Co-

COLUMBIA WEATHER						
In degrees Fahrenheit						
	Jan.	April	July	Oct.	Rain	Snow
Daily highs	50	72	88	72	43"	5"
Daily lows	32	50	69	50		

COLUMBIA COST OF LIVING					
Percentage of national average	Overall	Housing	Medical	Groceries	Utilities
	97	91	92	98	122

lumbia is different. The British needed a capital city for South Carolina, so in 1686 they designed the first planned city in the colonies. The city's broad boulevards and architectural gems attest to its early beauty. Robert Mills, one of the pioneers of U.S. architecture, designed several buildings here as well as many in Washington, D.C. (One of his more famous works is the Washington Monument.)

Another educational center of the South, Columbia has the University of South Carolina as its focal point. The university, with 28,000 students, is a major source of cultural enrichment. Along with a nearby two-year college, the school attracts academics from around the nation, many of whom later join the ranks of Columbia's retired. All South Carolina state colleges and technical institutes waive tuition for residents older than sixty years of age (on a space-available basis). Retirees can also take full advantage of this benefit at regional campuses in Beaufort, Lancaster, Allendale, Sumter, Union, Aiken, Conway, and Spartanburg. Special low-cost spring and summer residential academic programs are also available for senior citizens.

This is a popular retirement location for military families because of the town's proximity to Fort Jackson and the obvious advantages of retiring near a military installation. Many who were stationed here fondly recall the mild weather and friendly South Carolinans. These memories are bringing the ex-GIs back to Columbia for their retirement careers. These two out-of-state groups, academic and military, contribute toward making the Columbia area heterogeneous, with open, accepting feelings toward newcomers.

We found several retirees who had started out intending to retire elsewhere, but somehow wound up happily retiring in the Carolinas. For example, one retired couple admitted that they had always planned on retirement in Florida. "Every year, as we made our annual trip to Florida, we broke our trip up with a stopover in Columbia," they explained, "and again on the way back. Then, one day, just before retirement, we realized that we really liked Columbia better than Florida!" They decided to rent an apartment, just to "see how Columbia feels." They found low living costs and friendly, cultured neighbors. "We never made it to Florida," they said with satisfied smiles. "We still go there for vacations, though."

I asked him how he felt as a Yankee moving into a Deep South town. Did he find any prejudices? "To tell you the truth, I haven't noticed anything like that," he said. "My neighbors are just as nice as the ones we had back home, but they're definitely more friendly. Other Northerners warned us, 'They'll be neighborly, yes, but they'll never invite you to their daughter's debutante party unless you were born in Columbia.'" He shrugged his shoulders and said, "That's a relief to me, because the last place I'd want to be invited would be to some teenager's debutante party! I'd have to invent an excuse why I couldn't go."

Another advantage they pointed out—aside from the low cost of quality housing—is the excellent medical care available. (As a pharmacist, he was aware of such things.) About thirteen hospitals serve the area with more than 500 doctors to treat your ills.

There's always something happening around Columbia. Ten golf courses can be found in the area. For spectator sports Columbia has a minor league baseball team. Open-air concerts and festivals are held at frequent intervals, and the nation's oldest community theater presents drama productions.

Aiken   Aiken (pop. 25,000) is a genteel Old South town located in the western corner of South Carolina's Piedmont region, with the majestic Blue Ridge Mountains a short drive away. Aiken's robust business district makes it look larger than it actually is, because it's the shopping and employment center for a large area. Aiken County has about 135,000 people.

One way Aiken differs from many other Southern towns is that so many out-of-state people have moved here that distinctions between natives and newcomers have blurred. Townspeople are used

AIKEN WEATHER					
In degrees Fahrenheit					
	Jan.	April	July	Oct.	Rain	Snow
Daily highs	57	77	91	77	43"	1"
Daily lows	33	49	69	50		

AIKEN COST OF LIVING					
Percentage of	Overall	Housing	Medical	Groceries	Utilities
national average	93	78	94	104	92

to different accents and other lifestyles; a cosmopolitan mix has broken through all but the most inbred social barriers. Where did these outsiders come from? Initially people came to work for the Department of Energy's high-tech, atomic-energy facility in Aiken. The department imported engineers, physicists, technicians, bricklayers—you name it—from all over the country.

When the energy project was finally up and running, many workers moved elsewhere to new jobs. Others—some nearing retirement anyway—elected to stay. The word soon got around about this beautiful little city with mild winters, friendly people, and low real estate prices. This brought even more outsiders into Aiken. The result is an eclectic collection of people from all over the country.

Aiken isn't all single-family homes, mansions, and honeysuckle. Modern condominiums, apartments, and gated communities are home to many families. Away from town you'll find small farms and homes on acreages for horses or garden hobbies. Luxury communities—Kalmia Landing, Woodside Plantation, Midland Valley, Cedar Creek, and Houndslake—offer country-club retirement accommodations and an atmosphere of studied elegance.

From its inception Aiken was known as a health resort. Wealthy people from Charleston and the coastal plantations came here to escape the sultry, lowland summer heat and malaria-bearing mosquitoes. The Civil War and its aftermath of poverty put a temporary halt to Aiken's role as a summer health resort. But by the 1890s Aiken entered a new golden age when wealthy Northerners, seeking pleasant, quiet places for their winter homes, "discovered" the town.

At an altitude of only 527 feet, the town had a climate mild enough to permit year-round grazing and was a perfect place to raise thoroughbred horses. Soon the ordinary rich, the filthy rich, and the disgustingly filthy rich bought old mansions and built new ones of their own designs. They bought farms for their racehorses and enclosed pastures with white fences. They established the Palmetto Golf Club in 1893 and were slicing drives into the lake by the time the first thoroughbred colts were frisking in the meadows.

These activities quickly established Aiken as a rich man's playground, mostly a haven for wealthy Yankees from New York and Connecticut. These newcomers brought prosperity to Aiken and, with it, a return to a genteel lifestyle that had disappeared with the Civil War. Aiken's old, aristocratic families quickly accepted the winter residents into local society despite different customs and accents. This established a tradition of openness and hospitality that has characterized Aiken ever since. Today the super-rich Northerners have gone elsewhere, yet the legacy of hospitality and friendliness remains.

Aiken boasts a campus of the University of South Carolina and Aiken Technical College. This means free, or nearly free, courses for senior citizens and entry into the academic community of the town. There's a 190-bed medical facility that, we were told, has an excellent reputation. There are VA hospitals in both Columbia and Augusta for military retirees and their dependents.

Recreational choices abound; because the weather is generally mild, year-round outdoor activities are possible. Nineteen golf courses within a 20-mile radius of Aiken make this sport convenient; several feature senior citizens' clubs. The famous Masters Tournament is played every year in nearby Augusta. Each autumn on the shores of Lake Hartwell, Clemson University conducts a camping program for senior citizens. Fishing, swimming, even water-skiing for all those old-timers who go for that sort of nonsense, are available at any number of nearby ponds or lakes. Hunting and fishing permits are free to residents older than age sixty-five.

Cheraw   Cheraw is one of South Carolina's oldest and most picturesque inland towns. Named for the Cheraw Indians, whose main town was nearby, the town began as a small trading post.

CHERAW WEATHER					
In degrees Fahrenheit					
	Jan.	April	July	Oct.	Rain	Snow
Daily highs	52	74	90	74	43"	3"
Daily lows	29	46	67	48		

Cheraw was as far upriver as steamboats could travel on the Great Pee Dee River and was the scene of busy steamboat traffic in the nineteenth century. The area of the original plan is now the nucleus of a 213-acre historic district, listed in the National Register of Historic Places, and is rich with gardens, trees, and parks and the architectural legacy of more than 200 years.

Cheraw is located on the edge of the Carolina Sandhills that stretch from Pinehurst, North Carolina, to Warm Springs, Georgia. The town is located less than two hours from Columbia and Charlotte, three hours from the mountains, two hours from Myrtle Beach, and one hour from Pinehurst. Today Cheraw is a beautiful, prosperous town of close to 6,000 people who take pride in taking the best of the past and making it an important part of the future.

Citizens here have been involved in preservation efforts for almost a century. Well known for its trees for more than 150 years, Cheraw has been named a "Tree City" by the state tree-preservation program every year since the program's inception.

Cheraw is another of those towns that go out of the way to welcome newcomers. The head of Cheraw's welcoming committee says, "We are proud of our wonderful retirees who have become a vital part of our community. The town's people are committed to the arts, recreation, good schools, and government." She went on to point out that in Cheraw, as in many small Southern towns, the best way to immediately become involved in the community is by joining a church. Cheraw is home to almost all denominations, and any congregation is delighted to welcome new members. Joining Cheraw's chamber of commerce also provides a good chance to meet the community at the bimonthly Business After Hours.

Cheraw has beautiful antebellum neighborhoods as well as newer subdivisions. Prices here are about average for towns of similar size in South Carolina, about 10 percent less than national averages.

On the Ocean

Most of South Carolina's Atlantic Ocean coastline is lowland country, sparsely populated and suitable for rice cultivation. Generally the major roads and highways run far inland, with occasional roads meandering toward the ocean. Except for Hilton Head, the Charleston area, and a few isolated oceanfront towns, South Carolina's most logical beachfront retirement choices occupy a 60-mile stretch of spectacular coastline known as the Grand Strand. It begins at Little River, on the North Carolina–South Carolina border, and stretches south to the Santee River, just beyond Georgetown.

The warm waters of the Gulf Stream flow about 40 miles offshore, which explains the Grand Strand's mild weather. It's said that winter temperatures here are only two degrees cooler than the northern Florida coast. However, local residents qualify this by saying, "We do get some right smart cold spells from time to time." Snows are rare.

Sparsely settled a few years ago, the Grand Strand is blooming with new residential developments. Timber plantations along the shore are being replaced by several upscale resorts, some complete with golf courses and clubhouses. Some of the developments are priced well within the average retiree's budget.

Myrtle Beach   Myrtle Beach sits in the center of the accessible beach areas of the Grand Strand. With about 30,000 year-round habitants, Myrtle Beach doesn't sound like such a big town, but seasonal visitors can boost the population more than tenfold. The full length of the Grand Strand has a permanent population of

MYRTLE BEACH–GEORGETOWN WEATHER						
In degrees Fahrenheit						
	Jan.	April	July	Oct.	Rain	Snow
Daily highs	60	75	89	75	51"	2"
Daily lows	40	53	71	53		

MYRTLE BEACH COST OF LIVING					
Percentage of national average	Overall	Housing	Medical	Groceries	Utilities
	98	95	92	103	98

about 60,000, a large percentage of whom are retired, but visitors expand the population to more than 300,000. Spring and fall have always lured golfers to enjoy the more than ninety golf courses along the Grand Strand. And summer traditionally draws crowds of vacationers to delight in beach sun and fun. Each summer seems to bring more and more tourists. Retirement here means you will be living in a really busy tourist resort. The compensation is that you don't have far to go for golf or other tourist attractions.

When we first researched Myrtle Beach about ten years ago, I described the town as South Carolina's equivalent of a Florida Panhandle resort: tourist-frenzied in the summer and somewhat relaxed in the winter. In fact many restaurants and small businesses closed down when tourists deserted for the winter. Inexpensive homes were almost the rule, and rentals were plentiful. I reported that after Labor Day, "the town drops its frantic, super-hero role and changes to its mild-mannered, sleepy identity for the rest of the year."

Since that time the population of the Grand Strand has doubled. All seasons are busy. Myrtle Beach has become one of the South's premier golfing meccas, drawing visitors from all over the country. According to the chamber of commerce, Myrtle Beach has the greatest number of golf courses per square mile in the world! People who live in country-club developments in other parts of the South routinely organize excursions to play golf on the Grand Strand. Besides golf courses you'll find an assortment of golf schools, golf shops, and a wide range of golf vacation packages should you decide to come here to test the water (or the sand traps for that matter).

A proliferation of country-and-western entertainment centers, modeled after Missouri's Branson and Tennessee's Grand Ole Opry, have joined golf to make full-tilt tourism a year-round business. Adding to the momentum are events like the annual Harley-Davidson motorcycle rally and the Sun Fun Festival. The increased tourism is nice for commerce, but it creates traffic congestion and additional strain on summer-season facilities already under pressure. With an increased workforce and long-term visitors competing for housing, bargain real estate is out of the picture today.

Despite the aforementioned drawbacks, folks are still coming here to retire. A look around tells why. Between Myrtle Beach's main thoroughfare (which used to be Highway 17) and the ocean, several blocks of beautiful homes on spacious, well-landscaped lots provide neighborhoods of gracious living, and other equally nice areas are found away from the business centers. Other choices are golf-course communities and upscale subdivisions as well as more modest homes between the main street and the Highway 17 bypass.

Georgetown   At the end of the Grand Strand, halfway between Myrtle Beach and Charleston, the small city of Georgetown (pop. 8,950) offers a fascinating snapshot of the colonial and antebellum past. Actually Georgetown's rich history goes back even further than colonial times. Many readers will be surprised to know that Winyah Bay was the site of the earliest European settlement in North America. Colonists from Spain established a settlement at Winyah Bay in 1526, a century before the Pilgrims landed on Plymouth Rock. By 1729 Georgetown was a thriving shipping port for the highly successful indigo and rice plantations in the region. By the time of the American Revolution, Georgetown was an important city with a well-developed class of prominent and influential planter families. Thomas Lynch Jr., one of Georgetown's most vocal patriots, was a signer of the Declaration of Independence. Another area planter, Christopher Gadsen, is remembered for the flag he designed: "Don't Tread on Me." Georgetown resident Francis Marion was the legendary "Swamp Fox," who led a ragged band of followers to handily defeat the British in this area.

I hate to use the timeworn cliché "a town where time stood still," but the saying fits Georgetown perfectly. This is a virtual treasury of colonial, antebellum, and Victorian architecture. You can't help but feel humble as you tread silent, tree-shaded streets past historic homes, each one more ancient than the last, some more than 250 years old. It's easy to picture men wearing tricornered hats and ladies dressed in long skirts and petticoats ambling along the streets. You begin to wonder how life in South Carolina must have been before the American Revolution, before the Civil War, before the invention of automobiles, electricity, and miniature golf.

Georgetown is small and soft-spoken, yet immensely proud of its historic business district. The main street that faces the harbor has an Old World appearance, with ancient buildings in rows of pastel colors in the style of the colonies. The town clock tower sits atop the old Market Building, dating from 1842. Today the building houses a museum depicting the days of rice, indigo, and slavery.

Although Georgetown is technically located on the Grand Strand, it isn't on the ocean. The town's waterfront is Winyah Bay; the nearest ocean beaches are found at Pawley's Island, some 22 miles away. Pawley's Island is one of the oldest beach resorts in the country, having been used for recreation since the late 1700s. It also has the distinction of being one of the few South Carolina sea islands where original antebellum and Victorian beach homes have survived the occasional hurricanes that bruise the coast. Housing prices on Pawley's Island are well above average, whereas Georgetown has much more affordable places for sale, about 10 percent below the national average.

This is a place for people who used to like the old-time atmosphere of Myrtle Beach, but who are appalled at the changes in population density and proliferation of highway mall businesses. Folks who've relocated here from Ohio, Long Island, and elsewhere feel protective of their discovery; they don't want to spoil their piece of utopia. To protect the town from tourist clutter, Georgetown has some strictly enforced zoning laws that should guard against glitz and sleaze. You needn't drive to Myrtle Beach for golf—there are a dozen courses in Georgetown County. Health care is localized as well; Georgetown Memorial Hospital, a 142-bed facility, uses the latest technology. More than fifty physicians and twenty surgeons staff the facility, most of whom also maintain private practices.

Charleston   After its settlement in 1670, Charleston quickly became one of the most prosperous cities in the thirteen colonies. Charleston was the standard against which people measured other cities in terms of beauty, culture, and riches. Located in what today is called the Low Country, the land was rich and fertile. Planters, acquiring wealth from fantastically productive rice plantations, began designing mansions as lavish as money could provide. They built with such loving attention to detail and such devotion to quality and style that future generations of Charlestonians have resisted all temptations to exchange those prizes for new fashions. At least 240 homes are known to have been built before 1840 and 76 predate the American Revolution, with some dating back to the 1720s. Hundreds more date from the time of the Civil War and Reconstruction.

Today Charleston vies with Savannah for the title of most beautiful city on the Atlantic seaboard. Each scores high marks, and each claims to be the "cultural center of the South." It's difficult to

CHARLESTON WEATHER					
In degrees Fahrenheit					
	Jan.	April	July	Oct.	Rain	Snow
Daily highs	61	78	90	77	49"	—
Daily lows	38	54	71	55		

CHARLESTON COST OF LIVING					
	Overall	Housing	Medical	Groceries	Utilities
Percentage of national average	102	104	102	102	104

choose between them. Charleston is so steeped in history that a walk through its downtown streets is an adventure in time travel. It's easy to imagine fine carriages jaunting along the cobblestone streets or fashionably dressed women and nattily attired men strolling the sidewalks. A pause in front of a home built in 1720 evokes a feeling of humility as one mentally recreates the setting almost three centuries in the past. In California, where I live, any building more than one hundred years old is considered a priceless antique.

Built on a narrow peninsula, the downtown section isn't very large; the total population is approximately 100,000. The peninsula is so narrow that it's almost an island between two rivers that empty into the ocean at the city's east end. The emphasis is on private homes rather than on commercial activity. The most important enterprise (from my standpoint as a lover of seafood) in this old section is the superb collection of fine restaurants. As major tourist attractions Charleston's restaurants fully live up to their reputation for excellent seafood and Southern gourmet dishes of all descriptions. (We can never pass through town without a pause for our favorite culinary delight: she-crab soup.)

Charleston living isn't for everyone. It can be terribly formal, paced with the tempo of Southern society, intellectual pursuits, and traditional manners. We've been told that the social whirl is a closed affair, with few outsiders ever invited in.

Even if you aren't into buying historic mansions and entering the social whirl, some alternatives might be an adventure for a part-time living arrangement. You can do as the old-time planters did: live in Charleston most of the year and somewhere else for the summer. Many old mansions in Charleston's Historic District were long ago converted to apartments, which at one time rented at unusually affordable rates, given the enchanted, historic atmosphere. Carriage houses behind the mansions were remodeled into studio apartments or charming cottages with lofts converted into upstairs bedrooms. However, as Historic District real estate becomes more and more valuable, more homes are being restored to their days of antiquity, and prices for rentals have risen to match the more expensive housing.

All is not lace curtains and fresh paint in old Charleston. As in many cities the curse of urban blight hovers. Not very far from the prosperous streets described here, you'll find rows of abandoned houses, so old and uncared-for that they look as if they might collapse from old age and decay. It's unfortunate that there's not some way to preserve these old mansions. Some stand three stories high, with beautifully crafted balconies and balustrades rising the full facade. Porches, high columns, and carved woodwork add to the impression of museum pieces from an irretrievable past. Within a decade these will probably all be gone. Most neighborhoods bordering the downtown area do not look to be appropriate retirement possibilities.

More than half of the city's population lives in West Ashley and James Island, which lie just to the west of the peninsula. These locations are a mixture of old and new; older neighborhoods with brick homes and graceful oak trees settle in with newer subdivisions and commercial centers.

If you don't care to live in or near a city center, or if you can't afford one of the historic places, you should check the outskirts of Charleston or one of the outlying towns, where you can live outside the city but visit Charleston for dinner or a play any time you feel like it. Nearby places where people choose to retire are Charleston's islands or nearby towns such as Summerville (described later).

With five major hospitals, the Charleston area enjoys some of the finest medical care in the region. University of South Carolina's Medical University is a leading biomedical, teaching, patient-care, and research center.

Isle of Palms   Just east of Charleston, bordered by the Atlantic Ocean and the Intracoastal Waterway, two semitropical islands and one luxurious resort community are popular places for relocation. Miles of sandy beaches, pastel homes, and warm, friendly people make relocation pleasant. The Isle of Palms is a classic family-oriented beachfront community offering a wide variety of accommodations and recreation options. Wild Dunes, located on 1,600 acres at the northeastern end of the Isle of Palms, is a premier resort community with championship golf and tennis facilities, a full-service marina, and a full selection of homes and villas for sale.

Sullivan's Island   This is the Isle of Palms's sister island. More of a residential beach community, Sullivan's Island is located just south of the Isle of Palms, across Breach Inlet. There are beautiful beaches and an impressive selection of homes on this island. Natives describe the difference between the two islands this way: Isle of Palms is "more of a resort island," whereas Sullivan's Island is "more of a beach town."

Sullivan's Island offers much more, however, than a quiet beach-town atmosphere. Here you'll find a quaint restaurant area, historic Fort Moultrie, a working lighthouse, public tennis courts, and an old-fashioned community playground complete with a grandstand gazebo! Of course Sullivan's Island offers all the natural amenities you could want: wide sandy beaches, fishing, swimming, boating, sunning, and more.

Johns Island   More rural in character, Johns Island combines an intricate network of waterways with fertile farmland, residential property, and limited commercial development. Daniel Island and the Cainhoy Peninsula, which lie east and north of the peninsula, are among the most recently annexed areas of the city. The pristine Daniel Island, a full 4,500 acres in size, is just beginning to reflect the thoughtfully planned, environmentally sensitive community mapped out in the Daniel Island Master Plan. It is sure to be the future complement to Charleston's historic downtown.

Summerville   Summerville, a small city of 27,000 people, is about 20 miles from Charleston—near enough to take advantage of all that the Southern jewel offers, yet far enough away not to be bothered by the frenzy of the city. Located on a relatively high, pine-encrusted ridge, the town was first inhabited in the late 1700s. Traditionally, from May to September, families along the nearby Ashley River and from coastal Charleston fled the malarial lowlands to enjoy their forest colony. Because they spent every summer here, what more logical name could it have than Summerville?

After the Civil War the town gained a reputation as a health center and winter resort. Today it is gaining favor as a place for retirement. Much of its charm derives from the natural beauty of the historic architecture—with 700 buildings on the National Register of Historic Places—and the profusion of azaleas, camellias, and wisteria that line the streets and provide seasonal blooms. Its rambling streets, which deliberately wind around large pine trees to avoid destroying them, also add charm to Summerville.

Early on Summerville realized that these pines were among the town's biggest assets. So when the village incorporated as a town in 1847, elected officials passed a law that prohibited the cutting of trees without permission and fined offenders severely. The town's motto was born, and still holds strong today: *Sacra Pinus Esto*–"The Pine Is Sacred." The ordinance is one of the oldest of its kind in the United States and is still on the books.

Summerville's special hometown feeling bubbles over during the Christmas holiday season. A special tree-lighting ceremony in the town square starts things off, and every Thursday until Christmas the town enjoys strolling carolers, late-evening shopping, free hot cider and cookies, free gift wrapping, Santa in the Square, and horse-drawn carriage rides through the historic district.

Hilton Head Island   Still in South Carolina, just 40 miles north of Savannah, Georgia, Hilton Head Island is the epitome of a luxury retirement area. The island is divided into eight gated developments (called "plantations") centered around active living—golf, tennis, boating, and 12 miles of white, sandy beach.

This semitropical island is defined by its tidal rivers and streams, and by its unspoiled forests of moss-draped live oak, magnolia, and palmetto. Its white, sandy beaches, quiet lagoons, meandering creeks, and expanses of sea marsh symbolize the romance and mystery of the Carolina coastline.

Hilton Head Island was discovered in the 1600s and through the years managed to preserve its natural heritage because of the residents' sensitivity to the island's pristine beauty. Development has been a model for forward-looking planning and conservation. Custom homes and villas are interspersed with open areas and wildlife preserves. Commercial zones are free of garish signs and billboards, and the beaches are pristine and clean. More than a million visitors come here every year, yet the island is refreshingly tranquil. Traffic, commercial, and recreational facilities are coordinated to allow visitors and residents to coexist nicely.

Golfers love the courses here and the 425 holes of golf spread over twelve locations on Hilton Head and nearby Daufuskie Island. For tennis buffs there are more than 250 courts, ranging from major complexes that host national championships to one or two courts adjoining a condo or apartment complex. Five hundred acres are reserved as a forest preserve with an astonishing 260 species of birds, alligators, deer, raccoon, and wild turkey. (A small gate fee is required to enter.) Hiking, shrimping from the shore, biking, and boating fill out the menu of outdoor activities. The list of gourmet restaurants is also impressive. According to the chamber of commerce, about 200 restaurants, cafes, and fast-food emporiums serve everything from gourmet cuisine to stand-up pizza and egg rolls.

The bottom line: This is a place for those who can afford to pay top dollar for a high-quality lifestyle. Housing prices, although not the most expensive in the country, are certainly not for the fainthearted. Also be aware that not too long ago, a new city administration was elected on a platform of shutting off the flow of retirees into the island. Apparently many feel that "now that I'm here, we can lock the gates."

Hilton Head Island supports a large community of doctors, dentists, and other health-care professionals. The local sixty-eight-bed Hospital Medical Campus has a medical staff that represents more than thirty specialties and subspecialties, a number frequently found in hospitals several times its size.

Sun City Hilton Head   The Del Webb corporation's Sun City retirement development began in the Southwest several decades ago and quickly became synonymous with planned retirement concepts. The first development was an Arizona desert setting that featured home designs appropriate to the climate and style of the Old West. Before long Sun City clones began appearing in other parts of the country with appropriate motifs and designs to match different environments.

Now South Carolina has its own Del Webb development: Sun City Hilton Head. Located on 5,600 acres of what had once been a pine forest, Sun City eventually will have 8,000 homes with

35 percent of the land dedicated to lakes, lagoons, and woods. Since its beginning in 1994, more than 3,900 residents have moved here, and construction is under way for more homes. Sun City Hilton Head is located 13 miles from the island of Hilton Head, 6 miles off Interstate 95. Like other Del Webb projects, this one features golf and tennis, and emphasizes an active community lifestyle.

This new development fulfills much of the original Arizona concept, but with a motif adapted to South Carolina's gracious Southern traditions. The community is focused on a town center designed to resemble a traditional Southern town square, complete with a picturesque clock tower. The Village Center offers indoor/outdoor swimming pools, a tennis club, bocci courts, a bowling center, a huge fitness complex, and other amenities you would expect to find in a Sun City.

Two eighteen-hole golf courses are in place, with a 10,400-square-foot clubhouse; another clubhouse and an additional nine holes are planned. The arts and cultural life includes live theater, dance, and a variety of galleries. The well-respected Savannah Symphony and other cultural delights of Savannah are a short drive away, and those of Hilton Head Island are even closer. The advantage to this type of retirement—besides quality surroundings and excellent facilities—is the carefully planned social structure already in place when newcomers move in. You'll find instant involvement in bridge clubs, golf foursomes, hobbies, travel clubs, and much more. It eases the effort of making new friends in the adopted community. Everything is in place for you to start a new life.

Georgia

The state of Georgia is trying hard to tempt out-of-state retirees into moving here rather than continuing on to Florida, and a growing number of folks discover that they like the state's varied menu of locations and its sunbelt climate. The largest state east of the Mississippi, Georgia stretches from the golden beaches of

GEORGIA TAX PROFILE

Sales tax: 4% to 6%, drugs exempt
State income tax: graduated, 1% to 6% greater than $7,000; can't deduct federal income tax
Property taxes: taxed on 40% of market value minus $2,000 homestead exemption; typically 0.98%, plus variable local taxes
Intangibles tax: yes
Social security taxed: no
Pensions taxed: excludes first $10,000 for older taxpayers
Gasoline tax: 7.5¢ per gallon, plus 3% sales tax

the Atlantic to the foothills of the Appalachians. The Blue Ridge Mountains taper off in the northern end of the state, but not before rewarding the region with rich valleys, forested hills, and scenic mountains. Another good prospect for retirement is Georgia's Atlantic coast, characterized by barrier islands with moss-draped oaks and magnificently preserved colonial towns, affordable retirement choices that once were domains of millionaires. To the south is the Plantation Trace with its early spring, delightful small cities, and nearness to both the Gulf and Atlantic. Another popular retirement area is around Augusta, which enjoys the benefits of two geographical areas: the Piedmont Plateau and the Atlantic Coastal Plain. This is golf and thoroughbred country.

Valdosta   In their haste to get to Florida, many vacationers zip right past the city of Valdosta (pop. 44,000), never suspecting that a delightful little city sits undiscovered just a short skip away from Interstate 75. Some tourists stay overnight in motels, maybe getting in some shopping at the manufacturers' outlet stores before steering their cars back onto the interstate to resume the high-speed parade to the saltwater beaches a couple of hours down the cement pavement.

Valdosta is set in Georgia's Plantation Trace, a region marked by fertile plains, bountiful woods, and hundreds of blue lakes. Steeped in Victorian history and architecture as well as modern subdivisions, Valdosta stands out as south Georgia's dominant city. Featuring immaculately maintained neighborhoods shaded by enormous trees and enhanced by landscaping that emphasizes flowering plants, Valdosta's residential sections are exceptionally inviting. One retiree affirmed that this well-groomed, upscale ambience influenced his decision to choose Valdosta as a place to settle, saying, "You can tell Valdostans respect their town by the way they treat it. It's a joy to live among people like that."

To be fair I'll have to admit that our first Valdosta research co-incided with the first riotous days of spring in the midst of an outrageous explosion of blossoms splashing color from every tree, bush, and garden. It's no coincidence that Valdosta is called "the Azalea City." Yet the overall quality of these neighborhoods tran-scends mere flower beds and magnolia trees. In Valdosta the phrase *quality living* is not a shopworn cliché; it's an apt description.

A glance at cost-of-living charts indicates that Valdosta's is less than the national averages, with housing costs 16 percent below av-erage. The region benefits from a recession-proof economy based on military and university payrolls, which don't vary a great deal. Be-cause of a high turnover of Air Force families (mostly officers) who are transferred in and out for training, there's a wealth of apartment complexes scattered about town—more than one hundred.

As I visited neighborhoods, noticing beautiful, quality brick homes on half-acre lots, a theme kept recurring: This is a place where a couple cashing in equity in overpriced sections of the country could move up and live in a fabulous neighborhood, in a style never dreamed of—and probably still bank some of their profits from the sale of their house.

The downtown area, too, shows that Valdosta residents care. An ambitious renovation of an already nice-looking town center is going to make this one of the showplaces of the South. To finance this project a special sales-tax measure passed with an overwhelming margin, a refreshing vote of confidence in Valdosta and its future.

An important consideration for those retiring from other parts of the nation is Valdosta's cosmopolitan retiree community; they come from everywhere! Large numbers of Air Force officers spent

VALDOSTA WEATHER

In degrees Fahrenheit

	Jan.	April	July	Oct.	Rain	Snow
Daily highs	70	80	94	83	49"	1"
Daily lows	45	54	71	59		

VALDOSTA COST OF LIVING

	Overall	Housing	Medical	Groceries	Utilities
Percentage of national average	95	90	92	99	91

training time at Moody Air Force Base. Naturally when retirement draws near, when military families begin discussing favorite towns, they remember this area with fondness.

This is a university town, too, and Valdosta State University's grounds and campus are in keeping with the upscale look of its surroundings. The university offers continuing education, with low-cost fees, in classes ranging from calligraphy to tai chi. Transportation is another strong point here.

The surrounding countryside's woodlands and numerous lakes make hunters and anglers happy. The federally owned Grand Bay Wildlife Area provides 5,900 acres of hunting preserve. With a wildlife management stamp firmly affixed to their state hunting licenses, sportsmen decimate ducks and geese as they make their way south each fall.

Three hospitals provide excellent health-care services to the Valdosta area, totaling more than 359 beds and about 125 doctors. Several health-related firms and nursing homes provide auxiliary care as needed. Smith Hospital is a seventy-one-bed acute-care hospital in nearby Hahira, with twenty-four-hour emergency services.

Savannah Georgia was the last of England's thirteen colonies to be settled, and Savannah was the first British settlement in the state of Georgia. It all started in 1733, when England was anxious to secure her claim to the territory against Spanish encroachment from Florida. General James Edward Oglethorpe selected a spot to settle on the Savannah River, 10 miles from the Atlantic, on the edge of Yamacraw Bluff. Savannah's historic city hall now sits on the same bluff overlooking the Savannah River where Oglethorpe landed. Besides a military outpost, Oglethorpe hoped to create a planned city—a center of agriculture, manufacturing, and export. He was eminently successful. Instead of allowing a traditional, haphazard village layout to develop, Oglethorpe designed a system of street grids, broken by a series of public squares. From the beginning, Savannah was designed to be beautiful as well as defensible. This was the country's first planned city, a masterpiece of urban design.

Instead of Charleston's ostentatious one-of-a-kind showpieces, which were built as winter residences for inland planters, Savannah's antebellum mansions were owned by merchants, shippers, and townspeople. They preferred the dignified, formal expression of

SAVANNAH WEATHER						
In degrees Fahrenheit						
	Jan.	April	July	Oct.	Rain	Snow
Daily highs	60	78	91	78	49"	—
Daily lows	38	54	72	56		

SAVANNAH COST OF LIVING					
Percentage of	Overall	Housing	Medical	Groceries	Utilities
national average	101	102	96	100	108

Italianate, English Regency, and Gothic Revival. Homes in Savannah were designed to harmonize with each other, precisely arranged around parklike squares. Many homes in Savannah's historic district are so well preserved and fit so perfectly in the scheme of things they look as if they were constructed last year. Of the original twenty-four squares in the master plan, twenty-two still exist. Today these squares—tastefully landscaped with live oak, azaleas, fountains, and statues—give Savannah that charming flavor that sets the city apart as unique as well as beautiful.

Our first research visit to Savannah was about fifteen years ago, when the historic city center was in the first stages of renovation; at that point Savannah had a long way to go. Crime statistics looked dismal, the downtown was not someplace you would care to walk after dark, and rehabilitation seemed impossible. How things have changed!

With loving care and determined community action, Savannah's downtown historic district (the largest of its kind in the country) has been not only restored, but made exceptionally livable. It changed from an area of above-average crime to a safe place to be. In fact *Walking Magazine* nominated downtown Savannah as one of "The Ten Top Walking Cities in the U.S." You can stroll the historic district, the cobblestone riverfront area, or City Market.

Four blocks in the heart of Savannah's historic district have been renovated to capture the authentic atmosphere and character of the old marketplace. Restaurants, open-air cafes, jazz clubs, theme shops, and crafts and gift shops blend to create a pleasant place to pause during a walk, have lunch, and enjoy the scene. The market features artists working in their lofts and exhibiting their works for sale. Savannah's determination to protect and improve its historic sites presents a model for historic-preservation efforts.

For a flavor of Savannah, read John Berendt's book *Midnight in the Garden of Good and Evil*, which is set in the heart of the historic district. Tourism in Savannah increased more than 13 percent in 1996; folks wanted to see the places described in the novel. The motion-picture version of the book was filmed on location in Savannah, with lovely old mansions as backgrounds.

Savannah has 150,000 inhabitants, which makes it too large for some tastes. But Savannah is surrounded by some very livable communities, probably more suitable for retirement than the city's historic center (as well as more affordable). The greater Savannah area comprises a 50-mile radius of Chatham County and has a total population of nearly 520,000. In the Savannah area the range of real estate varies from the very expensive properties on Skidaway Island, where building lots run into six-figure prices, to livable neighborhoods in nearby towns where acceptable places can be purchased for less than $100,000.

One of Savannah's fastest-growing residential areas is on the fringes of the south side, only 6 miles from the historic district. A collection of attractive neighborhoods offer quality single-family housing as well as a number of apartment complexes, townhouses, and shopping centers. To zip downtown is a matter of minutes.

Savannah's Islands

Eighteen miles east of downtown Savannah, Tybee Island is the prototype of a summer beach community. People from Savannah and tourists from all over come here to enjoy sunning and shell collecting on the island's 2 miles of white sand beaches on the Atlantic. However, the 3,000 year-round residents enjoy the vacation atmosphere all year long. Accommodations are divided into short-term rentals of condos and apartments and permanent-resident housing, which tends to be older and not fancy. Other island communities on the way to Tybee Island are Wilmington, Whitemarsh, and Talahi. Like most Georgian islands, they are not crowded and have several nice-looking developments.

The ultimate in upscale living hereabouts can be found at Skidaway Island, the Isle of Hope, Southbridge, and a few other developments. Many of these are gated communities, very posh, and usually offer private golf-course membership as a part of ownership fees.

Brunswick and the Golden Isles A hundred years ago—when being a millionaire meant more than having equity in an above-average Connecticut home—millionaires from all over the country converged upon the Golden Isles and encouraged their contractors and interior decorators to enter the competition for the fanciest homes possible. The objects of their affection were the islands of St. Simons and Jekyll on the south Georgia coast.

The mainland base camp and supply for the islands is the conservative old town of Brunswick. Compared with its rich island cousins, Brunswick is a rather ordinary community of approximately 20,000 inhabitants. But there's a charm about the place that money can't buy.

The town was founded before the American Revolution, with the names of streets and squares such as Prince, Gloucester, Norwich, and Newcastle honoring English nobility of the time. Property here is reasonable (if not downright cheap), and the homes are well kept. Streets are sheltered by overhanging oak trees hung with Spanish moss—quiet and peaceful. Some antebellum homes with columns and balconies grace the side streets, mixed in with more modern cottages. We saw a few mobile-home parks, but none had the class of Florida parks. These seem to be more for economical living, without extensive landscaping and organized clubhouse activities. All in all Brunswick looks like the place to live for those who want to enjoy the fishing, beaches, and amenities, if not the ambience of nearby Jekyll and St. Simons without paying the higher cost of actually living on the islands.

Development on the islands began in the 1880s when opulent families like the J. P. Morgans, Rockefellers, and Goulds formed the Jekyll Island Club. Only club members were permitted to live on the

BRUNSWICK–GOLDEN ISLES WEATHER						
In degrees Fahrenheit						
	Jan.	April	July	Oct.	Rain	Snow
Daily highs	61	78	91	78	49"	—
Daily lows	38	54	71	56		

island, making this one of the most exclusive resorts in the entire world. Historians estimate that at one time Jekyll Island Club members represented one-sixth of the world's wealth!

Because Jekyll Island is now a state park, and because all the lovely homes here are situated on state-owned land, the homes are purchased, but the land itself must be leased from the state of Georgia. Although homeowners don't pay property taxes (after all, they don't own the property), their lease payments for the land equal what taxes would normally be. Technically a real estate transaction on Jekyll Island involves buying a lease instead of a deed. But this doesn't affect the price, because the cost of the lease is equal to the value of a home on a conventional piece of land.

Nearby Sea Island is another mind-boggling upscale development, this one dating from the 1920s. The country's most successful barons of industry and finance constructed enormous mansions in the style of the Roaring Twenties that the Great Gatsby would have adored. These gorgeous homes are the island's hallmark, but since the end of World War II, a few less-ambitious homes have made their appearance (less ambitious in style, perhaps, but not in price!).

St. Simons Island Homes on Jekyll Island and Sea Island are not places the average retiree can afford, especially Sea Island. But St. Simons Island is another story. Here you'll find many affordable neighborhoods and charming rural areas interspersed with the higher-cost spreads.

Originally named San Simeon by sixteenth-century Spanish colonists, St. Simons is the largest of Georgia's fabled Golden Isles. Britain took over in 1736, and the island flourished as rice, indigo, and cotton plantations expanded. Later islanders actively participated in the revolution against British rule. The revolutionary warship Old Ironsides was clad with iron-hard planks from live oak trees hewn on St. Simons Island.

Today sprawling plantations of the nineteenth century have become beautiful residential areas, golf courses, tennis courts, and quaint commercial areas with numerous shops and restaurants. The island's original town center is called the Village, a quaint district at the island's southern tip. The Village includes a 200-year-old working lighthouse, a great fishing pier, shops, boutiques, and a coastal history museum. Many handsome homes—both large Victorians and cute cottages—sit within walking distance from the Village, often set back from the road under spreading oak trees festooned with Spanish moss. The northern portion of St. Simons Island is less crowded, with homes set on wooded acreage along the lightly traveled road. Several developments are under way here, with upscale housing set among oaks and palmettos.

Instead of rice or cotton, the major harvest today is tourists. They come here year-round to swim and sail along St. Simons's miles of lovely beaches, to challenge its eighty-one holes of golf, and to dine in gourmet restaurants. Island residents manage quite well coexisting with tourists. Several shopping areas hide behind shrubbery, partially hidden from view from the main road that curves along the beach side of the island. Several miles of fine public beach invite picnics and sun bathing.

Georgia's Blue Ridge Mountains

The Appalachian range pushes into north-central and northeastern Georgia with a mountainous plateau that rises to the state's highest elevations. With a total land mass of 1,400 square miles, this picturesque and uncrowded three-county area has only 71,000 residents, many of them retirees who have come from all parts of the country to relocate in this beautiful Blue Ridge setting.

With lovely mountain scenery everywhere, you're never far from lakes, rivers, and state parks. The Chattooga Wild and Scenic River is nearby, with dramatic waterfalls and spectacular rapids and other natural beauties. Deep canyons like the 1,200-foot chasm of Tallulah Gorge, high peaks like the 3,600-foot Blue Ridge Crest, and the spectacular 729-foot plume of Amicalola Falls all combine to create some of the most dramatic and stirring scenery of the Appalachian chain. The famous Appalachian Trail traverses the counties. All this wilderness thrives here, yet is 90 miles or less from Atlanta. South of here the Blue Ridge Mountains dwindle into foothills and finally change into gentle hill country as you approach the fringes of metropolitan Atlanta.

Successful publicity has taken its toll in northeast Georgia because of the number of people who've decided to relocate here. Although not overwhelming, the influx of newcomers to a sparsely settled area naturally pushed up real estate prices. Once at bargain basement levels, it's no longer a buyer's market here, especially in Rabun County. In fact the campaign to attract retirees

was so successful that the Clayton Chamber of Commerce was be-
sieged with so many requests for relocation packets they had to start
charging money to send them out—printing costs, postage, and
handling got out of hand. But this doesn't mean homes are expensive; they're just not bargains any longer.

Rabun, Lumpkin, and Habersham Counties have several delightful towns suitable for retirement. Clayton, in Rabun County,
has attracted the most attention, probably because it's one of the
more picturesque in Blue Ridge Mountain country. Other locations—such as Clarkesville, Demorest, Helen, and Dahlonega—
haven't achieved quite the same popularity. To date the demand for
homes in these locales hasn't quite reached the level in Clayton. The
terrain around these latter towns can be more accurately described
as Blue Ridge foothills rather than Blue Ridge Mountains, but this
doesn't detract from their charm.

None of the dozen locales that make up this region are very
large. Clayton, with a population of 1,700, is the largest town in
the high-mountain region of Chattahoochee National Forest.
Dahlonega is the largest in the three-county area, with a population of 3,100. Many places here are mere villages. Helen, for example, has only 300 year-round residents. For this reason folks
hereabouts don't think in terms of towns; when you ask where
they live, they'll reply "Rabun County" or "Habersham County"
rather than mention a specific locality. But the commercial districts in these towns are larger than one would expect because
they serve customers from the surrounding countryside. For example, Clayton is the commercial center for Rabun County's
12,000 residents; as such, it provides an unusually good selection
of shopping, business, and medical services.

A natural getaway near the town of Clayton is an area called
Sylvan Falls. Next to the Chattahoochee National Forest, about 600
homes are tucked away in the forest here, some with lookout van-
tage points from a 2,500-foot-high ridge. Not all homes are blessed

RABUN COUNTY WEATHER						
In degrees Fahrenheit						
	Jan.	April	July	Oct.	Rain	Snow
Daily highs	52	69	84	69	60"	10"
Daily lows	32	45	65	46		

with such breathtaking views, but each enjoys its own little natural paradise of rustic beauty. I once visited a couple, retired here from New Orleans, who live on the apex of the ridge. As we gazed out over the view, Marjorie said: "We feel like we're on the edge of Heaven here in the Blue Ridge Mountains of northeast Georgia. It has to be one of the most beautiful spots in the country!"

One feature all residents point out proudly is their four-season weather with gentle summers. As local boosters say, "This is where spring spends the summer." Flowering trees in the spring, delightful summers, and fall colors keep you aware of the seasons, yet comfortable enough to enjoy them.

Few communities the size of Clayton can support a senior citizens' center, and here is no exception. As an excellent substitute the chamber of commerce organized a club called the Silver Eagles. About 200 enthusiastic members hold monthly meetings, elect officers, arrange social activities and tours, and share their expertise with others in the community. The camaraderie developed among the members is contagious. This is the place for newcomers to come and meet their new neighbors and forge all-important community connections. The program is such a success that it's being emulated in other parts of the country.

Clarkesville (pop. 1,400), the county seat of Habersham County, is another town often praised by retirement writers. A tourist brochure claims it is just an hour's drive from Atlanta, but I'd hesitate a long while before getting into a car with anyone who makes the 75-mile drive in an hour! The countryside here is made up of rolling hills rather than low mountains, and although not as picturesque as Clayton, it has a rural charm.

Another major retirement destination is Dahlonega, the location of the first full-blown gold strike in the United States. Gold was discovered here in 1828 and can still be panned today. Dahlonega boomed until gold was discovered in California in 1849. Suddenly the local miners deserted their claims en masse and hot-footed it out West. The restored county courthouse now has a gold museum.

Athens Athens is located approximately 70 miles east-north-east of Atlanta—only an hour and a half drive on the interstate—providing the sophistication of a big town with the coziness of a

ATHENS WEATHER					
In degrees Fahrenheit					
	Jan.	April	July	Oct.	Rain	Snow
Daily highs	62	75	91	74	48"	2"
Daily lows	33	51	70	51		

small town. This is yet another excellent example of how the presence of a university can transform an ordinary city into an exciting blend of academia, cultural events, and entertainment, all leading to a quality lifestyle. The population of 50,000 contrasts with about 26,000 students, creating a demand for a high level of services and nice shopping facilities. Because students are chronically short of money and because retirees don't like to be extravagant, prices naturally remain at reasonable levels.

Downtown Athens looks exactly as a university town's downtown should. The main street is called College Avenue and is arched over by large trees, with old-fashioned wrought-iron lampposts with globes, and has sidewalk tables and chairs in front of cafes. Exotic restaurants specialize in everything from traditional southern-style cooking to wood-fired pizza, from Mexican enchiladas and Indian tandoori to exotic Japanese cuisine. Folks from nearby towns come to downtown Athens to browse bookstores and specialty shops for articles not normally found in small Georgia cities. A mixed crowd of students, residents, and tourists strolls the streets browsing stores and restaurants, or lounges on wrought-iron benches, observing the passing world with the unhurried casualness only students and retirees can afford to have. Downtown Athens is the central focus of activity for students and residents alike.

A university atmosphere also pervades Athens' residential districts. Lovely neighborhoods packed with Greek Revival mansions and Victorians are interspersed with modern ranch-style homes and bungalows. You'll also encounter an occasional antebellum homestead with massive columns, magnolia-shaded gardens reminiscent of the way of life enjoyed by the planter class of the Old South. Because of the large student population, visiting scholars, and temporary faculty, Athens offers an ample supply of apartments, condos, and rental homes. Two private golf-course communities, with upscale homes peering over the fairways, provide alternative housing for golf nuts. Several other golf courses are open to the public. Of course the University of Georgia can be relied upon as a source of year-round athletic events, everything from football and basketball to intramural sports.

Medical care here is superb. Two major hospitals located in Athens support more than 150 physicians in all medical specialties. Both facilities provide twenty-four-hour emergency care. Of interest to military retirees, the Navy Corps Supply School provides medical and dental facilities to veterans.

Virginia and West Virginia

Originally one state, Virginia and West Virginia were separated into two after the Civil War. In some ways they blend together, with Virginia starting with an Atlantic coastline, moving westward with a gradually rising landscape and becoming more hilly as the foothills of the Appalachians rise higher and higher. Then West Virginia takes over to complete the scenic drive with some of the loftiest mountains east of the Rockies. Driving from one extreme to the other takes you through not only some of the East's most varied panoramas but also a wide variety of possible re-

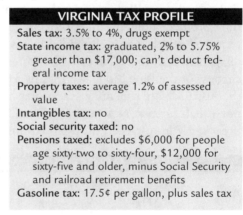

VIRGINIA TAX PROFILE

Sales tax: 3.5% to 4%, drugs exempt
State income tax: graduated, 2% to 5.75% greater than $17,000; can't deduct federal income tax
Property taxes: average 1.2% of assessed value
Intangibles tax: no
Social security taxed: no
Pensions taxed: excludes $6,000 for people age sixty-two to sixty-four, $12,000 for sixty-five and older, minus Social Security and railroad retirement benefits
Gasoline tax: 17.5¢ per gallon, plus sales tax

tirement lifestyles. You'll see everything from wild stretches of Atlantic beaches, tidewater wonderlands, rolling fields and farms stocked with thoroughbred horses, and finally, the legendary Appalachian Mountain majesty.

The state of Virginia is the most diverse. Lifestyles include highly sophisticated and dignified suburbs near the nation's capitol, modern cities, rural crossroads communities, university towns, tidewater communities on coastal inlets and bays, and small towns tucked away in the Blue Ridge Mountains. Yet curiously Virginia, as a rule, doesn't attract a large number of retirees. In fact Virginia has one of the highest ratios of outbound retirees compared with incoming retirees of any state. This exodus can be explained in large part because people come from all sectors of the country to pursue careers in Washington, D.C. An enormous number choose to live in the numerous smaller suburbs with a short commute to the office. Most of them are there because they must be, not because they really want to be. When they retire (or when their political party is voted out of office), they tend to go home.

Once away from the hustle and bustle of the capital, the scene quickly morphs into pristine rural areas with small towns and villages tucked away between wooded ridges and fast-running rivers. Several tempting examples of retirement lifestyles can be found throughout the region. And—important for those who plan on working occasionally during retirement, maintaining consulting connections, or keeping a hand in political affairs—many locations are within a feasible commuting distance from the capital.

Charlottesville   The central portions of Virginia are similar to the Carolina Midlands: miles of rolling hills checkered with grassy pastures, woods, and well-tended farms. A particularly interesting retirement location is historic Charlottesville, a college town in the shadow of the Blue Ridge Mountains. Hiking and backpacking on the Appalachian Trail are just minutes away from town and skiing not much farther. Not far from Charlottesville's town center, retirees settle in to raise thoroughbred horses; it's claimed that more

CHARLOTTESVILLE WEATHER					
In degrees Fahrenheit					
	Jan.	April	July	Oct.	Rain	Snow
Daily highs	62	75	91	74	48"	2"
Daily lows	33	51	70	51		

CHARLOTTESVILLE AREA COST OF LIVING					
Percentage of	Overall	Housing	Medical	Groceries	Utilities
national average	108.7	113.7	97.1	111.4	108.4

than 10,000 horses are pastured on homesteads in the area. More than a dozen wineries dot the surrounding countryside.

Thomas Jefferson loved Charlottesville; he called it "the Eden of the United States." This is where he decided to build his famous home, Monticello, and where he founded the University of Virginia in 1819. The campus buildings he designed are considered to be among the finest examples of classic American architecture. The school consistently ranks in the top ten of public universities, enhancing community lifestyles as it serves as the area's hub for cultural and sporting events. Fortunately Charlottesville's 70,000 residents aren't enough to overwhelm the university's 17,000 students, as well as a large faculty and staff who also participate in the city's economy and social life. The school offers a wide range of cultural amenities: drama, concerts, lectures, visiting dance troupes, and summer opera. Many events are open to the public free of charge.

Medical care is superb here. The University of Virginia Health Sciences Center, a 651-bed hospital, and the 200-bed Martha Jefferson Hospital are more than ample in supplying the most modern health care.

Tidewater Region   The Tidewater Region is one of Virginia's more interesting locations. It's defined as that area bordered on the north by the Potomac River and south almost to the North Carolina state line. Several tidal rivers crucial to early American history run through the region as they flow into the Chesapeake Bay. The James, York, and Rappahannock Rivers served as highways of commerce for early British colonists, enabling plantations to access European markets for cotton and tobacco crops. The Tidewater Region became the keystone of colonial trade and is rich in history. The ill-fated first British colony in the New World was established at Jamestown. The Tidewater Region is where the British suffered the final defeat that resulted in the independence of the United States and where the most battles in the War of 1812 were fought. During the Civil War approximately 70 percent of the major battles of the war were fought in this area.

The countryside is naturally oriented toward river and sea. Every cove and bay appears to have docks where commercial and pleasure fishing boats tie up. Good seafood restaurants are more than a tradition here; they're considered essential to quality living. Boats and yachts are ubiquitous.

Tidewater living offers several distinct lifestyle possibilities, depending on the locale and cultural traditions. You'll find historical and intellectual places near Colonial Williamsburg, as well as outdoors-oriented, gated golf developments scattered throughout the region. But our favorite lifestyle example is found in a wonderfully rural and sparsely settled area along the James River. The countryside looks pretty much as it must have appeared in colonial times, changing little from the Civil War era. Many homes and buildings indeed date from those periods. You'll frequently see remains of tobacco barns and slave quarters falling into disrepair behind stately old plantation homes, now occupied by couples recently moved in from out of state.

Instead of reporting on a particular retirement location here, let's investigate living in one of the many tiny communities in this region. These are special places within easy commuting distance to a city, where folks may enjoy rural living but not cut ties to employment, and where out-of-state retirees will feel comfortable and welcome. We combined our research with a visit to some good friends who live in this region. The couple lives in one of many tiny crossroads communities of about 150 people, almost an hour's commute from Richmond. (It's probably too small to find on a map, so the name doesn't matter.) Our friends dearly love their home, a 150-year-old farmhouse sitting on five acres of partly wooded ground. The property includes a barn, a chicken house, and a rabbit hutch. One acre is cultivated as a truck garden, supplying veggies for their kitchen. Their pride and joy is an asparagus patch and adjoining lettuce bed.

Normally an isolated, rural location like this could be culturally stifling. All too often native residents and newcomers find little in common with each other; their worldviews and backgrounds are worlds apart. Not here. It turns out that almost everyone here is a newcomer, an escapee from an urban environment, either commuters or retirees. They've moved from the city to enjoy the peace and quiet of the Tidewater countryside. Socially they are little different from those who still live in a city neighborhood and therefore share much in common. Neighbors here are much closer than they would ever be in a city neighborhood. They know everyone in the community and they are all friends.

The downside of living in an isolated Tidewater crossroads community is the total lack of services. Purchasing a can of tomato sauce or a roll of paper towels entails a 20-mile round-trip. The nearest doctor is 15 miles away, the same distance as the video-rental store. But as one resident says, "It's worth it. We don't have many neighbors, but the ones we have are quality. They're more than neighbors, they're friends we can count on if we need them. We don't need a big city to be happy."

Virginia Beach This is a retirement destination that receives frequent endorsements as "Top Ten Places to Retire" or "Best Places to Live in America" from magazines such as *Ladies' Home Journal, Money Magazine,* and *Entrepreneur Magazine.* Residents are drawn to Virginia Beach for a variety of reasons, not the least of which is an outstanding, water-oriented, high quality of life. Residents enjoy 38 miles of shoreline on the Atlantic Ocean and the Chesapeake Bay, 28 miles of public beaches, and 79 miles of scenic waterways. They find plenty of opportunity for water sports, boating and sailing, fresh- and saltwater fishing, and tennis. The city has eleven public golf courses, eighteen marinas with public access, three fishing piers, and 60 miles of biking trails.

Virginia Beach's temperate maritime climate is created by the nearby Gulf Stream, which explains its mild winters that rarely drop below freezing. Swimmers enjoy great beach weather that extends from spring through fall. Residents like to point out that personal safety is high here; for the tenth consecutive year, Virginia Beach has had the lowest crime rate in the nation for a city of its size. And the area enjoys an outstanding reputation for quality health and medical

NORFOLK–VIRGINIA BEACH WEATHER						
In degrees Fahrenheit						
	Jan.	April	July	Oct.	Rain	Snow
Daily highs	62	75	91	74	48"	2"
Daily lows	33	51	70	51		

NORFOLK–VIRGINIA BEACH COST OF LIVING					
Percentage of national average	Overall	Housing	Medical	Groceries	Utilities
	99	94	93	95	124

care. Nearby Hampton Roads also has a well-coordinated regional health-care system with state-of-the-art equipment and facilities and specialists in every field.

Virginia Beach residents enjoy cultural amenities such as symphony, opera, performing arts, and museums. The Virginia Marine Science Museum in Virginia Beach recently completed a $35-million expansion and is one of the most attended aquariums in the nation. Education in the region plays a prominent role, with eleven colleges and universities serving the community.

Housing is pretty much upscale here, although many neighborhoods with affordable housing can be found. Virginia Beach takes much pride in its many well-preserved seventeenth-, eighteenth-, and nineteenth-century homes, historic churches, and public buildings. Housing costs are below national averages, but utilities have jumped sharply since the last edition of this book.

Appalachian Retirement Discovery in Virginia and West Virginia

In past editions of *Where to Retire,* we've occasionally discovered "sleepers," locations where quality retirement lifestyles can be enjoyed on exceptionally low budgets and where nice homes sell at rock-bottom prices. Our latest discovery is the Four Seasons Country, a charming Appalachia locale bordering the states of Virginia and West Virginia. Four towns—two on the Virginia side, two on the West Virginia side—have joined forces to lure retirees into their communities to replace residents who moved away because of an economic slump. The cost of living is among the lowest in the country, and quality housing is going for a song—truly a buyer's market.

The idea of communities luring newcomers into their midst as a way of bolstering the economy has become rather common in today's small-town America. Four Seasons Country's two-state, two-county, and four-city pooling of resources to attract retirees is unique. It's awfully nice to feel wanted! And the low cost of living is just one of the enticements here.

At the risk of repeating myself, I must remind you that just because a place is inexpensive, that doesn't mean you'll enjoy living there. Seems there's usually some "catch" to living in a bargain-basement neighborhood. Sometimes the surroundings are bleak or boring, or even dangerous. Often the climate is so extreme that most families wouldn't live there unless their jobs required it. The locations are poverty stricken and inhabited with uneducated and unfriendly natives. But trust me, none of the above applies to the Four Seasons Country!

In this Appalachian wonderland you'll enjoy truly breathtaking surroundings, with mountains, rivers, and forests as background and friendly, sophisticated folks who will welcome you as new neighbors. The climate lives up to the region's self-styled nickname: four seasons, with glorious springs, warm summers, colorful falls, and winters with soft and short-lived snowfalls. Several retirees we interviewed here came from Florida or California in search of just such a four-season climate.

What happened here to make retirement living a bargain? Two problems: one, an economic disaster; two, a public relations dilemma. The economic meltdown began about twenty years ago, when the region's major industry, coal mining, decided to automate, installing elaborate, labor-saving devices that displaced workers and decimated the workforce. As jobs were eliminated, families moved away in search of work. The economy never fully recovered.

The public relations problem is battling the conventional stereotype of what coal-mining towns are. The image is poverty and substandard living conditions. People tend to picture coal-mining families living in trailers or tumbled-down shacks, wearing bib overalls, and shopping at a dreary company store. To our delight we found this not true. Instead we found exceptionally nice-looking communities with housing ranging from above average to elegant. The countryside is dotted with small farms with historic Victorian mansions and modern ranch-style homes. You'll find gated golf-course developments, as well as lovely, tree-shaded neighborhoods with friendly small-town ambience.

So what happened to the stereotype? It turns out that coal miners in this region have long been unionized. They've always

FOUR SEASONS COUNTRY AREA WEATHER					
In degrees Fahrenheit					
	Jan.	April	July	Oct.	Rain	Snow
Daily highs	39	65	83	65	37"	48"
Daily lows	22	47	60	39		

earned exceptionally high wages. With incomes equal to middle-management personnel elsewhere, coal-mining families had sufficient disposable income to afford any kind of housing they desired. It's no surprise that they preferred high-quality homes on large lots and that they led comfortable, middle-class lifestyles. (Please note that although this standard of living is true of the locale described here, by no means is this true of all of the region! In fact some parts of West Virginia are famous for occasional pockets of poverty.)

As jobs evaporated workers received generous severance pay and ample pensions. Some retired here; others took the cash and moved away to take other jobs. Real estate prices plummeted; the market never fully recovered. Nice 1,500-square-foot homes often sell for about half the median price of homes in Florida, Arizona, or California. Larger, more upscale homes on landscaped and wooded parcels can be found for double that amount. An outlay of $250,000 buys a stately five-bedroom brick home on an acre of land.

Excellent medical facilities are another legacy of the old days, before machines displaced people. The miners' union negotiated for excellent company-paid health plans with comprehensive benefits for coal-mine employees. This created a high demand for medical services that was filled by a surprising number of hospitals and clinics accustomed to using high-tech technology. Five hospitals serve the four towns described here, with 870 beds plus specialized physicians of all types providing a level of medical care found in few nonurban areas anywhere in the country.

The Appalachian foothills and forested mountains enjoy a four-season climate that's perfect for outdoors lovers. Spring, summer, and fall provide white-water rafters and kayakers the chance to explore deep river canyons and float through stretches of calm waters. Skiing, snowboarding, and hunting fill the winter sports calendars. An hour's drive or less takes skiers to some of the best slopes in the southeastern United States. A dozen challenging golf courses are available to Four Seasons Country residents.

Unlike many semirural areas throughout the nation, the Four Seasons Country has superior transportation facilities. The local airport has several daily commuter flights to regional cities. Intercity buses and nearby AmTrak passenger trains make it easy for the grandkids to visit. For those who prefer automobiles, these communities are within a one day's drive of half the population of the

United States. Interstate 77 runs right through the heart of Four Seasons Country, and both Interstate 64 and Interstate 81 are nearby.

Let's take a look at the four communities in West Virginia and Virginia who are so eager to have you come and visit. These are the West Virginia towns of Bluefield and Princeton and the Virginia towns of Tazewell and Richlands.

Bluefield   Straddling the Virginia–West Virginia state line, Bluefield is technically two separate cities, each governed by its own municipal government. The two Bluefields nevertheless consider themselves as part of the same community. Originally known as Higginbotham's Summit, residents eventually changed the name to Bluefield in honor of the profusion of blue chicory flowers that covers the surrounding countryside each spring.

Bluefield is the region's largest town, with about 14,000 inhabitants, and for years it was the business center for the other communities. However, like many similar small cities around the nation, Bluefield conceded its central shopping focus to the inevitable strip-mall shopping centers. Yet Bluefield still has a downtown center that looks as if it belongs in a much larger city.

The 2,600-foot elevation here creates such a pleasant summer climate that the city of Bluefield calls itself "Nature's Air-Conditioned City." To bolster this claim the city serves free lemonade whenever the temperature reaches ninety degrees. Because of mild summer temperatures, some years lemonade never gets served. Pure, fresh air and beautiful surroundings are among the first things newcomers mention when explaining why they chose to retire here.

The two Bluefields are located in a lovely valley setting, with mountains looming on either side of the scenic Bluestone and East Rivers. Residential neighborhoods are neat and attractive, with plenty of affordable homes in quiet surroundings. Many stunning Victorian mansions in the nearby Bramwell stand as reminders of the affluent era when coal was king. Several newer subdivisions of upscale homes are under way on the outskirts of town, on rolling hills, with lovely views.

A rich offering of cultural activities is available between the region's communities, with symphony concerts, museums, country music jamborees, professional baseball, theater performances, and classes at four local colleges that offer nontraditional education tailored for mature residents. Bluefield State College is quite active in community affairs. Besides being a place of higher education, the school reaches out to the community with its special Creative Retirement Center. Modeled after a similar successful program at the University of North Carolina–Ashland, this program brings a concept of lifelong learning to mature residents of nearby communities. Students fifty years or older are encouraged to enroll in courses ranging from computers and Internet to creative writing to genealogy.

Princeton   Princeton, West Virginia, was founded in the early part of the 1800s, but was largely destroyed during the Civil War and was slow to rebuild. Most of its older buildings date from the early part of the 1900s, with a handful of earlier Victorian homes. The town's growth accelerated in 1908 with the arrival of the Virginian Railroad's first passenger train. Princeton enjoyed great prosperity during the heyday of coal mining, but like neighboring communities saw its population leave as efficient machines began replacing skilled labor. According to the latest census, Princeton has a population of approximately 7,000.

Princeton provides the region's only retirement village, with a full spectrum of services that allow folks to adjust their living conditions as they grow older. The facility begins with independent living homes, then assisted living quarters, and finally a nursing home. Princeton's town center, like that of nearby Bluefield, was somewhat weakened by businesses moving to the strip malls, particularly the large mall between Princeton and Bluefield. But being a county seat, the downtown maintains its lively look, and the town is investing money and energy into renovation and relocating suitable businesses. Some lovely wooded residential developments are located here—dating from the affluent boom era—and they feature tastefully designed homes that make quality lifestyles somewhat affordable. Starting on the outskirts of town, many country roads meander through woods and fields, where ranch-style homes sit on huge lots or on small farms just minutes from Princeton's town center.

Tazewell   In the state of Virginia, 15 miles southwest of Bluefield, the town of Tazewell is the third of the four Four Seasons

Country towns. It has 4,176 residents within the town limit; however, many retirees prefer to live in pastoral settings, in rolling foothills or small villages very close to Tazewell. The county is lightly populated with just more than 20,000 inhabitants.

Tazewell is the idealized town you picture when you think of small-town living. This is a place where folks greet you on the street, whether they know you or not. Yet it doesn't have a rural or unsophisticated atmosphere; the town is up to date and lively. Its large strip mall brings in shoppers from far and wide.

We were impressed by some upscale developments under way in and around the town of Tazewell. Our favorite is a group of high-quality homes, each surrounded by a half-acre or more of wooded land bordering a golf course, complete with country-club facilities and a restaurant, which all comes with ownership. Selling prices for a 3,000- to 3,500-square-foot home are about what an ordinary tract home would sell for in Southern California. When we asked a contractor why almost no smaller houses seemed to be under construction, he answered, "We already have too many low-price custom homes on the market. It's the upscale places that are in demand."

Richlands West of Tazewell an 18-mile drive along a four-lane highway brings you to the town of Richlands, the southernmost of the Four Seasons Country towns. Richlands is slightly larger than neighboring Tazewell, and it shares all of the advantages of small-town living, peace, and tranquillity. The scenic Clinch River runs through town, and many charming recreational areas are found nearby.

Although both towns are sophisticated on one level—with plenty of modern services, shopping, and cultural activities—they are also small enough to be places where neighborhood picnics and the friendliness of small town living are still enjoyed by all. One retiree remarked, "As long as I've lived here, I still can't get used to perfect strangers saying 'hello' when we pass on the street."

People here are justifiably proud of Richlands's Southwest Virginia Community College. The school does an excellent job of providing cultural events of a quality normally found only in much larger metropolitan areas. Regular drama and musical productions are sponsored by the college—everything from ballet to satire and comedy. The fifty-plus crowd is welcome to participate in classes tailored for their needs, with such courses as pottery, jewelry, leather, and computers.

Although Richlands sits at the far end of the Four Seasons Country, medical care is near at hand. Besides its own community of medical specialists, Richlands boasts a 200-bed hospital as well as two other medical facilities nearby, one with seventy-six and the other with fifty beds.

West Virginia

Beckley   Due north of the Four Seasons Country, another location with many of the same benefits and conditions awaits your investigation. Beckley is larger than any of its southern neighbors, with a population of almost 19,000. Situated at the intersections of two interstate highways (I-64 and I-77), Beckley serves as a hub of southern West Virginia, with a trade area of more than 200,000 people. You get the feeling that you are in a real city, small and compact, but with all the facilities.

Founded in the 1830s Beckley remained a sleepy crossroads farming village until the beginning of the 1900s, when railroads and coal mining transformed the community into a modern and thriving little city. With the mechanization of mining, Beckley lost population, as did other communities in this part of the state. Today retirement has become one of the "industries" that is reviving the town. The local chamber of commerce and city officials are quite naturally interested in inviting retirees to fill the gap.

Beckley's downtown sector seems to be alive and thriving despite the usual fleeing of major "shopping" to the strip malls on the highways. This is partly due to several small colleges located in town, with students, faculty, and schools' staff supporting the downtown merchants.

Besides the usual fishing, hiking, golf, and other typical West Virginia outdoor recreation, the Winterplace Ski Resort is located 15 miles from Beckley. The facility offers outstanding skiing to residents of the region. Seven local golf courses serve Beckley, and another twelve are within an hour's drive, including three at the world-famous Greenbrier. More than 80 percent of the county is forested, with twelve major trails maintained by the National Park Service.

Housing is a buyer's market here with some great real estate buys. For more upscale homes nearby Glade Springs Resort is a new addition to the region's housing selections. This gated community sits on 4,100 acres and is built around an eighteen-hole golf course. Located about twenty minutes from downtown Beckley, residents are also only about ten minutes from skiing at Winterplace ski resort.

Lewisburg   West Virginia never ceases to provide us with surprises and discoveries. The historic town of Lewisburg (founded in 1751 as Lewis Spring) is one of our more interesting retirement surprises. Nestled in the heart of West Virginia's Allegheny Mountains, and close to the Greenbrier, with its famous and historic golf course complex, Lewisburg is one of the region's retirement success stories. The town plays a delightful role as a virtual time capsule, steeped in traditions of colonial and federal architecture. Artists, shopkeepers, residents, and, of course, retirees casually reside in homes built of native stone, some dating from the time of the Revolution. A casual stroll along Lewisburg's tree-shaded streets takes you past native limestone buildings built in the 1700s, antebellum mansions, Victorians, and cottages so old they defy dating. Antiques stores, excellent restaurants, boutiques, and art galleries seem to be the only modern touches. You almost expect to see horse-drawn carriages and powdered wigs here.

Of course newcomers to Lewisburg fully appreciate the ambience and some hope to keep it a best-kept secret. As we interviewed one lady, she smiled, held a finger to her lips as she whispered, "We love it here, but don't tell anybody else!" I solemnly promised her I wouldn't tell. (But everyone knows how we travel writers lie!)

Retirees come to Lewisburg from all sections of the country and from all walks of life, often from artistic or professional endeavors. Some find an excuse to keep busy by dealing in antiques, creating artwork for galleries, or starting some small, laid-back

LEWISBURG–SULPHUR SPRINGS AREA WEATHER					
In degrees Fahrenheit					
	Jan.	April	July	Oct.	Rain	Snow
Daily highs	40	65	84	68	39"	13"
Daily lows	18	36	59	40		

business enterprise. So many artists have relocated here that Lewisburg occasionally makes the ranks of "one hundred best small art towns in America." All of this makes for a sophisticated mix of people and an interesting social milieu. No matter where you are from, you could very possibly find your neighbors come from your part of the country.

With a population of 4,000, Lewisburg is large enough to have all needed services and shopping, yet still retains an elegant, small-town feeling. Home prices here reflect the general higher-class neighborhoods and antique quality of some homes. Yet not far from the town center you'll find truly affordable homes, and a ten-minute drive over a narrow highway, winding through rolling farmlands, you'll discover nineteenth-century farmhouses and manor houses, as well as modern ranch-style homes surrounded by large parcels of semiforested land.

Florida:
A Retirement Tradition

WHEN DREAMING OF RETIREMENT many people automatically picture Florida. They've vacationed there for years, so retirement there seems logical. Visions of warm weather, snow-free streets, and easy living dance temptingly through their retirement fantasies. Soft, sandy beaches with swaying palm trees and balmy January days complete the vision. Beginning in the 1920s retirees moved south in such numbers that Florida retirement became almost a cliché.

Because Florida is a high-profile state, it receives a lot of media attention. Sometimes it seems as if the only news coming out of the state deals with crime, hurricanes, violence, overcrowding, and disrepair. Does this mean we should write off Florida as a viable choice? Not by any means! From our research we are convinced that of all the states, Florida still offers some of the best bargains in quality living and affordable retirement for the average retiree. Regardless of what you see on television, most Florida communities are as safe as other popular retirement destinations. If this book were to give ratings, many Florida towns would receive ratings far above towns of similar size elsewhere, both in livability and safety. Even though it isn't for everyone, Florida is still a great place to retire. That is precisely why so many retire here!

Isn't Florida Overcrowded?

Florida is the fourth-most-populous state in the Union. New residents move here at the rate of 900 a day, most of them retirees. Since the 1990 census the state's population grew by three million!

With all those retirees moving in, isn't Florida overcrowded? That depends upon which part of Florida we're talking about. Certainly some parts of Florida are heavily populated, with high-rise apartments and condos clustered together with nothing but shopping centers and parking lots to break the monotony. Yet large sections of Florida are sparsely populated. Thousands of square miles have virtually no presence at all. Herons, egrets, ducks, storks, and wildfowl of all description share vast expanses of land with other wildlife ranging from panthers to rabbits and alligators to turtles. Deer abound in the open countryside and in the state's large system of national forests.

Lightly populated central Florida features rolling, wooded terrain dotted with small towns and crossroad communities comparable to those in small-town Ohio or Illinois. They are quiet, safe, and rural. Were

FLORIDA TAX PROFILE
Sales tax: 6% to 7%, food, drugs exempt
State income tax: no
Property taxes: approximately 1.6%
Intangibles tax: yes
Social security taxed: no
Pensions taxed: no
Gasoline tax: 4¢ to 10¢ per gallon

it not for an occasional palm tree, you could easily forget this is Florida. These places are often overlooked in retirees' enthusiasm for living close to beaches and excitement. Surprisingly most locations in the interior are less than an hour's drive from a beach. No place in the entire state is more than 70 miles from salt water. Some towns in the very center of the state give you a choice: A drive of an hour or so in either direction takes you to the Atlantic Ocean or to the Gulf of Mexico. You can spend a day playing in the sand and return home in time for dinner. And the state is well endowed with coastline—8,426 miles of it!

Florida offers a wide range of choices. You can select the convenience and excitement of a city, or you can choose a small-town atmosphere with slow traffic and rural tranquillity. Florida has it all, except perhaps mountain climbing and downhill skiing.

Florida Weather

The near-tropical climate of Florida's peninsula has always been the main attraction for those in the North and Midwest who want something better to do with their winters than shoveling snow and staying indoors to watch television. January afternoon temperatures generally climb into the sixties or low seventies, with nights dropping to the forties and fifties in some areas. Summers are hot, to be sure, but aren't summers in the Midwest and North scorchers, too? If you insist upon cool summers *and* mild winters, you need to think Pacific Coast—California, Oregon, or Washington. But that's in another chapter. In the summer early-morning temperatures are usually in the seventies, giving you plenty of opportunity to exercise outdoors. Summer afternoons are why God gave Florida swimming pools and iced lemonade.

Florida's tropical setting is an accident created by a huge flow of warm water—a kind of oceanic river—known as the Gulf Stream. This balmy current sweeps up from the Caribbean, hooks around the Florida Keys, and then brushes across Florida's east coast. Its benevolent warmth flows close to shore, bestowing its blessings on the Atlantic coast until a point near Vero Beach, where it swerves out to sea.

The entire state benefits from the Gulf Stream, but the 80-mile stretch of southeastern coast known as the Gold Coast is the biggest beneficiary. Summers here aren't quite as hot because of the ocean's constant temperature and some cloud cover. The best part is winter; this part of Florida is warmer than anywhere else in the continental United States. This dreamy weather explains why you see several million people crowded together along the Gold Coast.

Florida Real Estate

If high-quality yet inexpensive real estate is an important consideration, then Florida should rank high, because dollar for dollar and feature for feature you'll find the best bargains here of anywhere in the country. True, you can find homes selling for less in Oklahoma or Idaho, but as I continually stress, cheap housing should not govern your retirement choices.

Florida offers virtually every kind of housing imaginable. Condos, townhouses, and apartments are common along the coasts or wherever land costs are high. Mobile homes and manufactured homes (mobile homes on foundations) allow for downscale, economical housing. Traditional subdivisions are common, particularly away from the beaches, as are custom homes. A common type of arrangement is a gated community, often reserved for folks older than age fifty-five and built around a clubhouse and tennis courts, sometimes with its own private golf course and other facilities.

Coastal Retirement

For many folks, tourists and retirees alike, Florida's beaches are what it's all about. Condos rent by the day or week and motels, hotels, and glitzy restaurants abound, mostly catering to the needs of vacationers and weekend visitors. Yet just a few miles away from the beachfront crush—sometimes just a few blocks away—a different world presents itself: the world of residents.

It's entirely possible to live in a quiet, normal neighborhood and then, whenever you choose, slip away to join the hedonistic, suntan-crazy world of the tourist just a few blocks away. When the sun starts to set, you can walk home to peace and quiet. With beaches on three sides of Florida—east, west, and south—no matter where you decide to settle, you can be near the coast.

Not all beachfront real estate is devoted to tourism; most coastal properties are residential. Some of the fanciest housing is found along sandy beaches, screened from the road by thick stands of palms and tropical shrubbery. Some areas are so exclusive that the only research we did was to drive past and sigh enviously. Yet happily, there are beach areas where houses are definitely affordable.

Golf and Boating Properties

One of Florida's top retirement benefits is year-round outdoor recreation. Not surprisingly some of the most successful retirement communities here are those focused on exercise and recreation. Thus we find country-club developments featuring Olympic-size pools, exercise rooms, jogging paths, and golf courses. The more desirable homes edge expanses of greens and fairways, giving a wide-open feeling as well as access to the game. In addition to the first tee sitting just a three-iron shot away from your back door, you probably won't have to wait long for a starting time, because residence in the development usually includes membership in the club.

The good part about some golf complexes is that membership is optional, so if you play golf as badly as I do, you don't have to pay for upkeep of the golf course and feel obligated to humiliate yourself on a regular basis. Often these courses are open to the public, with affordable greens fees for nonmembers. A typical monthly fee (without golf) might be about $100, for which you receive cable TV, lawn maintenance, and membership in the community club, com-

plete with tennis courts and swimming pool, social activities, hobbies, and dinners. Not only are houses and condominiums commonly bundled with a golf course, but some of the more expensive
mobile-home communities often feature their own links.

Another Florida innovation is boat-canal living: homes built
along a waterway, with sailboats, powerboats, and yachts tied up in
their backyards. Residents of canal developments enjoy the ocean or
gulf in ways that beachside folks cannot. Some boating communities are locked-in or gated arrangements, but most are in open
neighborhoods. I'm continually surprised that homes backing up to
a canal are often priced not much higher than similar places in "dry"
neighborhoods.

Developing a boating community isn't as expensive or extravagant as it might seem. Because so much of Florida's real estate is
low-lying—just a few feet above sea level—a practical way of re-
claiming marshland is to dredge drainage canals and use the
dredged material as fill to raise the level of the land. Canals must be
constructed anyway, and boating access is a natural result of the
preparation of the land for housing. All that remains is to place a
wooden dock at the rear of each home and put up signs pointing the
way to the salt water.

Although country club–type golf, tennis, and boating communities would appear to be expensive and luxurious, they can be surprisingly affordable. In fact compared with some parts of the
country, these houses can be downright cheap! To be sure there are
monthly maintenance fees, but because the golf courses, swimming
pools, and tennis courts serve the entire country-club community,
the costs and upkeep are spread among hundreds of families.

The Mobile-Home Alternative

Those who are able to move to Florida and buy any property they
choose with little regard for price are usually those fortunate people
who bought a home in the 1960s or 1970s for the going price, then
sold it in 2003 for many times their investment. Perhaps they realized a 1,000 percent profit; that's not unusual. These folks pay cash
for their retirement homes and stash the rest of their profits in the
bank, with the monthly interest helping to pay expenses.

But we all weren't that lucky or that far-seeing. If you've lived in
an apartment or rented a house all these years, you'll probably be

renting when you move to Florida. There is another option, however: a mobile home. Although you can pay as much for a Florida mobile home as you would for a conventional home, you can also buy one for the same price as a used car. At that price it won't be elegant, but it will be yours.

Mobile-home parks come in all levels of luxury, from the strictly utilitarian, with no amenities except a laundry room, to the ultraluxurious, complete with eighteen-hole golf courses, Olympic-size pools, and deluxe country-club surroundings. Prices can be remarkably low or exorbitantly high, depending upon the level of park you choose. Most of the better ones also sell new mobile homes and will set one up to your specifications.

Most parks we inspected included lawn maintenance in the rent. This makes it nice for those who spend the winter months in an inexpensive mobile home and then leave it for the rest of the year. But it isn't just snowbirds who live in the less-expensive units. The majority in the parks we visited were full-time Florida residents. It was comforting to realize that people of limited means have the opportunity to retire in their own homes in Florida so inexpensively.

North-Central Florida

Although attractive retirement places can be found all over the state, an area often overlooked for retirement possibilities is Florida's interior. The north-central part of Florida is a different world, as distinct from either coast as you can imagine. This is Florida with a four-seasons climate. Instead of being ironing-board flat, as is most of the state, central Florida sits at a

higher elevation on rolling hills covered with dense woodlands, meadows, and hundreds of lakes. Forests of oak, pine, maple, flowering dogwood, and azalea make this a unique cosmos, a place where palm trees and other tropical flora seem out of place. Yet the fun beaches of either the Gulf or the Atlantic are within easy driving distance. Because of its slightly higher altitude and distance from the water, you'll find true changes of season, with cooler summer nights, even an occasional dusting of snow in the winter.

This part of Florida attracts more retirees from Midwestern and Northern states than from New York and New England (whose residents seem to prefer Florida's Gold Coast). Residents here tend to duplicate the ambience of their hometowns. By and large, the state's interior is more peaceful, more rural, and safer; it feels more like home to them than the hectic beachfront zones. Generous lawns and single-family homes make this a re-creation of small-town America, with a slight Florida flourish. Homes here come equipped with the pools, sundecks, and outdoor rooms so important for Florida outdoor lifestyles. Were it not for an occasional orange grove, many neighborhoods would look right at home in Peoria or Terre Haute, where their owners came from. Part of this openness is due to lower land costs that encourage large building lots, which are routinely measured in acreage rather than square feet.

The climate is different here, too. In this region the weather-stabilizing Gulf Stream is far off Florida's coast, headed toward the open Atlantic. Consequently summer days are hotter and winters are a few degrees colder. Slightly less rain falls as well. These temperature differences can be significant when you consider Florida's high humidity. Miami averages thirty days a year with temperatures higher than ninety degrees, whereas inland it's more like 100 ninety-degree-plus days. This is enough to encourage many who retire in central and west coast Florida to return north for the summer.

Nevertheless, if you love warm weather (like me), ninety-degree days aren't bad, even with the 75 percent humidity you find in most of Florida. As one person from Rochester, New York, pointed out, "Coping with hot weather is simply a matter of changing my living patterns. Back home in New York I stayed indoors all winter. I only went outside to go to work or to shovel snow. Here I stay indoors during the *summer,* yet every morning and evening it's comfortable outdoors for golf or bicycling."

Orlando Area   At one time I considered Orlando one of Florida's better retirement ideas. That was before it became so busy. In a short time the city made a remarkable transition from a sleepy crossroads of citrus orchards and cattle ranches into a dynamic city, the fastest-growing in the state. Actually, for such a booming economy, Orlando managed to make this transition fairly painless by diversifying commerce and concentrating on clean, high-tech industry, gaining the nickname "Silicon Swamp." Another nickname for Orlando is "Hollywood East," because of the film industry's focus on this area. Disney, MGM, and Universal Studios invested millions in soundstages, production entities, and tourist attractions; apparently, this is just the beginning. There is much, much more to come!

The bottom line is that newcomers do not appear to be put off by growth; the city of Orlando has increased by 25,000 just in the past five years to approximately 195,000 inhabitants. And many more have settled in the smaller towns scattered around Orlando's city limits. Even though Orlando has grown into a real city—and the best places to live are near rather than in the city—there are nevertheless some tranquil neighborhoods not too many blocks from downtown. Residents live quietly and oblivious to the hubbub of the tourist attractions, which are mercifully some distance from the city. Ancient oak trees arch over the streets, and restored homes from the early 1900s qualify some neighborhoods for historic status ("historic" meaning one hundred years ago, when the city's population was 2,481 inhabitants).

Orlando's major problem, as far as retirement is concerned, is that it grew too much and too fast. With tourist super-attractions like Disney World and other Hollywood-style promotions, throngs of visitors create enormous traffic jams and encourage the proliferation of fast-food joints, souvenir stands, motels, and business areas, which can be depressing to those who live here year-round. This shouldn't detract from the fact that Orlando has many won-

ORLANDO AREA WEATHER						
In degrees Fahrenheit						
	Jan.	April	July	Oct.	Rain	Snow
Daily highs	72	84	92	84	48"	—
Daily lows	49	60	73	65		

ORLANDO AREA COST OF LIVING					
Percentage of national average	Overall	Housing	Medical	Groceries	Utilities
	99	87	101	102	107

derful services and attractions that are worth a day visit for local residents.

Orlando is a golfer's paradise, with almost eighty golf layouts in the metropolitan area and another sixty or so within driving distance. Some courses were designed by golf greats such as Arnold Palmer, Jack Nicklaus, Tom Fazio, Dick Wilson, and Gary Player. It's no coincidence that thirty PGA Tour players make Orlando their homes, including Tiger Woods, Corey Pavin, and Ernie Els.

The Orlando metropolitan area is surrounded by small, pleasant towns that are truly pastoral, yet close enough to downtown to take advantage of big-city offerings. The countryside is rolling, with orange groves and lemon blossoms to sweeten the air. More than fifty lakes dot the landscape, many with gorgeous, tropical shores edged with cypress, pines, and tall palm trees. Fish abound in the lakes, along with an occasional alligator.

An inviting place for retirement outside Orlando is Winter Park, a scenic little college town with curving brick streets and charming Mediterranean-style architecture. The town boasts a chain of seventeen lakes with a parklike setting of Spanish moss–draped live oaks. A little more expensive than some neighborhoods in Orlando, the town demonstrates its quality in a downtown that features a main street bustling with al fresco cafes, upscale boutiques, arts-and-crafts galleries, posh clothing shops, and other shopping pleasures.

Leesburg/De Land   The best retirement bets near Orlando are found north of the city in a fan-shaped area starting at Orlando's northern edge. A dozen small towns are scattered throughout this triangle, from De Land on the east to Leesburg on the west, places little publicized as retirement locations. Most towns are long settled, with established neighborhoods and mature shade trees along quiet streets, plus great real estate bargains. Leesburg is the largest of these communities, with a local population of approximately 16,000 and about 50,000 in the shopping area. It sits on the Lake Wales Ridge, a range of hills that runs north and south, in the heart of the Florida peninsula. Leesburg is about an hour's drive from Orlando, with the Ocala National Forest nearby.

Most homes in these smaller towns are located in conventional neighborhoods, and larger retirement developments can be found

in the surrounding countryside. We looked at a very impressive retirement complex near Leesburg. Because country property is inexpensive in this area, the developer was able to purchase a huge tract
of land—a mixture of rolling hills, pastures, small lakes, and marshland. Because homes can't be placed on wetlands, much of the land
is open, giving most homes unobstructed views and privacy. The facilities (completely owned by the homeowners' association) are top
quality and include an Olympic-size pool, a huge clubhouse, tennis
courts, and large areas of parkland. The development has a golf
course, and you'll find half a dozen links within a 16-mile radius.

Winter Haven   Another possibility that shouldn't be neglected is the area southwest of Orlando and east of Tampa, a
group of small communities around Winter Haven. Lakeland
(pop. 72,000) is the largest and newest of the cities and Frostproof
(pop. 3,000) the smallest and probably the oldest. Winter Haven
(pop. 27,000) is the best known, because it's received much positive publicity as a retirement center. Besides being the spring
training camp of the Cleveland Indians and the home of Cypress
Gardens, a famous tourist attraction, Winter Haven bills itself as
the water-skiing capital of the world. For good reason: A series of
eighteen spring-fed lakes known as Chain O' Lakes, intercon-
nected by navigable canals, provides unlimited opportunities for
water-skiing, boating, fishing, and swimming. Forty percent of
the city is covered by lakes or canals, which contributes to cooling
in the summer and warming in the winter.

Housing is affordable, with homes selling way below national averages, and Winter Haven ranks as the fortieth most-
economical city in the nation and possibly the lowest in Florida
with regard to real estate. Much lakefront is open and parklike,
but boat access is almost unlimited. Lakes away from Winter
Haven commonly have homes with private docks. Health care is a
major industry, with seven hospitals and ten medical centers scattered about the county.

Interstate 4 hustles traffic to Tampa or Orlando for serious
shopping in short order, but shopping is more than adequate in
Winter Haven and environs, with a large mall just off the interstate that rivals those in larger cities. The area is lucky to have
daily Greyhound bus service to Tampa, Orlando, Jacksonville, and
Miami. Disney World is thirty-five minutes away, Sea World forty-

five minutes away, and Busch Gardens sixty minutes away. Granted, these distractions are not nearly as far away as one might wish.

Gainesville   The home of the University of Florida, Gainesville is one of the most culturally stimulating cities in the state. It's interesting how much one university town can resemble another, with the same kinds of businesses, services, students, even similar street names. Large, old homes on tree-shaded streets, some converted to fraternity houses, along with unobtrusive university construction, recall memories of my own college days. The city's official nickname, "The Tree City," is appropriate.

You needn't be a student to participate in the many activities connected with the university. Theater for all tastes is highlighted by the Hippodrome, one of only four state theaters for the performing arts. Miracle on 34th Street is a cultural complex with museums of art and natural history as well as an 1,800-seat performing-arts center. The university's ongoing program of public lectures and other cultural events entertains many retirees in the area.

Gainesville was originally planned as a health resort. Described as the "Eden of the South" by its founder, the town was visualized as a community with a "regular body of skilled physicians in attendance." In a way this dream was fulfilled, because Gainesville is number one when it comes to Florida health care. Four full-service hospitals serve the area, including the university's nationally renowned Shands Hospital, a 548-bed nonprofit facility.

Nearby wildlife areas provide great pleasure to bird-watchers and to those interested in ecology. About 65 percent of the county's 965 square miles is a wilderness of forests and wetlands dotted with scenic lakes.

As in most college towns, rentals are at a premium, except for the summer quarter, when many students leave town. If a town of 100,000 is too large for you, the nearby communities of High Springs and Archer are a fifteen-minute drive away. Housing costs less there, and small farms are affordable. Haile Plantation, an upscale golf-course development, offers miles of walking/bicycle trails, tennis courts, swimming pools, and other recreational amenities in addition to a new eighteen-hole golf course. This is but one of several such entities.

Besides the 35,000-student university, there's the two-year

Santa Fe College with a student body of about 7,500. A walk through its pleasant campus reveals a large percentage of students here with gray hair. Tuition is free under most circumstances to those age sixty and older. The extensive curriculum covers classes such as dog training, computers, and antiques collecting. If you're looking for Florida retirement in an intellectual climate, Gainesville is the place to investigate.

For outdoors people there's plenty to do. A dozen nearby lakes invite anglers—six of the lakes have boat ramps. For golf Ironwood, an eighteen-hole, par-seventy-two, public golf course, is one of four public or semiprivate links. Thirty parks, many with tennis courts, are publicly maintained. And, of course, either the Gulf or the Atlantic is a short drive away. The closest saltwater fishing is in Cedar Key, a 49-mile drive to the Gulf. Driving time on Interstate 75 is about two hours to Tampa Bay. The University of Florida Gators football team draws fans from all over the nation and creates great excitement with local residents. If indoor shopping is your favorite sport, there's the million-square-foot Oaks mall, an enclosed shopping facility with five department stores and 150 other shops and boutiques.

Ocala   Another of Florida's fast-growing areas, Ocala (pop. 48,000) comprises a rapidly expanding retiree population. About one in four adults is age sixty-five or older. Its quiet, laid-back lifestyle attracts those who hate Northern winters, yet want to avoid the traffic jams and insanity of the beach cities. The cost of living here is the lowest in Florida, and the average selling price of real estate is the third lowest. New-home subdivisions as well as conventional homes in comfortable-looking neighborhoods offer a range of housing choices.

Ocala's downtown business district is rather orthodox, looking very much like a typical Midwestern agricultural town, with a traditional downtown square. This isn't surprising, because Ocala is an agricultural center. Modern malls and chain stores haven't totally killed the town center as they have in some small cities.

The countryside is checkered with farms, especially horse farms. The area around Ocala is one of the most important thoroughbred-breeding areas in the country. There are even "farm subdivisions," developments where you can buy a few acres, a barn, and a house, and do small-scale farming or horse raising as your retirement hobby.

GAINESVILLE–OCALA WEATHER						
In degrees Fahrenheit						
	Jan.	April	July	Oct.	Rain	Snow
Daily highs	66	81	90	81	52"	—
Daily lows	42	55	71	59		

GAINESVILLE–OCALA AREA COST OF LIVING					
Percentage of	Overall	Housing	Medical	Groceries	Utilities
national average	95	84	85	100	101

One retiree told us that he chose to live here because Ocala reminded him of the countryside where he grew up in northern Illinois. "The only thing it lacks is the ice and snow in the wintertime," he added. When asked about northern Florida summers, he replied, "I don't believe they are any hotter than they were back home. Anyway, whenever we get the notion, the wife and I drive an hour and twenty minutes to Daytona Beach and cool off in the Atlantic Ocean. We can get there by nine in the morning and be home with sunburns by suppertime!"

Real estate in and around Ocala is affordable, with a trend toward restored homes in Ocala's historic district as well as in new developments away from the town center. Single-family homes in nice neighborhoods sell for what condominiums go for elsewhere, and a lakeside home on a golf course is not too much more. Prices like these account for the influx of retirees, with about 25 percent of the population age sixty-five or older. A new retirement development, with a projected 5,000 homes, will be under way soon. The Del Webb Corporation has also purchased land here, and plans for a new layout are under way.

Several inviting mobile-home parks surround Ocala. We inspected one park just an eight-minute drive from the Ocala city limits that had a country setting worthy of the name, yet with a Florida accent. Shaded by spreading oak trees, the mobile homes rest on large parcels along paved drives that wind through the park. A radio-operated gate keeps out high-pressure salespeople. The park's ample clubhouse hosts senior citizens' activities plus a swimming pool and tennis courts, creating an atmosphere conducive to quiet, slow-paced retirement.

Not only do Ocala's mobile-home parks range from ordinary to deluxe, but it's also possible to buy a few acres, or just a small lot, and install your own mobile home. Many small farms of five to fifty acres dot the countryside, with nothing but a mobile home and a barn on the property.

The Atlantic Coast

Palm Coast Let's take a look at one of those multiple-use communities, one with beach, golf, tennis, and boating facilities all in one. This is not to be considered an advertisement or an endorsement of this particular community, but rather an example of similar communities found all over the state. Some are much more ex-

pensive and most are smaller. Palm Coast is interesting in that it evolved from a large-scale development into an actual city of almost 33,000 residents; it is now a conventional community with no ties to the original developer.

Palm Coast is located halfway between St. Augustine and Daytona Beach—22 miles each way. A private ocean beach club (open to residents) is an easy walk or bike ride across the Intracoastal Waterway bridge. The planned community was developed by ITT Community Development Corporation over a two-decade span and is still under way.

As you exit Interstate 95 to enter the Palm Coast development, you immediately feel as if you have entered a park. The landscaped, four-lane parkway through residential and commercial areas is bordered by lush forests of oak and native palms. Bicycle and jogging paths meander through the landscaped commons and are fully used by Palm Coast residents and visitors.

Great pains were taken to preserve the semitropical aspects of the Florida natureland, with its magnificent tall trees, tangled vines, and indigenous palm trees. Housing and businesses are skillfully hidden behind the vegetation so that it appears to the casual visitor

PALM COAST WEATHER					
In degrees Fahrenheit					
	Jan.	April	July	Oct.	Rain	Snow
Daily highs	68	80	89	81	48"	—
Daily lows	47	59	72	65		

PALM COAST AREA COST OF LIVING					
Percentage of	Overall	Housing	Medical	Groceries	Utilities
national average	97	91	100	101	100

that most of the developments are natural parklands. The business district and shopping centers are tastefully landscaped and surrounded by a buffer of trees to keep noise and traffic away from residential areas. Of the original 42,000 acres in the development, 5,000 acres are set aside as a nature reserve.

This development wasn't planned solely as a place for retirement. Provisions were made for business parks and light, technology-oriented industry to provide jobs for the residents of Palm Coast. These areas are located near the interstate and screened from the residential areas by nature preserves, yet close enough for workers to walk or ride bicycles to work. The infusion of young couples and children adds a freshness to the face of Palm Coast, taking it out of the category of a retirement center.

Scattered through the complex are five championship golf courses, two of them designed by Arnold Palmer. The community tennis club is one of only four clubs in the country with clay, grass, and hard surface within the same complex. Sixteen hard-surface courts draw players of all skill levels. The club is complete with an aerobics room, lockers, and restaurant.

Boating enthusiasts can have their own private marinas at their back doors. The canals vary from 60 to 125 feet wide and are about 8 feet deep. Homes here are of course priced higher than houses on ordinary streets but are surprisingly good values, considering the amenities. Because the development is mature, many older places are on the market, helping to hold prices down somewhat.

All Florida retirement communities are not created equal. Across the Intracoastal Waterway is another development (also by

ITT Community Development Corporation) called Hammock Dunes. It also features golf courses and natural Florida landscaping, but on a lavish scale, along 5 miles of oceanfront. An impressive 32,000-square-foot clubhouse overlooks the Atlantic and a spectacular golf course. Prices for homes start at the mid-$200,000 range. Building lots vary from $150,000 to $875,000. "Exclusive" is the appropriate description here.

Daytona Beach   Daytona Beach is about 65 miles south of St. Augustine and is situated partly on the peninsula and partly on the mainland. Daytona's main tourist section is on the peninsula's ocean side rather than on the mainland. The city population is 65,000, with 100,000 in the metropolitan area. The 23-mile-long white sand beach is perhaps its most famous feature, one of the few places in Florida where autos are permitted to drive along the beach. The only time to drive it is during low or outgoing tide, when it is hard packed and pavementlike. Many speed records have been set on this beach. Overnight parking or camping is not allowed.

The famous tourist area—on the peninsula—has a wide promenade, an amusement park, and a fishing pier to entertain vacationers. To keep tourism alive during the slow tourist months, automobile and motorcycle racing were instituted. Over the years these events have gained wide media recognition, bringing racing enthusiasts from all over the nation. During important races the fans outnumber the residents. This creates welcome revenue for Daytona Beach and the surrounding communities, but also pro-

DAYTONA BEACH WEATHER					
In degrees Fahrenheit					
	Jan.	April	July	Oct.	Rain	Snow
Daily highs	68	80	90	81	48"	—
Daily lows	47	59	73	65		

DAYTONA BEACH AREA COST OF LIVING					
	Overall	Housing	Medical	Groceries	Utilities
Percentage of national average	100	102	100	96	103

duces some marvelous traffic jams. Local people pay close attention to the schedules and avoid the peninsula during races.

Daytona Beach is one of Florida's nicer-looking Atlantic cities, with graceful buildings on both the peninsula side and on the mainland, where the commercial district is located. As you drive across the connecting causeway, rows of mature tropical trees outline a pleasant view of downtown in the distance. Housing prices are among the lowest in the state, about 14 percent below the national average.

The Halifax River is part of the Intracoastal Waterway, which stretches from the Florida Keys north to Chesapeake Bay. It's wide and sheltered—a perfect place for learning how to handle a sailboat before venturing into open water. Everything from fishing dinghies to freighters uses this channel to follow the coast. You can make it to the Florida Keys with very little exposure to the open ocean. A new development in Daytona Beach is the recently completed Halifax Harbor Marina, which is now the largest marina between Baltimore and Fort Lauderdale.

Rents in the tourist sector vary widely, depending upon the season, the view, and access to the beach. When buying something near the beach, always make sure you aren't buying into a party pad. Any complex where most units are rented to tourists by the week is liable to mean trouble. A clean-cut college student can invite the whole fraternity house for an around-the-clock animal party. Retirement-type housing is available on the peninsula, but most retirees prefer to live in the comparative peace and quiet of the mainland.

Some nearby communities worth investigating are Ormond Beach—where the famous daredevils like Barney Oldfield raced automobiles in attempts to break the one-time 60-mile-an-hour speed barrier—and New Smyrna Beach, which is as far as autos can be driven on the sand. This is where Canaveral National Seashore wildlife preserve begins, the refuge of alligators, turtles, manatees, and a marvelous variety of birds.

Where the wildlife preserve ends, the Canaveral Peninsula and the John F. Kennedy Space Center begin. New Smyrna Beach, by the way, is one of the oldest settlements in America. Historians believe Ponce de Leon landed here in 1513.

Cocoa Beach to Melbourne   The "Space Coast" derives its name from the John F. Kennedy Space Center on the Canaveral Peninsula. All along this section of coast, from Cocoa Beach down to Melbourne and Melbourne Beach, is an attractive group of towns just made for retirement.

Cocoa Beach's commercial center is much larger than its actual population of 13,000 might indicate. Its downtown streets are lined with flower boxes and old-time village shops where folks can watch potters at work, leathersmiths making belts and hats, and skilled craftsmen restoring antiques. Cocoa Beach serves as a focal point for nearby cities such as Cocoa, Merritt Island, and Rockledge. The Canaveral Pier at Cocoa Beach extends almost 800 feet into the ocean, a great place for fishing, dining, and nightlife.

Cocoa Beach is home to many space-center workers and military families from nearby Cape Canaveral and Patrick Air Force Base. Cocoa Beach and the nearby towns have attracted a large share of military retirees, folks who liked the area when stationed here.

According to the local chamber of commerce, a good percentage of the population are retirees, and they are very active in politics. The number of services available to senior citizens reflects this. Thirteen apartment and housing complexes are for senior citizens. A good public transportation system is augmented by the free van service for wheelchair-confined residents provided by a local surfing shop.

A community college and a state university are located here, with plenty of activities that involve retired residents. Hospitals are within 45 miles and air transportation is 45 miles away.

The area has an interesting mixture of very expensive and very ordinary homes. All in all prices seemed a bit higher than in other sections of the state, probably because of the nearby air bases and space industries. Even so, plenty of inexpensive homes and condos are on the market. Some developments and mobile-home parks near the ocean are having problems with water; be sure to check for drinkability before buying on the beach.

COCOA BEACH–MELBOURNE WEATHER						
In degrees Fahrenheit						
	Jan.	April	July	Oct.	Rain	Snow
Daily highs	72	81	89	83	51"	—
Daily lows	52	62	72	67		

Sitting at the lower end of this famous coast is the largest of the towns, Melbourne, with a population of 72,000. Palm Bay, Merritt Island, and Satellite Beach are also part of Melbourne's shopping area. This is a relatively quiet area, at least compared with the hectic, tourist-clogged pace of nearby Orlando.

Melbourne itself is on the mainland; a causeway takes you to the beach town of Indiatlantic. And what a beach it is, with 33 miles of sandy, uncrowded Atlantic shore! At one time this beach was nicknamed the "Treasure Coast"; when a hurricane shipwrecked a fleet of Spanish ships against the shore, millions of Spanish doubloons spilled into the sea. The survivors—some 1,500 men, women, and children—spent three years trying to recover the treasure. Today divers still keep their eyes peeled for coins and bullion.

During the summer, from May until September, loggerhead turtles visit the beaches to dig nests and lay eggs. As many as 12,000 nests are dug each season. Retirees are invited to join the Sea Turtle Preservation Society. The elusive manatee is often sighted around here, as well.

This coast is liberally endowed with attractive apartments, complete with swimming pools, tennis courts, and social directors, starting at $450 and going up. Single-family housing and condos are comparably priced.

Florida's Gold Coast

It all started back in the 1880s when two starry-eyed promoters, John and James Lummus, bought a barren spit of sand that jutted offshore from the southern Florida main-land. Lying in the indigo waters be-tween Biscayne Bay and the Atlantic Ocean, their new purchase inspired a dream. They were convinced they could turn this worthless piece of land into a fabulously productive coconut plantation. They planted

thousands of trees and sat back, waiting for them to mature and for tropical winds to shake the harvest to the ground.

However, things didn't work out that way. Blight cut the harvest

GOLD COAST WEATHER					
In degrees Fahrenheit					
	Jan.	April	July	Oct.	Rain	Snow
Daily highs	75	82	89	84	60"	—
Daily lows	56	65	74	70		

potential, and tree rats harvested more than did the plantation owners. Mosquitoes and other insects drove workers away, and finally the dream died. But the coconut trees survived. Later promoters saw a different promise: tourism and retirement. They called their new development Miami Beach.

The boom started in the 1920s and spilled from Key Biscayne north to Fort Lauderdale, Pompano Beach, Boca Raton, all the way to Palm Beach and beyond. By the 1930s it was in full swing as a winter retreat and retirement haven. This is Florida's famous Gold Coast. A drive along the coastal highway will explain how it received its name. It certainly took a lot of gold to build it and more to maintain it.

Individually the cities from West Palm Beach down to Coral Gables don't appear to be particularly large. But together the more than forty towns comprise one long, enormous metropolitan area of almost 3 million people. These many communities spread along the beach have no chance of having a central focus or a common "downtown" area. Broken into a string of suburbs without an urban area to be suburban to, each has its own shopping center, stores, businesses, and its own small political entity. In this unconsolidated way, Florida's Gold Coast resembles Los Angeles.

Except for the classy sections along the beaches, most housing is single-family bungalows, low-profile condominiums, and expansive apartment complexes. In some of the less intensely developed areas, where things aren't so tightly packed, it's easy to forget that you are part of an urban sprawl. People commonly don't go shopping away from their area; they have no need to.

Along the Gold Coast you'll find the biggest contrasts in all of Florida. From tall forests of condominiums and apartments that remind you of New York's Park Avenue to rows of tract houses reminiscent of Los Angeles, you'll find almost every imaginable type of housing and neighborhood—all within miles or sometimes yards of each other. Then just 10 to 20 miles to the west, the land is uninhabited, totally the domain of wildlife.

The Miami Complex   This is the Florida you usually read about in your newspaper's travel section, the Florida you see on television and in movies. For some folks the thought of living in such a crowded area is a turnoff. But for others the amenities of a metropolitan area—combined with a mild climate and gorgeous beaches—add up to ideal retirement living. They adore everything about the Gold Coast. They love the convenience of well-stocked shopping centers, good medical facilities, and a wide array of restaurants. Folks here enjoy apartment living, having someone else wash windows, mow lawns, and trim shrubs. As one lady put it, "We've lived all our lives in or near Manhattan. We couldn't survive in some dinky, one-horse town where they roll up the sidewalks after dark!"

Curiously, in the midst of this densely packed, tropical replica of Manhattan, distinct concepts of neighborhood and community emerge. We've visited several large condominium developments and are always fascinated by the way folks create their own islands of interests and community. A typical complex, this one in Pompano Beach, has a dozen eight-story buildings set apart in a parklike setting. Each building has complete laundry facilities and an exercise room. Jogging paths, swimming pools, and tennis courts are strategically placed about the grounds, and a clubhouse dominates the center.

In effect the development corresponds to a small town, or an intimate neighborhood in a larger city. The condo owners' association substitutes for city politics back home. Residents have a great time voting for officers, running for election, lobbying for pet projects, or trying to recall those who aren't doing their job. "I feel like I have a helluva lot more control and say-so about my neighborhood now than I ever could hope for back in New York," said one resident who was in the middle of a fight to redecorate the clubhouse and install more outdoor lighting.

Another example is a condo development in Deerfield Beach, a place called Century Village East. It seems to be populated primarily by former New Yorkers, many of whom knew one another back home. Century Village is not only large, but well organized—so

MIAMI AREA COST OF LIVING					
Percentage of national average	Overall 102	Housing 89	Medical 122	Groceries 100	Utilities 116

much so that it puts out an impressive forty-eight-page newspaper every month to carry news of the development's activities to the 8,000 residential units in the development. Residents have their own shopping center, golf course, even buses and trolleys. They elect members to serve in positions analogous to mayor, city council, etc.

As in any metropolitan area, living in the Gold Coast area has drawbacks. Higher crime rates, traffic jams, and crowded stores are pretty much standard. However, the crime picture is somewhat distorted in the Miami area because of vigorous commerce in illegal drugs. Presumably you are not into drug dealing and won't be participating in car chases, revenge killings, and Mafia shoot-outs as featured on television shows. Therefore, statistics on drug busts, drive-by shootings, and gang-related activities should not affect you significantly—as long as you stay away from the dangerous neighborhoods. Robberies of tourists obviously will occur in tourist-clogged areas, places you would avoid under normal circumstances.

One important point: What metropolitan areas lack in peace and quiet, they more than make up for in services and conveniences for retirees. The larger the population, the more and better senior citizen centers, health-care facilities, libraries, educational opportunities, and other advantages.

Coral Gables   You'll find numerous affordable communities in the Gold Coast complex, and also some upscale, moderately expensive places. The city of Coral Gables (pop. 43,000) is a fashionable suburb of Miami, situated at the southern edge of the Miami metro complex. It's conveniently located 6 miles from downtown Miami, 3 miles from Coconut Grove, 5 miles from Miami International Airport, and not distant from Little Havana and Bayside Marketplace. Transportation connections to the Gold Coast cities are facilitated by two Metrorail stations serving Coral Gables, as well as a commuter train running 67 miles from Miami International Airport to West Palm Beach.

Coral Gables was one of Florida's pioneer developments and boasts "historic landmarks" dating back to the early 1900s, buildings in the Mediterranean Revival style. This set the trend for the future. In 1921 Coral Gables became one of the state's first planned communities with elaborate plans calling for classic Spanish and Italian architecture, requiring new buildings displaying styles of old Malaga and Granada. The result is today's wide, tree-lined avenues, monumental buildings, winding roadways with generous green space, ornate plazas and fountains, plus landscaped waterways. There are a few glass-sheathed modernistic buildings bucking the trend, but for the most part Coral Gables has held fast to its Spanish architectural roots. In 1925 the University of Miami located here, with its buildings continuing in a Mediterranean mode. The university is the city's largest employer today and affects the community's cultural as well as economic life.

Coral Gables's picturesque environment is somewhat insulated from Miami's metropolitan bustle and is popular with commuters because it is near the action, yet slower paced. However, this popularity causes housing to be on the expensive side of the ledger, attracting working executives and middle-management families more than retired couples. But for those who can afford it, Coral Gables is worth investigating. Two-bedroom condos can cost as much as a four-bedroom home in ordinary Florida developments.

Florida Keys: The End of the Line   Except for Hawaii, this jumbled string of islands and reefs is the most tropical part of the United States. A highway follows the route of an old railway line, an engineering marvel in itself, 110 miles to the last of the accessible islands, Key West. The highway skips from one coral atoll to another over numerous causeways and bridges, across islands festooned with palm trees, hibiscus, and bougainvillea and bearing such romantic names as Key Largo, Islamorada, and Matacumbe.

Substantial numbers of retirees, both snowbirds and regular residents, populate these islands. Boating and fishing are top attractions, with year-round tropical weather the frosting on the cake. When it comes to snorkeling and diving, these islands are a virtual paradise. Folks here boast of the longest living reef in the western hemisphere, crystal-clear waters with visibility up to 100 feet, and more than 500 wrecks to explore.

Yachts are "in" throughout the Keys, large ones and small ones. Resident sailors simply cut berths into the coral and limestone backyards of their homes and tie up. Other houses are set back against networks of canals, where their occupants can dock after a day's adventure of fishing or treasure hunting in the warm waters of the Gulf Stream. You'll even find mobile homes with sloops moored at their floating patios.

At one time Key West developed a reputation as a retreat and retirement spot for writers and artists. Wallace Stevens fell in love with Key West back in 1922, and in his poem "The Idea of Order in Key West" he praised it as "a summer without end." Having let the cat out of the bag, Stevens soon found himself in the company of other intellectuals who wanted to participate in this "summer without end." Ernest Hemingway, John Dos Passos, and Tennessee Williams all maintained houses in Key West. Some of their homes are now major tourist attractions.

The tradition of an artist colony continues, but in a somewhat diminished form. Key West has become incredibly crowded and overrun with tourists and weekending college students. Finding a parking place becomes a treasure hunt. Key West's tolerant openness to varying lifestyles and its "live and let live" attitude has encouraged the establishment of a considerable gay community. Because it's such a long drive from the mainland, over a snail's-pace, two-lane highway, and because housing costs in Key West are hardly bargains, our recommendations lean toward retirement farther up the line, in places like Key Largo or Marathon.

A perpetual problem facing those living on the Keys is the threat of hurricane-driven tides—another reason for living closer to the mainland. Everywhere you look you'll find some (not all) homes and businesses raised off the ground 10 or 12 feet. Storm tides are the obvious reason; they simply wash underneath the houses without causing much damage. Flood insurance rates are considerably less with this type of construction. That's good. But being up in the air raises the chances of wind damage, so storm insurance is higher. That's bad.

One of the major complaints by residents of the Keys, besides the continual influx of newcomers, is a steadily rising real estate market. At one time, they reminisce, you could rent an apartment or small home for next to nothing, but today the tariffs are becoming higher than on the mainland. This is particularly so in Key West, where space is at a premium and tourists arrive to become residents at a rate that appears alarming to residents. I saw a bumper sticker there: KEY WEST IS A DRINKING TOWN WITH A TOURIST PROBLEM. On both Key Largo and Marathon we checked out several homes, some with canals in their backyards, where motorboats, launches, and yachts were tied to individual docks.

Florida's West Coast

Like Central Florida, Gulf Coast retirees tend to come from different parts of the country than the northern Atlantic Coast. Instead of drawing its newcomers from New York and New England, a higher percentage of residents emigrate from Midwestern and Northern states. Therefore, it isn't surprising that architecture and lifestyles are more disposed toward Midwestern values.

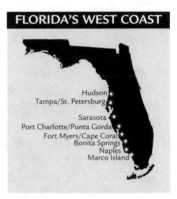

Instead of tall condos and apartments, the preferred style is low profile, informal, and conservative. Single-family homes are the norm, sitting on lots often measured in acres rather than in square feet, with generous areas of lawn and landscaping.

The climate is different here, too. The weather-stabilizing Gulf Stream misses Florida's west coast. The result: Summers along the gulf are hotter and winters a few degrees cooler than along the Gold Coast. But the folks who've retired here say it's worth it, and they point out that the relative humidity is lower than on the other coast.

This southwestern part of the state is one of our favorites. From Fort Myers/Cape Coral on down to Naples and Marco Island you'll find a wide assortment of neighborhoods as inexpensive as any developed part of Florida, or as luxurious as you might wish. Cape Coral's average sales price for existing homes is one of the lowest in the country, whereas Naples and Marco Island are among the most expensive in Florida. Sanibel Island also ranks up there in expense and carries an added handicap of not having any place to park.

Fort Myers and its sister city of Cape Coral are separated by the Caloosahatchee River. (No, I'm not making that up.) Neighboring Pine Island lies across a saltwater pass from Cape Coral. Fort Myers Beach is also an island, one of a string of them that shelter the coastline all the way south to Naples. In the middle are Bonita Springs and Bonita Beach, two excellent choices for in-between expensive and affordable retirement.

Formerly a cattle-growing area, population growth here is nothing short of phenomenal, an astonishing 600 percent in the last twenty years! Good transportation accounts for some of this growth; Interstate 75 shoots through the area, making it a snap to drive east to the Gold Coast or north to the Tampa Bay area in two and a half hours. Fort Myers also boasts an international airport. Medical care is excellent with the new Gulf Coast Hospital's discounts for senior citizens. A half dozen other hospitals and several nursing facilities serve the area as well.

This is definitely a winter snowbird haven—the population doubles between the first of November and Easter week. Then, when summer's humidity and ninety-plus-degree weather sets in, the comfort-loving snowbirds fly home to cooler northern climes. But year-round residents protest when I suggest that summer might be harsh. "Check it out; it's just a little bit warmer than Miami Beach," they point out, "and it's a lot safer living around here!"

In addition to the usual saltwater sports associated with Florida's west coast, those with a fondness for gambling will enjoy greyhound racing at the Naples–Fort Myers Greyhound Track. Betting on the doggies is fun and not very expensive at two bucks a bet.

Fort Myers/Cape Coral   Discovered early in the century by Henry Ford and Thomas Edison, Fort Myers has been booming since. The city's landscaping is a unique heritage left by Thomas Edison. He loved to experiment with trees and shrubs, particularly palm trees. Older residential areas are full of them, grown tall and mature over the decades since the great inventor planted them around town. It's claimed that more than seventy varieties of palms grace the streets of Fort Myers. Some stand tall and stately; others are short, with bottlelike trunks. A few flaunt astonishing leaf patterns that look as if they were created by fashion designers.

FORT MYERS–CAPE CORAL WEATHER						
In degrees Fahrenheit						
	Jan.	April	July	Oct.	Rain	Snow
Daily highs	74	85	91	85	54"	—
Daily lows	53	62	74	68		

FORT MYERS–CAPE CORAL AREA COST OF LIVING					
Percentage of	Overall	Housing	Medical	Groceries	Utilities
national average	98	92	97	104	106

The overall theme of this area is one of prosperity, with very few sections of town looking seedy. Well-manicured lawns, flowering bushes, and magnolia trees give residential areas of Fort Myers a quiet, homey look. Edison Community College offers a profusion of classes, almost free, in their Lifelong Learning Center. Naturally landscaping is one of the more popular courses.

Fort Myers and North Fort Myers have a combined population of approximately 94,000, about the same as sister city Cape Coral. The island of Fort Myers Beach—population 14,000—fronts the city of Fort Myers and provides open access to the Gulf, making it a popular place for homes with boat docks. The 7-mile-long island is tightly packed with small homes, condos, and beachfront properties. It's only about three-quarters of a mile wide. For being close to such a popular beach, prices are affordable, but winter traffic on the island can be horrific and the number of tourists along the beachfront appalling. Be aware that Fort Myers Beach's population *triples* during the winter. A few blocks off the beach, confusion and noise greatly diminish, that's true, but this is a place for the young at heart and possibly the hard of hearing.

Throughout the area is a profusion of condos, some sitting on the edge of their own nine-hole golf courses. Condo styles seem quite practical: mostly two stories with bedrooms upstairs and no other families living overhead or underfoot. Condominium developers have been generous in providing spacious lawn areas between the condos, so you don't have the cramped, hemmed-in feeling that comes with east Florida multistory skyscrapers and asphalt parking lots.

Mobile-home parks are plentiful. Most are beautifully landscaped and offer organized activities in their clubhouses and recreational facilities. Some are downright luxurious, some super-expensive, and others quite affordable.

For quiet, rural island retirement, Pine Island is the place. Seventeen miles long and about 2 miles wide, this is the largest of the barrier islands in these parts. Its shores are almost completely ringed with mangrove estuaries, many in wildlife preserves. As its name implies, the island is rustic, covered with pines, and retirement housing is inexpensive. Approximately 8,000 year-round residents are joined by another 4,000 during the winter months.

Pine Island is accessed from Cape Coral via a fishing bridge that crosses over to Matlacha and Little Pine Islands. This is known as "Florida's Fishingest Bridge," and at almost any time, day or night, you are apt to see fishermen dipping their lines into Matlacha Pass. This area is a throwback to the time when tiny fishing villages were the norm along the southwest coast. The western shore sits in the lee of Captiva Island, which makes the water safe for sailing and peaceful fishing.

Naples/Marco Island/Bonita Springs   Those accustomed to going first-class will want to check out Naples and nearby Marco Island. Naples dominates a stretch of public beaches 41 miles long. It's one of the fastest-growing upscale communities in Florida. One section of Naples, appropriately called Venice, is a modern-day recreation of its Italian namesake, with luxury condos and some of the finest shops and boutiques on Florida's west coast built right down on the water line.

Naples has the reputation of being super-expensive, and it is if compared with nearby Florida communities. Yet many impressive neighborhoods of lovely landscaping, mature shade trees, and upscale housing look like bargains to folks from some parts of the country. A home costing $350,000 here couldn't be duplicated for twice that amount in the spiffy parts of California or New York.

This is the western terminus of the Tamiami Trail, a famous highway that cuts right through the Everglades. In addition to golf and the usual Florida pastimes, swamp-buggy racing is popular in the Marco Island–Naples area. Hopped-up swamp machines are run in special events in October to mark the beginning of the Everglades hunting season.

Bonita Springs, about fifteen minutes north of Naples and twenty minutes south of Fort Myers, is a mixed affordable/luxury community. The year-round population is around 33,000. Great beaches are about four minutes from town at Bonita Shores, which is a kind of "less expensive Naples." My impression is this beach is patronized more by local folks rather than tourists, which makes it much less zoolike. The entire area is much more laid-back and quiet than the northern beaches. The water temperature of the Gulf is about seventy-one degrees in the winter and eighty-four in the summer, which translates into pleasant swimming.

Many homes are built on canals with open-water access, thus making boating and yachting popular pastimes here. The average selling price of these places is about 50 percent higher than homes in conventional neighborhoods. Overall home prices in this area are higher than Florida averages and higher than national averages as well.

Port Charlotte/Punta Gorda   Not far north from Fort Myers, on expansive Charlotte Harbor, the cities of Punta Gorda and Port Charlotte display interests different from their neighbors. Beaches aren't the big deal here; instead residents focus on the miles of man-made canals and waterways that cut through their neighborhoods like boulevards. More than 150 miles of these man-made waterways provide easy access to the Gulf for thousands of boating and fishing enthusiasts. As one resident pointed out, "The water is so clean and unpolluted here, we don't hesitate to swim or water-ski right here in town." The Myakka River and the harbor make possible some of the best fishing and boating in the state.

Having a boat tied up in the backyard is as common as having an automobile in the garage. Prices for these waterside residences are surprisingly affordable, probably because they are so common, and you'll notice some rather ordinary houses backed up to the waterways with more invested in the sailboats and yachts than in the homes. Boaters are quick to point out, however, that waterways in neighborhoods to the west of the Tamiami Trail—the main highway that bisects Port Charlotte—must pass under low bridges. Only boats with low profiles—motorboats or small sailboats with masts that can be lowered—can make their way to salt water. So if you're a fan of tall-masted ships, better look on the saltwater side of the river, otherwise you'll never make it out to open water. Perhaps this is why some neighborhoods on Port Charlotte's west side benefit from such exceptionally low property prices. Everyone wants to be on the "saltwater side."

PORT CHARLOTTE WEATHER					
In degrees Fahrenheit					
	Jan.	April	July	Oct.	Rain	Snow
Daily highs	74	85	91	85	54"	—
Daily lows	53	62	74	68		

Port Charlotte is large (pop. nearly 100,000), but it doesn't have a city feeling. It spreads out along the Tamiami Trail (Highway 41) with businesses and malls scattered along the highway rather than concentrated in a downtown civic center. Just a block or so off the main thoroughfare, tranquil neighborhoods offer peaceful havens.

Punta Gorda, a smaller place with fewer than 14,000 inhabitants, sits just across the Peace River from Port Charlotte. It's older and more sedate, and housing can be fairly expensive. This is because most homes are built on one of Punta Gorda's 85 miles of navigable canals, all of which can provide access to the Gulf.

Every February local people commemorate Ponce de Leon's reputed visit to Charlotte Harbor with a festival complete with conquistador costumes. They reenact the Spaniard's historic landing on the shore of Charlotte Harbor in his stubborn search for the Fountain of Youth.

From Port Charlotte, along the 30 miles of highway down to Fort Myers, are some most impressive mobile-home developments. Some parks are country clubs in every sense of the term. They aren't cheap, but they are well worth a visit even if you can't afford them, just to see how the other half lives. In some developments you purchase the lot your home sits on, in other places you lease, and in still others you rent. Each system has its own advantages and drawbacks, as explained earlier.

Tampa–St. Petersburg   Separated by Tampa Bay, the twin cities of St. Petersburg and Tampa are connected by three causeways. Interstate 275, the area's main link to southern Florida, crosses the wide mouth of Tampa Bay on yet another long causeway as it heads south to Bradenton. Together the cities and their suburbs have about 1.6 million people, making it the second-largest metropolitan area in Florida. Although many retire here, the best places are nearby.

St. Petersburg (pop. 250,000) is famous for its proclaimed year-round sunshine; the local newspaper has a standing pledge to give away a newspaper every day the sun doesn't peek out at least some. On one visit it was overcast all day. I'm still waiting for my free newspaper. According to the U.S. Weather Bureau, the Tampa–St. Petersburg area can expect an average of 127 cloudy days a year and 107 days of rain. This surprised me, especially when I compared these figures with San Francisco, a place famous for foggy and overcast days. Turns out that San Francisco averages 100 cloudy days and only 67 days with rain.

St. Petersburg entered into the retirement business long ago, advertising in newspapers around the country, stressing its great climate and emphasizing the pleasant retirement possibilities here. It worked so well that the city soon became overrun with senior citizens. The city fathers then changed the advertising campaign to attract industry and younger people. The story goes that the city even removed park benches in an effort to discourage senior citizens from "hanging out." Perhaps they were concerned about gangs of geriatric delinquents getting out of hand. That didn't discourage retirees; they kept on coming, probably bringing their own park benches.

The emphasis on retirement here is not necessarily either St. Petersburg or Tampa, but surrounding, smaller locations, using the metropolitan area as a central focus. The nearby towns of Sarasota and Bradenton to the south and Clearwater, Indian Shores, Tarpon Springs, and a dozen other communities north of St. Petersburg are all pleasant places for retirement. Clearwater is famous for its stretch of pure white sand beach. North of Tampa, along Interstate 75, you'll find another series of great prospects, particularly for inexpensive mobile-home living, in farming communities with affordable acreages and a down-home country atmosphere, yet minutes from big-city life.

Sarasota is our particular favorite in this area. Apparently others agree with us, for *Money* magazine ranked Sarasota among the "Top 20 Places to Retire" and fourteenth on its "Best Places to Live in the U.S." list, and *Southern Living* named Sarasota County "the nation's per capita arts capital."

With its own opera and symphony, bolstered by the Ringling Museum and School of Art and the Asolo Theater, Sarasota can be considered the culture capital of the state, attracting a population—many of them retirees—that supports the arts. We have a friend who resides here, a portrait artist, who has lived in and visited just about

TAMPA–ST. PETERSBURG WEATHER					
In degrees Fahrenheit					
	Jan.	April	July	Oct.	Rain	Snow
Daily highs	70	82	90	84	47"	—
Daily lows	49	61	74	65		

TAMPA–ST. PETERSBURG COST OF LIVING					
Percentage of	Overall	Housing	Medical	Groceries	Utilities
national average	97	94	100	99	88

every part of the country, including Hawaii, but chooses to live here because of the city's comparatively low population density and leisurely pace.

You'll find a wide selection of housing choices here, from small cottages in renovated neighborhoods to luxury condominiums and mansions on the Gulf, to smaller apartment complexes throughout the city. Miles of beaches are within a few minutes of almost any residential area, and a protected bay and marina make boating and fishing popular activities. Golfers and tennis enthusiasts enjoy the city's many public and private golf courses and tennis courts.

Saltwater fishing is one of Tampa Bay's outdoor attractions. Anglers are out in early summer for silver king tarpon and then kingfish in early fall. By the way, fishing licenses aren't required in Florida for residents older than age sixty. Baseball fans might be interested to know that this coast is the winter home for the New York Yankees, Toronto Blue Jays, Tampa Bay Devil Rays, Pittsburgh Pirates, and the Philadelphia Phillies. Another popular sport in St. Pete is greyhound racing. Admission is reasonable; the track makes it up on the pari-mutuel (rabbits get in free). For golf addicts about seventy golf courses dot the surrounding area.

For cultural balance the metropolitan area supports two theater groups, a ballet, and an opera company. Nine art museums, including two at the university and the Museum of Fine Arts, complete the schedule. Numerous hospitals and medical specialists ensure good health care.

Sun Coast North of Tampa–St. Petersburg is another area largely ignored by retirement writers. Local public relations folks

SUN COAST WEATHER					
In degrees Fahrenheit					
	Jan.	April	July	Oct.	Rain	Snow
Daily highs	70	82	90	84	47"	—
Daily lows	49	61	74	65		

call this area Florida's Sun Coast. In our estimation this is one of the more practical retirement areas in the state from several angles. Long stretches of Highway 19 are largely undeveloped, with many patches of affordable and quality housing. As Highway 19 goes north from Clearwater, it passes through several moderately settled areas and finally thins out into open farmland and untouched forest. Parts of it are as rural as you'll find in the state.

New housing developments and livable mobile-home parks spice up pleasant towns such as Hudson, Crystal Springs, and Homosassa. We especially liked the name of one town: Weeki Wachee. (As you've probably already guessed, Weeki Wachee is just south of the town of Chassahowitzka and is within easy striking distance of nearby Withlacoochee State Forest.)

Roadside signs and billboards clearly affirm the Sun Coast's dedication to retirement services. Large billboards announce items of interest to senior citizens: services such as cataract surgery, arthritis clinics, hearing aids, and cardiac care. A billboard announces a large-print book fair; another advertises supplementary Medicare policies.

From Clearwater north, stores and businesses crowd the main route (U.S. Highway 19) and begin thinning out past New Port Richey. Even though much of this portion of the route sometimes seems to be one long shopping center, just a block off the highway in either direction you will find quiet residential areas.

But then, as you drive further north, population becomes sparse. Abandoned gift shops, motels, and restaurants give mute testimony that tourist traffic along this highway has fallen away drastically. My guess is that construction of Interstate 75, which parallels Highway 19, drew the flow of tourist traffic away onto its faster, 65-mile-an-hour route. For those entrepreneurs who hoped to make a killing from selling milkshakes and souvenirs to tourists, this must have been devastating, but for the retiree who hates heavy highway traffic, it is a boon. This is the lightest-traveled highway I've yet to drive in Florida—with divided pavement and few competing autos. The most important roadside signs caution motorists to watch for deer crossing the road.

Florida's Panhandle

Starting from Tallahassee, the state's capital, and stretching westward to Pensacola, Florida's Panhandle is different from most of the state. Pure white sand beaches and enterprising resort towns clearly remind you that you're in Florida, but the Panhandle also borrows from nearby Georgia and Alabama. There's a "down-home" atmosphere here; the native accent is Deep South, the thinking is pure country.

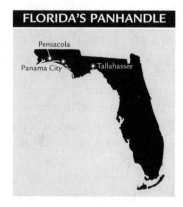

FLORIDA'S PANHANDLE

Many Southerners and Midwesterners feel especially comfortable with this combination of resort-country retirement living. Our research shows many Panhandle locations have personal safety statistics similar to those of Alabama and Georgia, which contrasts pleasantly with statistics for the Gold Coast.

The main tourist and retiree attraction is a 100-mile length of beach that begins at the little town of Mexico Beach and runs westward to Pensacola. Many folks who eventually retire along this coast are those who regularly spent their summer vacations here with their families. They fondly remember summers on the white sand beaches and fishing expeditions far out on the Gulf's blue waters.

Panama City   About 20 miles west of Tallahassee, the land ends abruptly at Cape San Blas, and the highway makes a right-angle turn north toward Port St. Joe. From here all the way to the Alabama state line, two main features characterize this part of Florida's Panhandle: military bases and powder-white beaches.

From Port St. Joe to Pensacola are more than a dozen little towns that cater to tourists and retirees. Often no more than a few blocks wide, the towns string along the highway and beach in a very laid-back manner. Single-family homes, duplexes, and small apart-

PANAMA CITY AREA COST OF LIVING					
Percentage of	Overall	Housing	Medical	Groceries	Utilities
national average	99	93	95	99	97

ments are available for either seasonal or year-round rental. Some stretches of high-rise construction would do justice to Florida's Gold Coast, however. During the winter months these little towns are quiet, but summers make up for this bustle deficit. The largest population center is Panama City (pop. 36,417). Like many towns in this area, Panama City has a dual personality. One side is that of a happy summer resort, the other a peaceful winter retreat. From November until March, the beaches are uncrowded and quiet. About the only tourists you'll see are speaking French with a Quebec accent. So many French Canadians congregate here in the winter that one begins to wonder who's tending to business in Montreal. But with warmer weather the French Canadians go home just as Midwesterners arrive for their turn at the beaches.

An offshoot of the Gulf Stream known as the Yucatan Current moves close to Panama City. It tends to warm the water in the winter just a tad. This flow also brings nutrient-rich waters from the Caribbean and, with it, schools of sport fish. Fishermen haul in marlin, sailfish, tuna, and dolphin, as well as buckets of panfish. A fishing pier extends about 1,600 feet into the Gulf for the convenience of anglers. To a certain extent the Yucatan Current moderates summer weather, but not to any appreciable amount. This doesn't deter the tourists, because as one of the natives pointed out, "It flat cain't get too hot for tourists!"

You needn't live on the beach to enjoy Gulf Coast living. Many folks reside in nearby towns just a twenty-minute drive from the sand and surf. Callaway, Springfield, Lynn Haven, and others are preferred by many retirees, particularly those who aren't captivated by the busy beach scene.

Part of the dual personality is the question of seasonal apartment and home rentals. In the off-season most rents drop rapidly, just as you would expect, but beach condos vary wildly, depending on season and demand. Housing prices along this coast are among the lowest in the nation, a good 12 percent below national averages.

The Emerald Coast   Between Panama City and Pensacola stretches a selection of towns ranging from ordinary to luxurious. A particularly interesting area circles a large body of water known as Choctawhatchee Bay. This is the self-styled Emerald Coast. It includes the town of Navarre and a dozen other little towns, but does not include Seagrove Beach. Some places look very comfortable, and living isn't too expensive. Other towns look as if they coddle tourists to the *nth* degree. The skyscraper-type condo towers would look right at home on Miami Beach. Despite the tourist factor, the area enjoys an unusually low crime rate.

Major towns on the bay are Fort Walton Beach and Destin, which seem to blend together into one city with a combined population of approximately 40,000. Valparaiso is the second city across the bay. Personnel at Eglin Air Force Base account for much of the off-season business activity as well as the high numbers of retired military who live around Choctawhatchee Bay.

The long string of beaches here is famous for having some of the whitest, cleanest, and softest sand in the world. According to geologists, the beaches are composed mainly of quartz washed down from the Appalachians via the Apalachicola River, some 130 miles east of Fort Walton Beach. By the time they get to Fort Walton Beach, the grains have been polished into tiny ovals that cause the sand to squeak when you walk along the dry part of the beach. Local residents are conservation minded and are working hard to prevent erosion. Fishing is said to be wonderful both on the beach side and in the bay itself. A fishing pier at Navarre Beach, on Santa Rosa Island, is a popular loafing place for local retirees.

Okaloosa Island, where Fort Walton Beach and Destin are located, is one of several barrier islands that protect the mainland. The bay is sheltered and makes for great swimming, boating, and picnicking. This is the place to look if you insist on living within blocks of the water. Winter rentals are inexpensive and plentiful during the off-season, but expect to pay your dues during the rest of the year.

EMERALD COAST AREA WEATHER						
In degrees Fahrenheit						
	Jan.	April	July	Oct.	Rain	Snow
Daily highs	61	77	90	79	61"	—
Daily lows	43	59	74	59		

For the area's best bargains in housing and rentals, check around Niceville and other communities on the mainland side of the bay. About a 25-mile drive along a divided highway is Crestview, near Interstate 10. Real estate prices here are also favorable for retirees, and the interstate brings Pensacola's hospitals and services within a forty-five-minute drive.

Pensacola   The Spanish recognized Pensacola as an excellent seaport when they settled here in 1559. With both an offshore island and a peninsula barrier against storm-driven tides, the town is quite secure from the scourge of hurricanes.

Pensacola has a checkered history, its political allegiance changing thirteen times—among Spain, France, England, the Confederacy, and the United States. (Flag-making must have been a bustling cottage industry.) Its growth from when I worked here in 1952 has been phenomenal, changing from a small town into a modern city of more than 60,000.

Its beaches are extensive, with pretty white sand. But they're becoming covered with condos. Summer sees a greater influx of younger people than in other parts of the Panhandle coast. You'll find an emphasis on things like discos and bars that might be downplayed elsewhere. That shouldn't deter retirees, because they'll be living away from the hustle and bustle of the beach scene.

Pensacola is the choice of many military retirees. Eglin Air Force Base, Whiting Field Naval Air Station, and the Pensacola Naval Air Academy ring the town. Upon retirement pilots who've served here naturally recall the attraction of the Panhandle's "Riviera" beaches and the convenience of military medical and base-exchange privileges.

PENSACOLA AREA WEATHER						
In degrees Fahrenheit						
	Jan.	April	July	Oct.	Rain	Snow
Daily highs	61	77	90	79	61"	—
Daily lows	43	59	74	59		

PENSACOLA AREA COST OF LIVING					
Percentage of	Overall	Housing	Medical	Groceries	Utilities
national average	97	88	99	97	100

Other Panhandle towns also have military bases. Tyndall Air Force Base, with 6,300 personnel, starts just west of Mexico Beach and extends to Panama City. There's also a Naval Coastal Systems center in Panama City, with about 2,300 personnel. Next is Eglin Air Force Base, and finally Pensacola's Naval Air Station. The military presence is significant indeed, with large payrolls supporting the economy because many civilians work on the bases.

CHAPTER 4

The Gulf Coast States

FIVE STATES CURVE AROUND the Gulf of Mexico's 2,000 miles of northern shoreline, forming a sort of private sea. Western Florida and the Panhandle account for more than a third of the Gulf's coastline; the other states are Alabama, Mississippi, Louisiana, and Texas. Long strands of sparkling beaches alternate with miles of saltwater marsh, the home of egrets, herons, roseate spoonbills, and dozens of other shorebird species. Wildlife sanctuaries abound. Fishing ports, sheltered bays, and natural harbors protected by offshore islands make saltwater sports convenient and productive. Gulf waters teem with life: shrimp, pompano, flounder, speckled trout, plus weird specimens like blowfish, rays, and robbinfish. No telling what might attack your bait.

Sometimes a highway will run along the coast, just a few yards from the water. Other places are accessible only by boat or swamp buggy. Some towns are tourist oriented, with large throngs of summer vacationers crowding the beaches. Other towns are quiet and reserved primarily for the enjoyment of residents. Not everyone chooses to live by the beach; more find their retirement inland, where other, nonmarine attractions entice them to live.

Large, modern cities provide cultural and medical facilities prized by retirees. Quaint towns with friendly neighbors make transitions into retirement easy. Gracious old Southern mansions, moss-draped bayous, and Southern hospitality are all part of the setting. To all of this add a four-season climate that varies from semi-tropical to warm temperate, and you have a formula that spells successful retirement.

The cost of living in these states is as favorable as you'll find anywhere in the nation, and personal safety in the smaller towns is also gratifying. Some parts of the Gulf Coast states offer the most inexpensive housing we've ever seen. Wages are lower, to match the living costs. These economic benefits are offset somewhat by above-average utility costs in some locales.

Many people have images of the South that aren't so idyllic. The news media of thirty-five years ago highlighted a dramatic struggle for civil rights—complete with violence and tragedy—as citizens of color fought for the right to vote and to be treated with dignity as equals under the law. These impressions of conflict, social injustice, and poverty were vivid and fade slowly.

This lingering bad press is unfortunate, because the South has undergone tremendous change over the past three decades, resulting in a 180-degree turnabout in the general conscience of the region. The younger generations often express difficulty understanding just what the fighting was all about. Few can imagine a world in which people should be prevented from participating in society because of skin color or should drink from separate water fountains or sit in designated sections of buses and theaters.

I don't believe that all Southerners have suddenly changed into color-blind liberals, totally free of racism and full of brotherly love. My point and opinion is that the overall Southern attitude toward race relations has taken a dramatic turn for the better. From my perspective the South today harbors no more racism than the rest of the country. I'm convinced of this. You might well accuse me of damning with faint praise, because as we know from media reports, some regions of our country harbor extremely racist organizations and militants dedicated to racial hatred. And in some northern states, such as Michigan and Pennsylvania, extreme racist organizations stoke fires of hatred. According to the Southern Poverty Law Center, many regions in the United States harbor greater amounts of racial prejudice than most Southern locations.

Alabama

This is one of the nation's most active states when it comes to seeking out retirees and creating a welcoming environment for them. According to state officials, over the past fifteen years, Alabama's share of retirement immigrants climbed from twentieth in the country to fifth. Part of this is due to a state-funded program called Alabama Advantage for Retirees, which works intensively at getting the news out about retirement opportunities within the state. Many Alabama communities participate in this program and deserve special mention as retirement destinations.

Alabama's convenient location midway between the northern states and Florida, its mild winter climate, and crime rates as much as 20 percent lower than the national average are important to many potential retirees, but there's much more. Among other enticements Alabama combines quality living with one of the country's most favorable living costs. Tax burdens are lowest in the nation. For example, the property tax on a $100,000 home (approximately the median sales price here) assesses out at about $300—often less, depending on the community. No, that isn't $300 each *quarter*, it's $300 for the *year!*

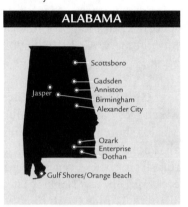

Real estate is among the most affordable in the nation, with average new and resale home prices less than $90,000. Other economic advantages for retirees include most pensions being exempt from taxes and free fishing and hunting licenses for residents sixty-five years of age and older. Alabama's colleges and universities offer free or reduced tuition to residents age sixty or older. Some private schools offer tuition discounts, special classes, and access to recreation and cultural programs for retirees.

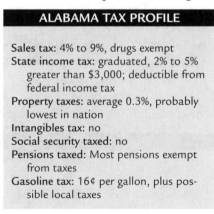

ALABAMA TAX PROFILE

Sales tax: 4% to 9%, drugs exempt
State income tax: graduated, 2% to 5% greater than $3,000; deductible from federal income tax
Property taxes: average 0.3%, probably lowest in nation
Intangibles tax: no
Social security taxed: no
Pensions taxed: Most pensions exempt from taxes
Gasoline tax: 16¢ per gallon, plus possible local taxes

But Alabama's more than just a low-cost place to live; it's a state of multiple lifestyle choices and retirement opportunities. As more and more "outsiders" take up residence, the population becomes more cosmopolitan, making transition into the community easier.

Each Alabama community mentioned in this book has a welcoming committee to help newcomers assimilate into the social whirl of the town. Although this won't ensure that you'll find successful retirement, you know you'll be welcome and won't be considered a stranger. For information call (800) 235-4757 or write to Alabama Advantage for Relocation and Retirement, P.O. Box 5690, Montgomery, AL 36103-5690 for a free Alabama Advantage guidebook.

Gulf Shores/Orange Beach   Because of the rude manner in which Florida's Panhandle elbows Alabama aside to hog the Gulf of Mexico shoreline, you wouldn't expect Alabama to have any beach at all. Look at a map and you'll see what I mean. Florida's Panhandle runs from the Georgia state line almost to Mobile in the west. However, visitors are flabbergasted at the quality and beauty of Alabama's 32-mile beach that fronts the Gulf between Pensacola and Mobile. It clearly matches anything Florida has to offer, and it's peaceful and relatively uncrowded.

Mobile—Alabama's only large Gulf Coast location, with almost 200,000 inhabitants—like most large cities is best considered as a commercial center, a place for serious shopping and entertainment, with ideal retirement away from the metropolitan area. Traditional candidates for nearby retirement are Fairhope and Daphne. But because the city of Mobile is only about 15 miles distant, these towns have become "bedroom communities" for those working in the city. As such, property has become more costly, and the percentage of retirees has fallen off in recent years.

On the other hand the two small towns that comprise Alabama's Gulf Coast "Riviera" are fast becoming a choice destination

GULF SHORES–ORANGE BEACH WEATHER

In degrees Fahrenheit

	Jan.	April	July	Oct.	Rain	Snow
Daily highs	61	78	91	79	64"	—
Daily lows	41	58	73	56		

GULF SHORES–ORANGE BEACH AREA COST OF LIVING

	Overall	Housing	Medical	Groceries	Utilities
Percentage of national average	93	85	84	91	101

for retirees, particularly with golf nuts and anglers. Traditionally a roost for thousands of snowbirds each winter season, Gulf Shores (pop. 5,000) and Orange Beach (pop. 3,000) entice winter visitors to become permanent residents when they retire. White sand beaches, great fishing, and friendly neighbors are persuasive arguments that help retirees make up their minds about Alabama's Gulf Coast. Luxury retirement villages are making an appearance to accommodate newcomers.

World-class saltwater fishing is a strong drawing card. The largest charter-boat fleet on the Gulf Coast is located in Orange Beach, and seven golf courses are within a twenty-minute drive. There is an emphasis on golf communities, with seven golf courses nearby. As one resident put it, "We're becoming a mini-Myrtle Beach, minus the traffic, noise, and flash."

An interesting diversity of retirees gives Gulf Shores and Orange Beach a cosmopolitan flavor not common in smaller resort towns. Because retirees come from all parts of the country, they bring a rich mixture of interests and talents. Year-round residents love to participate in art shows, theater, concerts, and other cultural pursuits. Winter tourists bring a blessing to Gulf Coast businesses: This means seasonal part-time jobs are available for those who want them.

Even though the population is small, health care is adequate. Because of the number of elderly tourists each season, this area has an unusual number of paramedics, perhaps the highest per capita in the nation. A hospital is located in nearby Foley, just 5 miles from Gulf Shores. Foley, by the way, is a popular place because of its manufacturer's outlet stores of the "shop-till-you-drop" genre. For big-ticket items Pensacola is just a 30-mile drive, and Mobile is about an hour away.

Dothan   Before we discovered some of Alabama's better retirement locations, we kept hearing about a town called Dothan (pronounced *DOE*-than). Readers would ask, "Why don't you mention Dothan in your books?" We checked our Alabama road map and were puzzled why a place in the corner of southeast Alabama should have something special going for it. We received so many inquiries that we decided to take a look for ourselves. We're glad we did.

Dothan (pop. 56,000) and its neighboring communities combine a pleasant Alabama location with an unusually diverse retiree population. Folks come from all over the world to settle here. This is partly due to nearby Fort Rucker, home of the world's largest international helicopter-training center; military families from around the world remember Dothan when making retirement plans. Post-exchange privileges and access to military medical services make it a natural.

But there's another interesting source of Dothan's unique diversity: a growing colony of civilian retirees from the Panama Canal Zone. Between 100 and 120 families have moved to Dothan to begin (or resume) their retirement careers. With the canal now having been transferred to Panama, more families are on the way.

How did such an unlikely place as southeast Alabama become a mecca for folks who lived most of their lives in tropical Panama? It started some years back when one canal zone employee convinced his wife to retire in his home state of Alabama instead of staying in Panama, as most others did. When they returned for visits, they talked so much about the charms and advantages of Dothan that others began visiting and eventually moving here. The treaty between Panama and the United States, which returned control over the canal to Panama, really started the ball rolling. With an unclear future ahead and no roots any place outside Panama, many decided to look more closely into Dothan.

The city and its businesses sensed a trend and, in an effort to draw as many retirees into the community as possible, sponsored emissaries to Panama to spread the word about the advantages of moving to Dothan. Obviously it worked.

However, the influx of retirees here is more than just an accident. The biggest draw is the high quality of life, which is reflected in the lovely neighborhoods throughout the area. Quiet, tree-shaded streets with large lawns and elegant homes reflect well-kept neighborhoods and pride of ownership. The flowering trees in the spring and colorful leaves in the fall make changes of season a delight here. Visitors come every spring to follow the trail of pink during the Azalea–Dogwood Trail event.

As is the case in most of Alabama, housing is very affordable, with home prices from 10 to 20 percent below national averages.

The cost of living is also way below average. Real estate taxes are almost ridiculous. Example: Taxes on an owner-occupied home valued at $65,000 amount to about $224 a year, but if the owner is older than 65 years of age, there's a rebate.

For a town its size, Dothan has a surprising inventory of cultural events and establishments, including a symphony, ballet, community theater, and so forth. The region enjoys a low crime rate.

The Dothan area supports the usual outdoor recreational opportunities, including hunting, fishing, and golf. Golfers are pleased that one of the new Robert Trent Jones thirty-six-hole golf courses is located here. When I asked my chamber of commerce guide what her husband does, she replied, "He plays golf nine days a week." The city sponsors thirty-seven public tennis courts and many parks.

Providing medical care to the cities of Enterprise, Ozark, and Dothan are four hospitals plus the medical facility at Fort Rucker. Ozark has Dale Medical Center, with ninety-two beds. The Enterprise Medical Center is a fully accredited hospital with 135 beds and has recently added all the newest high-tech equipment. Dothan has two hospitals: Dothan Southeast and Flowers Hospitals.

Ozark   Everything said about Dothan can be repeated about Enterprise (pop. 21,000) and Ozark (pop. 17,000). Of course they are smaller, and those who value small-town qualities will adore Enterprise and Ozark. Why retire here? One retiree from Ozark put it this way: "This area is the best of all worlds. We live far enough south to avoid winter cold, far enough away from the ocean to escape destructive humidity. We enjoy a small-town atmosphere, yet we're close to the Gulf Coast and great fishing. We're only minutes from Dothan."

Ozark retirees appreciate the fact that they can drive around a charming city with no traffic jams and few stoplights. A relatively inexpensive, full-service country club with a challenging eighteen-hole golf course is only 2 miles from the courthouse square in the center of town.

Actually our first visit to Ozark wasn't exactly fair, because it was in February, a time when flowering trees were exploding with color, birds were trilling songs of joy, and the world was turning emerald green. Our travels through the neighborhoods here and in nearby Enterprise were admittedly influenced by this early spring frenzy. Yet in neighborhood after neighborhood, even the more humble places, we found quality housing and pride of ownership.

During our visits here, we found residents particularly open to newcomers, with an active retirement welcoming committee looking to bring retirees into the community. This makes it much easier to relocate and make friends in your new neighborhood. Housing in Ozark is high in quality and affordable in price. Impressively large homes situated on half-acre lots seem to be the norm, although you'll also find smaller homes in attractive neighborhoods.

Enterprise   The closest town to Fort Rucker, Enterprise is a favorite retirement location of ex-military families. They remember the town with favor and think about it when retirement plans are discussed.

A wide variety of housing is available in Enterprise, and the town is continually expanding its inventory of homes. A recent development is a group of "garden" homes and townhouses. These are smaller, maintenance-free places for folks wishing to downsize their house size and their house chores. Always moving ahead, Enterprise is in the process of building a new park with lots of walking trails and passive recreation.

Enterprise is also famous for an unusual landmark, a serious monument dedicated to an insect: the boll weevil. In the early part of this century, many parts of the South went from the height of affluence to economic disaster because of the boll weevil. Within one season the insects all but exterminated cotton, the crop responsible for the state's prosperity. But Enterprise/Ozark farmers didn't surrender to despair; they plowed under cotton and planted peanuts. This change in tactics restored prosperity and then some. The relieved citizens decided to give credit where it was due, to the boll weevil, who forced them to make their communities even richer than before.

Whether you enjoy living in a planned subdivision or a tranquil rural setting, Enterprise provides a variety of options, including quality rental property. Housing in Enterprise is plentiful and affordable. Several new housing developments will have entities such as lakes, golf courses, two-acre lots, walking trails, and neighborhood shops.

Recreational opportunities abound among these three cities. Within a short drive are five public golf courses, plus one of the famous thirty-six-hole Robert Trent Jones courses. Strong recreation

DOTHAN–OZARK–ENTERPRISE WEATHER						
In degrees Fahrenheit						
	Jan.	April	July	Oct.	Rain	Snow
Daily highs	57	77	91	77	49"	—
Daily lows	36	53	72	53		

DOTHAN–OZARK–ENTERPRISE AREA COST OF LIVING					
Percentage of	Overall	Housing	Medical	Groceries	Utilities
national average	90	77	85	97	85

departments oversee twenty parks, six public swimming pools, forty public tennis courts, four recreation centers, a softball complex, and numerous organized team sports. The lure of fishing is available on nearby lakes or in the Gulf of Mexico, only 80 miles to the south.

The region has a surprising inventory of cultural events, including a symphony, ballet, and community theater. Wallace College offers a free tuition program for citizens sixty years or older who meet the admissions standards. Through the college's community services program, citizens, regardless of academic background, can take a wide variety of courses. Troy State University offers one course tuition-free to adults who have been out of school for at least three years and who qualify for admission to the university.

Scottsboro   Sitting up in Alabama's northeast corner, Scottsboro is a picture-book version of a retirement town. An antique courthouse and old-fashioned town square, tree-graced neighborhoods of substantial brick homes, reasonable housing, and lakes galore all contribute to making this a pleasant community for retirement. For those who enjoy fishing, boating, and other water sports, Scottsboro sits on one of the Southeast's largest lake complexes (Guntersville Lake), with more than a thousand miles of shoreline just in the county. Even though its population is only about 15,000, it is far enough away from the nearest large city to have ample shopping and facilities. Huntsville is forty-five minutes away by car, Chattanooga an hour, and it's three hours to Atlanta or Nashville.

Scottsboro is a city that believes in parks. Goosepond Colony, the largest of twenty-one parks and recreational areas in the county, is a complete recreational facility and is city-owned and -operated.

Sitting on the edge of a gorgeous lake, Goosepond Colony boasts an eighteen-hole championship golf course, a lakeside restaurant, rental cottages, meeting rooms, marinas, and camping and picnic facilities.

Why should Scottsboro be described here, instead of one of a dozen other beautiful, economical, lakefront retirement areas that crowd northern Alabama? It was difficult to make this decision, but I submit two justifications. The first is the cosmopolitan makeup of Scottsboro's population. It seems that several years ago, Revere Corporation moved its plant down here from someplace in the North, transplanting hundreds of employees along with its manufacturing facilities. For some reason or another things didn't work out, and when Revere moved away, many employees liked Scottsboro so much, they refused to transfer away. They either took early retirement or found other jobs. Later on other Northern companies selected Scottsboro as a place to move their operations and brought along their employees, too. The result: a pleasant mixture of Northern and Southern neighbors.

My second reason is the community's dedication to betterment of their surroundings and quality of life. A case in point: an ultra-modern community recreation center, which serves a wide spectrum of citizens, from preschoolers to the elderly. Its construction came at a time when voters around the country were refusing to pass school bonds or fund libraries, yet Scottsboro voters didn't hesitate to allocate money for this impressive recreational and cultural facility. It comes complete with an Olympic-size pool that doubles as a training center for students as well as for senior citizen water aerobics, a gymnasium, an indoor walking track, racquetball courts,

SCOTTSBORO WEATHER					
In degrees Fahrenheit					
	Jan.	April	July	Oct.	Rain	Snow
Daily highs	49	73	89	73	54"	—
Daily lows	31	50	69	49		

SCOTTSBORO AREA COST OF LIVING					
Percentage of	Overall	Housing	Medical	Groceries	Utilities
national average	94	83	94	97	81

handball and a game room, plus meeting rooms and hobby shops. Another expensive project under way: An already substantial-looking hospital is undergoing an $11-million expansion, which will make Scottsboro a leading medical center of the region.

An example of an event that reinforces its small-city feeling: At a monthly happening called the First Monday Trade Day, the courthouse lawn fills with residents selling arts and crafts, antiques, flea market items, locally grown produce—anything that can be traded or sold. The first Monday in every September—Labor Day—the event grows so large they have to move it to a park.

This is an area that makes the most of its blend of mountains, forests, and lakes. Residential areas show taste and charm in this setting. Real estate selling at 18 percent below national average also makes retirement here affordable. Personal safety here is exceptionally high, ranking in the top 15 percent in the nation.

Alexander City/Lake Martin   Back in the mid-1920s, the Alabama Power Company decided to place a dam across the Tallapoosa River. Residents at that time were devastated and totally convinced that the rising waters would create swamps and breeding grounds for flotillas of mosquitoes and armies of bugs. Resigned to disaster, they sold out at $5.00 to the acre, feeling lucky to get anything at all for such worthless land. Little did they realize! Lakeshore lots now go for a minimum of $25,000, up to more than $500,000!

Today travel writers describe Lake Martin as one of the most beautiful recreational lakes in the South. It's also become one of east-central Alabama's prime retirement destinations, having received numerous recommendations by retirement and relocation experts.

Scattered around the lake are nine or ten developments, which range from relatively inexpensive places nestled among the woods to elegant gated communities with private golf courses. Almost 22,000 people make their homes on the 750 miles of shoreline—on sandy beaches, in secluded coves, or on rocky knolls with magnificent views. Officially designated one of Alabama's cleanest lakes, residents proudly refer to Lake Martin as "44,000 acres of pure drinking water." Golf, boating, water-skiing, and fishing—the lake has it all. Residents rave about the quality of their new surroundings.

With golf and water recreation the central focus, newcomers have a wide choice of lifestyles, from exclusive golf-course developments, where homes cost a small fortune, to a mobile-home park with spaces that rent for as little as $100 a month. Don't expect super-bargains in real estate, however; after all, if you live on a lake as pretty as this, you'll pay for the privilege. Strict building codes ensure that the housing is high quality—no shacks or fish shanties are permitted.

Nearby Alexander City (pop. 15,000) is an alternative for those who would like to be near the lake, but prefer more inexpensive housing in town. Alex City (as people here call it) is a charming place in its own right. The town owes its prosperity to the Russell Corporation, a local company that made good as a Fortune 500 textile giant.

Just 50 miles from the state capital in Montgomery and 30 miles from Auburn University, the Alexander City–Lake Martin area is conveniently located for the occasional big-city shopping and cultural fixes. Birmingham is a 70-mile drive via a superhighway.

Quite naturally recreation here centers on golf and water sports. Swimming, fishing, water-skiing, and boating are favorites. Many residents keep powered pontoon boats tied at their lakefront homes, ready for fishing, loafing, or a trip across the water to dine at a first-class restaurant. The original championship golf course at Willow Point has thirteen of its eighteen fairways edging the lakeshore. Two other courses are similarly located on the water. Alexander City also has an eighteen-hole municipal golf course.

The cultural and entertainment offerings of Montgomery and Birmingham are within an easy drive; however, Alexander City provides its own entertainment. There's a little theater group that stages several productions a year, and the Alexander City Arts

ALEXANDER CITY–LAKE MARTIN WEATHER

In degrees Fahrenheit

	Jan.	April	July	Oct.	Rain	Snow
Daily highs	56	76	91	77	58"	—
Daily lows	36	55	70	54		

ALEXANDER CITY–LAKE MARTIN AREA COST OF LIVING

Percentage of national average	Overall	Housing	Medical	Groceries	Utilities
	90	78	88	92	85

Council uses the Central Alabama Community College facilities to bring plays, musicals, and concerts to the community. The college has special programs, free to students age sixty and older.

Russell Hospital, in Alexander City, is a modern, nonprofit seventy-five-bed hospital with twenty-four-hour, acute-care facilities. For military retirees there's a regional hospital at Maxwell Air Force Base in Montgomery, about an hour's drive.

Anniston   From the moment of its inception, Anniston was a planned model city. Back in 1879 two entrepreneurs decided this is where they would build their textile mills and blast furnaces. They needed a town and commercial center to go with their enterprises, so they hired a team of well-known architects to design a company town. They insisted that the new town must be modern as well as pleasing to the eye. Of course "modern" in those days meant Victorian, and that's what we see today. Most of these historic structures are still in use, well preserved and reflecting Anniston's rich heritage.

Anniston, with of 27,000 inhabitants, is the population center of Calhoun County. Immediately adjacent, the city of Oxford has another 10,000 residents. The two cities form the major shopping center for the surrounding area's total population of 120,000. Thirteen miles away, not quite close enough to be considered an Anniston suburb, the town of Jacksonville provides a university setting. Including students, Jacksonville has a population of 11,000. The university has continuing-education programs as well as Elderhostel programs for folks from all over the country. Because the region is centrally located between Atlanta and Birmingham, the local slogan is: "Near Atlanta. Near Birmingham. Near Perfect."

We particularly liked Oxford as a retirement possibility. Originally it was called Lick Skillet, but when time came to incorporate into a town, residents wanted a more dignified name. Can you get more dignified than "Oxford"? Essentially part of Anniston, Oxford has several unusually attractive neighborhoods that appear to be ideal for retirement living. The Calhoun County medical community includes more than one hundred physicians, forty-five dentists, and three hospitals.

Fort McClellan, an Army base occupying 15,000 acres of prime land, is one of the military installations that was decommissioned.

It's a beautiful place of woods and landscaped grounds. At the moment the federal government, the state of Alabama, and the city officials of the surrounding cities are trying to decide what to do with the valuable land. One purpose that seems fairly certain is to devote a percentage of the surplus property to retirement housing.

Silver Lakes Anniston and its neighboring city, Gadsden, both have enthusiastic retirement attraction committees ready to assist newcomers. The headquarters for the retirement committees is located at a golf development at Silver Lakes, between the two cities. Silver Lakes is a gorgeous setting of rolling terrain and lakes near the edge of Talladega National Forest. This is an experiment in retirement attraction because this is the first time one of Robert Trent Jones's Golf Trail courses has ever been placed within a private development. This is a thirty-six-hole, world-class golf complex, and it's always open for public play.

Gadsden Gadsden (pop. 39,000) is located in the southern foothills of the Appalachian Mountains, where Lookout Mountain and the Coosa River meet. This is probably Alabama's most successful city when it comes to recruiting out-of-state retirees. A few years ago Gadsden realized that it was losing its industrial base. It needed something to replace the disappearing factories, but didn't want to "chase smokestacks." Joining with several other cities in Etowah and Calhoun Counties, Gadsden's retirement committee set a goal of attracting fifty retired couples a year. The first year they exceeded their goal; sixty-three couples moved to town. The next year forty-eight couples joined the party. Gadsden has been

ANNISTON–SILVER LAKES–GADSDEN WEATHER						
In degrees Fahrenheit						
	Jan.	April	July	Oct.	Rain	Snow
Daily highs	62	75	91	74	48"	2"
Daily lows	33	51	70	51		

ANNISTON AREA COST OF LIVING					
Percentage of	Overall	Housing	Medical	Groceries	Utilities
national average	94	93	84	95	96

GADSDEN COST OF LIVING					
Percentage of national average	Overall 90	Housing 79	Medical 85	Groceries 90	Utilities 87

growing ever since, with more than 4,000 newcomers, many of them retirees.

The impact of new residents on Gadsden's economy has been a dramatic textbook example of how communities benefit from out-of-state relocation. Because of the newcomers, jobs were created for health-care specialists, construction workers, and retail businesses. Restaurants, motels, and service businesses blossomed. These new jobs were of a clean, nonpolluting "smokeless-industry" nature. This helped the area to free itself of dependency on a handful of manufacturing facilities.

The downtown's pride and joy is the huge 44,000-square-foot Gadsden Center for Cultural Arts. When a downtown department store closed its doors—a victim of strip-mall syndrome—Gadsden decided to do something with the large multistory building. Rather than allow the edifice to disintegrate, they converted it into the Center for Cultural Arts, one of the most impressive downtown monuments to rehabilitation we've seen. Besides expansive rooms for community meetings, private parties, proms and dances, and concerts, the center has an experimental arts programs in which kids from a nearby housing project are paid to study art.

Two popular residential areas on Gadsden's outskirts are the towns of Rainbow City and Attalla. Attalla has a population of approximately 7,000 and a thriving commercial center. This was the bedroom community for employees of Gadsden's heavy industries before they closed some years ago. Much affordable housing is available here. For a while Attalla's downtown section all but died. Then city officials encouraged the establishment of antiques shops and specialty boutiques. This seems to have turned the corner economically for Attalla, because folks come from miles around to shop, and storefronts are beginning to find tenants once again.

Rainbow City is slightly larger, with 8,000 inhabitants, and the residential areas are a bit more upscale. When Gadsden's industrial life was booming, this is where the white-collar and executive employees lived. Some exceptionally lovely homes are located here. Both towns are within minutes of downtown Gadsden.

Gadsden State Community College, Alabama's largest two-year college, and the University of Alabama–Gadsden Center provide educational opportunities. If that's not enough, Jacksonville State University is about 18 miles away.

Birmingham Area   Birmingham is the center of a large industrial and technical complex. Skilled technical and executive personnel are always in demand here, often as consultants or for part-time duties. It's also set in a lovely region of hills, forests, and lakes. For these reasons many of those forced into early retirement look favorably toward the Birmingham area and its booming industrial environment. However, retirees today tend to prefer a smaller city rather than a big metropolis like Birmingham. Therefore, we'll focus on a couple of towns near enough to take advantage of what the city offers, yet far enough away to avoid big-city living.

On Birmingham's southern flank the hustle and bustle of a large population center fades away into busy suburbs and finally disappears into a countrylike atmosphere in Shelby County. Well, not really country, because you are within a half-hour drive to Birmingham, with all its cultural and commercial amenities. And it's rare you'll need to drive to the city: The suburbs of Hoover, Pelham, Helena, and Alabaster have shopping centers that would make most small cities envious. The crime rate in the county is one of the lowest in the state, and there are many middle- and upper-class neighborhoods to choose from.

BIRMINGHAM AREA WEATHER

In degrees Fahrenheit

	Jan.	April	July	Oct.	Rain	Snow
Daily highs	52	75	91	43	52"	2"
Daily lows	33	51	70	51		

BIRMINGHAM AREA COST OF LIVING

	Overall	Housing	Medical	Groceries	Utilities
Percentage of national average	98	93	90	100	105

A popular relocation choice here is Pelham, with a population of 15,000. The city of Hoover is of similar size and is also desirable as a place to live. Other nearby cities offer more or less the same attractions as Pelham. This is a place for those who want to live in an upscale suburb, yet be close to a metropolitan center for the cultural and entertainment bonuses. In twenty years population has doubled, yet much of the growth isn't apparent. Many new homes are hidden in woodlands or on large lots with so many trees it's hard to see the houses.

Developers are busy carving fancy developments into the steep foothills adjoining Oak Mountain Park and clearing enough trees to place attractive homes. Although you'll find all kinds of housing—"from cottages to castles," as the chamber of commerce puts it—this is not a place to expect an abundance of economical housing. In 1997 the average price of homes sold in Shelby County was more than double that of most other Alabama communities. That says something for the quality and amenities.

Jasper   A different retirement lifestyle option on the opposite side of Birmingham, the small city of Jasper (population 14,000) sits in a peaceful countryside of forested hills and small farms. Birmingham is currently a 40-mile drive over Highway 78. A high-speed superhighway called Corridor X, an Appalachian Regional Limited Access Highway, is being built through Jasper from Memphis to Birmingham. It is under construction now around Jasper. When completed, the drive to downtown Birmingham will be twenty-five minutes. Like Pelham, Jasper is sometimes described as a bedroom community for Birmingham, but on a more moderate scale. This has traditionally been a blue-collar city, where coal mining was king until the black gold mineral fell out of favor as an energy source. This turned the region into a real estate buyer's paradise.

Like most small cities, Jasper's downtown suffers from strip-mall syndrome; shoppers patronize large malls and stores on the town's outskirts. As a result the town center is quaint, quiet, and laid-back, a nice place to stroll.

Jasper is working hard to attract more residents. One of the community's efforts to lure retirees is the Newcomers' Club. The group invites new residents to join in cultural and service programs and make friendships through shared social gatherings. The Newcomers' Club holds monthly luncheon meetings to plan activities

JASPER AREA COST OF LIVING					
Percentage of national average	Overall 90	Housing 75	Medical 84	Groceries 93	Utilities 91

for the group. As an example of how out-of-state people are received: In a recent election for mayor of Jasper, voters chose Don Goetz, a Yankee who relocated here from Milwaukee.

Although Jasper does have some areas of expensive homes, most housing—located in quiet residential neighborhoods with lots of trees—is priced a bit lower than typical low Alabama prices. In town as well as on the outskirts you'll find a few neighborhoods of stately old homes—residences of mine owners and supervisory personnel. Just a few minutes from the town center, newer subdivisions and wooded acreages are for sale at affordable prices.

Mississippi

For most folks from outside the South, Mississippi comes as a pleasant surprise. They expect cotton fields and dreary farming communities where "outsiders" might not be welcome. These stereotypes will fade away upon your first visit to Mississippi. You'll find a delightful landscape of great diversity, from picturesque Appalachian foothills in the northeast to sandy beaches on the sunny Gulf of Mexico. In between are affluent towns and cities graced with lovely pre–Civil War mansions on landscaped grounds as well as contemporary houses, ranch-style homes in golf-course communities, and developments situated on fishing lakes or surrounded by forested hills.

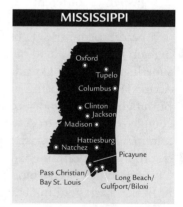

Mississippi's cities jealously preserve their Old South heritage of lovely homes to complement modern subdivisions and tasteful commercial centers. Classic university campuses and medical centers are just as prominent as graceful residential districts and upscale restaurants and shopping. In short the state of Mississippi has everything most retirees might need for a successful and pleasant retirement. I suppose you could find cotton fields if you look hard enough, but offhand, I don't recall seeing any.

The best part about Mississippi for retirement: In our experience it's the most welcoming state in the South, perhaps in the nation. From the governor's office down to the neighborhood level, the people of Mississippi are working hard to convince out-of-state

MISSISSIPPI TAX PROFILE
Sales tax: 7%, drugs exempt
State income tax: graduated, 3% to 5% greater than $10,000; can't deduct federal income tax
Property taxes: average 1%, but for older than age sixty-five, homestead exemption could be as much as $700
Intangibles tax: no
Social security taxed: no
Pensions taxed: no
Gasoline tax: 18¢ to 20¢ per gallon, plus local taxes of from 2¢ to 3¢ per gallon

folks to relocate here. The backbone of this campaign is a well-funded and professionally managed state program called Hometown Mississippi Retirement. The state allocates more than a half-million dollars a year for this program, spending more than any other state for retirement attraction. This money isn't spent on a mere propaganda barrage to lure warm bodies to the state. The message isn't just "Come to Mississippi" and leave the results up to chance. On the community level hometown residents follow through with a well-considered program to welcome new individuals into each community.

I interviewed a wide range of retired couples who moved to Mississippi from places like California, New Jersey, Minnesota, and Florida. All attested to the genuine hospitality and friendliness of their new neighbors. Typical were comments such as, "We've only been here a year, but we have more friends now than we ever had in thirty years of living in our old neighborhood."

To further enhance Mississippi's status as a retiree-friendly place, the legislature voted to exempt retiree income from state income tax. Along with low property taxes and favorable living costs, this provides more dollars to be spent on recreation, travel, or investments. For those older than age sixty-five or disabled, the exemption from the assessed value of their home is such that a home valued at $60,000 would owe no property taxes.

Mississippi's Gulf Coast   Long a favored retirement destination for military personnel, the area around Gulfport and Biloxi combines a summer carnival atmosphere with sedate Old South values. The complex of beach towns stretching between Florida and Louisiana is known as Mississippi Beach. The total population here is approximately 90,000, and the cities are so closely connected that it's impossible to tell where one ends and the next begins.

It's obvious why this is such a tourist attraction. Vast stretches of sugary beach with gentle waves lapping at the sand are complemented by streets arched over by branches of majestic oak and magnolia trees, fine restaurants, and lots of sunshine. Large, formal estates survey the scene with Southern majesty. Here was—and is—the mansion where Jefferson Davis chose to live out his days, writing memoirs of his days of glory as president of the Confederacy.

A recent innovation is the appearance of a dozen or so glittering gambling casinos that energize the coastline with bright lights, blackjack and roulette, and slot machines. Gambling provides tourists from surrounding states an additional excuse to congregate here; golfing and sunning on the beaches by day and shouting at the dice by night. In the winter regular tourists are replaced by snowbirds, a large percentage of them Canadians, who don't mind the cooler water and occasional nippy days. Compared with Montreal or Moose Jaw winters, Gulf Coast's coldest days are tropical paradise.

Don't let gambling prevent you from considering Mississippi's Gulf Coast, because the way things are going, gaming palaces, riverboat casinos, and even oceangoing gaming ships are popping up all over the Gulf Coast, Mississippi River towns, and Florida ports.

MISSISSIPPI'S GULF COAST WEATHER

In degrees Fahrenheit

	Jan.	April	July	Oct.	Rain	Snow
Daily highs	61	77	90	79	61"	—
Daily lows	43	59	74	60		

MISSISSIPPI'S GULF COAST COST OF LIVING

	Overall	Housing	Medical	Groceries	Utilities
Percentage of national average	94	90	90	97	105

You're not going to avoid them. Gambling's effect on the local economy brings a mixed bag of assets and deficits. It has created more than 5,000 jobs in the Gulfport–Biloxi area (including much part-time work for retirees) and has warmed the hearts of many local businesses.

Many military couples choose to retire here because of convenient medical and base-exchange privileges at Keesler Air Force Base. Most of these military retirees were stationed in the area at one time or another and developed a fondness for the beaches and the climate.

Nearby Communities   Although Gulfport and Biloxi both offer attractive neighborhoods for relocation, we believe that the best bets for retirement around here are towns nearby the Gulfport–Biloxi complex. When people speak of retirement on the Mississippi coast, they usually mean the towns of Long Beach, Pass Christian, and Bay St. Louis. With the convenience of good hospitals and other emergency facilities in the twin cities, many retirees look for reasonably priced housing and pleasant neighborhoods away from the hustle, bustle, and tourist world. A bonus is exceptionally low crime rates in these towns; according to FBI statistics, they are among the lowest in the country, although those areas around the gambling casinos quite naturally score higher (in a negative way).

The quiet and peaceful atmosphere is one of the benefits of suburban living that local residents usually point out. "Gulfport–Biloxi is too crowded and too honky-tonk," said several retirees in Pass Christian, Long Beach, and Bay St. Louis. "Here we have 26 miles of quiet beach, all to ourselves."

Long Beach (pop. 22,000) is a former farming community to the west of Gulfport, whose quiet residential areas attract retirees who enjoy the quality neighborhoods. In all of these towns, old homes are treated like valuable jewels, continually polished and restored to yesterday's splendor. The city of Long Beach has strict local ordinances against cutting live oaks or magnolia trees without permission of the planning commission.

Pass Christian (pop. 6,500) is the elegant member of the retirement trio. Long a vacation center for wealthy New Orleans residents, Pass Christian is rich in history and past opulence. At one time steamboats regularly made the 55-mile voyage from New Orleans, bringing high-society families to their second homes. The original families are gone, but their homes remain, as do the gracious lifestyles of the last century. Mansions with manicured lawns line the beachfront and invitations for afternoon tea indicate social standing.

Called "The Bay" by local residents, Bay St. Louis (pop. 8,500) is even older than neighboring Pass Christian. It was founded in 1699 by the French and named after the king of France. Its historic downtown features palm trees towering over the streets, Victorian mansions, and an old Catholic seminary, all contrasting with modern shopping and commercial centers.

Oxford   Were I to rank places as to the "best place for retirement," Oxford, Mississippi, would surely rank in the top ten. I confess that as an author, I could be biased by a certain mystical literary connection between Oxford and the outside world. Oxford has fostered and developed writers from its very beginning as a university town—even before William Faulkner made his home base here—continuing today with several best-selling authors choosing to bask in Oxford's nurturing literary climate. It seems as if every third person we meet here has published a book!

Snuggled amid the forested hills of Northern Mississippi, Oxford is a picture-book example of a gracious Southern university town. Handsome antebellum mansions—partially concealed by flowering wisteria, redbud, and creeping ivy—hold court under ancient magnolias and magnificent oak trees. Oxford is positively saturated with history and Old South traditions. Quiet, tree-shaded streets, with silence broken only by the joyous song of a mockingbird and occasional barking of a dog in the distance, recall an era long forgotten in today's frantic rush toward urbanity.

Yet Oxford shows its modern side with a large shopping mall and all the usual businesses and home developments—mercifully located toward the outskirts of town. The outskirts, by the way, aren't all that far away. With a population of only 13,000, the town doesn't

OXFORD WEATHER						
In degrees Fahrenheit						
	Jan.	April	July	Oct.	Rain	Snow
Daily highs	51	75	93	76	56"	2"
Daily lows	31	50	69	49		

spread out to eternity. Oxford appears larger than it is because of an additional 20,000 living in the surrounding country.

The University of Mississippi's presence takes Oxford into another realm of being. Affectionately known nationwide as "Ole Miss," the school adds 11,000 students to double Oxford's population. This unique mixture of students and retirees creates a unique consumer demand: quality shopping, restaurants, and entertainment at affordable prices.

Oxford's charming downtown square is a perfect illustration of how the presence of a university can preserve the character of a town. Commerce generated by students and residents keeps downtown enterprise alive and healthy instead of abandoning it to strip malls and shopping centers on the highways, as happens in many small towns across the nation. Downtown Oxford looks the way a downtown should look. A classic 120-year-old courthouse, with massive columns and centuries-old oak trees, dominates the scene, complete with the obligatory statue of a Confederate soldier standing guard.

Across from the Confederate soldier's statue is a well-known Oxford tradition, the Square Book Store, which features a second-floor veranda that looks out over the square, where friends meet to sip capuccino and talk about books. The 25,000-volume collection, on every subject imaginable, makes you aware that the owner operates the store with a respect for books and literature rather than an eye for quick turnover and high profits—which seems to be the trend lately. On the staircase you'll find stacks of autographed copies of books by local authors. The Square Book Store's presentations by well-known authors who discuss their works and philosophical approaches in their literary accomplishments are favorite happenings.

Among the benefits of living in a university town like Oxford are the cultural attractions that become a tradition with the community. Residents of all ages are invited to participate in school activities. Those older than age sixty-five can take up to four classes free per semester. Many of the university's concerts, lectures, and drama productions are open to the public at no charge. Of course not all activities here are intellectual. Bass and crappie fishing in nearby Sardis Lake, outstanding basketball and football games at the school, and two public golf courses take care of outdoor recreation.

The Baptist Memorial Hospital is the regional health-care center. More than seventy physicians at the hospital represent thirty specialty areas of medicine to meet the specialized needs of individuals and families.

Natchez   Stately Natchez sits on a scenic bluff overlooking the mighty Mississippi River on land that was originally a tribal center of the Natchez Indians. The French constructed a fort here in 1716 after chasing away the Indians, making Natchez one of the oldest European settlements on the Mississippi River.

Very early the town blossomed as a prosperous cotton-raising and -exporting city. It became one of the South's wealthiest cities— possibly the richest in the entire nation. The large number of awesome homes and mansions testify to this. When war between North and South threatened, many Natchez plantation owners were staunchly opposed to secession. They fully realized that war would be a financial disaster as well as a tragic spilling of blood. Therefore, when the war descended upon the nation, Natchez's support was less than enthusiastic. When the first Yankee gunships drifted downriver, ready to bombard Natchez, they were greeted by a huge white flag of surrender fluttering on the bluff. The city of Natchez negotiated a peace that guaranteed the preservation of the magnificent mansions that graced the city.

After the war, its economy devastated, Natchez drifted into the doldrums. This had the further effect of preserving the antebellum homes from the catastrophe of modernization and urban renewal. Today Natchez is a virtual museum of Southern aristocratic architecture. Approximately 500 antebellum homes grace the quiet streets of the city, some dating back to the eras of Spanish and French rule. Throughout the expansive historic district, lovely Victorian homes add to the feeling of stepping back in time. The South has numerous towns with proud antebellum homes, many of them for sale at what seem to be bargain prices, but few have as many beautiful places at such low asking prices as Natchez. (I once said something like that about Oxford, but at last visit, prices have risen dramatically.)

Today Natchez is a quiet town of 19,000 friendly people with well-cared-for neighborhoods and affordable quality housing. Newer subdivisions and apartments are found on the fringes of

NATCHEZ WEATHER					
In degrees Fahrenheit					
	Jan.	April	July	Oct.	Rain	Snow
Daily highs	61	79	91	80	55"	—
Daily lows	40	58	73	56		

town and even in the thickly forested surrounding countryside—some on acre-sized lots carved out of the woods.

The wealthy aristocrats had their homes on the high ground, but the rough-and-tumble steamboat crowd, rogues, and river pirates strutted their stuff down by the riverbank at Natchez Under-the-Hill. This was a district of docks, saloons, and bordellos famous for gambling and illicit excitement. Today at least some of the excitement has returned to Natchez Under-the-Hill in the form of riverboat gambling. In addition to a casino and gambling aboard the ship, several unique restaurants have been embellished to keep alive the wicked, 1800s decor. Even if not your choice for retirement, Natchez with all its antebellum glory is well worth a visit.

In keeping with Southern traditions, the social scene in Natchez revolves about several "garden clubs." These usually exclusive, upper-strata social groups have less to do with gardening than with social activities and organizing civic events. Charities and volunteer work fall under the domain of these organizations. We were told to advise newcomers to seek an invitation to join. (Some of the more exclusive garden clubs probably require that your grandmother was a member.) However, a quicker way to meet new friends is to contact the Retire Partnership, a group specially dedicated to attracting retirees to the area and making them feel at home. Inquire at the local chamber of commerce.

Of course Natchez isn't all historic mansions; you'll find plenty of modern, conventional homes in pleasant residential neighborhoods. Newer subdivisions and apartments are found on the fringes of town. The forested countryside surrounding Natchez has numerous acreage-sized lots carved into the woods for small estates, custom homes as well as clusters of conventional homes.

Two modern, full-care hospitals and a large group of medical professionals serve the medical needs of Natchez. Between them the hospitals have 306 beds and employ the latest in medical technology. In addition to the hospital staff, fifty-four physicians practice in the area.

Columbus   This is a city of comfortable size with a population of 28,000 (add 2,000 to the total if you count the military personnel on the air base). Columbus is known for its historic old residences. Its antebellum homes were miraculously spared during the Civil War. Although 238 battles were fought in Mississippi, Columbus was never a prime military target and the city was never invaded by Union troops. Today the grand antebellum and Victorian mansions lining the old brick streets and tree-shaded lanes are the pride of the region. Each April the town conducts a Pilgrimage Tour of historic homes. Visitors are greeted by gracious hosts dressed in authentic period costumes, who conduct the visitors through their homes and proudly recite their histories.

The most famous of Columbus's historic homes is a wonderful yellow-and-gray Victorian, the birthplace of playwright Tennessee Williams. Some believe it was the setting of his play *Summer and Smoke,* and I can envision it as the set for *The Glass Menagerie.* Once when he returned to visit his boyhood home, he commented, "Home is where you hang your childhood, and Mississippi to me is the beauty spot of creation." The Tennessee Williams house is now used as the Mississippi Welcome Center. Another famous home is 12 Gables, a Greek revival built in 1838. This is where the ladies of Columbus met in 1866 to honor the fallen soldiers of the Civil War, Union as well as Confederate, a meeting that was the origin of our present-day Memorial Day commemoration.

It isn't surprising that many military families decide to relocate in Columbus upon retirement. When service personnel leave the military they naturally remember the more pleasant tours of duty and long to return. Retirees can take advantage of the commissary, base-exchange, and recreational opportunities on the post. This is the home of Columbus Air Force Base, one of only three pilot-training facilities in the United States. Although the base hires 1,500 civilian workers and pumps $2.5 million a week into the local economy, Columbus isn't just a "military gate" town. More than fifty manufacturers, two universities, and a healthy agricultural sector make for a diversified economy. For those who have reached retirement age but aren't quite ready for the rocker, part-time work is an option in Columbus. Skills are valued and expertise is welcomed in a variety of fields. Like all Mississippi cities listed in this book, Columbus has a welcoming committee for newcomers. Columbus has adopted a Silver Eagles program for this purpose. The Silver Eagles are growing in popularity in other parts of the South as an organized social group bringing newcomers and residents together. They organize trips, potlucks, dances, and other congenial events. An important endeavor is offering visitors personally conducted tours of Columbus to help retirees make up their minds about relocation here. So when you visit, expect to be met by Silver Eagles.

The recreational jewel of Columbus is the scenic Tennessee–Tombigbee Waterway. Part of 16,000 miles of inland waters, it eventually connects with the Gulf of Mexico in faraway Mobile. Unlimited water and natural woodlands encourage boating, hiking, and fishing as well as hunting and camping. Columbus is ideal for year-round golf, with eight public and private golf courses within a thirty-minute drive. You'll find plenty of tennis and handball at public and private facilities.

Hattiesburg   Hattiesburg, a lovely town of 48,000, is another of the many surprises Mississippi seems to be continually pulling on us. Our first experience with Hattiesburg was during a research trip to the rolling, piney woods of south Mississippi. Fortunately our visit coincided with a dinner meeting of a group called the Hattiesburg Retirement Connectors. This is a group of retired volunteers whose main purpose is to make newcomers to Hattiesburg feel at home. Retirement Connection members are familiar with problems involved in relocating; all retired here from somewhere else. The Hattiesburg retirement relocation program is one of most successful in the state. It has welcomed 600 households from thirty-five states since the program began in 1993.

Unlike some Mississippi cities listed in this book, Hattiesburg doesn't have a collection of antebellum homes. This is because the town's development didn't get under way until some years after the Civil War. But Hattiesburg's twenty-three-block area of lovely, turn-of-the-twentieth-century homes in the Historic Neighborhood District truly compensates for the lack of pre–Civil War homes.

HATTIESBURG WEATHER					
In degrees Fahrenheit					
	Jan.	April	July	Oct.	Rain	Snow
Daily highs	51	75	93	76	56"	5"
Daily lows	31	50	69	49		

HATTIESBURG AREA COST OF LIVING					
Percentage of	Overall	Housing	Medical	Groceries	Utilities
national average	94	91	84	90	98

Residents are proud of these perfectly restored Victorian, Queen Anne, and Greek Revival–style houses.

Hattiesburg calls itself the "Hub City" because of its convenient location. Saltwater fishing and gambling casinos on Mississippi's Gulf Coast playground are only a 70-mile drive through the DeSoto and Brooklyn National Forests. The bright lights of New Orleans, with Bourbon Street fun and French Quarter restaurants, are less than an hour-and-a-half drive along Interstate 59. You can drive into New Orleans to watch an afternoon Saints football game, have dinner, and be home in time for bed. Mobile, Jackson, and Meridian are each about an hour and a half from Hattiesburg.

Hattiesburg is a golfer's paradise. Ten year-round golf courses are always ready for play, including a championship course described as one of the finest in the South, often hosting PGA events.

The University of Southern Mississippi and William Carey College enrich the community with theater, concerts, lectures, and exhibits. The university offers free auditing of classes for those age sixty-five and older. Of special interest is USM's Institute for Learning in Retirement. Located in a lovely, off-campus house, the program offers a relaxed setting for learning and sharing experiences. This is a great place to make new acquaintances in the community. Having no grades or exams takes the stress out of the continuing educational process.

Although the cultural ambience of Jackson is within easy driving distance—with opera, museums, and such—Hattiesburg residents don't have to leave town to enjoy a rich cultural life. Musical, theatrical, concert, and other events that you'd expect from a big city are enjoyed right here. The Hattiesburg Civic Light Opera produces

Broadway musicals; Just Over the Rainbow entertains with dinner-theater productions. A gallery featuring works of Mississippi artists is maintained by the Hattiesburg Arts Council.

You'll find a wide variety of homes here to fit any lifestyle, and because Hattiesburg real estate is about 10 percent below national averages, prices are affordable. We looked at one very stylish development featuring large wooded lots arranged along the shore of a private lake. Amenities include tennis, boating, and trails for hikers, with homes selling for less than many California tract homes.

Hattiesburg is rightly proud of its two state-of-the-art hospitals, which serve as the health-care center for the southern Mississippi region. Between them they boast 738 beds and are staffed with 300 doctors.

Jackson   Mississippi's capital is not only the capital city, but it's also the state's cultural, financial, and population center. Jackson is a beautiful city in its own right, and for many folks, a good retirement choice. It is a large city, however, and when we find a place as nice as Jackson, we like to look for retirement places just outside the metropolitan center. In the course of our research, we discovered two delightful small towns, both within a few minutes' drive of Jackson's center—a compromise between living in the city of Jackson and living in the "country," yet close enough to enjoy all the cultural and civilized amenities to be found in the city.

These two communities are Clinton and Madison. Both have a lot to offer retirees, both communities have active welcoming committees, and both towns have female mayors. Because we couldn't decide which we liked best (both the towns and the mayors), we decided to include both places. Clinton sits beyond the western limits of Jackson, and Madison is to the northeast. We'll start (in alphabetical order) with Clinton.

Clinton   Because Clinton is just a short commute from Jackson, its suburban quality is unmistakable. Quiet streets and quality neighborhoods make for tranquil living. Choosing a place like Clinton is like finding the best of two worlds: a place with a peaceful, small-town disposition, yet only minutes away from the convenience and action of the city.

JACKSON–CLINTON AREA WEATHER						
In degrees Fahrenheit						
	Jan.	April	July	Oct.	Rain	Snow
Daily highs	57	78	93	79	53"	1"
Daily lows	35	53	71	52		

JACKSON AREA COST OF LIVING					
Percentage of national average	Overall	Housing	Medical	Groceries	Utilities
	89	89	75	84	98

In keeping with its small-town image, the charming downtown area has been restored, complete with historic brick streets and tasteful shops, and named Olde Towne. Clinton isn't strictly a bedroom community, however; several manufacturing facilities provide jobs and add to the overall feeling of prosperity. Clinton is also a college town. With the founding of Mississippi College in 1826, Clinton became known as the "Athens of Mississippi." One of the oldest universities in the country, the school prides itself on community involvement in a variety of activities, from collegiate sports to concerts and pageants.

Folks who've retired here swear by the small-town friendliness, yet they appreciate the nearby big-city conveniences. One retiree from Ohio said, "When my company moved us down here, we liked Clinton so well that I turned down promotions in order to stay. When retirement came around, we didn't even think of leaving."

Because Clinton is just a ten-minute drive from Jackson, residents here enjoy a rich, year-round source of cultural entertainment such as symphony concerts and chamber music recitals. There's always something going on at Jackson's Museum of Art and the Jackson Zoo, and there are even street parties with downtown stages for blues, rock, country, and gospel music. There's a full calendar of events year-round.

In Clinton, the city's arts council keeps cultural and fun events going. Among its activities is the Brick Streets Festival, which starts in April with a monthlong series of festivities. The brick streets of Clinton's restored Olde Towne are enlivened by music, food, and arts and crafts displays as well as a Shakespeare festival.

Because Jackson is just minutes away, Clinton residents have access to some of the finest medical care in the South. Six major medical facilities are located in the Jackson metropolitan area, with specialists in just about every medical field.

Madison   The second suburb of Jackson that caught our eye is the small city of Madison. Located about the same distance from Jackson as Clinton, where the Natchez Trace skirts to the north of Jackson, Madison is smaller than Clinton, with about 15,000 residents, and it has a totally different flavor. For one thing Madison is definitely upscale; the homes and developments are tops in quality as well as price. Residents have the highest per capita income in the state. Shopping districts and outlying residential development clearly show this affluence.

One of the first things you'll notice about Madison is the lack of strip-mall clutter—no blinking signs, flashing lights, or bright plastic decor. Strict regulation of signs and business architecture should make Madison a model for other small cities—an example of how downtowns should be kept alive and well. (Unfortunately it's too late for most towns; their depressed downtowns are filled with closed shops and painted-over display windows. Their shops, markets, and businesses were forced to go out of business or join the movement to the highway on the edge of town.) I urge city planners to visit Madison to see how it's done.

The city complex now includes more than sixty carefully planned subdivisions, among the most upscale (and expensive) in Mississippi. As a planned community Madison places emphasis on safety, comfort, and maintaining a quality small-town atmosphere.

Madison is also a favorite spot for antiques shoppers. Those in search of something special from a bygone era will fall in love with the pieces of antebellum and Victorian grandeur found in Madison's shops. Twice a year 30,000 crazed antiques-shoppers descend upon the Madison area for the Canton Flea Market, which features 1,200 vendors of arts and crafts, antiques, and collectibles.

The inevitable result of restrictive zoning and building codes is plenty of high-quality homes but a dearth of low-cost housing. You won't find mobile-home parks or inexpensive tract homes here. Apartment rentals are all but nonexistent, and we saw no condominiums. The average price of houses sold here is about $25,000 to $50,000 higher than in most Mississippi communities. But if you can afford higher prices, you definitely get your money's worth. Madison has at least one lovely golf-course development, complete with a country club–type center for residents.

Tupelo   When Hernando DeSoto's expedition entered northeast Mississippi in the 1500s, present-day Tupelo was the site of a large Chickasaw Indian village. No longer a village Tupelo has become a prosperous town of 34,000 inhabitants, where warm smiles and hometown hospitality are the rule, not the exception. This place has one of Mississippi's most enthusiastic retiree welcoming committees eagerly waiting to bring you into the fold, to make sure you get settled in your new home and are introduced all around. They'll have you working on a community project before you know what happened.

Nestled in the scenic beauty of northeastern Mississippi's rolling countryside, Tupelo sits on the Natchez Trace, about halfway between Natchez and Nashville. Memphis is an hour-and-a-half drive via Interstate 78, and Mississippi's lovely state capital at Jackson is a pleasant three-hour drive along the scenic Natchez Trace. The Trace, by the way, is a nature wonderland you'll not want to miss. You'll see wild turkeys, deer, and birds, and enjoy light motor traffic (no trucks allowed). A leisurely drive along the Natchez Trace is truly a pleasure. We've driven this road many times, occasionally pausing for a picnic or a hike along one of the historic pathways that branch off from the Trace.

Twice named an All-American City by the National Civic League, Tupelo enjoys a prosperous base as a manufacturing, retail, and distribution center, and its furniture industry rivals that of North Carolina. Our impression is that this is an exceptionally pleasant place to live, with welcoming neighbors and plenty of opportunities for community participation. And in case you didn't al-

TUPELO WEATHER					
In degrees Fahrenheit					
	Jan.	April	July	Oct.	Rain	Snow
Daily highs	57	78	93	78	53"	5"
Daily lows	34	51	70	50		

ready know it, residents will proudly inform you that Tupelo was the birthplace of Elvis Presley.

Five public and private golf courses and mild winters make for golfing pleasure year-round; there's also excellent golf at the Tupelo Country Club. The city has tennis courts in abundance, with instructors available to help you learn or sharpen your game. The 1,600-mile-long Tennessee–Tombigbee Waterway is minutes away from Tupelo, providing outdoor fun in the form of fishing, boating, picnicking, or camping.

Tupelo has two colleges, a branch of the University of Mississippi and the Itawamba Community College. Those older than age sixty-five do not have to pay tuition! In addition to continuing-education opportunities at the colleges, the Lee County Library offers year-round lecture series and "brown bag luncheons" (informal presentations for workers on their lunch break and retirees on their shopping break).

Tupelo has a wide range of homes in a variety of comfortable neighborhoods. From stately, older homes to new residential construction, Tupelo provides choices for every budget and lifestyle. Neighborhoods are peaceful and tend to be closely knit, with residents benefiting from well-trained, professional fire and police protection.

Picayune   In the southern part of Mississippi, we made a surprising discovery in small-town retirement: Picayune. Conveniently situated an hour's drive from either New Orleans's French Quarter or the glittering casinos on the Gulf of Mexico, the town manages to hold onto an old-fashioned hometown atmosphere. Rolling, wooded hills and numerous lakes contribute to a high-quality retirement environment. The current population is 12,500 and growing.

We were impressed both by the comfortable, home-town feeling of Picayune's downtown and by the quality of its residential areas. From expensive and plush neighborhoods to more humble areas, you'll find good value for your housing dollar. Just a few minutes from downtown, the landscape becomes rural, dotted with homes on large, wooded lots commonly ten acres or more. Some places have acreage for horses, with part of the land in small farms. The surprising thing is that the cost of a quality home on a large piece of land is similar to that of a small subdivision home in many other areas of the country.

Picayune's name derives from that of the local newspaper, the *Picayune Item,* which in turn comes from the New Orleans paper of the same name. Both newspapers were owned by Eliza Jane Poitevent Nicholson, a local resident and probably the only woman publisher of a major daily newspaper in the country at that time. A picayune, by the way, was a tiny coin circulated in New Orleans when the territory belonged to the Spanish Empire. A picayune was the original cost of a copy of the newspaper.

Recreation and entertainment are part of Picayune's heritage. Hunting and fishing in south Mississippi are said to be superb because of the pristine woodlands and numerous lakes, ponds, and streams. For saltwater fishing the Gulf beaches are 29 miles away. Golfers enjoy the Millbrook Country Club, with its eighteen holes of golf, tennis courts, and Olympic-sized pool. To enjoy the world-famous Mardi Gras, Picayune residents don't have to worry about finding a place to stay—New Orleans is only 40 miles away across Lake Pontchartrain. Similarly Saints professional football is easily accessible to Picayune sports fans. Finally the local community college offers a wide array of tuition-free classes to senior citizens on a space-available basis.

Louisiana

If you're looking for Gulf Coast beach property in Louisiana, you are out of luck. Except for a short stretch of sand in the western part of the state— humorously referred to as the Cajun Riviera—most of coastal Louisiana is swamps, mudflats, and bayous. People in Texas claim they can tell Louisianans by the high-water marks on their legs. Beaches start when you get to Texas,

and Texans feel smug about that. Of course, Louisianans enjoy making snide remarks about Texans, so they're even.

Nowhere in the United States can you find such a rich diversity of people, customs, and worldviews as in Louisiana. These differences aren't imaginary. You can travel 50 miles in almost any direction and you'll hear distinct accents, slang, music, and possibly even different languages. The cuisine is different, too. With eight ethnic groups tracing their ancestors back through Louisiana's history, it isn't surprising that many people here are bilingual, sometimes with Eng-

LOUISIANA TAX PROFILE
Sales tax: 4% to 10%, drugs and some food exempt
State income tax: graduated from 2% to 6% greater than $50,000; federal income tax deductible
Property taxes: local taxes average of 1.15% of market value, with $75,000 exemption; no state property tax
Intangibles tax: no
Social security taxed: no
Pensions taxed: private pensions taxable, $6,000 exemption
Gasoline tax: 20¢ per gallon, plus sales tax

lish as their second tongue. Visiting Louisiana is almost like visiting a foreign country.

Louisiana has an eclectic collection of nationalities and cultures. Of course France quite naturally left the strongest influence, as evidenced by the widespread use of Cajun French. Other artifacts of French influence are the concept of *parish* instead of *county* and Louisiana's legal procedures, which bear a stronger resemblance to the Napoleonic Code than British common law.

Louisiana's unique property tax system is highly praised by residents who relocate here from other states. Because the state derives most of its revenues from taxes on petroleum, there is no state property tax on residences. Furthermore there's a $75,000 deduction from local property taxes. Because real estate prices are low, the generous tax exclusion is often higher than the value of the average home. Except for more expensive properties, the homeowner pays little or nothing in the way of property taxes.

Acadiana (Cajun Country)

Louisiana's most famous ethnic group is the Cajuns, those French Canadians who were evicted from the Canadian province of Acadia (today's Nova Scotia) back in 1755. The English authorities—with the typical British tact and understanding of the time—insisted that the Acadians not only swear allegiance to the Crown, but that they renounce their Roman Catholic faith and join the Church of England. Or get out. The mass exodus that followed was recounted in Henry Wadsworth Longfellow's *Evangeline*. (Somehow I always assumed the Acadians fled Canada rather than submit to English cooking. Ever notice how the Brits boil everything they can't fry?)

The exiles went through terribly difficult times. Some families were shipped to the West Indies, some to the New England colonies, others went back to France. Many wandered, homeless for twenty years, before finding a welcome in the French-speaking environs of Louisiana. They established small farms along the Mississippi River, Bayou Teche, Bayou Lafourche, and other streams and bayous in the territory's southwestern section. The word *Cajun* comes from a modification of the original French pronunciation of Acadian (*A-ca-jan*), describing their French Canadian origins.

From the perspective of someone who loves good food, a big plus for living in Cajun country is the connection with Cajun cuisine. A first cousin to the Creole cuisine of New Orleans, Cajun cooking is way ahead in terms of creativity of its dishes and the artistic inspiration of its seasonings. Favorite Cajun dishes include jambalaya, gumbo, *cochon du lait* (suckling pig), *boudin* (a blood, pork, and rice sausage), soft-shell crab, stuffed crab, crawfish étouffée, crawfish bisque, crawfish pie, and shrimp fixed every possible way a Cajun chef can imagine. That's just for starters.

Upscale restaurants all over the world are jumping on the Cajun cooking bandwagon. They've discovered that simply tacking the term *Cajun* to a menu item works miracles. Should the chef make a mistake and burn something, it's advertised as "Cajun Blackened Broccoli," or whatever. One Cajun, angry at worldwide plagiarism of cherished recipes, declares: "My Mama never blackened anything in her life and put it on the table. If my Mama ever blackened somethin' it was a pure mistake, and she wasn't ashamed to *call* it a mistake. She'd feed it to the *dogs!*"

Lafayette and Vicinity   Lafayette is often called the "Cajun Capital City," and it offers a full range of activities and services, anything seniors need for quality retirement. Housing of all kinds in all price ranges is available, including several specialized housing developments with independent and assisted living arrangements, such as Azalea Estates and Courtyard at South College. New developments are under way away from the center of the city, with some impressive "plantation manor" homes on half-acre lots.

For those who feel that Lafayette is too much like a city, with a population of 54,000, there are several delightful choices away from

LAFAYETTE WEATHER					
In degrees Fahrenheit					
	Jan.	April	July	Oct.	Rain	Snow
Daily highs	62	79	91	79	54"	0.5"
Daily lows	42	58	73	59		

LAFAYETTE AREA COST OF LIVING					
Percentage of	Overall	Housing	Medical	Groceries	Utilities
national average	96	103	88	92	85

town. Southwest of Lafayette the charming little city of Abbeville (pop. 13,900) is known for its two quaint town squares. Abbeville claims to be the "most Cajun place on Earth." Then there's New Iberia (pop. 33,000) to the east, set among the breathtaking plantations and gardens of Shadows-on-the-Teche. Another major center of Cajun culture is Opelousas (pop. 22,500), the third oldest city in Louisiana, famous as the site of Jim Bowie's residence and well known for having produced many fine Creole and Cajun chefs. The nearby towns of Marksville, Bunkie, Simmesport, Bordelonville, and others are wonderfully steeped in history, yet lie quietly and unpretentiously as places for peaceful living.

Lafayette and the surrounding Cajun heartland offers horse racing, boat tours of the Atchafalaya Basin Swamp, and facilities for golf and tennis. Nearby Abbeville is known for excellent duck and goose hunting, hosting a duck festival every Labor Day. Golf courses, although not numerous, are scattered throughout Cajun country, so that you can play if you don't mind a thirty-minute or so drive.

Besides a branch of Louisiana State University, Lafayette has a local community college, affectionately known as "Gumbo U," which provides excellent adult education programs for cultural enrichment. Festivals are big here, with one taking place nearly every weekend. There's a crawfish festival in Breaux Bridge, a French music festival in Abbeville, a rice festival in Crowley, even a *boudin festival* (*boudin* is a special Cajun sausage) in Carencro. Lafayette is host to the South's second-largest Mardi Gras, complete with parades, balls, masquerades, and more.

Lafayette has six hospitals, with a total of 1,134 beds.

Opelousas General Hospital serves as a referral medical center and offers a comprehensive community health-care facility with a wide range of medical specialties and state-of-the-art technology.

Baton Rouge   Not really in Acadiana, Baton Rouge received its French name well before the Cajuns entered the bayou country. French explorer Pierre Le Moyne (Sieur d'Iberville) organized the first permanent European settlement here back in 1682. The site he selected for the village had a tall, bloodstained cypress tree on the riverbank that marked the hunting territory of two Indian tribes. The villagers christened the area *Baton Rouge*, "red stick."

As you might expect Louisiana's state capital—Baton Rouge (pop. 232,000)—is a handsome city. With neat, prosperous-looking neighborhoods, attractive subdivisions, and one of the prettiest university campuses in the country, Baton Rouge fulfills its role as political and educational center of the state. Its distinctive blend of French, Creole, Cajun, and Old South traditions makes it as much a part of Louisiana as the great river on which it thrives.

Until the real estate market pushed up prices, Baton Rouge had one of the lowest costs of living of any city of its size in the country. Living costs and housing prices are now about average for the nation. But it's the quality of the setting that makes it a bargain.

Most university towns have lots to offer retirees. Baton Rouge's Louisiana State University (LSU) is no exception. Its cultural offerings and its enrichment of the intellectual aspect of the community are quite important, but additionally the school attracts scholars, professors, and university employees from all over the country. The narrow, conservative atmosphere of many Southern cities is absent

BATON ROUGE WEATHER						
In degrees Fahrenheit						
	Jan.	April	July	Oct.	Rain	Snow
Daily highs	61	79	91	80	55"	—
Daily lows	41	58	73	56		

BATON ROUGE COST OF LIVING					
Percentage of national average	Overall	Housing	Medical	Groceries	Utilities
	104	98	100	110	113

in Baton Rouge. Students, faculty, support personnel, and families of these outside people nourish fresh views and lifestyles throughout the community.

My distinct impression is that most residents do *not* use the thick Southern accent one expects from such a deep South location. This shouldn't be surprising, because so many people come from places where Midwestern accents are the norm. I attribute the university's influence for this leveling of accents. Among the natives a slight Cajun twist of pronunciation is common, but this is totally different from a conventional Southern accent.

The university touches the community in other ways, culturally as well as educationally. A slogan here is "Art Is the Heart of Baton Rouge." Using the talent in theater, music, and fine arts that LSU attracts, the community has organized some commendable programs. Every year a 10-block stretch of downtown is blocked off so people can see potters at their wheels, musicians entertaining, and artists at their easels. Mimes entertain the crowds, and craftspeople of all kinds sell their wares. Two ballet groups bring stars from major companies to work with local students; the Baton Rouge Opera is in its tenth season. Two light opera companies, a symphony orchestra, and a professional theater company round out the cultural offerings. The city is quite proud of its historic past and is taking vigorous steps to preserve and restore two downtown neighborhoods, historic Beauregard Town and Spanish Town.

As a retirement location, Baton Rouge has a lot going for it. It's a cosmopolitan community, and it's centrally located. It's just 70 miles by interstate to New Orleans for those extra-special nights on the town or for the hilarity of Mardi Gras. You can reach the beaches at Pass Christian in two hours by car. Fifty miles to the north is the nineteenth-century atmosphere of historic Natchez. For riverboat gambling you don't have to go far. Baton Rouge has two riverboat casinos, the Belle of Baton Rouge and Casino Rouge.

Natchitoches This is another place we would never have found had it not been for Louisiana's retirement welcoming program: the town of Natchitoches in the north-central part of the state. Strangers always have problems pronouncing the name. We usually try to pronounce it as it's spelled, which brings polite smiles to the faces of natives, if not outright guffaws. It's pronounced *NAK-*

NATCHITOCHES WEATHER						
In degrees Fahrenheit						
	Jan.	April	July	Oct.	Rain	Snow
Daily highs	56	78	92	79	58"	0.7"
Daily lows	36	55	73	55		

a-tish. This is an Indian word meaning Place of the Paw Paw, or Chinquapin nut.

History buffs will find plenty to marvel at in this fascinating little city of 17,000 inhabitants. Natchitoches has one of the most picturesque and authentic downtown sections of any place we've yet seen in this region, reminiscent of the French Quarter in New Orleans. To get an idea of what the town looks like, rent the movie *Steel Magnolias* from your local video store. The picture was produced on location here, using homes in the downtown area as stages and local people as extras.

Natchitoches has the proud distinction of being the oldest settlement in the entire Louisiana Territory. French explorers first made contact with the Natchitoches Indians in 1700 and fourteen years later established a trading outpost on the Red River. Natchitoches soon became a bustling river port and an important crossroads. Wealthy planters not only built imposing plantation houses along the river, they also maintained elegant showplaces in town.

Sometime in the 1830s the U.S. government decided to clear the logjam so river barges could travel upstream to what is now Shreveport. Theoretically this would make Natchitoches even more prosperous. But to the dismay of Natchitoches residents, the Red River changed its course, leaving the once-thriving river town high and dry, several miles from the new river course. The town's future as a bustling port town became history as the river became a spring-fed creek. Although this disaster isolated Natchitoches, it safeguarded its historic buildings from the curse of progress and urban renewal. It also preserved the deeply ingrained traditions of its residents.

Fortunately Natchitoches came up with a great idea. Why not dam the old channel and create a lake? Today a 26-mile oxbow lake, called Cane River Lake, runs through upscale Natchitoches residential areas and is the showpiece of the downtown National Landmark District. Cane River Lake looks very much like a river but aesthetically is much better. The lake-river doesn't flood or become silty in rainy weather. It doesn't have a current or carry flotsam and debris from upstream, and it provides a place for peaceful boating and good fishing in its clear, spring-fed waters. Best of all it lends an air of Old South dignity to Natchitoches, with huge oak and magnolia trees arching over the lake's bank and weeping willows trailing branches into the still water.

Natchitoches's rich historical background encompasses French, Spanish, Native American, African, and Anglo-Saxon influences. Contemporary residents take pride in this colorful palette of tradition and carefully maintain their ties with the past by preserving the older part of the city. Large antebellum town homes of cotton planters sit next to ornate Victorian houses and substantial homes dating from the early 1800s. Some have been converted to bed-and-breakfast inns. (In all, Natchitoches has twenty-one B&Bs.)

These historic buildings are more than museum pieces; they are homes of residents who enjoy being within a short walk of the fascinating downtown. At first we suspected that Natchitoches's commercial district might be a clever remodeling project. The brick streets, wrought-iron balconies, and storefronts—all in the style of the 1850s—looked too authentic to be real. But several stores display photographs taken of downtown businesses more than a century ago. They clearly show that, indeed, this is how Natchitoches looked in its prime.

Natchitoches's further claim to being a good retirement choice is enhanced by the presence of Northwestern State University. In addition to its symphony, dinner theater, ballet, and other entertainment, the school offers many interesting continuing-education programs for mature adults.

Compared with the national average, Natchitoches's housing prices seem low. Historic homes sell for half what similar places would fetch in Charleston or Savannah. But for this region prices are probably $10,000 above average. This is understandable when the setting is considered.

Toledo Bend Lake   Toledo Bend, a 186,000-acre man-made reservoir created by damming the Sabine River, is the fifth-largest man-made lake in the country. The body of water stretches north-south for 70 miles, with 1,100 miles of irregular shoreline. Inlets and

TOLEDO BEND WEATHER					
In degrees Fahrenheit					
	Jan.	April	July	Oct.	Rain	Snow
Daily highs	56	77	94	79	44"	0.7"
Daily lows	36	55	73	54		

bays make great places for lakeshore homes and boat docks, though some sections have dead trees and stumps sticking out of the water. Apparently local fishermen prefer these areas because that's where the fish are. However, the Sabine Recreation Authority has three cutting barges working full time clearing stumps and trees in addition to improving existing boat lanes. Eventually most of the lake will be pristine.

The Toledo Bend region is in the first stages of development and is anticipating growth in the near future. In the meantime the lake affords sports fun and excitement for tourists as well as low-key and quiet retirement living for residents.

Living in an isolated and rustic area like Toledo Bend has certain drawbacks. It's still sparsely populated, so depending on where you live, you must travel to the nearby towns of Shreveport, Many, Leesville, or DeRidder for your medical services and major shopping. The way the area is developing, however, it may only be a matter of time until Wal-Mart, Walgreens, and Wendy's make their appearance. Residents hope not.

The real surprise in recreational facilities is the new public golf course at Cypress Bend. The $3-million, eighteen-hole championship layout fronts on the lake and was funded as a joint project by the federal and state governments. Plans are on the drawing board for a multimillion-dollar resort, complete with a one-hundred-room hotel, condominiums, and a convention center at Cypress Bend. If this comes to pass, you can be sure there'll be a proliferation of jobs and new residents to swell the population.

The area surrounding Toledo Bend is home to many species of birds: pelicans, egrets, cranes, bald eagles, ducks, and a host of migratory species. Other wildlife in the area include white-tailed deer, fox, armadillo, opossum, raccoon, coyote, beaver, and wild hog.

The lake is said to have a fish population of 300 pounds per square acre. Local residents swear that the lake is so full of bass, crappie, and catfish that the fish regularly engage in fistfights to see who gets to be next on your hook. In order to promote catch-and-release protocol, fiberglass replicas of lunker bass are awarded those sportsmen who catch and release the big guys. We've seen these fiberglass replicas; they look very natural, but local anglers complain that they're difficult to clean, and you have to cook them a long time to make them tender.

Residential and business construction in the Toledo Bend area is on the increase. In the past few years there has been a significant increase in population, with more than 900 new homes constructed as well as almost 600 mobile homes to house new residents. Real estate offerings vary from rustic fish camps by the water's edge to gorgeous lakeview homes. Building costs here can be higher than in the larger towns, simply because workers and materials must be brought in from neighboring cities. This will change as the volume of building accelerates.

Leesville and DeRidder   When World War II exploded, the government hurriedly constructed a large Army post in an almost deserted part of western Louisiana. They called it Fort Polk. Generals Eisenhower, Patton, and Clark used the region to train several million soldiers. The first draftees pushed through Fort Polk for training retained bad memories of those rustic early days, so it's understandable that the installation acquired a poor reputation among the military. Over the years the government gradually improved conditions. They constructed quality off-post quarters in Leesville and DeRidder and added amenities to the post itself, such as a championship golf course, parklike landscaping, and quality housing. Those who did tours of duty at Fort Polk in later years look back with fond memories of Leesville and DeRidder. One retiree from Klamath Falls, Oregon, said, "The first time I came to Fort Polk, the Army dragged me here kicking and screaming. But six years ago, I decided to retire here!"

LEESVILLE–DERIDDER WEATHER						
In degrees Fahrenheit						
	Jan.	April	July	Oct.	Rain	Snow
Daily highs	56	77	93	79	44"	2"
Daily lows	36	55	73	55		

In line with recent Pentagon policy, Leesville's Fort Polk has been downsized. Local residents were delighted that the fort wasn't shut down entirely, something which would have been disastrous for the economy. As part of the cutbacks, however, the government ordered all enlisted men to live on base. This created a buyer's market for quality housing in Leesville and nearby DeRidder. These favorable real estate prices, along with the presence of a retirement welcoming committee in both Leesville and DeRidder, prompted our research for relocation opportunities here. Retirement committee volunteers are available to take visitors on a tour of their area and share their pride in the community.

A small city of about 12,000 residents, Leesville has well-designed homes, mostly of brick construction and set on generous plots of tree-shaded land. The historic downtown center, off the highway going through Leesville, is undergoing a dramatic renovation. An old theater has been beautifully restored as a special-events place for banquets, proms, parties, and meetings. Electric lines are now underground and attractive lighting has replaced old lightposts. Because of community efforts, Leesville won first place in the district's Cleanest City contest.

The older residential section immediately around the town center is stocked with prewar traditional white frame homes, mostly suitable for low-cost housing. There's a potential for restoration here, as well. These places would be suitable for people who like being within walking distance of downtown.

The golf course at Fort Polk is the local pride and joy, and its beautiful eighteen-hole layout is always open to the general public. With all the lakes, rivers, and forests nearby, outdoors people have plenty of opportunity for fishing and hunting or just enjoying a hike or boat ride. Leesville/Fort Polk is also blessed with a branch of Northwestern State University for adult education. The school offers courses in several professional fields in addition to leisure learning classes. Seniors may take one course per semester tuition-free, with an application fee of $15.

Down the highway 20 miles, DeRidder is slightly the smaller of the two towns, with an estimated population of approximately 10,000. DeRidder has a section of old, elegant homes, a legacy of the bounty the town realized through timber harvests in the early part of the century. These elaborate showplaces attest to the wealth of the timber barons and merchants. Several modern neighborhoods have more upscale housing, and some are showplaces in their own right.

Like Leesville, DeRidder is a home-buyer's market because of the downsizing at Fort Polk. The city is also in the process of revitalizing its historic downtown section. The center is starting to look as if it might make a comeback, with several businesses flourishing. The historic old railroad depot has been converted to a museum with a unique collection of antique dolls, bringing tourists to the downtown.

One of the absolute jewels of DeRidder's downtown renovation project is its new library. The library is fast becoming the heartbeat of the community. This is one of the first places newcomers should check in. An exciting part of the library is a program called the Cyberspace Launch Pad, an innovative approach to community involvement in computers and the Internet. Thanks to a generous grant from the state, a sophisticated computer network offers free computer connections to all county residents. The emphasis is on communications via the Internet. For retirees, this means staying in touch by e-mail with children and grandchildren anywhere in the world. Those seniors who don't have computers can use the library's equipment and are issued their own e-mail accounts. Those who don't know how to use computers are given lessons and hands-on training. An example of the library's innovative approach is the Cyber-Grandparent Program. This project links grandparents and grandchildren by e-mail and Web pages so they can work together to perform school projects. The cyber-grandparents help their grandkids with homework as they maintain close relationships.

DeRidder also has several upscale neighborhoods, with prices about the same as Leesville. Bargains are to be found in either community because of the present buyer's market.

Alexandria Between 1988 and 1995 the U.S. government closed down 536 military bases, handing over a total of six million acres to state and local control. This is the largest transfer of land since the Oklahoma Land Rush. From what we hear this is just 30 percent of the planned closures; there are more to come. The big question is: What are we going to do with these multibillion-dollar properties?

Of course all military bases aren't exactly prime real estate. Many were constructed in deserts, swamps, or inaccessible back country. They'll probably sit and gather sagebrush until the next war. But many bases are ideally located for residential and industrial development. Over the years the government spent untold billions on these bases, constructing homes for officers and enlisted men, building PX facilities resembling Wal-Mart, top-quality golf courses, swimming pools, and other amenities that made the bases resemble self-contained cities.

However, many localities feel highly threatened by these abandoned housing units. If sold to the public, these units could glut the open market, causing real estate values to plunge through the floor. Bad enough the military pulled many thousands of consumers from the region without adding more chaos. Yet it's a shame to let all of these expensive amenities go to waste.

The solution to this dilemma: Convert base housing to senior housing, and bring in folks age fifty-five-plus (and their money) from outside the community to rejuvenate the local economy. The incoming retirees occupy homes that would otherwise be left to deteriorate and will be boosting the economy to boot.

When England Air Force Base, on the outskirts of Alexandria, was decommissioned, the city turned the airfield into its major commercial airport, renaming it Alexandria International. Warehouses and repair facilities were leased to manufacturers, and some buildings were converted to offices and warehouses.

This left a large collection of housing, mostly two- and three-bedroom homes, in good shape and ready for occupancy. Because the redevelopment authority didn't want to damage the local real estate and rental markets, they decided to restrict the base housing to two categories of tenants: retirees and employees of businesses located on the former air-base property. They named the complex England Oaks, because of the live oak trees that abound here. As an experiment, it was decided that the homes should be leased, rather than sold (as is the case in most other senior developments).

Therefore England Oaks is aimed at a distinct niche of retirement service: an independent living facility for middle-income seniors who don't care to invest a lot of money in their retirement homes. Additional advantages are the security and convenience that go with a maintenance-free lifestyle. Retirees combine sub-

ALEXANDRIA WEATHER					
In degrees Fahrenheit					
	Jan.	April	July	Oct.	Rain	Snow
Daily highs	56	79	93	79	42"	0.7"
Daily lows	36	56	74	55		

ALEXANDRIA COST OF LIVING					
Percentage of national average	Overall	Housing	Medical	Groceries	Utilities
	94	88	96	95	111

urban home life with group social and recreational activities, without sacrificing comfort, space, and privacy. Social life in England Oaks is centered around the development's clubhouse (the former officers' club), where regular meetings, potlucks, and social hours are held.

The two- and three-bedroom homes (formerly noncommissioned officers' housing) have been remodeled with a view to attracting active seniors whose health is such that assisted living is somewhere down the road. Homes are equipped with emergency-response systems, safety features for the elderly, and even telephones with large, easy-to-read pushbuttons and a voice that echoes back the number so that a person with poor eyesight can know he or she has made the right connection. This is a pleasant, secure neighborhood of homes shaded by oak and pecan trees, with a golf course, hiking and bike trails, and a gated community that gives you a feeling of security.

An arrangement like this especially appeals to retired military because they're familiar with military retirement complexes like Air Force Village in San Antonio and elsewhere. The new concept here is that instead of large, nonrefundable deposits of many thousands of dollars, England Oaks requires only a refundable deposit of less than $500 and $595 to $725 per month on a year's lease (at time of writing).

CHAPTER 5

The Midsouthern Hills

IF YOU LOOK AT A MAP of the United States, you'll notice a curious east-west line that cuts the country almost in two. From the point where Nevada, Arizona, and Utah intersect, state boundaries form a line that runs eastward until it hits the Atlantic Ocean near Norfolk, Virginia. This line bisects the nation, separating Virginia from North Carolina, Kentucky from Tennessee, Missouri from Arkansas, Kansas from Oklahoma, Colorado from New Mexico, and Utah from Arizona. Except for a slight deviation around the southern edge of Missouri, the demarcation is almost perfectly straight.

Why the line runs as it does is something only historians or geographers can explain. A long stretch runs through what I call the "Midsouthern Hills"—through the heart of the Appalachians, the Tennessee–Kentucky hill country, the Ozark Mountains of Missouri and Arkansas, and into Oklahoma's Ozark section. Straddling this line is an interesting swathe of woodlands, hills, plains, and mountains, places that offer prime retirement conditions for those who like four seasons and a woodsy and slow-paced lifestyle. A low cost of living, inexpensive housing, and high personal safety are bonuses.

Industry and modern agriculture characterize the country to the north of this strip of semiwilderness. Below is the Deep South. Life in the Midsouthern Hills moves at its own pace, always a little out of sync with the rest of the nation. Until World War II this was one of the most poverty-stricken segments of the nation. Cartoonist Al Capp located his imaginary town of Dogpatch here, the home of indigent Lil' Abner, his family, and his girlfriend, Daisy Mae. Although the cartoon strip amused folks who didn't have to live in Dogpatch, real-life circumstances were anything but funny. Roads were often gravel and dirt. Subsistence farmers lived in flimsy shacks as they raised families and tried to coax a living from the rocky soil.

The change in living standards since the war years has been nothing less than miraculous. Change began with the government building dams and water-power projects to provide cheap electricity. Manufacturing industries and businesses relocated to take advantage of inexpensive power as well as low labor costs. Local people no longer had to move to the north to find employment.

Fortunately progress didn't destroy the Midsouthern Hills's natural beauty; it actually improved things. With the dams came lakes—hundreds of them. The combination of Ozark and Appalachian scenery with new lakes—perfect for fishing, boating, water-skiing, and just plain looking—created an overnight tourist sensation. Vacationers brought money, and retirees brought even more dollars, which further contributed to economic growth. Today small farms are more often a hobby or a sideline than a means of survival.

Because of its porous limestone base, the Ozark formation is honeycombed with underground caves, sometimes storing so much water that rivers gush from the cavernous depths as if by magic. One example: In Missouri's Big Spring Park, a full-fledged river surfaces at the rate of 286 million gallons a day! Ozark soil—typically rock-studded, rust-red in color, and nutrient-poor—doesn't lend itself easily to plows or farm machinery. For this reason large portions of this country escaped agricultural development; they remain rustic, unspoiled, and delightful places for retirement hideaways.

Climate

Every retiree we interview here emphasizes the four-season climate as a major plus. "I like to know what time of year it is," said one lady who had lived in California before retirement. "Here I get the feeling of seasons. Summer is nice and hot, fall is beautiful and colorful, winter is short and merciful, and then comes spring!" She sighed in ecstasy.

Make no mistake: Winter does bring chilly winds, creeks ice over, and your furnace gets a workout. Still it doesn't begin to compare with winters farther north. Summers are humid, but not unbearable, with ninety-degree highs normal. Enough rain falls in the summer to keep the landscape looking green and fresh, streams flowing, and fishing good to excellent year-round.

Transportation

As mentioned earlier in this book, many small towns lack intercity bus service and air transportation. This is particularly common in the Midsouthern Hills area. Without intercity buses or passenger trains, you are totally dependent upon an automobile. The nearest airport could be 75 miles away. When the grandkids come to visit, how do they get to your place from the airport? If you don't drive, and if you're used to public transportation, don't take it for granted when looking for a retirement destination. Make it a point to determine the situation before locking yourself in.

Arkansas

Arkansas is a major beneficiary of today's retirement trends. After Florida, Arkansas is one of the fastest-growing states in number of new residents older than age sixty-five. Throughout the state almost a fifth of the population is older than sixty, with percentages much higher in popular retirement locations.

Newcomers from Chicago or Indianapolis find it easy to make friends, because they find that many of their neighbors have come from the same part of the country, have similar interests, and have common things to talk about. This is convenient because, believe it or not, many Arkansas natives have never even *heard* of the Chicago Cubs, much less spent time discussing their pennant possibilities for the season.

What is the attraction here? Arkansas's mild, four-season climate, low taxes, and personal safety. Inexpensive housing and friendly people figure into the picture, but the catalyst for retirees settling in Arkansas is the glorious Ozark environment. These low, ancient, thickly forested mountains symbolize many retirement dreams. The Ozarks represent a rebirth of simplicity, a purging of city life, and a new mode of relaxation.

Besides clear-running streams, squeaky-clean air, and lakes swarming with fish, many retirement dreams also picture an isolated cabin with a boat dock at the back door and lazy days of casting for bigmouth bass or lake trout. But don't worry— even nonanglers enjoy the Ozarks's beautiful surroundings.

The southern part of Arkansas, below the Ozarks, is rarely the choice of folks coming from other states. They prefer the northern half above Hot Springs and

ARKANSAS TAX PROFILE
Sales tax: 5.5%, plus 3.5% on fast food
State income tax: graduated, 1% on first $3,000 income to 7% on $25,000 and greater
Property taxes: average 3.9% of assessed value, set at 20% of appraised value
Intangibles tax: no
Social security taxed: no
Pensions taxed: excludes $6,000 from government and private pensions
Gasoline tax: 18.5¢ per gallon

Little Rock. This is important to know. Without a substantial number of out-of-state retirees or other outsiders for neighbors, you could find yourself isolated among folks with whom you have little in common. Not that people would be anything but friendly and neighborly, but unless your cultural background is basically agricultural and small town, you could have a difficult time adjusting.

Arkansas state policy on college education is to waive general student fees for credit courses to persons age sixty and older on a space-available basis. State vocational and technical schools also waive fees.

Following are some northern Arkansas towns we've visited and that we feel confident have potential for retirement. All have a significant number of nonnatives living there. Some places are small, but none are isolated from medical and other important services. Intercity transportation is sometimes a problem, something you'll have to look at if you don't drive.

Fayetteville   Up in the northwest corner of Arkansas's Ozark Mountains, two great candidates for senior relocation await your consideration. On either side of 28,000-acre Beaver Lake, Eureka Springs and Fayetteville have both received favorable publicity as great places for relocation. Between them is the small city of Rogers, and to the north of Fayetteville is one of the earliest planned developments in Arkansas: Bella Vista.

Fayetteville is the largest, a city of about 58,000 people plus almost 15,000 students at the University of Arkansas. This part of Arkansas also shares in some of the most beautiful Ozark scenery in the entire region. It starts just a few miles from downtown Fayetteville.

One way you can tell you're in a college town: Look for a collection of offbeat gourmet restaurants. Fayetteville has 'em all. Besides a tempting selection of Japanese, Mexican, and barbecue restaurants, downtown Fayetteville offers esoteric eating establishments with names designed to grab your attention, such as Gumbo Joe's Cajun Grill, Penguin Ed's, Armadillo Grill, and Schlegel's Bagels. I can't imagine a restaurant named Penguin Ed's in a farm town in flatland Arkansas. The chef would be arrested and handcuffed by the local sheriff before the first penguin-on-rye sandwich ever left the grill. (They might accept armadillo, however, if served with red-eye gravy and biscuits.) When Bill Clinton was first running for Congress back in 1974, he and his campaign committee used to meet at a popular place in Fayetteville called the D-Lux Café. (Now doesn't *D-Lux Café* sound more like down-home Arkansas?)

The University of Arkansas is Fayetteville's heart and soul. Without intentionally doing so, the school, its students, and professors add excitement and vigor to the city. To fully savor the magnetism of the resident student community, you must visit Dickson Street, near the campus. This colorful, entertaining street is filled with bistros, restaurants, and art galleries. It's a place to dance the night away to your favorite music. (Doesn't sound like Arkansas, does it?) Dickson Street is also home to the splendid Walton Arts Center.

Fayetteville's downtown is a delightful combination of a healthy business sector combined with a well-preserved historic district, which local residents refer to as "the Square." Commercial and

FAYETTEVILLE WEATHER						
In degrees Fahrenheit						
	Jan.	April	July	Oct.	Rain	Snow
Daily highs	48	74	94	76	40"	7"
Daily lows	27	49	71	49		

FAYETTEVILLE COST OF LIVING					
Percentage of	Overall	Housing	Medical	Groceries	Utilities
national average	92	92	85	87	92

residential buildings have been lovingly restored to their nineteenth-century glory. They contrast nicely with contemporary architecture containing shops and offices. Local farmers and craftspeople are encouraged to bring their wares to the laid-back farmers' market on the square, which takes place three times every week. A tourist trolley provides free transportation for shoppers and visitors to move around Fayetteville's downtown on their leisurely errands.

Homes around the Fayetteville historic district are very much in demand, with potential buyers asking to have their names placed on a waiting list. Most homes have been completely renovated and are large, from 2,500 to 4,000 square feet. Downtown historic homes can be relatively expensive. By way of contrast, a few blocks away is Wilson Park, a safe, homey neighborhood with houses built in the 1950s and 1960s with much lower price tags. A dozen attractive areas around town, farther away from the city center, offer affordable housing in secure-feeling neighborhoods. Seven upscale developments are in place. One of these is a golf-course subdivision, with residents' backyards touching the greens. In short the range of real estate is wide here, from Arkansas-inexpensive to more than you'd like to pay.

Bella Vista   About 20 miles north of Fayetteville is the planned community of Bella Vista. One of the earlier experiments in Ozark development, Bella Vista started thirty years ago and now has more than 16,000 year-round residents and thousands of seasonal residents. It was created by the same developers as Hot Springs Village, employing the same concepts, although it's older. Originally intended as a retirement and vacation resort, it became popular with commuters to Fayetteville who didn't mind the drive over the new four-lane highway. When you buy into Bella Vista, you automatically belong to four country clubs and recreational complexes. Residents have access to tennis courts, swimming pools, eight lakes, and seven golf courses.

Eureka Springs   This delightful town in northwest Arkansas started with a retirement boom more than a century ago. The word *eureka* means "I have found it," and this is how many visitors felt when they decided to convert their vacation visits into permanent retirement here. The population of year-round residents is 2,270.

People started coming to Eureka Springs around the turn of the twentieth century because of the "magical" healing qualities of the spring waters that gushed out of the canyon's grottoes. Perhaps the mineral water helped, but getting away from the crowds and squalor of the city, breathing the pure mountain air, and seeing the lovely Ozark surroundings probably had more than a little to do with the miracle cures.

Of course the waters were known and appreciated by Native Americans long before the white man muscled into the region. The palefaced newcomers began arriving in large numbers in the 1880s, when the Frisco Railroad ran a line into town to carry visitors from Chicago, St. Louis, and Kansas City. Several large and luxurious hotels accommodated the crowds. Wealthy families built ambitious Victorian mansions that duplicated their big-city homes. Before long the town's winding streets were lined with houses, hotels, and commercial buildings, many displaying the fancy gingerbread styles of that era.

During World War I folks stopped coming to Eureka Springs. The town's bonanza was put on hold; its popularity declined as new residents moved away or died. Lovely homes were boarded up and forgotten as absentee owners lost interest in the town. The Great Depression was the final blow; Eureka Springs almost became a ghost town. At the time townsfolk must have viewed this abandonment as extreme misfortune, but today's residents see it as a stroke of luck. Otherwise Eureka Springs would have suffered from modernization, with the old buildings gradually replaced by modern structures. This temporary loss of popularity created a virtual time capsule of Victorian architecture.

Your first glimpse of Eureka Springs is a guaranteed surprise. Solid limestone and brick buildings, wrought-iron fancy work, and gracefully styled mansions with winding carriageways make the town a fascinating window into yesterday. Boutiques, restaurants, art galleries, and other businesses occupy the downtown's street-

EUREKA SPRINGS WEATHER						
In degrees Fahrenheit						
	Jan.	April	July	Oct.	Rain	Snow
Daily highs	48	73	90	76	44"	6"
Daily lows	27	49	69	49		

level stores with second- and third-floor apartments for those who live downtown.

Majestic residences line the streets that twist and climb the mountainside above the business district. This incredible collection of Victorians rivals and perhaps even surpasses the finest that San Francisco has to offer. Some have fluted columns rising three stories in front of dignified brick facades and wrought-iron balconies—homes that look as if they belong on the set of *Gone with the Wind*. It's difficult to describe Eureka Springs without slipping into clichés, because the entire town *is* a cliché, a magic peek at yesterday.

The town and environs offer all the amenities retirees seek: good medical facilities, a quaint, artistic cultural atmosphere, friendly neighbors, recreational opportunities, and inexpensive real estate. Eureka Springs has become both a retirement mecca and an artist colony.

An interesting aspect of Eureka Springs is that you often can buy a historic Victorian for about what you'd pay for an ordinary tract house in most parts of the country—even less. Several retired couples have converted their spacious old mansions into delightful bed-and-breakfast inns. In the old days not all Victorian homes were mansions, however. Ordinary folks lived in modest-sized houses just as they do today. These places are exceptional bargains, and conventional housing on the town's outskirts is similarly priced well below national averages.

Holiday Island   A half-hour's drive from Eureka Springs takes you to an ambitious golf/country-club resort known as Holiday Island. Located on Table Rock Lake, the resort is set on 5,000 acres of natural beauty. The lake is narrow at this point, following the twists and turns of an old riverbed, thus creating a large number of lakefront lots. Two golf courses (one a nine-hole layout), a number of tennis courts, two swimming pools, and most of the facilities expected of a resort community are in place. Ninety percent of the residents are from other states, mostly from Illinois, Missouri, and Texas.

Golf seems to be excellent here, so much so that enthusiastic golfers purchase inexpensive lots and pay the $283 annual assessment for unlimited use of the courses. Owners of lots also have the right to stay in the development's campground and use all the facilities.

Mena   Small towns have the reputation of being exceptionally low-crime areas. However, crime waves can strike anywhere at any time. Recently a serial auto thief struck the western Arkansas town of Mena. Faced with an emergency Sheriff Mike Oglesby asked the local radio station to broadcast an emergency warning. The warning: "Don't leave your car keys in the ignition! Someone is stealing cars!" Fortunately the culprit was quickly apprehended—and turned out to be a high school student who liked joyriding. A good thing, too, because Mena citizens aren't used to heavy-duty crime waves. They probably wouldn't remember to remove their keys.

Sitting in a valley surrounded by western Arkansas's Ouachita Mountains, Mena is a pleasant town of 5,700 in a county of 17,000. It's near the Oklahoma border, about 77 miles west of Hot Springs and 85 miles south of Fort Smith. Local boosters call their town "the pride of the Ouachitas." (Pronounce it this way: *WAH-shi-taw*!)

Mena is surprisingly prosperous looking, with several upscale neighborhoods where housing sells at scandalously low Arkansas prices. Another surprise: Mena is a college town. Students and faculty always brighten a community, adding a touch of energy and spirit. The college influence shows in the way the downtown is still alive and breathing: The old railroad station, refurbished and restored, is now a museum and chamber of commerce office. Stores, businesses, and restaurants are open and thriving, not boarded up and collecting cobwebs as in some small Arkansas towns.

Part of Mena's economic well-being is due to local industries that employ skilled workers and consequently pay better-than-average wages. U.S. Motors, a division of Emerson Electric, provides a large number of jobs. Another skilled-worker employer is a large facility that repairs and maintains aircraft for major U.S. and Canadian airlines. Its technicians are all FAA qualified and can work just about anywhere in the world they choose. But they like it here in Mena. One man said, "We were looking for a good place to raise our children, and we couldn't find a better place than Mena."

Good wages have a multiplier effect on the economy in precisely the same way as retired people's incomes do. When spent in the community, wages and incomes turn into profits and wages for other residents. They, in turn, have more money to spend, which benefits still others. The money goes 'round and 'round. Mena's community leaders understand this very clearly. That's exactly why they are so enthused about sharing their community with retirees rather than going after marginal, minimum wage–paying industries as many other Arkansas cities have done.

Mena is surrounded by 1.5 million acres of the Ouachita National Forest, the South's oldest and largest national forest. There are thirty-two recreational areas in the forest where you can enjoy picnicking, camping, hiking, horseback riding, mountain biking, swimming, fishing, hunting, and boating.

For a small town Mena surprised us by having two public golf courses as well as a private golf course at the local country club. Like most Arkansas small towns, Mena is in a dry county; however, for those who enjoy a glass of vintage grape with their steak, the local country club is allowed to serve. Also the Oklahoma state line is less than 10 miles away. Ironically Oklahoma was one of the last states to permit legal sale of liquor, and now it's the first place people from neighboring states go to stock up their liquor cabinets.

Rich Mount, Mena's college, is a small school but has lots of get-up-and-go about it. The school's library has twenty computers, plus three computer labs, which the community is welcome to use between classes. Free tuition is offered to anyone older than age sixty, for either credit or audit.

Housing costs in Mena are pretty much standard for Arkansas. (That means very low.) The difference between Mena and the average Arkansas small city is a higher number of affluent neighborhoods than you'd normally expect. One couple I interviewed (retirees from Wisconsin) were absolutely delighted with their home: a three-bedroom, two-bath, modern log cabin sitting on nine acres of wooded property with a stream flowing through it. "We always wanted to live in a log cabin," they said, "and we absolutely fell in love with this one. When the seller told us he was only asking

MENA WEATHER						
In degrees Fahrenheit						
	Jan.	April	July	Oct.	Rain	Snow
Daily highs	48	74	94	76	39"	7"
Daily lows	26	49	70	49		

$65,000 for everything, we didn't even think about making a counteroffer. Then we found out taxes were only $300 a year!"

Greers Ferry Lake Area   About 60 miles north of Little Rock, the Greers Ferry Lake area is one of Arkansas's retirement success stories. Three towns share in this success: Heber Springs, Greers Ferry, and Fairfield Bay. They sit on the shores of a 40,000-acre lake created by an Army Corps of Engineers dam. (One of President Kennedy's last official acts was to dedicate Greers Ferry Dam while on his way to Dallas.)

This 300 miles of wooded shoreline—encompassing a lake filled with bass, stripers, walleye, catfish, and lunker trout—soon caught the attention of folks considering an Ozark retirement. Inexpensive property, low taxes, a temperate climate, and an almost nonexistent crime rate added to the attraction of retirement here. Folks from Chicago and St. Louis paid particular attention, for the lake wasn't so far from their grandchildren and old friends that they couldn't go home for a visit whenever they pleased.

In a matter of twenty years, Heber Springs, the largest of the communities, zoomed from a population of 2,500 to more than 6,000. The vast majority of newcomers were retired couples. Their pension money and savings pumped up bank deposits more than twentyfold, and the extra purchasing power boosted retail sales, created jobs, and generated tax money for local improvements. Home-building activity continues today, with lovely new neighborhoods materializing in low-density clusters, hidden in wooded, lakeshore settings.

Actually the area's population increased much more than the figures indicate. Many small neighborhoods are located *outside* town limits, nestled in wooded glades, often invisible from roads and highways. Typically a development consists of a grouping of from ten to fifty homes, sometimes with lake views. This arrangement cuts the expense of utility installation as well as construction costs. There could be as many as 150 of these mini-neighborhoods scattered through the forests. Although building lots are usually half an acre or more, the setting creates a sense of closeness among the neighbors. "We never worry about leaving our home vacant during the winter," remarked one resident, "because our friends watch the place for us."

GREERS FERRY LAKE AREA WEATHER						
In degrees Fahrenheit						
	Jan.	April	July	Oct.	Rain	Snow
Daily highs	50	74	96	75	49"	4"
Daily lows	29	51	71	50		

Construction quality is high, most homes are of brick, and low labor costs keep the selling prices affordable for retirees. Properties on the lake are priced higher, but not remarkably so. This is because the Army Corps of Engineers prohibits ownership of land directly on the water beyond a determined high-water line. This means no boat docks or direct access, and no immediate advantage to being next to the water. Lakeside homes enjoy the view, but so do places set farther back. Unlimited water access is provided by public docks, ramps, and marinas. A unique type of retirement development that appeals to those who fly small planes is Sky Point Estates, where you can build your home next to an airstrip.

For even smaller small-town retirement, Greers Ferry sits invitingly on the other side of the lake. The community provides all the basic services needed for day-to-day living, yet it's so small and uncongested that it doesn't require traffic lights. Greers Ferry has grocery stores, craft shops, and three branch banks. As a consideration for retirees' health care, the community has two full-time doctors and provides free ambulance service to Cleburne Hospital in Heber Springs.

Fairfield Bay, at the far end of the lake, is for those who prefer a more upscale setting where they can own a home near a golf course. This resort/retirement community features round-the-clock security and all the advantages of an exclusive, gated complex. Its parent company has built several other developments around the country.

One of the advantages of living in the Greers Ferry Lake area is its proximity to Little Rock, an hour's drive away. With a metropolitan area of nearly 250,000, Little Rock provides the health services that smaller towns cannot. Libraries, museums, and other cultural attractions fill a void for those who are used to larger cities. Little Rock is also the closest place to stock up on wine and beer to serve your guests, for like most smaller Arkansas areas, this is in a dry county.

Housing prices here have risen along with the improving economy, but prices and quality are remarkably better than where the retirees come from. A typical remark by new residents is, "Our new home is twice the size as the one we sold back home, and it cost half the money." Property taxes come as a pleasant shock when new residents receive tax bills just a fraction of what they paid back home.

Bull Shoals/Mountain Home   In the north-central part of Arkansas, along the Missouri border, a forested area of lakes and rivers has become a miniature melting pot, with retirees moving here from all over the country. Even traditional retirement areas like California and Florida are represented by former residents taking advantage of an exceptionally low crime rate, inexpensive living, and gorgeous scenery.

Surrounded on three sides by water, Bull Shoals and Lakeview sit on the shore of a lake that stretches for almost 100 miles. Its deep, blue waters are legend among bass fishermen, and the rivers and streams feeding the lake are considered premier spots for rainbow trout fishing, which in the spring and summer is done at night under lights. There are no closed seasons here; you can fish year-round. Sports aren't restricted to fishing or hunting; several challenging golf courses in the area will test your skills, whether you're a pro or a duffer.

The lake's shore is off-limits to construction up to the high-water mark, but the public has free access to both lake rivers. This restriction protects the lake's pristine quality, keeping it from being cluttered with sagging docks and scruffy-looking boats. The shoreline always looks clean and natural. Public marinas will house your boat for less than $400 a year, so you don't have to keep pulling your boat out of the water after every fishing trip.

Mountain Home is 15 miles from Bull Shoals and Lakeview, over a highway that winds through picturesque Ozark woods. This small city of about 10,000 is the commercial center for the lake com-

BULL SHOALS–MOUNTAIN HOME WEATHER						
In degrees Fahrenheit						
	Jan.	April	July	Oct.	Rain	Snow
Daily highs	46	73	92	74	42"	8"
Daily lows	25	47	67	48		

munities and the surrounding county of nearly 30,000 inhabitants. Mountain Home has a real downtown area, including an archetypal, old-fashioned town square. Major shopping and consumer businesses are located on the highway and around the major crossroads. Stores here supply any consumer goods for which anyone could reasonably ask. A community college serves the area, and retiree organizations offer opportunities for volunteer work. A hospital accommodates the area's population, and an airport runs shuttle services to the nearest large cities. The Area Agency on Aging operates a local bus service.

The county in which Mountain Home is located allows the sale of package liquor, and cocktails are permitted to be served in at least one restaurant. Bull Shoals is dry except for one private club.

According to couples who retired in this area, major attractions are mild winters and low living costs. One couple from just north of Chicago said, "We cut our property taxes by $2,000 a year by coming here, and we cut our heating bills by more than half." They explained that they spend less than $100 a month for heat, whereas the colder Lake Michigan winters had whacked $250 out of their monthly budget during the coldest months. The husband said, "The money we save makes the difference between struggling to stay within our budget and having money to spend for luxuries."

Hot Springs   This fascinating little city, situated partially within Hot Springs National Park, is one of the more attractive retirement possibilities in Arkansas. Hot Springs combines the spirit of a 1920s resort with that of a 1990s city. It is as different from the previously described towns as can be, yet its rustic setting on the lower edge of the Ouachita Mountains lends it an Ozark feeling.

The old part of town sits in a canyon with buildings and homes clinging to the sloping-to-steep sides of the ravine. During the decades before, during, and shortly after World War II, Hot Springs maintained a reputation as a lively nightlife town. Roulette, blackjack, and slot machines were as much an attraction as the gushing hot springs. Nightclubs and fancy restaurants flourished in a kind of midcountry Monaco atmosphere. Wealthy and famous citizens rubbed elbows with ordinary workers and the elite of the crime syndicates. Gambling, drinking, and dancing the night away preceded health-restoring soakings in the hot springs the next morning.

During its heyday Hot Springs was considered as sumptuous a resort as Las Vegas or Palm Springs is today.

Casino gambling and nightclubs are just memories today. The action now is bathing in the soothing waters and enjoying the quiet atmosphere of the Ozark Mountains. After casino-style gambling was prohibited, the old town, in the steepest part of the canyon, gradually fell into disrepair. When high rollers stopped visiting, money ceased flowing. Local folks preferred to shop in the malls away from downtown. But a new wave of retirees and a revival of tourist interest in the hot springs stirred a renewal of the downtown. Once-abandoned buildings now sport fine restaurants, art galleries, and quality shopping. The motif is turn of the twentieth century, with antique globe streetlamps, Victorian trim, even horse-drawn carriages for sight-seeing. A new breed of visitors comes to Hot Springs today, bringing retirement money instead of casino gambling money, and they tend to stay permanently.

Residential areas are located on higher levels, where the land is rolling and hilly but not steep. A good thing, too, because the canyon is subject to flash floods. Not long ago newspapers reported that a 6-foot wall of water crashed its way down the main business street, flooding stores and wreaking havoc. Hot Springs business people are used to this. After cleaning out the mud, bathhouses, boutiques, and restaurants opened for business with little delay.

Volcanic springs pour steaming hot water from grottoes and crevices in the canyon floor. Neither drought nor rainy seasons affect the water's copious flow. For generations the elderly and infirm praised the waters' healing and revivifying powers. The young and healthy (unaware of what revivification entails) simply enjoyed sit-

HOT SPRINGS AREA WEATHER						
In degrees Fahrenheit						
	Jan.	April	July	Oct.	Rain	Snow
Daily highs	52	75	93	77	55"	3"
Daily lows	31	52	71	53		

HOT SPRINGS COST OF LIVING					
	Overall	Housing	Medical	Groceries	Utilities
Percentage of national average	91	80	94	96	101

ting in the hot water and relaxing. The bonus for all is the fresh mountain air and the smell of pines and sassafras trees. The bewitched waters are reputed to heal everything from rheumatism to dandruff.

Residential neighborhoods fall into two distinct categories: Victorian and modern. The older sections have ample yards and large homes—often with enormous lawns and large shade trees. Other neighborhoods are more modern, with conventional bungalows, duplexes, and low-profile apartment buildings. There are several new, quality senior citizens' developments and some excellent mobile-home parks. Not only is the cost of living well below national averages, but also homes sell for 20 percent below national average.

There appear to be more apartments than usual for a town of this size, probably because of the seasonal tourist invasions, which encourage temporary housing. Since the demise of gambling and the subsequent tourist scarcity, apartment owners have been forced to become competitive with rents.

Hot Springs Village Fifteen miles from the city is one of the more impressive retirement complexes in Arkansas: Hot Springs Village, one of those Florida-style, self-contained, and guarded enclaves with 13,000 full-time residents. The assurances and dreams of the promoters have been realized here; the promised improvements are in place, including a shopping center that would do justice to a good-sized town.

Property in Hot Springs Village is not inexpensive, at least not for Arkansas, but it is certainly first class and returns full value for the money. Condo prices start in the low $60,000 range, three-bedroom homes at $80,000. These compare favorably with similar developments we've investigated in Florida, Arizona, and California.

Situated on 26,000 acres of rolling-to-steep Ozark foothill wilderness, the property is covered with a hardwood forest of oaks, hickories, and a scattering of evergreens. Roughly one-third of the property has been converted into lakes and golf courses. There are four par-seventy-two golf courses and one par-sixty-two layout, each with its own clubhouse, restaurant, and pro shop. Another third of the land is devoted to homesites, and the remaining third is natural forest.

Hot Springs Village is not exclusively a retirement complex; people who work in the nearby city of Hot Springs also buy houses here. But because there are no schools (residents voted down a school tax to avoid having schools), families with younger children rarely purchase property. According to the salespeople, the majority of the residents come from large Midwestern cities in Illinois, Missouri, and Kansas.

Missouri

Of course, Ozark hills and forests do not stop at the Arkansas border. They extend into Oklahoma on the west and about halfway up the state of Missouri before fading into plains and prairie country. Although the Ozarks indiscriminately bestow beauty upon all three states, Missouri's share is the largest, with 33,000 square miles of low mountains, verdant valleys, and rolling plateaus. The Missouri River marks the northern boundary of the Ozark range, Springfield the western edge, and the mountains taper out before they reach the Mississippi River in the east. Even in the midst of the mountains, plateaus can stretch for miles, with flat-to-rolling country reminiscent of the prairie to the north and west.

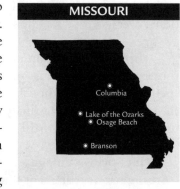

MISSOURI

Columbia

Lake of the Ozarks
Osage Beach

Branson

MISSOURI TAX PROFILE

Sales tax: 4.3% to 7.3%, drugs exempt
State income tax: graduated, 1.5% to 6% greater than $9,000; federal income tax deductible
Property taxes: average 1.1%
Intangibles tax: no
Social security taxed: half of benefits taxable for higher incomes
Pensions taxed: excludes $6,000
Gasoline tax: 15¢ per gallon

One of the more scenic areas is the 86,000-acre Current and Jacks Fork River country, set aside as the Ozark National Scenic Riverways. I cherish fond childhood memories of camping along the Current River and watching my father fly fish for trout. Memories like this are probably why people dream of retiring in an angler's paradise like the Ozarks.

Most Missouri Ozark rivers have been impounded by dams, forming long chains of lakes. They sprawl and twist through wooded valleys, covering a great part of both Missouri and Arkansas with water. The largest lakes are the Lake of the Ozarks—in the middle of the Missouri mountain range—and the Table Rock–Bull Shoals–Lake Tane complex on the Missouri–Arkansas state line.

Lake of the Ozarks/Osage Beach The largest lake in the Ozarks originated with the construction of Bagnell Dam across the Osage River in the 1930s. Ninety-four miles long, the lake boasts more than 1,000 miles of shoreline for fishing and recreation. Ozark forests climb from the water's edge, up and over low mountains, as far as the eye can see.

Years ago, before World War II, most outsiders who owned Ozark property expected, and demanded, rustic accommodations. They preferred log cabins for use as summer retreats or as fall hunting lodges. Most cabin owners lived in St. Louis or Kansas City, occasionally coming from large cities as far away as Chicago. City folks prized their backwoods hideaways and wanted to keep things rustic. Ozark natives were few in number and culturally isolated from the outside world. Natives and outsiders had little in common and lived in separate worlds even though they might be next-door neighbors every summer.

Things have changed around the Lake of the Ozarks. The site of my family's vacation cabin, where we drew buckets of water from a well, cooked freshly caught fish on a woodstove, and ate dinner by the orange glow of a kerosene lantern, is now the site of a bustling motel complex complete with a gourmet restaurant and marina. Across the highway is a shopping mall. In contrast to sleepy lake towns in other parts of Missouri and Arkansas, Missouri's Lake of the Ozarks is jumping. Kerosene lamps are out, contemporary living is in.

Osage Beach is the largest town on the Lake of the Ozarks and by far the most commercialized, with shopping malls, classy restaurants, and all the other amenities that come with full development. Vacationers, weekenders, and retirees come from all over the Midwest. Newcomers spend dollars that attract more businesses and more employees in a circular growth pattern. Instead of a summer

LAKE OF THE OZARKS WEATHER						
In degrees Fahrenheit						
	Jan.	April	July	Oct.	Rain	Snow
Daily highs	42	68	90	71	40"	17"
Daily lows	21	44	66	46		

resort with businesses that close every winter, Osage Beach has become a year-round city of approximately 6,000, the commercial center for an unknown number of lakeside residents and cabin owners outside the city limits.

One couple, who retired to Osage Beach from St. Louis, said, "We're used to shopping malls, nice restaurants, and big-city conveniences. We couldn't stand living in a small, isolated village where we would have to settle for whatever the stores *have* rather than what we *want*. Yet we want to live on a lake and be away from it all." The couple's home is fifteen minutes from a shopping mall, but it couldn't be more private. It sits on a large lakefront lot surrounded by a forest of northern red oak, black oak, shagbark hickory, and basswood. They can't see a neighbor in any direction. Because this is not an Army Corps of Engineers lake, a private boat slip is permitted at the lake's edge. Roads follow the lake's twisted arms to reach large, luxurious homes, ordinary houses, and rustic, unsophisticated cabins, most within easy shopping distance of town.

A few years ago a financial crisis in St. Louis's largest high-tech manufacturing firm caused a large number of employees—executives and factory workers alike—to seek employment elsewhere. This had a profound effect upon real estate prices around the Lake of the Ozarks. Weekend homes were unceremoniously dumped on the market. Bargains were legion, and the real estate market never fully recovered from the shock.

Of course lakefront homes can be as expensive as you care to consider. Some areas are quite prestigious, with homes commonly approaching half a million bucks in price. We looked at one (briefly) for $579,000 in Hawk Island Estates that had five bedrooms, four baths, what seemed to be an acre of deck overlooking the water, and a four-car garage. In contrast two-bedroom condos on the water were moderately priced. Away from the lake prices drop dramatically.

Branson   For years Branson, Missouri, has been an enormously popular vacation destination for families living in the Midwestern and Southern regions. The entire family—kids, parents, and grandparents—enjoy vacationing together in a unique combination of "neon and nature." By day vacationers enjoy nature with three scenic Ozark lakes, including Lake Tanycomo (accessible from the center of Branson), where some can swim, ski, boat, sail, scuba dive, jet ski, or parasail while others fish for trout or lunker bass. Evenings are devoted to the neon and bright lights of forty theaters with nationally celebrated musicians, singers, and entertainers performing on stage. Thus Branson has become the Ozarks's counterpart to North Carolina's family-friendly Myrtle Beach (with its combination of golf courses, theme parks, and theaters). And like Myrtle Beach, Branson has become a popular locale for retirement. It's a place where grandchildren eagerly anticipate visits with their grandparents.

One feature about the Branson/Lakes area that many retirees appreciate is the opportunity for part- and full-time work. Those who aren't ready for the rocking chair have numerous choices for employment. Jobs are usually there, whether working in the theater box office or as an usher, greeting guests at a hotel, demonstrating a craft skill, or holding one of the many other positions in the retail, restaurant, and hospitality industries. Working is a great way to become acquainted with other residents of the community.

Beyond the recreational, entertainment, and part-time employment opportunities, the moderately priced housing market is a good reason for retirement here. Finding a home on a golf course costing half of what might be asked in other vacation destination cities is an appealing concept. A wide variety of homes and prices can be found, running the gamut from multimillion-dollar lakefront estates to moderately priced in-town single-family homes—something for every budget. As a result the population from 1990 to 2002 almost doubled, from 3,700 to 6,000 inhabitants. Seniors account for a large measure of this growth, with an astounding 32 percent of the population age fifty-five and older. Revenue from tourism is a major factor in keeping city taxes low. The cost of living in Branson is actually about 6 percent below the national average.

One major hospital and several specialty clinics provide a full range of health-care services for residents and visitors. The 107-bed

BRANSON–LAKE TANYCOMO WEATHER					
In degrees Fahrenheit					
	Jan.	April	July	Oct.	Rain	Snow
Daily highs	41	63	89	75	39"	9"
Daily lows	23	48	69	52		

Skaggs Community Health Center, recently rated among the top ten hospitals in Missouri by the Center for Healthcare Industry Performance Studies, offers a full range of medical services. The hospital just completed a $20-million outpatient facility expansion that houses cardiac rehabilitation.

Columbia   Although not exactly in the Ozarks, the small city of Columbia is just a short drive from the Ozarks' outdoor recreation and rustic mountain scenery. With a population of 70,000, Columbia is large enough to supply all the amenities and conveniences of a modern city, yet not so large that it suffers from the inherent congestion, crime, and pollution of the big cities.

As a place to retire, Columbia is popular with folks from large Midwestern cities such as St. Louis, Chicago, and Kansas City. Just as visiting the Ozarks is convenient from Columbia, so are visits to places like Kansas City or St. Louis. Either city is a two-hour interstate drive, giving Columbia residents access to major league professional sports, stage plays, and all the good things offered in a large city. Then they return to the refuge of a safe, quiet, clean hometown.

Making the decision to retire in Columbia is made easy by a unique program provided by Columbia's chamber of commerce. Volunteer retirees give newcomers an hour-and-a-half "windshield tour" of the city. The tour visits residential neighborhoods ranging from economical to deluxe. They drive you past the three colleges in town as well as by the golf courses and hospitals. You'll see the best shopping areas and visit Columbia's delightful downtown. This way potential retirees check out neighborhoods, home styles, and amenities without being pressured by a real estate agent.

Despite Columbia's upscale appearance, housing costs are below national averages. The most popular retiree housing choice here is the split-level ranch, usually of brick construction, with a large lawn. Condominiums are available for those who don't care for mowing lawns. Because of the college population, apartment rentals are often scarce. During the summer, however, temporary housing is easily found for those who want to savor the atmosphere of Columbia as a final test for livability. At least three developments are aimed at the retiree market. One development under way will feature golf-course living.

The economy here is solidly based on education, with three institutions of higher learning: the University of Missouri, Stephens College, and Columbia College, the city's major employers. This translates into a high level of prosperity, stability, and an almost recession-proof economy. The academic milieu enhances the city's cultural and social life with school activities that spill over into the community. It seems as if something is always happening for the public to participate in—lectures, concerts, sports events, or celebrations, some of which are free. The huge university library is open to the public for browsing and research, and although you can't check out books, the staff is very accommodating in helping you locate material. As you might guess Columbia is a great place for continuing education. Many retirees choose Columbia specifically for that purpose; a myriad of adult education programs reaches out to mature residents and encourages them in their quest for lifetime learning.

Education flows through all sectors of the community, even in law enforcement; 90 percent of Columbia police officers are college graduates. That may have something to do with the city's low crime rate, which is 30 percent below national average.

The university, with its medical school, confers another blessing on the community by leading the way in health care. In addition to the university hospital, seven other hospitals serve the

COLUMBIA WEATHER						
In degrees Fahrenheit						
	Jan.	April	July	Oct.	Rain	Snow
Daily highs	36	65	89	68	36"	23"
Daily lows	19	44	67	46		

COLUMBIA COST OF LIVING					
Percentage of	Overall	Housing	Medical	Groceries	Utilities
national average	98	95	95	95	102

community along with so many health-care personnel that one in five workers in Columbia is employed in a health-related occupation. A unique service provided by the university is the Elder Care Center. Its major goal is to keep patients out of nursing homes by providing activities to help them maintain high functional levels. The daily fee is often covered by Medicaid—which is less than half the usual nursing-home cost in the area. University students in physical, occupational, and speech therapy benefit from their experience from the center, and patients benefit from more robust health and postponement of nursing-home care.

Outdoor recreation is more than adequate. Besides two municipal golf courses and two private country clubs, there's the Twin Lakes Recreation Area, complete with boating, fishing, and swimming. A relatively new hiking and recreation trail follows the abandoned MKT Railroad line and will eventually connect up with hiking trails that cross the state. This 4.7-mile stretch invites jogging and biking through dense woods, past streambeds, rock cuts, and open meadows—a small escape to the country, yet just yards removed from the surrounding city. For inclement-weather exercise, the university hospital has organized a mall walker's club. At six-thirty every morning, long before the huge indoor Columbia Mall opens for business, you'll find several hundred walkers working on their stamina and blood pressure. In thirty minutes you can do two full laps, equaling almost 2 miles of vigorous walking, and you don't get rained on.

Oklahoma

When people think of Oklahoma they imagine flat plains extending to the horizon, perhaps rolling hills studded with oil derricks or farm machinery, and cattle fenced in by barbed wire. True, parts of Oklahoma fit this description, for this is a state renowned for cattle, agriculture, and petroleum. But, just as New York State isn't all Manhattan, Oklahoma is not all flat farm country.

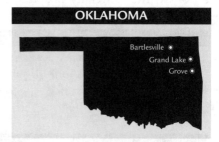

Parts of Oklahoma, particularly in the eastern and northern

portions, are hilly and
heavily forested, the tail end
of the Ozark Mountains.
Some places are even less
populated than the Mis-
souri and Arkansas Ozarks.
You can drive for miles with
barely a suggestion that
anyone might be living behind the solid mask of
forest that lines the high-

OKLAHOMA TAX PROFILE
Sales tax: 4.5% to 8.5%, drugs exempt
State income tax: graduated, 0.5% to 7% greater than $9,950; federal income tax deductible
Property taxes: about 0.7%
Intangibles tax: no
Social security taxed: no
Pensions taxed: excludes up to $8,000, depending on income level
Gasoline tax: 16¢ per gallon, plus possible local taxes

ways. Several dams take advantage of the deep river valleys to create
long, wide lakes that wiggle and squirm across the wooded landscape and through the hills. The largest, Eufala Reservoir, covers
more than 100,000 surface acres. At least eighteen lakes, most of
them built by the Army Corps of Engineers, provide recreation as
well as irrigation and power. This huge complex of water storage
changed forever the face of a state that once was in danger of drying
up and blowing away during the 1930s.

The desolation of Oklahoma's Dust Bowl, drought, and depression is a well-known piece of history. Those dismal times are far
behind as Oklahoma becomes a center for aerospace and aviation
industries. The latest agricultural technology, conservation, and
flood control protect the land from a repeat of the 1930s disaster.
Wonder of wonders: A deep river channel utilizing a system of dams
and locks links Tulsa with the Gulf of Mexico, making it an important seaport!

John Steinbeck's famous book, *The Grapes of Wrath,* dramatizes
the desperate condition of life in Oklahoma during the Dust Bowl
era. The book chronicles a dream of a good life in California and the
Joad family's struggle to get there. (Of course, that was before California suffered from graffiti, drive-by shootings, and Madonna.)

Today the children of those refugees who emigrated to California fifty to sixty years ago are old enough to retire. After suffering
the hardships of freeway traffic, high taxes, and idiotic politicians, the
Joad family dreams of a good life somewhere else. This time it's Oklahoma. Over the years they've kept in touch with relatives and friends
who didn't leave Oklahoma; visits between the two states were
common. So it seems natural that the second generation, now affluent, is making the reverse trek from the West Coast's "land of milk

and honey" to down-to-earth Oklahoma. Few have even a hint of an Oklahoma accent; they have no "country" mannerisms about them. Some don't even have relatives or family friends drawing them back here, yet Californians turn out to be Oklahoma's strongest boosters.

Grand Lake o' the Cherokees A series of lakes runs halfway down the state near the Missouri and Arkansas border. Each lake supports small towns that can be practical for retirement. One of the more popular areas is in the state's northeast corner, named after its largest lake, the Grand Lake o' the Cherokees. Sometimes it's called the Pensacola Dam Project or simply Grand Lake. The contraction "o" does not mean *of*, but *over*, to commemorate the Cherokee burial grounds that lie at the bottom of the lake. Sixty-six miles long, with 1,300 miles of shoreline and 60,000 surface acres of water, this is one of the Ozarks' largest bodies of water. Unlike many reservoirs created by the government, workers cleared trees and stumps before impoundment, greatly improving both navigation and aesthetics. The countryside around these lakes is not as rugged as the true Ozark mountains to the east or to the south in the Tenkiller Lake area, but the charm of the Ozark foothills is still evident.

The lake's wide stretches of water encourage sailboats, even full-fledged yachts capable of cruising in all kinds of weather. Some marinas specialize in sailboat moorings. Fishing is great; bass are so abundant that there's no size limit. Countless coves throughout the many crooks and branches of the lake make great places for picnics, should you become tired of torturing worms by sticking them with fishhooks. The rivers that run into the lake are famous for canoeing, an important tourist activity, with "canoe trails" as part of the Oklahoma park system.

The Grand Lake area supports more population than most Ozark waterways, with houses all along the lakeshore. Also, unlike many man-made lakes in the Midsouthern Hills, lakefront ownership is not restricted, and private docks are allowed. In addition to

TYPICAL RURAL OKLAHOMA COST OF LIVING					
Percentage of national average	Overall 90	Housing 77	Medical 92	Groceries 90	Utilities 100

simple fishing piers, some folks build flat docks like floating patios; other boat docks are covered and enclosed floating cabins of sorts. For years these lakes were considered the playground of Oklahoma oil patriarchs and big-city vacationers. They have long been popular weekend retreats for residents of northern Oklahoma, Missouri, Kansas, and Arkansas. Lately, however, the area is gaining prominence as a retirement destination.

Grand Lake even has a country club–type development. The 600-acre Coves of Bird Island (actually a peninsula) has a golf course, clubhouse, restaurant, and about 150 homes, mostly owned by retirees. The usual swimming pools, tennis courts, and twenty-four-hour security are provided, a plus for those who like to leave their homes and travel. Don't expect to see mobile homes or trailers here; they're not permitted. Residents do their shopping in nearby Grove or in Langley.

A number of little towns sit on the shore of Grand Lake, the largest being Grove, with a population of almost 5,000. About twice that number living nearby consider Grove to be their hometown as well. Without large industry to provide employment, most folks either work in service jobs or are retired. An estimated 30 percent of the total population are retired—a very high percentage. Heavy shopping is available in Joplin (Missouri), a forty-five-minute drive, or 75 miles away in Tulsa. Grove is fortunate to have its own hospital. Another hospital is located in Vinita, a half-hour drive away.

Several properties were listed for more than $300,000, but they were top quality, with four or more bedrooms and deluxe docks with multiple slips. Most lakefront property starts in the low $100,000 range, although some smaller homes on the lake sell for as low as $80,000. Homes within walking distance of the lakes can be had for $60,000 and sometimes even below this amount.

Bartlesville   Not everyone is enamored of the idea of living in Ozark small towns, and many retirees rank hunting and fishing low on their must-have list. Bartlesville is our idea of Oklahoma small-city living, a place consistently given high marks for quality of life by national publications. Located in the gently rolling grasslands of northern Oklahoma, Bartlesville is just forty-five minutes from Tulsa International Airport and a short drive to Ozark lake environs.

The city is small enough (pop. 34,000) that newcomers can make friends throughout the community, yet Bartlesville is sufficiently

BARTLESVILLE WEATHER						
In degrees Fahrenheit						
	Jan.	April	July	Oct.	Rain	Snow
Daily highs	46	72	93	75	38"	9"
Daily lows	24	49	72	50		

BARTLESVILLE COST OF LIVING					
Percentage of national average	Overall 92	Housing 84	Medical 94	Groceries 97	Utilities 89

ample in size to afford amenities missing from more rustic sections of Oklahoma. In fact the showcase entertainment events that Bartlesville stages each year would do honors to a much larger city. Its famous community center, designed by Frank Lloyd Wright, hosts the internationally acclaimed OK Mozart Festival. This occasion lasts ten days in mid-June, hosting guest artists from all over the world. The entire populace is invited to participate.

Bartlesville Community Center is not one of those public buildings that sits idle between big-time events. More than 200 community-service groups stage art shows, performances, exhibitions, festivals, and parties. My wife and I attended a wedding dinner there—it was a fabulous evening! The seventy-five-piece Bartlesville Symphony is recognized as one of the best in the country. The Bartlesville Civic Ballet offers a mixed palette of music and dance, and the Theater Guild presents year-round entertainment. This is hardly what one would expect to find in small-town Oklahoma!

Bartlesville's overall cost of living is 8 percent below average. Housing costs fall 16 percent below national averages, making quality living in a nice neighborhood affordable.

Kentucky

The Mississippi River marks Kentucky's western border, and the deep valleys and rugged gorges of the Appalachians delimits its eastern. In between you'll find a wide selection of countrysides from which to choose: from gently rolling farming country to magnificent panoramas of the Blue Ridge Mountains; from quiet, rural crossroad communities to sophisticated cities and university towns. The first region west of the Allegheny Mountains settled by American pioneers, Kentucky epitomizes America's rugged frontier heritage. This is the country of Daniel Boone, the Hatfields and McCoys,

and good ol' mountain music. Today it's much more than that. With up-to-date services, neighborly people, and modern shopping everywhere, Kentucky is a great choice for retirement.

Modern-day transportation, with paved highways crisscrossing the state, has opened the backcountry to the world. A robust economic development since the end of World War II boosted most rural areas out of Al Capp's Dogpatch past. No longer are large parts of the state isolated and populated with illiterate mountaineers and moonshiners. Kentucky today is too open for that. This opening of the state also created retirement opportunities that didn't exist previously. But the entire state certainly hasn't become a carbon copy of middle America. Many charming areas back

KENTUCKY TAX PROFILE
Sales tax: 6%, food and drugs exempt
State income tax: graduated, 2% to 6% greater than $8,000; can't deduct federal income tax
Property taxes: average 1%
Intangibles tax: yes
Social security taxed: no
Pensions taxed: private pensions taxable
Gasoline tax: 15¢ per gallon

in the hills are almost as rustic and unspoiled as ever. And because most Kentucky counties have opted for prohibition, you can bet some of those piney hills still contain moonshiners.

Kentucky is particularly attractive for Midwestern and Northern retirees who see advantages in retiring close to their prior homes, in inexpensive, low-crime surroundings. The relatively mild, four-season weather easily satisfies requirements for those who insist on colorful autumns, invigorating winters, and glorious springs.

Bowling Green   About an hour's drive north of Nashville (65 miles by Interstate 65) and the Nashville International Airport is the delightful little city of Bowling Green. Because of its central location (within one day's drive of three-fourths of the U.S. population), this

BOWLING GREEN WEATHER						
In degrees Fahrenheit						
	Jan.	April	July	Oct.	Rain	Snow
Daily highs	41	68	88	69	43"	14"
Daily lows	24	46	67	46		

BOWLING GREEN AREA COST OF LIVING					
	Overall	Housing	Medical	Groceries	Utilities
Percentage of national average	96	88	100	108	96

is becoming a popular retirement location for fugitives from crowded Northern cities. The interstate, a major north-south artery, facilitates transportation and makes it easy for the grandchildren to visit.

Originally, the town was called The Barrens, after the Barren River that runs through the site, but in 1797 it was renamed something a bit more descriptive of the area: Bowling Green. The second name derived from the habit of court officials and visiting attorneys amusing themselves between trials by bowling on the lawn beside the old courthouse. The surrounding countryside is as green as its name—lush, with rolling meadows surrounded by white fences, with thoroughbred horses munching away at the Kentucky bluegrass. Bowling Green looks exactly as one imagines Kentucky should look.

Because of its location, Bowling Green serves as a regional hub for retail shopping and medical services. And because this is the only place between Louisville and Nashville where alcohol is served, Bowling Green's higher-quality restaurants attract folks from miles around for celebrating that special occasion. According to a recent survey, Bowling Green has more restaurants per capita than any other U.S. city except San Francisco.

Another factor in maintaining an upscale atmosphere is the presence of Western Kentucky University, with 15,000 students adding intellectual warmth. The university maintains a symphony orchestra and two theater groups, and it hosts frequent visits from touring artists and entertainers. Other cultural offerings are presented by the Capitol Arts Center and the Public Theatre of Kentucky.

Participation in university affairs is made easy by Kentucky's policy of senior-citizen scholarships that pay the full cost of tuition. This is true for both full-time and part-time students and applies toward either graduate or undergraduate courses. Numerous continuing-education programs are also offered, ranging from history of American presidents to motorcycle training.

Although Bowling Green is a fine example of a larger Kentucky town, it's not big enough to suffer from big-city problems. Crime rates here are low, pollution is almost nonexistent, and the cost of living is 7 percent below national average. Housing and utility costs are exceptionally low, with homes selling for 8 percent below average and utilities at 6 percent less than national averages.

Murray   Murray is a small city that consistently garners recommendations from retirement writers as a good place to relocate. It's also an excellent example of how good things can happen to a community when retirees move in. A few years ago Murray received a rash of national publicity when a popular retirement guide designated the town as the year's "top-rated" retirement location. This created an enormous amount of interest among folks planning retirement; before long, 250 couples made the move to Murray. Today's population is about 16,000.

As you might expect this had a snowball effect on the area's economy. The real estate market zoomed out of the doldrums and, before long, exhausted its inventory. Building construction increased to keep pace. At last report five new housing developments were under way. In short retiree immigration has proven to be an economic bonanza. Another positive side effect: These extra

MURRAY WEATHER						
In degrees Fahrenheit						
	Jan.	April	July	Oct.	Rain	Snow
Daily highs	42	68	88	71	47"	12"
Daily lows	25	48	69	47		

MURRAY AREA COST OF LIVING					
Percentage of national average	Overall	Housing	Medical	Groceries	Utilities
	88	77	85	93	82

retirees were enough to push the city into enlarging the senior citizens' center and adding more services. The staff at the local center, by the way, is dedicated and enthusiastic about plans for the facility's future.

What were the bad effects? Apparently none. Real estate sells at 14 percent below national averages, and although the cost of living may have gone up slightly, it is still 8 percent under most areas of the nation. People moving into the mid-South from most parts of the country feel like bandits as they sign the escrow papers. According to the FBI's last report, Murray came in very high in personal safety, with a record indicating that most criminals in Murray must have retired or moved away.

One of the volunteer workers at the Senior Center had retired from California and told of a special California Club composed of others like her who had also chosen Kentucky for retirement. It turns out that a colleague of mine, who had lived in California for the past two decades, recently retired in Murray. When I asked why, he and his wife explained that with children living in St. Louis and Nashville, they were within a few hours' drive of either place. They also liked fishing in the nearby lake. What were the drawbacks? They had to admit that snow and ice took some getting used to, but because they were originally from Canada, no problem there. The lack of good restaurants (this being a dry county) was the only other thing they missed from their California experience.

Danville   Kentucky's bluegrass region is world famous for its green pastoral beauty, with picturesque horse farms and wooded countryside. The college town of Danville (pop. 16,000) holds a key position as cultural and business center of the area. It's a place of wide, tree-lined streets, low crime, light traffic, and no parking meters. Danville's downtown is alive and well, convenient for those who live near the city center, and a great place for strolling and greeting friends.

The historic town center is well preserved, with wide streets and parks nearby. Stately old mansions, some dating back to the early 1800s, grace tree-shaded streets of the district known as Beaten Biscuit Row. You'll find antiques shopping, quaint restaurants, and charming bed-and-breakfast inns in this neighborhood, as well as many old homes that would be great for retirement living.

Senior citizens are a vital part of the Danville community. A new, well-equipped senior citizens center has recently been added to the area. The newly built structure includes an activity room, an exercise room, and a dining room. The facility provides activities, including lunches, speakers, shopping excursions, day-long outings, dancing and fitness sessions, and crafts.

Danville's Centre College provides community access to internationally recognized performing artists and world-class exhibitions in its Norton Center for the Arts. The school was the site of a presidential debate during the Bush–Gore campaign. In addition to multiple cultural offerings at the school, Danville has several theaters, including an outdoor dinner theater and several art galleries in the heart of its historic downtown.

Housing in Danville ranges from historic homes around the town center to newer homes toward the city's edge and tranquil rural homesteads on rolling farm and forest land. Even the most secluded regions of the county are only minutes away from shopping. Because of the school, a good supply of apartment and home rentals are available. Lakeside and golf course homesites are available just minutes from Danville. Real estate prices are well below national averages.

Old Bridge Golf Club, an eighteen-hole course open to public play on Lake Herrington, is reputed to be one of the best courses in the region. It has a country-club setting, with an Olympic-size pool and lighted tennis courts. Danville is in a dry county, but there is a country club where you are allowed to bring

DANVILLE–BEREA–LEXINGTON AREA WEATHER						
In degrees Fahrenheit						
	Jan.	April	July	Oct.	Rain	Snow
Daily highs	40	66	86	68	46"	16"
Daily lows	23	44	66	46		

DANVILLE–BEREA AREA COST OF LIVING					
	Overall	Housing	Medical	Groceries	Utilities
Percentage of national average	89	78	85	88	100

your own wine and liquor. Lexington, 35 miles away, does sell liquor.

Medical needs are served by a 177-bed, acute-care hospital. The facility offers comprehensive care representing more than twenty medical specialties, backed by state-of-the-art technology. Emergency care is staffed twenty-four hours a day.

Berea   About forty-five minutes east of Danville, just off Interstate 75 and nestled at the edge of the Cumberland foothills, you'll find another college town that is retiree-friendly. Berea is known as the "Folk Arts and Crafts Capital" of Kentucky's Appalachia region. Artists, weavers, potters, and other professional craftspeople have studios in town, especially in the old town sector of Berea. They carry on a tradition that started in the late 1800s. The historic section also features several interesting antiques stores, as well as shops and galleries displaying the finest in handcrafted work.

With a population of 12,000 inhabitants, Berea is located 39 miles from Lexington, where folks do heavy-duty shopping. Unlike many college towns, the "downtown" commerce has shifted to the strip-mall complex on the edge of town. Nevertheless, a small commercial area adjacent to the campus is thriving. The Berea Country Club, with a nine-hole golf course, is open year-round. Several other golf courses are within a short drive from town. Fishing lakes abound in the region, and the Appalachian foothills are heavily forested and full of wild game.

Berea College, founded in 1855, is very unusual in that students don't pay tuition but must work on campus about fifteen hours a week in lieu of tuition. Student crafts are featured at the historic Boone Tavern, near the campus. Because of the school's unusual orientation, adult classes for the community aren't offered on campus. However, the school's facility is used for Elderhostel classes, with many courses in arts, crafts, and music of the Appalachians. The school does make its recreational, cultural, and entertainment attractions available to the public, mostly at no charge.

Berea is divided into three types of residential areas. First is the old town historic district, with older, inexpensive homes priced from $65,000. Next are the homes around the campus, which are often stately, as you would expect in a college town. Finally newer homes away from the older sections can be purchased

LEXINGTON AREA COST OF LIVING					
Percentage of	Overall	Housing	Medical	Groceries	Utilities
national average	98	97	97	100	98

for as little as $85,000. Rentals seem to be plentiful, with one group of town homes starting around $300 a month for a one-bedroom unit.

Berea Hospital is the primary health-care facility. The facility has twenty-seven medical specialists on staff. The Berea Health Care Center is a forty-bed nursing facility.

Lexington   Lexington was founded in 1775, seventeen years before Kentucky became a state. By 1820 it was one of the largest and wealthiest towns west of the Allegheny Mountains. So cultured was its lifestyle, Lexington gained the nickname "Athens of the West." (In those days anyplace this side of Pittsburgh was considered "west.") Over the years Lexington's image hasn't tarnished.

Today Lexington is a modern, bustling city with a population approaching 250,000 and is the commercial focus of the region. This is the home of the University of Kentucky. The school's more than 30,000 students, faculty, and staff contribute greatly to the local economy as well as enhance the intellectual atmosphere. Among early students there were alumni that include Jefferson Davis and Stephen F. Austin.

Lexington Memorial Hospital helps covers the medical-care scene here. With a staff of 124 specialists in all fields of medicine, health-care availability ranks high. The Central Baptist Hospital provides a 383-bed facility. Real estate is slightly below national averages, with a wide variety of neighborhoods to choose from, as well as some delightful rural areas not very far from Lexington's center of town.

Tennessee

Tennessee is somewhat of a mirror image of Kentucky to the north and Arkansas to the west. Eastward the land slopes

gradually upward until the foothills finally become the Appalachian Mountains. They grow ever more rugged, reaching their highest peaks in eastern Tennessee, near the state's border with the Carolinas.

Near the Mississippi River, plains of fertile bottomlands alternate with dense hardwood forests. King Cotton once ruled this domain, a land steeped in the genteel traditions of the Old South. Flat-to-rolling land covers much of the eastern portions of Tennessee, with rich agricultural fields hedged with rows of trees, neat and prosperous-looking farmhouses, barns, and silos. Most smaller towns here look pretty much like any in Middle America. Memphis and Nashville are the large cities.

TENNESSEE TAX PROFILE

Sales tax: 6% to 8.5%, food, drugs exempt
State income tax: 6% on interest and dividends; older than sixty-five, $9,000 exemption
Property taxes: vary from 1.46% to 2.37%
Intangibles tax: no
Social security taxed: no
Pensions taxed: no
Gasoline tax: 21¢ per gallon

As you move eastward you come upon Tennessee's heartland, a region of gently rolling hills and bluegrass meadows. Continuing east, the landscape grows more scenic with every mile. Before long you find yourselves in foothill country and finally in Tennessee's high country, rugged, tree-shrouded mountains that cross into the Carolinas and the Blue Ridge Mountains.

Clarksville   Located on the northern border next to Kentucky, Clarksville sits conveniently on an interstate highway that whisks you to the big city of Nashville in less than forty-five minutes. This is one of our favorite Midsouthern Hills locations. Clarksville combines an atmosphere of small-town living with city and urban conveniences.

Don't misunderstand—Clarksville is no small town. An estimated 95,000 population places it into the realm of a city, yet it somehow manages to maintain the flavor of small-town life. This is a place where friends are constantly honking greetings to each other as they drive around town. Yet shopping malls and complexes are as large and complete as you could hope for in a much bigger city.

For those who cannot live without hauling fish out of the water or killing ducks, this is a great place to be, with all the conveniences

CLARKSVILLE WEATHER						
In degrees Fahrenheit						
	Jan.	April	July	Oct.	Rain	Snow
Daily highs	46	71	90	72	48"	11"
Daily lows	28	48	69	48		

CLARKSVILLE COST OF LIVING					
Percentage of	Overall	Housing	Medical	Groceries	Utilities
national average	91	82	94	91	94

of a city plus great hunting and fishing nearby. The Land Between the Lakes recreational area is 35 miles away, with 170,000 acres of public lands for hiking, camping, fishing, and seasonal scheduled hunting. The peaceful Cumberland River flows through Clarksville; pleasure boats cruise where huge paddle-wheelers once carried tobacco and cotton for European ports. A half-hour drive from pleasant residential neighborhoods can take you to thick forests or rich farms and bluegrass meadows where horse breeding is a major industry. This is where the Tennessee Walking Horse breed was developed.

For big-city life nearby Nashville offers fine restaurants, historical museums, and its famous Grand Ole Opry. Seems as if every country and western star from Minnie Pearl to Conway Twitty has a museum dedicated to them. But to me the most interesting museum is the home of President Andrew Jackson, where his original log cabin homestead still stands behind the stately Hermitage, the Greek Revival mansion he built during his more successful career.

A condition that makes Clarksville different from many Midsouthern Hills towns is the large number of out-of-state folks who retire here. This happens whenever you combine a pleasant area with a large military base like Fort Campbell, which straddles the Tennessee–Kentucky state line adjacent to Clarksville. The base covers 105,000 acres, mostly in Tennessee, but because the post office is in Kentucky, that state claims Fort Campbell as its own. Military retirees enjoy base PX privileges and medical benefits. The fort, almost a city in itself, has a population of 38,000, with a PX as large as a shopping center, plus seven on-post schools for military dependents.

The early-day prosperity of the tobacco plantations shows clearly in the beautiful antebellum mansions in town. Set back from the street among magnificent oak and magnolia trees, surrounded by acres of lawn, these old homes are among the best preserved in the South. This notion of large lawns carries over into modern housing. Big lots are in. Even humble two-bedroom homes sit on enormous lots with awesome expanses of lawn—awesome because of the amount of energy spent in keeping the grass mowed. Yet folks tell you with straight faces, "I really enjoy yard work. Cutting grass is relaxing." Yes, of course it is. That's why rich people are so tense; they hire someone else to cut the grass.

Our previous research showed Clarksville to be one of the housing bargains of the nation. Median sales prices are consistently below the national average. But conditions change here, depending upon what happens at Fort Campbell. When world conditions are peaceful, Fort Campbell operates with full staff and demand for housing is up. But when some military problems arise somewhere in the world, troops here are the first to go. When this happens vacancies become easy to find and For Sale signs sprout on lawns.

Clarksville offers a large range of activities. Austin Peay State University is located here, complete with an active theater department that produces five shows a season ranging from comedy to serious theater and even musicals. A jazz festival is held in March and a spring opera in May. Guest-artist recitals are offered throughout the year, with free admission. Fort Campbell has an entertainment-services office, and it produces seven theatrical productions a year, open to the public.

Thirty miles to the west of Clarksville is the little town of Dover. This is the gateway to the Land Between the Lakes, a 170,000-acre wilderness area that stretches over a narrow peninsula, 40 miles between Kentucky Lake and Lake Barkley. Almost 90 percent of this area is unspoiled forest, with just a few scattered farms and some facilities for boat launching, hunting, and fishing. Some retirees from Clarksville have moved into Dover, attracted by exceptionally low housing costs, peaceful living, and proximity to hunting and fishing in the Land Between the Lakes. Dover is an interesting town but verges on being provincial, with fewer outsiders in residence. To retire here happily, you'll have to love small-town living.

Crossville   East from Nashville along Interstate 40 or southeast on Interstate 24 brings you to the foothills of the Blue Ridge Mountains and the town of Crossville. While doing research in Crossville, we noticed that it looked somehow different from similar Tennessee towns. Much of the downtown construction seemed to be fairly recent, with fewer Civil War–era buildings than one might expect. Farms surrounding the town lacked older-looking houses and barns, the kind built before the Civil War. When we asked about it, a young lady who worked in a local business disagreed that the buildings are new, saying, "No sir, Crossville is a very old town. Almost nothing hereabouts is new." When we asked, "How old?" She replied, "Well, I understand that many buildings here date back to the days of the Franklin D. Roosevelt administration." We had to agree that was indeed a long time ago.

It turns out that until the Great Depression Crossville was pretty much woods and empty countryside. Despite rich soil and abundant rainfall, the district had been all but ignored. FDR's New Deal administration, searching for worthwhile projects to bootstrap the country out of the depression, seized upon a plan to develop the Crossville region as a model agricultural center. Government workers cleared forests, and homesteaders were given loans and seed money to get started. The plan evidently worked, because this is a very prosperous area today. Cheap electricity from the Tennessee Valley Authority Project lured industry into the area, adding jobs and even more prosperity.

As do most larger-sized towns in the South, Crossville enjoys friendly neighbors and inexpensive housing. The level of services for senior citizens is as good as anywhere in the state, with enthusiastic and imaginative folks running programs.

The town is dry, with residents routinely making the trek to Knoxville for alcohol—a 70-mile drive each way. When I expressed dismay that drunks should be free-wheeling down the interstate for their supplies, residents cheerfully assured me that bootleggers are plentiful in Crossville. "Why, you can buy anything you want, right here!" This weird custom of a community supporting prohibition and bootleggers at the same time never fails to puzzle me.

Property is quite affordable in Crossville and environs. Homes in town are usually on large lots with plenty of mature shade trees. On the town's outskirts larger lots are the rule, with small farms commonly used as retirement homes.

CROSSVILLE WEATHER					
In degrees Fahrenheit					
	Jan.	April	July	Oct.	Rain	Snow
Daily highs	47	71	87	70	47"	12"
Daily lows	29	48	68	48		

CROSSVILLE AREA COST OF LIVING					
Percentage of national average	Overall	Housing	Medical	Groceries	Utilities
	84	78	77	89	73

Fairfield Glade   When retirement writers speak of Crossville, chances are they have one of the special country-club developments in mind. There are several. Fairfield Glade is the oldest and the largest in the area, possibly the largest in the entire state. It's about 15 miles from Crossville and has been under development for two decades. Its year-round population is between 4,500 and 5,000, but thousands more enjoy the facilities on a vacation and part-time retirement basis. The corporation that put the package together has lots of experience—they have similar operations throughout the retirement areas of the nation.

Over the years Fairfield Glade has matured gracefully. It has changed from a glitzy promotion into a series of stable, pleasant neighborhoods scattered throughout the 12,000 acres. Eleven lakes and four championship golf courses with all the adjuncts—such as tennis, swimming pools, and restaurants—uphold the original country-club tradition.

Unlike some developments all promised facilities seem to have materialized. A large gymnasium offers everything from basketball to billiards to bicycle rentals. A riding stable presents complete equestrian facilities and miles of hiking and riding trails. There is a fully functional shopping mall (20,000 square feet under one roof) and a range of good-quality restaurants. Of course the better establishments serve cocktails to members of Fairfield Glade. A bus service takes residents into Crossville.

Homes surrounding this lake/golf course complex are well built, attractively priced, and architecturally pleasing. Acres of wooded and green space separate the various tracts. The closer to the golf course, the more expensive the homes.

Holiday Hills   Closer to Crossville, just a few miles from the downtown section, is the retirement development of Holiday Hills. It spreads over 1,200 acres of prime land around a lake and a golf course. Apparently this one also started as a time-share resort, but retirement homes have become the style. The tennis and clubhouse facilities are excellent.

Holiday Hills is newer than Fairfield Glade and more convenient to town. Homes are priced comparably to those in Fairfield Glade, and its natural setting is just as beautiful. An interesting feature is the Cumberland County Playhouse, located just outside the development's main gate. Dramas, musicals, and ballets draw visitors from all over the nation.

Nearby is another retirement development, a no-frills place called the Orchards. In recognition of retirees' propensity for recreational-vehicle travel, they build carports high enough to accommodate RVs. The Crossville area attracts retirees from Indiana, Ohio, and Illinois, but the hottest place of origin is Michigan, particularly from the Detroit area, which is an especially popular place to be *from*.

Cookeville   A tranquil and comfortable little city located about 80 miles east of Nashville and 100 miles west of Knoxville on Interstate 40, Cookeville nestles in an area known as the Upper Cumberland region, a place of hills, valleys, waterfalls, and scenic country. The population here is nearly 26,000, augmented by numerous "commuters" who live in nearby small communities or on rural properties and who travel to Cookeville each day to work, go to school, receive health care, and participate in leisure-time activities.

COOKEVILLE WEATHER					
In degrees Fahrenheit					
	Jan.	April	July	Oct.	Rain	Snow
Daily highs	44	68	87	71	51"	8"
Daily lows	24	44	63	44		

COOKEVILLE AREA COST OF LIVING					
Percentage of	Overall	Housing	Medical	Groceries	Utilities
national average	83	75	79	90	75

Cookeville often scores high in popular retirement guides as one of the better retirement "off-the-beaten-track destinations." Not long ago the city was featured in a *Where to Retire* magazine article: "Six Great Low-Cost Towns." According to the latest ACCRA cost of living figures, Cookeville is well below national average. According to local people Cookeville also experiences Tennessee's lowest crime rate and lowest property taxes.

Five rivers, seven state parks, and three major lakes—all within minutes of Cookeville—offer camping, picnicking, hiking, and fishing. Cane Creek Park, a 260-acre facility with a 56-acre lake, is closest to Cookeville. Twelve golf courses, within a few minutes' drive, cater to golfers of varying abilities, and Cookeville Community Center has a half-dozen tennis courts available for public play.

The campus of Tennessee Technological University serves as a cultural center for residents of Cookeville and the Upper Cumberland region, hosting concerts, operettas, and recitals by professional artists. The school's Bryan Fine Arts Center hosts a symphony orchestra, art shows, lectures, music, and dance. The Cookeville Drama Center sponsors touring companies, as well as local performers belonging to two grassroots theater groups.

Cookeville Regional Medical Center has been the health-care provider for the Upper Cumberland region since 1950. This 227-bed hospital has a staff of more than ninety physicians with specialties in twenty-eight fields of medicine. A $20-million expansion is under way to provide a comprehensive cancer treatment center and an open-heart surgery center.

Chattanooga   Returning to Chattanooga for the first time in more than twenty years came as a pleasant surprise for this writer. Of course the lushly forested hills and mountains that surround the city will never change, and the peaceful Tennessee River meanders through the city, just as always. Lush forested mountains are the predominant feature here. Chattanooga is bordered by Signal Mountain to the north and Lookout Mountain to the south. Both areas are known for some rather upscale homes that enjoy spectacular views of Chattanooga and the wide bends of the Tennessee River in the valley below.

The big change is Chattanooga's rejuvenated city center. Twenty years ago the city was described as "having an ecological

CHATTANOOGA WEATHER					
In degrees Fahrenheit					
	Jan.	April	July	Oct.	Rain	Snow
Daily highs	48	73	89	72	53"	4"
Daily lows	29	48	68	48		

CHATTANOOGA AREA COST OF LIVING					
	Overall	Housing	Medical	Groceries	Utilities
Percentage of national average	93	83	89	97	93

heart attack," tortured by air pollution, urban decay, and social problems. But the residents took matters to heart and demanded a change. From a rundown, tired remnant of early-twentieth-century business failures, downtown Chattanooga has become an exceptionally viable, user-friendly—yes, even a beautiful—city. It's become a textbook example of how a city can be rescued and how its beauty can be restored.

The renaissance wasn't confined to downtown Chattanooga. Throughout the area neighborhoods have been busy sprucing up. Chattanooga is composed of so many distinct community-neighborhoods, each with its own distinct personality, that seven independent chamber of commerce offices serve the metropolitan area. The population today is close to 160,000, with another 300,000 persons residing in the surrounding countryside. This is a prosperous region, with average household income in the $40,000 range. Many lovely neighborhoods reflect this level of prosperity.

As you would surmise, outdoor recreation abounds in a region that is full of forested mountains, lakes, and rivers. But there are plenty of outdoor sports in Chattanooga itself, with some 200 tennis courts, both public and private, available throughout the city. Add to this seven public and ten private golf courses, and weather that allows outdoor play most of the year, and you have respectable recreational opportunities.

With five major health facilities serving the region, Chattanooga is proud of its hospitals. Among the four of them, they offer almost 1,600 beds and specialists in all conceivable fields. One hospital, Columbia East Ridge, specializes in women's health care.

CHAPTER 6

Texas: The B-i-i-g State

YOU DON'T HAVE TO BE TOLD that Texas is one enormous state. Give a Texan half a chance and he'll tell you all about it. Don't give him a chance and he'll tell you anyway. The truth is Texas is almost as large as Texans claim, and that's pretty darn big. It's bigger than any country in Europe except for Russia, and ten times larger than many European countries. Not only is Texas spacious, but it boasts some of the prettiest scenery you can imagine, as well as some of the most boring. This wide range of climate, scenery, and elevation presents a broad menu of retirement options, something for almost every taste.

Texas's range of climates varies wildly. The subtropical southern tip of the state never sees snow and thinks any temperature below sixty degrees is downright chilly. At the other extreme, the high plains of the northern Panhandle region can be one of the coldest conceivable places in the winter, yet it can also be one of the hottest places this side of Death Valley in the summer. The Gulf Coast is as humid as Florida, and west Texas is dry as the proverbial bone. You'll encounter large cities and small villages and medium-size places perfect for retirement. Landscapes vary from plains to deserts to seashores to mountains. Variety is the spice of Texas retirement choices!

TEXAS TAX PROFILE
Sales tax: 6.25% to 8.25%, food, drugs exempt
State income tax: no
Property taxes: about 2.2%
Intangibles tax: no
Social security taxed: no
Pensions taxed: no
Gasoline tax: 20¢ per gallon

The Texas Gulf Coast

With more than 600 miles of the Texas coast facing the Gulf of Mexico, one would expect beachfront developments galore. The fact is that most of the Texas waterfront is uninhabited. Furthermore, almost all the mainland faces not the Gulf, but offshore islands and narrow peninsulas that effectively shut off the open gulf waters. For the most part these islands are

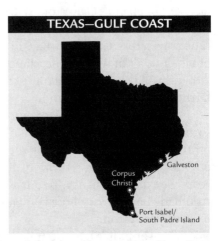

long and narrow, composed of sand dunes and unexplored beaches. Much of the actual coast is little changed from the days in the early 1800s when the French pirate Jean Lafitte used the islands as a base.

Long stretches of these islands, as well as parts of the mainland, are designated as wildlife refuges. Whooping cranes and Kemp's Ridley sea turtles are making a comeback after what once seemed almost certain extinction. Turtle eggs from Mexico planted on the Padre Islands about thirty years ago are beginning to show wonderful results. The hatchlings from the experiment have grown into adult turtles and are returning to their beach of origin to nest in a protected environment. When the new batches of eggs hatch and the baby turtles start for the sea, they are quickly captured and cared for in special pens until they're old enough to have a good chance for survival.

This is a fisherman's paradise. Both the channel and Gulf sides of the long islands teem with fish. From beaches and piers you can expect to catch redfish, speckled and sand trout, flounder, sheepshead, skipjack, croakers, and drum. Group boats offer bay and deep-sea fishing, with charter cruisers available for individual or small-party sport. The offshore game includes tarpon, sailfish, kingfish, marlin, mackerel, pompano, ling cod, bonito, and red snapper, among others. By far fishing is the major sport attraction for retirees who have chosen the Texas Gulf Coast for their home.

Galveston   On the entire Texas coast only one city actually faces the open gulf: Galveston. With a population of almost 60,000, it occupies one of those long islands and is reached via a lengthy causeway across Galveston Bay. Except for this 32-mile stretch of beach—not all of which is developed—there is little residential construction on the Gulf, just a tiny portion around Corpus Christi and farther south on Padre Island.

Many years ago Galveston was one of our favorite weekend resorts; we visited as often as we could, swimming in the surf, crabbing off the jetties, and driving along the beach with the waves playing at our car wheels. Upon returning, after an interval of almost thirty years, we expected change. To our surprise we discovered that Galveston had changed very little compared with the enormous changes in nearby Houston.

This shouldn't have been so surprising, because limited space on Galveston Island long ago filled to capacity with homes and businesses. The only new construction possible is replacing old buildings with new, something the local people are reluctant to permit. The old downtown section, instead of being replaced by slick new glass-and-steel monsters, has been preserved and restored to a charming, turn-of-the-twentieth-century state. Old brick and cast-iron fronts with wrought-iron balconies give the area a New Orleans French Quarter feeling. One street has been turned into a pedestrian mall, complete with restaurants, smart shops, and park benches for sunning and people-watching.

True, along the beachfront some older homes and buildings slowly give way to newer, more profitable construction focused on tourist dollars. But change is slow in coming. Most of the town is still the same: old-fashioned and comparatively inexpensive. Surf fishermen can try their luck almost anywhere along the beach. There are free municipal jetties and rock groin piers at regular intervals. If you fail to catch anything, markets sell the freshest catch found anywhere—right out of the Gulf into your frying pan.

People who don't live here think of Galveston as a weekend or vacation hot spot, a convention site, a place to go and blow off steam. However, there is a surprisingly intellectual air about Galveston. The University of Texas medical school is in downtown Galveston, as well as a branch of Texas A&M and a community college. These are serious students, some interested in art and literature to the exclusion of fishing (heaven forbid).

GALVESTON WEATHER					
In degrees Fahrenheit					
	Jan.	April	July	Oct.	Rain	Snow
Daily highs	59	73	87	78	40"	—
Daily lows	48	65	79	68		

Today the beach outside town is no longer deserted and wild, but is often lined with ugly, unpainted summer homes that are built on 15-foot stilts to avoid high waves during hurricane weather. (All along the Gulf Coast, from Key West to the tip of Texas, you find this stilt construction. Insurance companies insist on new buildings having stilts; it cuts their losses considerably.) Some owners successfully disguise the stilts by screening the lower portions of their houses, turning them into garages and storage spaces. This disguise makes the houses look like attractive two-story homes. But others don't bother, making stretches of beach look as if they had been invaded by spindly-legged monsters.

Corpus Christi   The only other major city on the Texas coast is Corpus Christi, a fast-growing metropolis of 277,000 inhabitants. It's actually not on the Gulf, but on a large bay, sheltered from open water by 30-mile-long Mustang Island. A major deepwater port, Corpus is large enough to mask the tourist crowds in all but the most hectic times (college semester breaks). For the most part, it looks like an ordinary, contemporary city—pleasant and unusually neat. It even has a modern, high-rise downtown. A seawall runs along the downtown area, with stairs that lead down to the water and a yacht basin. Palm-lined boulevards and cosmopolitan hotels and office buildings complete the picture.

Unlike Galveston, which sits exposed to the whims of hurricane-driven tides, Corpus Christi enjoys the protection of offshore islands. Thus construction work isn't impeded by the constant threat of flood. The town as a whole has a relaxed look about it.

Medical services are excellent here, with eleven hospitals as well as the military medical facilities serving the local naval air station. (Numerous retired military families live here.) Educational and cultural needs are met by a two-year college as well as a state university.

CORPUS CHRISTI WEATHER					
In degrees Fahrenheit					
	Jan.	April	July	Oct.	Rain	Snow
Daily highs	69	82	90	82	28"	—
Daily lows	52	67	75	66		

A new aquarium is becoming one of the major tourist attractions, with its 132,000-gallon deepwater exhibit.

Because the Corpus Christi area offers the only beach access along many miles of coastline, it has become quite popular as a resort. Not only are there beaches along the bay, but also there are 110 miles of sand and surf on the islands that shelter the mainland. Corpus has become almost as famous as Fort Lauderdale, Florida, for its assemblage of frolicking college students during semester break. As many as 100,000 tourists—an uncounted number of them college students—flock to Corpus Christi and Mustang Island to celebrate every spring.

Because of these sporadic visits by enthusiastic, youthful celebrants, local crime statistics can become distorted. The police are kept busy arresting drunks, breaking up fistfights, and stopping exuberant youngsters from destroying motel rooms. These offenses show up in the FBI's crime reports even though they are crimes that don't really affect ordinary residents or retirees, who neither live in nor frequent the tourist areas during the wild days.

South Padre Island   From time to time travel writers describe the coast between Corpus Christi and the tip of Texas—where it touches the Mexican border—as Texas's Riviera. Nothing could be further from the truth; this is one of the most deserted and unpopulated places in the United States. But that's its charm. Except for one solitary highway approaching the shore, Texas maps show a blank: no roads, no towns, nothing but beach wilderness. A Texas Riviera it is not.

Pavement penetrates North Padre Island for 5 miles; from then on you're looking at untouched dunes and deserted beaches for 75 glorious miles. Picnicking, camping, and driving are permitted on the seashore, except for a 5-mile stretch reserved for pedestrians. Four-wheel-drive vehicles are almost essential here, but they can't be used anywhere except on the beach. (No dune-running, please.) No bridge connects North Padre Island with South Padre Island. When the island terminates, that's it. The wilderness area continues on this neighboring island for many more miles until a highway heads south to the town of South Padre Island.

Approximately the same latitude as Miami Beach, the southern tip of South Padre Island has always stirred the imagination of developers and promoters as the next tourist and retirement bonanza. So far their optimism has been greater than their successes. To be sure a wealth of condos, hotels, and rental units compete for space with restaurants and souvenir shops, but the expected mass immigration just hasn't happened yet. Not long ago luxury condos that had been built to sell for $400,000 were going at auction for $70,000 and less. This has changed, of course, with the real estate market leveling out. Real estate brokers say there are still bargains on the market, but few distress sales at this time.

Although the town of South Padre Island looks like a city when first viewed from the causeway that crosses the Laguna Madre from Port Isabel, only about 1,500 residents live here year-round. That figure increases impressively during the season, because more than 3,000 condo units are rented out to tourists and visitors, and even in the off-season, a good percentage of the rentals are occupied. Unlike nearby Lower Rio Grande Valley, the peak season is summer rather than winter. At the crescendo of the tourist crush, during spring semester break, an unbelievable number squeeze into town. Fortunately miles and miles of camping on the beaches handle the overflow.

The developed portion of the island covers 6 miles of the southernmost tip, with the remaining 34 miles in deserted dunes and beaches inhabited by RVs, campers, and fishermen. The beaches seem endless and gently sloping—great for swimming and surf fishing. By the way, driving the beach is permitted (four-wheel-drive vehicle recommended) as far as Mansfield Pass. This artificial ship channel created two islands out of one. Local people will argue that an artificial channel doesn't make two islands out of one, but in 1964 the state of Texas officially pronounced it to be two islands, so that settles that. All along the beach anglers camp and cast bait into the surf for some really great sport fishing.

The Laguna Madre—those bay waters between the mainland and South Padre Island—is said to be jumping with fish such as sand trout, flounder, sheepshead, redfish, and croakers. In the town of South Padre Island and also in Port Isabel, you can find charter

SOUTH PADRE ISLAND–PORT ISABEL WEATHER					
In degrees Fahrenheit					
	Jan.	April	July	Oct.	Rain	Snow
Daily highs	69	82	90	82	28"	—
Daily lows	52	67	75	66		

fishing for sailfish, marlin, tarpon, kingfish, and pompano. For those who don't fish, there is plenty to do in the built-up, modern town. Several commercial RV parks accommodate visitors, and there is a county park, Isla Blanca, where you can park your rig while you beachcomb for lost pirate treasures.

Because South Padre Island lies at the most southern latitude of anywhere in the continental United States except for the Florida Keys, you might expect it to have a Florida-like climate, particularly because it enjoys a lower summer humidity. But because the Gulf Stream, the secret to Miami Beach's climate, misses the Texas coast, summers are hotter here and winters cooler. This is more than compensated for by the calm and peaceful atmosphere (except during semester break).

Port Isabel   On the mainland across a short causeway is Port Isabel (pop. 5,000). Many retirees choose to live here and make the 2.6-mile drive across the causeway to enjoy South Padre Island without paying premium prices for property. Another advantage to living in Port Isabel is that the island acts as a barrier against storm-driven seas, so stilt construction isn't necessary.

Like all South Texas towns that attract "Winter Texans," Port Isabel's population rises in proportion to the thermometer's fall in the colder sections of the United States and Canada. RV parks begin filling the last of October and stay packed until spring thaw lures the snowbirds back home. Because this is a year-round resort area, several large parks don't empty as they do in the winter resort areas. Those with self-contained rigs often prefer to boondock on the island beaches because they don't need electric or water hookups. Just north of town, and for miles up the coast, pristine beaches, all but deserted, invite campers and RV boondockers, offering good surf fishing and quiet times for reading or just sitting and contemplating whitecaps on the Gulf's blue waters.

In addition to the climate and beach location, local people point out the low crime rate, lack of rush-hour traffic, and serene living as reasons for retirement here. For traffic jams people need to travel elsewhere.

The Rio Grande Valley

After flowing 2,000 miles through Colorado, New Mexico, and Texas, the Rio Grande, the state's most famous river, finally empties into the Gulf of Mexico just below South Padre Island. This, the lower Rio Grande Valley, is the domain of motor homes, trailers, and campers. It is also the yearly destination of the Winter Texans, those warmth-loving folks who follow the sun south when arctic winds start blowing up north. Their winter target is a 90-mile stretch of valley starting at the Gulf of Mexico and westward to Rio Grande City. RV travelers and snowbirds from the United States and Canada who make the yearly migration call this place the "Poor Man's Florida." In many ways this part of Texas does resemble Florida. Lines of palm trees, fragrant citrus blossoms, bougainvillea, and other flowering shrubs provide a distinctly tropical flavor. Temperatures can drop, however, suddenly and dramatically.

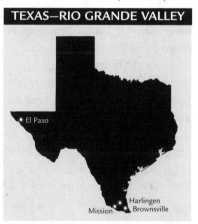

TEXAS—RIO GRANDE VALLEY

El Paso

Harlingen
Mission   Brownsville

The lower Rio Grande Valley would seem to be an unlikely place to become a popular retirement location because of its stifling summer heat. Many feel that it's all but unlivable from June through August. As evidence, witness the retirees leaving en masse every spring, not to return until summer has faded into late fall. In the coolest part of a summer evening, the temperature here rarely falls below seventy-five degrees, and it generally climbs into the high nineties during the day. Because of humidity, evaporative coolers are worthless; you must depend on refrigeration units. Yet despite the hot summers, many retirees are choosing to adopt full-time retirement along the Rio Grande. For them the pleasant winters make it all worthwhile, and they avoid the hassle of moving twice each year.

Winter is why folks come to the lower Rio Grande Valley. With seemingly endless sunshine, palm trees, and other tropical plants gracing the city streets, the ambience is unmistakably subtropical. Balmy breezes from the Gulf of Mexico caress the countryside, perfuming the air with the scent of orange and grapefruit blossoms. Meanwhile, back on the ranch, winds are whipping snowdrifts and dropping the chill factor to subzero records.

Although most retirees here start off as part-timers, or Winter Texans, more and more are making their stays permanent and becoming "Year-round Texans." According to the U.S. government, the number of Social Security checks being sent to the lower Rio Grande Valley went up by 16 percent over a three-year period. RV and mobile-home parks report twice as many spaces being occupied year-round as ten years ago.

South Texas winter retirement isn't a new concept, not by any means. Midwestern farmers have known about it for years. When snow and ice gripped their fields with bitter winter cold, they arranged for someone to feed the cows and hogs, hooked a house trailer behind the old pickup, and headed for the Rio Grande for a winter of leisure and sunshine. Orange groves, palm trees, and eighty-degree afternoons made for pleasant living while winter paralyzed farming country back home.

The bonus: Lower Rio Grande living was (and is) cheap. Local people used to joke that "farmers come down here with a five-dollar bill and a pair of overalls, and don't change either one the whole winter." You don't hear that joke nowadays. Winter retirement means big cash business in South Texas. Social Security, pension checks, and millions of outside dollars—American and Canadian—pump more than half a billion dollars into what could otherwise be a sagging economy. Alongside main highways roadside signs proclaim, WE LOVE WINTER TEXANS!

Farmers are no longer a majority today; retirees come from all walks of life and all parts of the continent. More come each year, mostly in RVs. A few years ago, 50,000 snowbirds wintering in the Brownsville–Harlingen–McAllen area was considered a record. But today the number tops 300,000! Don't worry, there's always room for one more. More than 500 RV parks compete for snowbird tenants; some parks have several hundred spaces each. In the town of Mission, just southwest of McAllen, fewer than 100 RV parks accommodate more than 10,000 RVs. Yet the year-round population of Mission is only 45,000!

This floating population has become a political force to reckon with. Because Texas requires only a thirty-day residence to become a legal voter, a significant number of folks register to vote as soon as they finish hooking up electricity and water to the motor home. These enthusiastic voters become involved in brisk political campaigning, providing swing votes to elect local officials and pass ordinances that affect their Winter Texan communities. You can be sure local politicians and city officials are responsive to the wishes of the Winter Texans. They aren't just retirees, they're *voting retirees!*

RV parks of all descriptions abound, with variety to suit everyone's taste. Some are extremely plush, others plain. The fancy resorts routinely offer refinements like Olympic-size swimming pools, indoor shuffleboard, tennis, dance halls, libraries, pool rooms, sewing rooms, and other special halls for recreation and socializing. Even bare-bones parks usually have a rec hall to go with laundry facilities.

Although many thousands of retirees come to this part of Texas in RVs, spend the winter, and move on, please don't get the impression that's all there is to Rio Grande Valley retirement. Motorhome or RV living isn't for everyone, and a vagabond lifestyle is inappropriate for most retirees. They insist on the security of a permanent home with an extra bedroom for guests, and perhaps a vegetable garden. They want a hometown or neighborhood where they can interact with the community as permanent residents, not as wandering strangers. Towns that welcome RVers—places such as Brownsville, Mission, and Harlingen—also offer inexpensive real estate and welcoming neighborhoods for those who would settle down to nonmovable homes.

Brownsville   Brownsville is Texas's southernmost city. Its history began in 1846 when General Zachary Taylor established a military base—calling it Fort Brown—to back up our claim that the Rio Grande should have been the western boundary of Texas. Mexico took offense at this, however, insisting that the agreed-upon boundary was the Pecos River, *not* the Rio Grande River. This misunderstanding touched off the Mexican War of 1846–48. Once the war was under way, our diplomats realized that, logically, neither the Pecos *nor* the Rio Grande should mark the western edge of the

BROWNSVILLE COST OF LIVING

Percentage of national average	Overall	Housing	Medical	Groceries	Utilities
	91	74	101	90	102

United States. What else could it be but the Pacific Ocean? Stands to reason. After our troops captured Mexico City and explained the revised negotiating position (at gunpoint), Mexican diplomats reluctantly recognized the logic of our argument. Thus we ended up with not only the Rio Grande but also the states of California, New Mexico, Arizona, Nevada, Utah, and parts of Colorado and Wyoming.

Brownsville is the Rio Grande Valley's largest city, with 140,000 inhabitants, an astounding increase of 48,000 (53 percent) since 1990. The cost of living here is favorable despite unusually high utility rates. Low housing prices account for the difference, with sales figures fully 19 percent below national averages. That's partly because the floating retiree population returns home every summer—they don't buy houses and settle down for the entire year along the Rio Grande Valley. Supermarket prices are generally moderate, especially for locally grown produce, because this area is the country's top producer of winter vegetables. Year-round apartment and home rentals are inexpensive, although those rented just for the winter are predictably pricey.

Wages are low, as in most border areas, partly because of the availability of eager workers from Mexico who are willing to cross the river and do a hard day's work for minimal wages. Job competition means lower wages, lower costs of goods and services, and a lower cost of living for visitors. Even so, the large influx of winter visitors creates a cornucopia of seasonal jobs for retirees. Employers like to hire employees they won't have to lay off when the season ends; they'll be leaving anyway.

Just across the river is the Mexican city of Matamoros, a favorite shopping target for Winter Texans staying in and around Brownsville. Nightclubs, restaurants, gift shops, and stores of all descriptions compete for the Yankee dollar, although some prices on the Mexican side have been creeping toward Texas price levels. You'll hear praise for Matamoros dentists, whose work is said to be both inexpensive and high quality. Of course the usual across-the-border doctors and medical clinics administer unorthodox treatment for diseases such as cancer and arthritis. Although the American Medical Association insists that unapproved remedies are worthless, many patients disagree. One man explained, "My doctor back home claims these Mexican clinics can't help my arthritis. Says I'm wasting my money. But he admits there's nothing *he* can do about arthritis, either. So, for a few dollars, I'm betting that the other doctor's wrong. I can't afford *not* to make the bet."

Another benefit of living along the international border is inexpensive prescription drugs purchased in Mexican *farmacias*. In Mexico—as in most foreign countries—many essential medications do not require prescriptions. Even though manufactured by the same companies that distribute in the United States and Canada, these drugs are significantly less expensive in Mexico. Just one example: A thirty-day supply of Enderal—a common medication for hypertension and heart irregularities—costs about a third to a half of what you would pay on the American side of the border. The Mexican government successfully controls drug prices and carefully monitors the sale of medications to prevent unfair profit-taking. (Is there a lesson here for our government?)

Mission   "Home of Winter Texans" is one of the ways Mission advertises itself, but the town can't seem to make up its mind, because it also claims the title of "Home of the Grapefruit." It's said that Texas's first citrus orchard started here when mission priests planted trees in 1824 (hence the name Mission). The area is indeed famous for its groves of Texas Ruby Red grapefruit. In addition to the sweet aroma of citrus blossoms in December, residents enjoy a particularly colorful Christmas because of the abundance of poinsettias throughout town. The joyful theme of "Tropical Christmas" is celebrated with profuse displays of these colorful plants in public buildings, parks, and private homes.

The Mexican city of Reynosa sits across the river from Mission. A popular shopping place for valley residents, Reynosa offers much the same attractions as Matamoros. Some excellent restaurants here serve cuisine rarely found in U.S. restaurants—wild game, for example. As is the case in all the border towns, tourist cards or passports aren't required for visits of less than seventy-two hours unless you travel to the interior of Mexico.

LOWER RIO GRANDE VALLEY WEATHER						
In degrees Fahrenheit						
	Jan.	April	July	Oct.	Rain	Snow
Daily highs	70	83	93	84	26"	—
Daily lows	51	67	76	66		

LOWER RIO GRANDE VALLEY COST OF LIVING					
Percentage of	Overall	Housing	Medical	Groceries	Utilities
national average	91	81	100	86	114

Harlingen   About 30 miles from Brownsville, Harlingen is somewhat smaller, with a population of almost 60,000. Like the rest of the Rio Grande Valley, Harlingen's population climbs dramatically during the winter. This city stands out because of its local beautification campaigns and recycling efforts, and thanks to the hard work of its citizens, Harlingen won the All-American City award from the National Civic League. Also a recent survey by *Money* magazine ranked the city the twentieth best place to live in the United States.

This is an area of truck farms, orange groves, and more of the prized Texas Ruby Red grapefruit. With a year-round growing season, one crop or another is ready to be harvested at any given time of the year. Harlingen's appearance is similar to that of Mission, with palm trees, colorful bougainvillea, and poinsettias brightening the warm Christmas season.

Overall Harlingen is a nice place for winter retirement even though it requires a longer drive for shopping in Mexico. A compensating attraction is a large greyhound racing park. (Dogs, not buses.) The city also boasts four PGA championship golf courses plus a twenty-seven-hole municipal course and several par-three layouts.

When comparing lower Rio Grande Valley housing and year-round rentals, Harlingen turns out to be the most economical of the towns mentioned here. Housing costs are among the lowest in the country.

El Paso   Just a little more than four centuries ago, the first Europeans pushed their way north from Mexico and found an easy crossing, or pass, across the Rio Grande into what is now Texas's upper Rio Grande Valley. Early Spanish explorers named the crossing El Paso del Norte. When Mexico relinquished claim to the crossing, the U.S. Army established a post here to protect American settlers from marauding Comanches and to oversee the growing business of international trade between Mexico and the United States. Over the ensuing years, El Paso grew from a dusty cow town into a modern city of more than 500,000, the largest city on the American side of the 1,933-mile U.S.–Mexico border.

That first military post established a continuing tradition of military presence in El Paso. Fort Bliss, in northeast El Paso, is the home of the U.S. Army Air Defense Center and contributes a huge payroll to keep the economy level. Military families and civilian support personnel live in all sections of the city and make the population very "middle America." When retirement time rolls around, military personnel quite naturally think of El Paso as one of their retirement possibilities. They remember the cleanliness and neighborliness of the city as well as the affordable real estate. Of course, being military, post-exchange privileges and medical facilities for retirees influence their final decisions.

El Paso has several good things going for it. First, the climate is mild, with summers far cooler than those of the lower Rio Grande Valley. You can usually get out in July or August and play a game of golf without risking sunstroke. Lower humidity and a 3,700-foot elevation makes a world of difference.

Another attraction for retirees is Ciudad Juarez, just across the Rio Grande. Juarez is more than just another border town like Reynosa or Matamoros; it is truly a city. It's even larger than El Paso, with an estimated population of nearly a million inhabitants. Juarez's downtown section, situated close to the border, is a bit grungy, with honky-tonks, bars, an occasional good restaurant, and the inevitable curio and souvenir shops. But when you get away from the old downtown section, you'll find modern areas with broad boulevards, nice restaurants, and nice clothing stores, and, depending upon the state of the economy, shopping in Juarez can be an experience in bargaining. Some commodities are always cheaper across the border, particularly items like booze, instant coffee, and some grocery items. Many retirees make weekly forays across the border to take advantage of bargains. Produce sells at giveaway prices; unfortunately you can't carry veggies across the border.

El Paso has a delightful way of blending Mexican and Anglo cultures, something that doesn't happen in the lower Rio Grande Valley. Instead of rigid social lines separating Anglo-Saxons and Hispanics, keeping a gulf between the United States and Mexico, you'll find a congenial mixture of Texas and Chihuahua. Radio and television announcers on both sides of the border often jump between Spanish and English, never missing a beat. Restaurant menus on both sides of the border do much the same. El Paso restaurants typically offer dishes like pozole or chiles rellenos, and Juarez restaurants are famous for steak-and-lobster dinners and Chinese food. Years ago, when I worked for the *El Paso Times*, my favorite lunch-break restaurant served a great chicken-fried steak. But instead of gravy on the steak, it came with chile con queso sauce!

American modern and old Mexican charm blend to give El Paso a distinctive character. The downtown's wide streets branch out in all directions, and Interstate 10 moves traffic quickly and efficiently through the center of the city. Commercial buildings are modern and crisp, avoiding the garishness and mirrored walls that seem to be in vogue elsewhere. As you move toward the outskirts of the city, you can't help but be impressed with El Paso's neatness and cleanliness. Most single-family neighborhoods favor brick construction, one-story homes, and neatly trimmed landscaping. Housing costs are 11 percent below national averages.

In El Paso's newer sections, away from downtown, you'll find a proliferation of apartment buildings. Like many Texas cities that participated in the savings-and-loan jubilee, condo and apartment construction has been overly enthusiastic, resulting in an oversupply. You'll often spy billboards shouting out special

EL PASO WEATHER						
In degrees Fahrenheit						
	Jan.	April	July	Oct.	Rain	Snow
Daily highs	58	79	95	78	8"	6"
Daily lows	31	49	70	49		

EL PASO COST OF LIVING					
	Overall	Housing	Medical	Groceries	Utilities
Percentage of national average	96	82	103	106	96

deals to entice renters. Some apartments offer the first month's rent free, or free utilities for the first year, maybe a color television to bring you into the fold. The best part is the advertised monthly rates are affordable.

Central Texas

San Antonio   It's difficult to think of San Antonio (pop. 1,150,000) as being in the south-central part of Texas, because it looks like west Texas to me. Only 28 inches of rain per year falls on San Antonio, compared with Houston's 45 inches or Port Arthur's 52 inches. Dry range country with thorny bushes starts not far from the city limits. Certainly, from here westward, we are looking at the kind of country one expects from the western United States, with brush, cactus, and sandy soil. If the "West" doesn't start in San Antonio, then where?

When white men first came here, a Coahuilecan Indian village occupied the bank of a beautiful river, where present-day downtown San Antonio is located. The river, life-giving and crystal-clear, was shaded by large poplar trees ("alamo" trees in Spanish). The Indians called the river Yanaguana, or "refreshing waters." Unfortunately the river didn't retain its pristine state once white men began using it to dump sewage and trash.

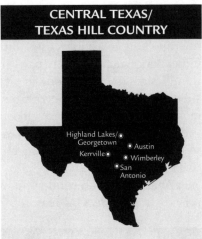

Today this river is a symbol of San Antonio's fight against urban decay. The downtown river project is a textbook example of how to remedy central-core blight. The city completely transformed the river—which was little more than a weed-choked garbage dump a few years ago—and turned it into an elegant shopping and restaurant area. Soaring cypress and cottonwood trees grace the riverbanks, shading shops, restaurants, and hotels. Tourists and residents alike enjoy strolls, boat rides, and nightlife along the riverbanks. The project has revitalized San Antonio's entire downtown section. The Coahuilecan Indians would be proud of the way their river has returned to its "refreshing waters" status.

San Antonio's weather is a plus retirees constantly brag about. Summers are warm, with highs typically in the low nineties. Yet summer evenings are delightful, with temperatures dropping into the high sixties or low seventies—just right for shirtsleeve evenings and for sleeping without the annoyance of air-conditioning. The humidity is moderate, so swamp coolers work efficiently and refrigerated air-conditioning isn't absolutely necessary. In the winter temperatures rarely drop below forty degrees at night, and afternoons are almost always in the mid-sixties, even in the coldest months. For all practical purposes there is no winter. Snow? Almost none; every three or four years San Antonio catches enough snow to measure, although in 1985 it snowed 13 inches! Rain? Just enough to keep lawns and shrubbery green.

San Antonio, like Austin to the north, enjoys a low cost of living. In fact San Antonio ranks lowest of the top twenty-five U.S. metropolitan areas; low-cost utilities and real estate at 17 percent under national averages are partly responsible for this happy condition. Residential areas flourish on the fringes of the city, with new subdivisions popping up everywhere. Most newcomers prefer to live in the outer ring of newer subdivisions, near one of several large shopping centers. These areas have comfortably high levels of personal safety, as opposed to the inevitably higher crime rate found closer to a city's center.

Apartments and condo units are overbuilt, with rentals appropriately reasonable. One reason for the abundance of rentals is the

SAN ANTONIO WEATHER						
In degrees Fahrenheit						
	Jan.	April	July	Oct.	Rain	Snow
Daily highs	62	80	95	82	28"	—
Daily lows	39	59	74	59		

SAN ANTONIO COST OF LIVING					
Percentage of	Overall	Housing	Medical	Groceries	Utilities
national average	88	83	101	86	80

enormous military population that is constantly on the move. A few years ago developers sized up this market and decided to increase the number of rentals. With abundant savings-and-loan money available, apartments and condos sprouted far quicker than tenants.

Medical care here is awesome. The University of Texas Health Science Center is located here, with schools in medicine, dentistry, and nursing, and research programs in cancer, cardiology, and other problems endemic to the elderly. This is one of only six sites in the nation that is approved for patients to try experimental cancer drugs. The South Texas Medical Center, a 700-acre complex, encompasses eight major hospitals, clinics, laboratories, and a cancer research and therapy center. Also there's the world-renowned Burn Unit at Brooke Army Medical Center at Fort Sam Houston, which receives burn victims from all over the world.

Since its beginning as a Spanish presidio almost three centuries ago, San Antonio has maintained a military tradition. Four Air Force bases circle the city: Brooks, Kelly Field, Lackland, and Randolph, plus Fort Sam Houston, an Army post. Brooks Air Force Base is famous in military circles for having one of the finest medical facilities in the country. This alone is an attraction for military retirees and would bring them here even if San Antonio weren't such a nice place to live. Our understanding is that almost 70,000 service personnel and families live in the San Antonio area and at least twice that many retirees. This may well be the largest population of ex-military folks in the country.

Texas Hill Country

The picture most of us have of West Texas is flat or rolling stretches of eternity, sparsely covered with prairie grass or low brush that extends to meet the distant horizon. Sometimes wheat replaces grass; occasionally a lethargic steer can be seen munching cactus. Nothing moves except the up-and-down rocking of oil pumps or perhaps a distant windmill. Texas flatlands do indeed flow pretty much undisturbed by mountains, except for the extreme western portion, where the Rocky Mountains march southward through Big Bend National Park.

This bleak picture is more or less accurate, with a notable exception: the Texas Hill Country. A geological formation known as the Balcones Fault has pushed the land a thousand feet above the surrounding plains, creating a mini-mountain range. This not only changes the geography of Texas, it also profoundly affects the state's climate. Moisture-laden breezes from the Gulf of Mexico can't easily lift over the Hill Country, so they release their rain on the southeastern part of the state and leave the western part arid. You can easily see this, for the great Southwestern Desert begins the other side of the Texas Hill Country.

This special part of Texas is a wonderland of large, limestone-cropped hills not quite large enough to be called mountains, mostly wooded and intersected by half a dozen clear rivers, spring-fed creeks, and lakes. Perhaps half a hundred small, friendly towns and cities are scattered through the lightly populated countryside, many of them holding great retirement potential. Because much of the Texas Hill Country is rocky, with high concentrations of limestone and caliche, the soil isn't suitable for extensive farming operations. Therefore, customarily the land is left in its natural state. Most acreage is covered by juniper thickets and wild cherry, gnarled oak, native pecan, and mountain laurel trees. Along the slow-moving rivers, magnificent cypress and elms shade the banks and provide cover for wild creatures. Cattle and sheep share the wilderness with white-tailed deer, turkey, javalina (wild pigs), and imported Russian boar.

The Texas Hill Country is as different from our usual view of Texas as can possibly be. Long considered one of the better living areas in the state, the region has been enjoying nationwide attention through retirement publications. One thing that makes it so different from other parts of West Texas is its year-round rainfall. The Hill Country receives more than 30 inches of rain each year, several times that of many Southwest locations. This accounts for its green, sometimes lush vegetation. The rain falls every month of the year, helping to keep things looking fresh.

Kerrville   Kerrville is often considered the "capital" of the Hill Country because it's the largest city in the hills and is centrally located among them. With a population of almost 21,000, Kerrville is the Hill Country's major shopping destination. Being close to Interstate 10, many residents find it convenient to commute to jobs in San Antonio, about forty-five minutes away. Thus Kerrville fulfills two roles: as a place to retire and as a bedroom community.

Kerrville shares in the Hill Country's panoramic views and is further blessed by the Guadalupe River flowing softly through the heart of town. Kerrville's location at 1,600 to 1,800 feet above sea level, the Hill Country's highest, contributes to its good climate, providing cooler summers and more clearly defined seasons than Austin or San Antonio. Local people are happy with July and August days, always several degrees cooler than the lowland cities. One source of retirees stems from those summer residents who later decide to move to the Hill Country when embarking on new careers as retirees.

Because of the area's growing population of retirees (almost 30 percent of county residents are older than age sixty-five), many Kerrville social and business events focus on seniors. The local chamber of commerce is one of the few we've seen that really goes all out for retirees and deserves high praise. An interesting example is the annual Senior Job Opportunity Fair that the chamber of commerce conducts. One recent year local businessmen and more than 200 seniors joined together in a half-day seminar to explore employment possibilities. Together they worked out ways to create a large number of part-time and permanent jobs for retirees and supplied valuable employees for area businesses.

Kerrville holds a reputation as the Hill County's preeminent art colony. The picturesque surroundings naturally encourage artistic development and act as a magnet to draw working artists, many of whom display works in local galleries and boutiques. One of Kerrville's galleries, the Cowboy Artists of America Museum, is the nation's only museum whose exhibitions are restricted to America's Western and cowboy artists. Artistry isn't restricted to visual arts; there are also outdoor theater productions and a performing arts group that brings concerts and other live shows.

Another popular cultural presentation is the annual Kerrville Folk Festival, held in late spring. Residents and tourists enjoy eighteen days of musical events, which include original works performed by artists in an outdoor theater, evening concerts around campfires, and a songwriter's competition.

Camp Verde, 11 miles south of Kerrville, was the eastern terminus of a camel route that stretched all the way to Yuma, Arizona. This was part of an experiment in overland transportation, an idea whose time has never quite arrived.

Wimberley Wimberley is another Hill Country town that's been basking in the warm light of national publicity as a new discovery in retirement destinations. Its photogenic qualities make wonderful color layouts for magazines. This is where the clear, cool waters of Cypress Creek join the warmer waters of the slow-moving Blanco River, a place where large trees and old homes of native stone harken back to another era. This was a popular getaway during World War II, when rich folks from Houston and San Antonio didn't have enough gasoline to travel to their second homes in the Blue Ridge Mountains. So they built summer homes—"camp houses" as they called them—in Wimberley. When they retired these summer places became permanent homes, thus starting a retirement trend. As a result Houston transplants are well represented here. It's properly called a "village," because it's never been incorporated, and folks hereabout like it that way.

Wimberley is strategically located between Austin and San Antonio, not far off Interstate 35. The population here is a little more than 8,000 (including adjacent crossroads comunities), large enough for essential services, but Wimberley enjoys a small-town atmosphere, with low crime and friendly neighbors. Because it's only 12 miles to San Marcos, that's where most heavy-duty shopping is done, or 45 miles (about an hour) away in Austin. San Marcos is also the nearest place to purchase bottles of wine or liquor; local restaurants do serve wines and cocktails by the drink.

Although there is no Greyhound bus service, the county sponsors a service called CARTS, which takes disabled and senior citizens to medical appointments and even into Austin for shopping and special medical needs. A volunteer ambulance group takes emergency cases to the hospital in nearby San Marcos.

Wimberley sits at an altitude of 1,100 feet—twice as high as Austin—and therefore enjoys slightly cooler summers and a few inches more rainfall. Like other towns in this part of the country, snow is a rarity. Homeowners choose among properties on rivers or hills, on city-size lots or acreages, with homes selling for slightly less than national averages. Nearby Woodcreek is a planned community with an eighteen-hole golf course, tennis courts, clubhouse, and other amenities. Rentals are almost impossible to find, because there are no apartments, just single-family homes.

A summer community tradition is an outdoor movie theater (bring your own chairs). The Blanco River, lined with huge old

HILL COUNTRY WEATHER						
In degrees Fahrenheit						
	Jan.	April	July	Oct.	Rain	Snow
Daily highs	56	77	90	79	30"	2"
Daily lows	36	57	74	59		

HILL COUNTRY COST OF LIVING					
	Overall	Housing	Medical	Groceries	Utilities
Percentage of national average	94	95	92	80	84

cedars and oak trees, passes one edge of town and intersects with Cypress Creek on the other. The rivers are crossed by one-lane bridges, which residents refuse to widen because that would mean cutting some beautiful cypress trees. The Blanco River's turquoise waters are excellent for swimming, tubing, fishing, and canoeing.

Austin   The capital of Texas, Austin sits 80 miles north of San Antonio on Interstate 35. Austin (pop. 643,000) is about half the size of San Antonio, but equally charming. Its downtown centers on an ornate state capitol and its extensive grounds.

Not as level as most Texas cities, Austin sits on the fringe of the Texas Hill Country and is surrounded by a circle of low hills. Unlike San Antonio, which developed from a haphazard grouping of trails converging at a river crossing, Austin began as a carefully planned city designed to be the state's capital. The downtown has an interesting mixture of modern and older buildings, creating an air of informality.

Austin is becoming widely known as a country music center, second only to Nashville. Not only country music but everything from jazz to reggae can be heard in the clubs around the city, particularly on Sixth Street, the renovated nineteenth-century historic district. The city is also proud of its reputation as a cultural center in arts other than music. Museums, theaters, and art galleries are well attended throughout the city. A symphony, ballet, and lyric opera complement the cultural offerings. Medical services are more than adequate, with a dozen hospitals and numerous specialists in attendance.

Austin is also known for its universities and colleges. The University of Texas at Austin is the largest in the state system. Adult

AUSTIN AREA WEATHER						
In degrees Fahrenheit						
	Jan.	April	July	Oct.	Rain	Snow
Daily highs	59	79	95	81	32"	1"
Daily lows	39	58	74	59		

AUSTIN COST OF LIVING					
Percentage of national average	Overall 104	Housing 110	Medical 104	Groceries 96	Utilities 94

education classes are widely available. Almost twenty golf courses are open to the public, plus another fifteen private clubs, the mild climate permitting fairway use throughout the year.

Real estate costs in Austin are above national averages by 2 percent, which may be explained by the large number of quality homes being sold in the many pleasant-looking neighborhoods on the fringes of the city. Popular retirement areas such as nearby Georgetown or San Marcos have similar housing selling for almost 10 percent lower.

Highland Lakes   Austin's outdoor recreation centers on the Highland Lakes area. This has long been considered one of the better retirement areas in the state. With 150 miles of water wonderland, a series of lakes stair-step down toward Austin. The lakes area offers abundant fishing and boating as well as wonderful scenery for retirement living. Buchanan Dam (pop. 4,000) is a small resort and retirement community that grew at the construction site of the lake by the same name. This is the largest of the lakes and also the highest. The altitude is 1,025 feet (approximately 500 feet higher than Austin), high enough to be cooler in the summer but not so high as to have heavy winter snows. Roads circle the lake, giving access to retirement homes, RV parks, and rental properties.

Another retirement possibility, Marble Falls (pop. 4,500) takes its name from the dam that created this particular lake. Sheer bluffs of limestone, granite, and marble encompass the lake at this point. Hunting, fishing, and camping are popular activities. White-tailed deer and wild turkey are said to be plentiful. Nearby Granite Mountain is the source of the distinctive pink-and-red granite used to construct the state capitol in downtown Austin. Other lakes in the area are Travis, Austin Town Lake, Canyon Lake, and Lake Georgetown.

Georgetown   Although sometimes billed as the "Gateway to the Hill Country," Georgetown's altitude is only 750 feet—not much higher than Austin—so it can't technically be considered Hill Country. That doesn't distract from its charm, however. Only 27 miles from Austin on the interstate, the community lies within easy commuting distance from the city. This makes it convenient for residents to enjoy Austin's conveniences, such as shopping, college sports events, and continuing-education opportunities. As far as personal safety goes, Georgetown ranks in the top 25 percent according to FBI statistics.

With a population of a little more than 28,000, Georgetown is proud of its history and delights in its wealth of Victorian architecture. The centerpiece is old, historic Courthouse Square, with antiques stores and boutiques. Residents take great care in the restoration and preservation of this historic town, with 180 homes and commercial structures designated as having historical significance. Some are now in use as restaurants and bed-and-breakfast inns. Georgetown is about 30 miles from downtown Austin on the interstate, within commuting distance for those involved in Austin's high-tech industries.

In addition to fourteen parks maintained by the City of Georgetown, Lake Georgetown offers picnic, swimming, fishing, and boating areas maintained by the Corps of Engineers. Residents enjoy walking the 5-mile hiking and bike trail, which begins at Blue Hole Park and travels along the riverbank, ending in beautiful San Gabriel Park.

As an indication of faith in Georgetown's future as a retirement location, the Del Webb Corporation is proceeding with one of its famous Sun City developments near here. Sun City Georgetown's 5,300-acre planned community features two scenic creeks meandering through fields of Texas wildflowers and stands of native pecans, walnuts, and majestic live oaks. Del Webb's first Texas venture, this will be an active retirement community designed for those age fifty-five and older.

Eventually 9,500 homes will be built, with 45 percent of the land remaining as open space and natural areas. Other recreational facilities include swimming pools, tennis courts, and extensive hiking and biking trails. Two eighteen-hole golf courses are open for play and boast a professional staff. Two more championship layouts are on the drawing board.

CHAPTER 7

Western Mountains and Deserts

FROM NEW MEXICO TO EASTERN CALIFORNIA, from the Mexican border to Colorado, the Southwest is a geological and scenic wonderland. Distinctive, dramatic arrangements of earth, water, and sky blend together, creating landscapes of unforgettable beauty. Sprawling, forest-covered plateaus scarred by awesome canyons contrast with endless expanses of sand, cactus, and sagebrush; great man-made lakes sparkle like aquamarine jewels in stark red settings. Badlands, with enormous monoliths, arches, and chiseled buttes, imitate mythical cities while snowcapped peaks preside over all. This is what draws retirees to the Southwest (in addition to snow-free winters).

It isn't all unspoiled natural paradise, however, because modern cosmopolitan cities rise over the shards of ancient Indian ruins and old ghost towns. In many areas Anglo, Spanish, and Native American cultures blend to create a spicy potpourri of something distinctly Southwestern. Huge retirement developments with golf courses and Olympic-size swimming pools (that look as if they've been magically transported from Florida) compete with small, comfortable localities of a few hundred homes.

The word *desert* incorrectly conjures images of Sahara-like sand dunes and desolate sweeps of barren land. True, North American deserts *can* be like that, but rarely are. Over eons plants and animals have adapted to living in dry country—even in places with 4 or 5 inches of rain per year. Trees and bushes survive on little water, flourishing miraculously in a dry desert or mountain environment. The first spring storm makes the desert bloom with an unforgettable explosion of colorful flowers and a profusion of green, all of which disappear when the plants withdraw into their water-conserving mode for the summer. Plants and animals have adapted quite nicely to living in the desert climate. The reptiles and mammals often survive hot summers by conserving body energy during the heat of the day and foraging and exercising in the cooler hours of the morning and evening. Therefore, it should come as no surprise that the famous species *Snowbirdus americanus* has also adapted to dry mountain and desert living. In the midst of the day they conserve body energy in air-conditioned homes and autos. They forage in enclosed shopping malls and play golf in the cooler hours of the morning and evening. Midday is for naps.

Arizona and New Mexico are favorite winter destinations, although a growing number of retirees choose to live there year-round. Two things you can count on: summer heat and abundant winter sunshine. Phoenix averages 295 days a year of sunny or partly sunny days. Winters are gloriously warm, but daily summer temperatures average more than one hundred degrees! We can't have everything. Fortunately relative humidity in Phoenix is as low as you can hope to find. This low humidity is why places such as Phoenix and Las Vegas are adding permanent residents like crazy, whereas parts of the Rio Grande Valley double in population each winter, only to lose it again in the summer.

Arizona

This is a state with scenic variety: evergreen-covered mountains; peaks with a foot of winter snow; deserts with forests of cactus; mineral-rich, shaded valleys; gently or rapidly flowing streams and rivers; and America's greatest natural wonder, the Grand Canyon. This

ARIZONA TAX PROFILE
Sales tax: 5% to 7%, food and drugs exempt
State income tax: graduated, 3.8% to 7% greater than $150,000
Property taxes: range between 0.8% to 1%
Intangibles tax: no
Social security taxed: no
Pensions taxed: private employer pensions taxed fully; government pensions receive $2,500 exemption; allows personal tax credits
Gasoline tax: 18¢ per gallon

is also a state with human variety: One-seventh of the United States's Native American population resides here. There are also generous numbers of Spanish speakers and newcomers from across the United States and Canada. Add to this the benefits of mild winters and a strong senior citizen political presence and support structure, and you have a state where retirement is a growth industry.

Speaking of growth, the U.S. Census report shows that most states grew in population over the past decade (the average state increased by 13.2 percent). But Arizona added an astounding *40 percent* to its population, an increase of almost a million and a half new residents!

Arizona ranks third in the nation attracting out-of-state retirees who seek new horizons for their retirement; Florida is first, California is second. It's interesting to note that of all the states sending retirees here, California and Florida send the most. Because California is conveniently nearby, this isn't surprising. But a good number of those coming from Florida are making a "second relocation" move—choosing Arizona after having first tried Florida retirement. So many retirees decide on Arizona retirement that about one-quarter of the state's residents are older than the age of fifty-five. That's one out of every four—most of them voters—so you can be sure senior citizen issues garner a fair share of attention, from the local city council to the governor's office.

Arizona has three basic choices for retirement lifestyles. The first is in the low desert climate found in the southern portion of the state, actually an extension of Mexico's great Sonoran Desert. As you would expect, summers are hot and winters pleasant. The second type of climate is high desert, where you'll find more pines than cactus and snows in the winter to create postcard scenery. And finally there are the mountains and plateaus of the northern regions, where winter snows can be deep and the summers cool and refreshing. Tall pines and deep canyons make northern Arizona as different from the southern parts as day from night. You have many choices here!

Southern Arizona's Sonoran Desert

Even though you have alternatives to Arizona's hot desert weather, the heat is exactly why many people retire here; they are fed up with battling ice and snow. Lovers of hot weather can't do much better than Southern Arizona short of moving to Death Valley. Sure, you'll spend many summer days enjoying indoor air-conditioning when it's one hundred degrees outdoors, but those warm and balmy winter days with seventy-degree January temperatures make up for it. No matter how hot it gets in the daytime, Arizona's dry air allows the heat to radiate rapidly so that the nights are usually pleasant, if

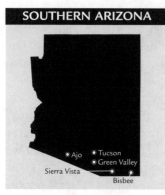

SOUTHERN ARIZONA

Ajo   Tucson
Green Valley
Sierra Vista
Bisbee

not cool. The air-conditioning system usually shuts down at night. With more than 300 days of sunshine each year and almost no rain, you have loads of opportunities to get outdoors. And just think about it: no snow shovels, no tire chains, no rubber boots, no windshield scrapers! The vast majority of those who retire to Arizona choose to live in the southern portion from the Mexican border up to Phoenix. So we'll start from the bottom of the state and work our way north with our descriptions of retirement living in Arizona.

Bisbee and Ajo   Economic disasters—such as a failing industry, a military base closure, or any other condition that causes a community to lose its vitality and for people to abandon ship—are bound to happen from time to time. Sometimes misfortune descends on places most people wouldn't choose to live unless they had jobs there, so having to seek employment elsewhere isn't exactly a tragedy. Occasionally an economic crash will affect a community that makes a great place for retirement. Home prices fall, families pack up and move away, and businesses fail from lack of customers.

Two such clouds descended on Arizona a few years ago, clouds with silver linings for those searching for inexpensive retirement Meccas. These towns were Bisbee, in the southeastern portion of the state near the Mexican border, and Ajo, somewhat farther west. Both were mining towns, and both saw their prosperity vanish when the mining company, without warning, ceased operation and fired its employees. Despair and pessimism reigned for a time but changed to optimism when the word got out and retirees began visiting to see what it was all about. Both towns regained their places in the sun and are admittedly grateful to their discovery and rescue by retirees.

Bisbee's surge of popularity brought its population up to 8,000, but after the initial rush the number of inhabitants began to decline. The 2000 census shows only 6,090 residents, a drop of 23 percent from 1990. Meanwhile the nearby town of Tombstone—of Wyatt Earp fame—increased population by 23.3 percent.

BISBEE WEATHER					
In degrees Fahrenheit					
	Jan.	April	July	Oct.	Rain	Snow
Daily highs	60	80	96	82	4"	2"
Daily lows	37	47	71	57		

When I first wrote about Bisbee, the town had just suffered financial disaster. At that time completely furnished homes sold for as little as $500. Homes were sometimes abandoned with unlocked doors. By the time we visited, things had taken a turn for the better, with retirees coming in to buy the cheap real estate and to rebuild the town. Bisbee made a dramatic switch from an abandoned mining town to its newer role as a retirement "discovery."

Revisiting a few years later, we found even more retirees had selected Bisbee for permanent homes. This increase in retiree population encouraged even more activity in services and organizations serving retired people. Of course this wave of bargain-hunting home buyers pushed selling prices up.

More than just a place of bargain housing, Bisbee's colorful history matches its picturesque desert-mountain setting. Tucked away in a canyon in the southeastern part of Arizona, only a few miles from the Mexican border, its narrow, winding streets present a classic style of mining towns of the late nineteenth century. The buildings are a mixture of authentic Victorian and Western mining camp, with brick and clapboard construction dating from the 1890s and even earlier. Because of its steep hills and ornate Victorian construction, people often describe the town as having a certain San Francisco atmosphere—without the cable cars, of course.

Be aware that the days of super-bargain homes are long gone. Of course, fixer-uppers can still be found, and satisfactory housing can easily be had for well less than national averages. Remember that the really old, historic places can require a lot of remodeling to bring them up to acceptable standards. Yet for many people renovating and rejuvenating an old house is enjoyable, a chance to allow artistic and creative abilities to run rampant. And at the price you pay for an old home, you can afford to be creative!

About 100 miles west of Tucson and 100 miles south of Phoenix is Ajo, another Phelps–Dodge mining town. Once a prosperous community of skilled miners and workers employed in the

AJO WEATHER					
In degrees Fahrenheit					
	Jan.	April	July	Oct.	Rain	Snow
Daily highs	66	82	100	86	6"	2"
Daily lows	40	50	74	56		

huge open-pit copper mine, the town boasted a population of more than 10,000 people. An oasis in the vast Sonoran desert, Ajo sits near the edge of the 300,000-acre Organ Pipe National Monument. The town centers on a pleasant garden plaza, with huge palm trees planted in 1917 when the copper company rebuilt the town. (Originally Ajo was located elsewhere, but when copper was discovered underneath the town, the mining company promptly moved everything.)

Suddenly, in 1984, the bubble burst—just as it did earlier in Bisbee. The mining company announced the closing of its mines and smelter operations. Caught without regular paychecks, the townspeople wasted no time in packing their belongings and leaving for greener pastures. The bustling town dwindled to 2,800 residents, a skeleton of its former self.

Because most houses in town belonged to the mining company, used as employee housing, there wasn't a mass abandonment of dwellings as happened in Bisbee. But the company homes went on the real estate market as low as $13,000 for a two-bedroom home. Privately owned properties also went for giveaway prices. A real estate broker said, "At one time we had 600 houses for sale. However, now all company-owned homes have been sold."

Even though distress sales have subsided and there aren't as many homes for sale today, Ajo's real estate market never fully recovered. Because retirees purchased most of these homes, the town has embarked upon a new career as a retirement center. Today, the population is reaching 8,000, about half retirees. "The nice thing about Ajo," said a retired couple, "is that we have a mixture of young and old. We have about 600 children in our school, and many young adults to balance out the social scene."

Sierra Vista   Near Bisbee—just 26 miles west—the high desert town of Sierra Vista is emerging as a popular retirement destination and one of Arizona's fastest-growing communities. With abundant sunshine, crystal-clear air, and an elevation of 4,600 feet, Sierra Vista enjoys an enviable climate. July high temperatures here average eighty-nine degrees (compared with Phoenix's 105 degrees), and Sierra Vista's July low temperatures are sixty-seven degrees (compared with Phoenix's eighty degrees).

The town's picturesque setting among the Huachuca, Dragoon, Mule, and Whetstone Mountains justify Sierra Vista's Spanish name: mountain view. The town owes its existence to Fort Huachuca (pronounced waa-CHOO-ca), established in 1877 as a cavalry post to secure the southern border to protect settlers from Indian attacks by the Apache chieftain, Geronimo. This was also the home base for the famous black troopers known as Buffalo soldiers of the 9th and 10th Cavalry. They pursued Pancho Villa's army in the 1916 expedition into Mexico led by General John H. Pershing.

From a small townsite around the fort, Sierra Vista has grown to more than 40,000 residents, including 11,700 military and civilian workers employed at Fort Huachuca. Several major commands now operate on Fort Huachuca, including the U.S. Army Information Systems Command, the Army Intelligence Center and School, and the Electronic Proving Grounds. Because of the military presence here and amenities available to retired personnel, Sierra Vista is naturally popular with military retirees and families.

Sierra Vista is the commercial center for Cochise County and parts of northern Mexico. To meet the area's growing needs, a 400,000-square-foot mall opened a few years ago with all major retailers represented. Fine dining is also available throughout the area.

SIERRA VISTA AREA WEATHER						
In degrees Fahrenheit						
	Jan.	April	July	Oct.	Rain	Snow
Daily highs	58	74	89	67	11"	4"
Daily lows	34	47	66	52		

SIERRA VISTA AREA COST OF LIVING					
Percentage of	Overall	Housing	Medical	Groceries	Utilities
national average	101	90	110	105	122

Sierra Vista's mild winters and warm summers encourage outdoor sports such as golf, tennis, hiking, and bike riding. Two championship golf courses are located here, and nine other golf facilities are within easy driving distance of town. You'll also find first-class bowling lanes, public and private tennis courts, and an Olympic-size swimming pool.

Housing is affordable and diverse, including country-club settings with homes bordering tees, ranchettes, apartments, and condos, as well as traditional neighborhoods. In early 2001 the median sales price of a three-bedroom home was 10 percent below national averages. A gated retirement community for age fifty-five-plus residents is available, as is an RV park with a section of "park models" (mobile homes) that people use for either summer or winter getaways (spending the rest of the year in retirement in their home towns).

Tucson   Sitting in a high-desert valley surrounded by mountains, Tucson's elevation of 2,375 feet guarantees an agreeable year-round climate. Its dry air and rich desert vegetation qualify it as one of the nation's finest winter resorts. Its 487,000 inhabitants make Tucson a moderately large city, and it is still growing. The fastest-increasing age group here is the sixty-plus crowd, which used to account for 20 percent of the population but is now pushing 30 percent. Because it's the sixty-plus group who are most likely to vote, it's no surprise that senior citizens get fair treatment in this city. The well-appointed Tucson Senior Citizens' Center clearly shows the attention that city politicians show retired people.

The University of Arizona, located in Tucson, greatly enriches the community's educational, cultural, and recreational life. Classes, lectures, plays, and concerts are an ongoing boon to retirees. The state's only opera company is based in Tucson, and a light opera company stages Broadway musicals.

Another favorable aspect of Tucson retirement is below-average housing prices. Buyers have a wide selection of neighborhoods, ranging from inexpensive to out of touch with reality. The warm and pleasant winters don't demand much in the way of heating costs, but this will be offset by air-conditioning in the summer.

Tucson is also a popular place for mobile-home living. The newspaper's classified section usually has listings from mobile-

TUCSON–GREEN VALLEY WEATHER						
In degrees Fahrenheit						
	Jan.	April	July	Oct.	Rain	Snow
Daily highs	65	81	98	82	12"	2"
Daily lows	38	50	71	56		

TUCSON AREA COST OF LIVING					
Percentage of	Overall	Housing	Medical	Groceries	Utilities
national average	98	91	104	104	110

home parks advertising spaces for rent, something rare in many metropolitan areas. A space in one of Tucson's adult mobile-home parks can often be found for half of what a nice two-bedroom apartment might cost.

With so many mobile-home parks to choose from, you would be well advised to do some shopping. Some parks are primarily for working people, and their interests and social lives are intertwined with friends who live somewhere else. Other parks have mostly retired folks, where you'll find plenty of activities and neighborly retirees. Visiting a park residents' meeting or attending one of the bingo sessions can tell you worlds about who your new neighbors might be.

Tucson is also known for its organized retirement and adults-only complexes. With beautifully designed homes, shopping and medical facilities, and extensive sports centers, these complexes are small cities in themselves. One adult community, Saddle Brooke, calls itself the "youngest adult community" because it sets its lower age limit at forty-five instead of the usual fifty-five. Housing prices in these adult communities range from $150,000 to $320,000. These complexes typically feature eighteen-hole golf courses, shuffleboard, bocci and tennis courts, cardrooms, jogging tracks, exercise rooms, and, of course, the ubiquitous swimming pools.

Smaller, apartment-type retirement quarters are available in and around Tucson. They range from places where renters must be "active" to those offering "senior care" concepts, a euphemism for "nursing home." You'll also find the growing concept of life-care centers, in which apartments are provided for those who are still active, then rooms with housekeeping care, and eventually nursing care for those who need it.

The Armory Park Senior Citizens Recreation Center (in downtown Tucson) is a model of its kind. Senior citizens take an energetic part in running the center and have no trouble getting all the volunteer help they need. At any one time several hundred volunteers are on call as they try to use everyone's special skills. For example: Retired accountants and tax practitioners give free income-tax assistance. Others teach handicrafts such as jewelry making, crocheting, and painting. A senior citizens' housing authority high-rise is across the street from the center and another is planned, making it convenient for everyone to participate.

Green Valley   Located 25 miles south of Tucson on Interstate 19 and 40 miles north of Mexico, Green Valley is an unincorporated adult retirement community. It sits at an altitude of 2,900 feet at the foot of the Santa Rita Mountains (an Apache hangout in the olden days). Green River has more than 18,000 residents, a high percentage of them retired, living in an area 8 miles long and 2 miles wide divided by the interstate.

Green Valley started off as an unlikely development dream on a somewhat elevated piece of desert land, miles from anywhere, a long way from a city or even a shopping center. The Green Valley concept turned out to be not so unlikely after all. Today more than 24,000 people call Green Valley home, the overwhelming majority of them retired. One source reports the average age here to be in the upper sixties. There are four shopping centers and more than 350 businesses serving Green Valley residents, including supermarkets, two major drugstores, discount department stores, apparel stores, restaurants, and other specialty stores. Tucson International Airport is only 23 miles away.

Green Valley is unincorporated, and folks seem to prefer it that way: fewer taxes, fewer bureaucrats, more time for golf. Residents boast that summer temperatures are consistently five degrees cooler than Tucson and ten degrees cooler than Phoenix. On the hottest July and August days, low humidity permits night temperatures to cool as much as thirty degrees below the afternoon's high. Green Valley winter temperatures are pleasantly similar to Tucson or Phoenix, averaging from the mid-sixties to the low seventies.

A study of the local telephone directory clearly demonstrates the melting-pot character of Green Valley. In addition to phone numbers and addresses, the local directory lists the residents' former hometowns as well as their occupations before retirement. The directory lists retirees from all fifty of the United States and ten Canadian provinces, as well as residents from twenty-six foreign countries, including Costa Rica, England, France, Ireland, Germany, and Sweden. Not all of Green Valley is restricted to fifty-plus folks. There's a sprinkling of youngsters around, just enough to keep the makeup of the community from becoming one-dimensional.

Complete facilities at Green Valley include a huge shopping center, which has a bowling alley. Three eighteen-hole public courses and two private courses, plus a couple of private nine-hole courses, satisfy that urge for hunting lost golf balls some retirees cannot shake. The rec center for Green Valley is quite comprehensive, with facilities for arts and crafts, sewing, lapidary, and photography. A swimming pool, Jacuzzi, sauna, and exercise room complete the recreational picture.

Green Valley has two highly rated nursing homes and a twenty-four-hour emergency clinic as well as two private clinics and a sixty-bed health care center. Tucson hospitals are 20 miles away via Interstate 19. There is also a volunteer organization called Friends In Deed (FID), which assists seniors in sharing their lifetime experiences and skills with one another.

Central Arizona: Between Phoenix and Flagstaff

Between the enormous urban sprawl of Phoenix and the modest northern city of Flagstaff, you'll experience some of the most varied spectacular scenes in the west. From Phoenix's desert landscape with cactus and sagebrush, through mountains clad with majestic pines, Indian reservations, and ski resorts, the variety seems unending. Higher altitudes are often covered with forests of pine, ju-

niper, and ponderosa, great habitat for deer, raccoons, and other denizens of the woods. The best part about both desert and mountain landscapes is they're accessible to everyone. About 45 percent of Arizona's land is owned by the federal government; it belongs to all of us. It isn't fenced and you'll not see any KEEP OUT signs. If you feel like strolling through government-owned deserts or forests, you can darn well do it.

Each of these Arizona regions offers its own temptations and advantages as retirement destinations. However, when considering retirement in Arizona, most people automatically think of the Phoenix area. Over the past two decades, population growth here has been enormous, almost as astounding as Las Vegas (another desert community). And when people speak of "retiring in Phoenix," they usually mean any one of a dozen communities on the expanding fringes of the metro area rather than Phoenix itself. They choose places like Mesa, Tempe, Scottsdale, and many more. Years ago most popular places—such as Scottsdale, Sun City, and Apache Junction—were stand-alone towns. Today you sometimes can't tell when you leave one and enter another without a city limits sign. (The combined population of this megametropolitan area is 1,320,000 according to the 2000 census.) This doesn't mean that each of these places doesn't have its own personality or that you are necessarily crowded cheek to jowl with neighbors as you might be in Chicago or New York. There is plenty of open space scattered in and between cities.

With such a large percentage of the population near or past retirement age, health-care servers have responded by providing some of the best facilities in the West. In addition to several excellent hospitals scattered all over the Phoenix area, this is the home of the new $50-million Mayo Clinic.

Given all the retirement choices offered in the Valley of the Sun, you'll need to do some in-depth investigation to find the community that suits your personality and your desired lifestyle. Let's take a look first at a couple of organized, seniors-only retirement communities in the Phoenix area: Sun City and Sun Lakes. Next we'll discuss two open, multigenerational communities: Scottsdale on the high end of the scale and Apache Junction on the economical end. When you visit, by all means do not confine your investigation to these communities. Take your time and make sure you're making the correct decision.

The Sun Cities   The concept of seniors-only, self-contained communities with homes clustered around recreational and social facilities began right here in the Arizona desert. About forty years ago the Del Webb Corporation unveiled its first retirement-oriented model homes in a community called Sun City. This was a nongated community that promised "an active way of life" for retirees. Before a single home was offered for sale, a shopping center, golf course, and recreational facilities were in place. The shopping center provided space for a supermarket, variety store, laundromat, barber shop, drugstore, and a service station. These facilities were essential, for at that time Sun City sat way out in the desert, a long, long way from the city. Today it is one solid metropolis with the Sun City complexes extending miles past the original location.

This highly popular concept of age-restricted and socially organized communities have changed the way many people view retirement. This prearranged lifestyle particularly suits those moving from another area, who have no acquaintances and who don't want to invest much time and energy trying to make new friends and to develop hobbies and recreational interests. It's all right here, in one package. As soon as the moving van unloads the furniture, a social director can have you out playing golf with your neighbors or working in the arts and crafts center.

Not everyone desires a planned and organized retirement. They want to do it themselves, preferring to live in a multigenerational neighborhood. They say, "I'd feel stifled, having all my neighbors the same age, with no children or teenagers in the neighborhood." Others enjoy having neighbors and friends of their own age, who share the same values and worldviews. When they want to play golf, their neighbors aren't busy working, hosting a Cub Scout meeting, or playing baseball with the kids. Not having youngsters around is a

PHOENIX–SUN CITY WEATHER						
In degrees Fahrenheit						
	Jan.	April	July	Oct.	Rain	Snow
Daily highs	65	83	105	88	7"	—
Daily lows	39	53	80	59		

PHOENIX AREA COST OF LIVING					
Percentage of national average	Overall 98	Housing 93	Medical 112	Groceries 101	Utilities 95

drawback for some, but others find it a blessing. "If I want to hear the pitter-patter of little feet," said one lady, "I'll put shoes on the damn cat!"

The original Sun City was so successful that thousands of additional acres were purchased, and soon three more Sun Cities appeared on the Arizona desert. Today more than 50,000 retirees are enjoying the benefits of four multimillion-dollar recreation centers, eight eighteen-hole golf courses, a 203-bed hospital, and a 7,169-seat performing arts center.

Home buyers have choices of model homes that vary from large four-bedroom places to small two-bedroom town houses. Because these homes are mass produced, they can be priced to sell. However, as the communities expand and people snap up the tempting new models, prices in the original Sun City fall. For retirees looking to join this lifestyle, homes in the older sections can be real bargains.

Sun Lakes   Not far from Phoenix is another example of a Sun City–style, adults-only development. However, Sun Lakes is a gated country-club community, on a somewhat more luxurious level than Sun City. A community of 12,000 residents, Sun Lakes is divided into four country-club neighborhoods, each with its own golf course and clubhouse. Although golf is Sun Lake's central theme, residents enjoy a multitude of opportunities for other activities such as tennis, swimming, fitness, and arts and crafts.

Sun Lakes sits in the desert, several miles from Phoenix, with a quiet atmosphere similar to that which characterized Sun City when it began years ago. This is just one of several places in the Phoenix area for those who enjoy country-club living. A surprising number of residents don't play golf; they just like the secure feeling of living in a luxurious, gated community. Of course you will pay a premium for these amenities. An impressive number of shopping facilities make it unnecessary to travel to Phoenix, not even for major purchases. But when you want to go to the big city, Interstate 10 access is just 2 miles away.

Scottsdale   The Sun City and Sun Lakes design appeals to those retirees who appreciate and need structured social and recreational environments. Not everyone wants this. Many retirees prefer to choose neighborhoods in which they may blend with residents of mixed ages, similar to the settings they left in their hometowns. This gives Scottsdale a different look, a distinct residential flavor that avoids mile after mile of similar dwellings.

Scottsdale has some of the most elegant and opulent shopping districts and residential neighborhoods we've encountered anywhere in the country. Majestically landscaped boulevards are lined with so many fabulous, prestige-name stores that your credit card vibrates as you drive past. Sumptuous residential neighborhoods display homes so elegant and palatial that you'll hate yourself for not being able to afford one. Scottsdale is a synonym for high-class, luxurious, and expensive, yet you'll find areas where housing costs aren't very much different from Sun City–type developments or ordinary neighborhoods in average communities.

If the Phoenix area sounds like a golfer's paradise, with 130 golf courses around the area, consider that twenty of these golf courses are located in Scottsdale, and several new layouts are under construction. Fourteen of them are public, including the Tournament Players Club of Scottsdale.

Cave Creek and Carefree, on Scottsdale's northeastern edge, epitomize tasteful desert-living lifestyles. The area is in the foothills, sitting above Scottsdale and Phoenix. The extra altitude makes an appreciable difference in the temperature as well as scenery. Most homes sit on large lots beautifully landscaped by natural desert plants. Large cactus of all description, flowering desert trees, and gnarled shrubbery surround upscale homes. Mountains loom in the background, and the air is pristine. This is one of our favorite retirement locations of all; we highly recommend it for those who can afford it.

Apache Junction   For those who feel like Sun Lakes, Cave Creek, and Scottsdale are too expensive, a lower-cost possibility for Phoenix area retirement is Apache Junction. It doesn't have the charisma or charm of Scottsdale (few places do), but it also doesn't have the price tag. Conventional housing sells for what is probably the lowest prices in the Phoenix area.

One of Phoenix's many commuter bedroom communities, Apache Junction is fast acquiring a dual personality in its role as a popular retirement destination for both permanent and temporary residents. Retirees from the Midwest and East are ending their retirement search when they discover Apache Junction's laid-back attitude and the area's year-round summer. Over the last ten years, the permanent population has doubled, almost to 20,000. Most of this increase can be attributed to retirees.

Only a half-hour drive via the fast-moving Superstition Freeway from downtown Phoenix and Sky Harbor Airport, the town can almost claim rural status because of its position on the border between city and open desert. In the distance the Superstition Mountains rise above the desert floor, presenting a mysterious fortresslike appearance. Once the stronghold of fierce Apache warriors, these mountains also are the source of the most famous "lost gold mine" story of all times. The Lost Dutchman's Mine has drawn adventurers for a century to search and explore the canyons and cliffs of the Superstitions, hoping to find the treasure. According to legend at least eight men have died mysteriously in their quest for the Lost Dutchman. But don't let this discourage you—by all means, have a look. (By the way, the mine was lost, not the Dutchman.) Every February the Lost Dutchman Days festival is celebrated with concerts, a rodeo, a parade, and a carnival.

Apache Junction's second role in retirement is with RV enthusiasts and snowbirds who travel to Arizona each winter. They enjoy it here because the town welcomes them (and their money) so warmly and because the city of Phoenix is easy to visit. More than forty mobile-home and RV parks accommodate some of these visitors. Their number is said to approach 35,000 for the season.

Wickenburg   About an hour's drive northwest from Phoenix, the town of Wickenburg is attracting retirees who don't want to accept the neatly arranged, orderly, and secure life of Sun City or the bustle of traffic-bound Phoenix. In small-town Wickenburg, they savor the tang of the Old West. The town has been famous for years for its guest ranches (they used to call 'em dude ranches), which go way beyond being simply ranches. They come complete with amenities such as swimming pools, tennis courts, and sometimes a golf course. Although guest ranches are still popular with tourists, the retirement emphasis is on small-acreage places where you can keep and ride your own horses.

Wickenburg has a population of 5,000—which almost doubles in the winter—and is the shopping center for 20,000 in the area.

WICKENBURG WEATHER						
In degrees Fahrenheit						
	Jan.	April	July	Oct.	Rain	Snow
Daily highs	63	79	103	82	11"	2"
Daily lows	30	48	70	52		

Health care is adequate, with a thirty-four-bed hospital and many doctors in private practice. Fifty minutes of driving takes you to excellent Sun City hospitals, which specialize in and cater to problems of the elderly.

Land here is abundant and inexpensive, so lots are typically sold by the acre. You may keep horses in your yard if you care to; the local horse population is considerable. You can saddle up and go for a ride through open desert and brush country in almost any direction you care to ride. Because almost all of the surrounding land is owned by the federal Bureau of Land Management (BLM) nobody can interfere with your rides. You don't know how to ride horseback? No problem—local saddle clubs with friendly members will help you get started. The clubs organize numerous social activities centered around horseback riding, from afternoon rides for beginners to the grueling Desert Caballeros Ride for seasoned horsemen, who come from all over the country to participate.

Wickenburg has several mobile-home parks, with many units used only part of the year, their owners choosing to live elsewhere during the hot summer months. At one time it was possible to buy a lot and install a mobile home, but nowadays this is frowned upon by the city council.

It does get hot in the summertime, with July and August posting highs of one hundred degrees and above. But like most Arizona desert country, low humidity takes much of the sting from the high temperatures. Winter nights can be cold, with frost common, but daytime temperatures are quite pleasant, with shirtsleeve weather being the noonday norm and January highs averaging sixty-three degrees at midday.

Sedona   Some folks choose their retirement locations because of beautiful surroundings. Sometimes people make decisions because of the weather. Occasionally you'll run across a town that combines both attributes in one neat package. Sedona is such a gem:

SEDONA WEATHER					
In degrees Fahrenheit					
	Jan.	April	July	Oct.	Rain	Snow
Daily highs	55	72	95	78	17"	9"
Daily lows	30	42	65	49		

mild four-season weather plus beautiful surroundings. Endowed with incredibly gorgeous views from any place in the area you might choose to live, Sedona is something you'll never get used to, even if you live there for the rest of your life. A friend who retired on the outskirts of town says, "Every morning when we wake up, we look through our kitchen window and drink in the view. We feel joyous, and we congratulate ourselves for being so lucky to live in Sedona." It's true. Enormous jagged red-rock formations, framed by a deep blue sky, sprinkled with rich green Arizona cypress and piñon trees, all majestically towering over the desert countryside—one can't help but draw in a deep breath and sigh.

On our first visit to Sedona several years ago—after taking our obligatory deep breath and emitting a long sigh—we experienced a curious feeling of déja vu. The view seemed strangely familiar, as if we'd visited here often. This odd feeling kept nagging at us until it suddenly hit us: *Western movies!* Sedona has been the location for hundreds of shoot-'em-up cowboy-and-Indian films. We'd seen these jagged cliffs and red bluffs over and over again, as cavalry troops chased Apaches or ran from them, as masked bandits robbed stagecoaches. Sedona has been a Hollywood tradition since the 1920s. In fact Hollywood artists and technicians came here so often that many decided to relocate here, either between films or as retirees. Several well-known personalities live here and don't hesitate to participate in local politics and community affairs.

The number of retirees who select Sedona as their home base is truly impressive. The head of the senior citizens' center estimates that around 40 percent of the population is retired. "This makes for an interesting mix of retired folks, artists, New Age devotees, and serious corporate people," he said. "Even some actors who liked working here and returned to retire."

Sedona is the place to cultivate latent talents or to appreciate the artistic talents of others. Between 200 and 300 resident artists reside here, accounting for the thirty-five art galleries and an exceptionally active community art center. Two theater groups present year-round performances, and there are several ad hoc performances by a senior-citizens' center group. Another theater group presents outdoor performances on summer evenings.

A local arts and cultural commission tries to focus the efforts of all talented people in the community into interesting, year-round projects. The theater and music wing of the Artists and Craftsmen Guild presents programs ranging from jazz to the classics, and the arts center holds monthly art exhibitions to augment the many art galleries in town.

The altitude at Sedona is 4,300 feet—that's 3,200 feet higher than Phoenix, only two hours away by car, and 2,700 feet lower than Flagstaff, which is less than an hour away. This altitude means warmer winters than Flagstaff and cooler summers than Phoenix. (Some guidebooks list Sedona as being at a 4,400-foot altitude. Because the town slopes downward, it all depends upon where you measure.)

The area's housing is predominantly single-family residences, with several condominium developments and many subdivisions toward and beyond the city limits. Several nice mobile-home parks provide alternative housing opportunities. Don't expect to find bargain real estate prices here, because the overall quality is high, and this is a very desirable location. On the other hand, when you consider what your dollar buys in Scottsdale and other high-quality and popular Arizona locations, Sedona looks somewhat reasonable.

Lest I make Sedona sound like paradise on earth and start a stampede, let's take a look at two downsides frequently mentioned by residents. First, real estate is relatively expensive when compared with other, nonscenic Arizona communities. Second, automobiles can be unusually prevalent on Sedona's main thoroughfares. Traffic is aggravated by the continual flow of tourists gawking at the scenery, grabbing parking spaces, and generally getting in everybody's hair. The other side of the coin: Sedona's quality of life and stunning landscape greatly lessen the impact of these inconveniences.

Prescott   Sedona's rival in Arizona mountain retirement is Prescott, a few miles to the southwest. Its setting is as spectacular as

Sedona's but with a different flavor. Instead of desert scrub, cactus, and dramatic red rock formations, Prescott is surrounded by jagged peaks, sometimes snow-covered, and a forest of ponderosa pines (reputedly the largest in the world) overlooks the city. Prescott's movie-set panorama not only equals Sedona's, but its residents claim the weather is better as well; the four seasons are more sharply delineated. The elevation here is about 1,000 feet higher, which means cooler summers, with daily highs rarely climbing out of the eighties and dropping to the sixties every evening. On the other hand, winters are colder, with several snowfalls every year.

One of our visits to Prescott was in January, two days after a 3-inch snowfall. The sky was brilliant, most of the snow gone after two sixty-degree afternoons, although it still looked pretty covering the ground among the ponderosa pines. We found housing prices somewhat lower than Sedona, with an abundance of rentals for those who want to try the area for a few months before making any decisions. This is an older town—founded back in the 1860s— and it has neighborhoods of Victorians and many areas of modest, smaller homes. Because the surrounding area is uneven, most homes are custom built, with few tract models constructed. For exceptional bargains in housing, nearby Chino Valley is the place to look.

Prescott likes to think of itself as a small town, but it's actually a good-sized place, with a local population of 34,000. In addition it is the shopping center for 70,000 people. As such it's able to provide a multitude of services for its citizens, including a museum, a concert hall, and a 110,000-volume library that would be the envy of many larger cities. Yavapai College, a two-year institution, offers a noncredit "retirement college" with 900 students older than the age of sixty-two. There are also a liberal arts college and an aeronautical university in the area. Health care is above average here, with nearly one hundred physicians and surgeons and a 129-bed hospital. Several golf courses are part of the recreational scheme, along with

PRESCOTT AREA WEATHER						
In degrees Fahrenheit						
	Jan.	April	July	Oct.	Rain	Snow
Daily highs	51	68	90	74	13"	16"
Daily lows	24	36	61	42		

hiking, camping, fishing, and horse trails. Should you be unable to control the urge, 7,600-foot Granite Mountain offers exciting rock-climbing opportunities.

Payson   A third candidate for Arizona mountain retirement is Payson, located to the east of Sedona and Prescott. Sitting at approximately 5,200 feet, the same altitude as Prescott, Payson shares the same four-season climate. It also is bordered by the Tonto National Forest with its ponderosa-pine wonderland. Summers are pleasant, as you might expect in a high altitude; winters are mild enough for hiking, fishing, or horseback riding, with occasional snows for cross-country ski treks. The town of Payson is more heavily wooded than its competitors to the west.

Retirees here have plenty of kids their own age to play with. Almost 25 percent of the population is older than fifty-five years of age. The chamber of commerce utilizes retirees, with twenty-nine volunteers working in the chamber office. "We couldn't operate without 'em," said the local chamber manager. Because of the older population here, the local hospital is in the process of enlarging and becoming a cancer treatment center for northern Arizona.

This is the place for outdoor sports, with the spectacular Mogollon Rim just a few miles to the north, where hunting, fishing, hiking, and sight-seeing are legend. For indoor sports, a nearby gambling casino operated by the local Indian tribe brings revenues to the community as well as affording entertainment at the casino's 476 slot machines. A bus service connects the area with Phoenix, some 94 miles to the south.

Because of Payson's natural beauty, more and more people are relocating here, so housing costs have a tendency to escalate. Yet prices still appear to be bargains compared with some other popular Arizona retirement areas. A golf development has homes starting in the $350,000 range, and a few upscale neighborhoods feature expensive homes, but most neighborhoods are relaxed, with afford-

PAYSON WEATHER					
In degrees Fahrenheit					
	Jan.	April	July	Oct.	Rain	Snow
Daily highs	59	78	95	80	13"	30"
Daily lows	26	40	66	45		

able housing available. Mobile homes are sometimes interspersed with conventional housing, particularly in the less-expensive areas; with plenty of tall pines and natural landscaping, they blend in just fine.

The local hospital has enlarged and become a cancer-treatment center for northern Arizona. Facilities are excellent, and it is the only round-the-clock hospital for nearly 25,000 full- and part-time residents of the Rim Country area. Payson is less than a two-hour drive to the Mayo Clinic in Scottsdale, as well as to numerous excellent medical facilities in Phoenix.

Flagstaff   North of Sedona, and close enough to be a strong cultural influence, is the city of Flagstaff. At 7,000 feet in altitude, it receives full mountain winters averaging 97 inches of snow annually. Because of the high altitude and sunny days, the melt-off is said to be rapid. Summer highs seldom top eighty degrees, while nearby Phoenix cooks at more than one hundred degrees. Summer evenings are always cool, with low humidity taking the bite out of a brisk winter. Housing costs are higher than normal, but some terrific buys can be found out in the country, nestled in pine forests.

Flagstaff is a beautiful, modern city with lots of tall pines. The San Francisco Peaks here rise 12,670 feet and provide a breathtaking backdrop to the city. For the outdoor sportsman, fishing and hunting opportunities are without equal. A midsize university and a symphony orchestra contribute to a cultural ambience under leadership of the Flagstaff Arts Council and its comprehensive performing-arts program.

FLAGSTAFF WEATHER

In degrees Fahrenheit

	Jan.	April	July	Oct.	Rain	Snow
Daily highs	42	57	82	64	21"	97"
Daily lows	15	26	50	30		

FLAGSTAFF AREA COST OF LIVING

	Overall	Housing	Medical	Groceries	Utilities
Percentage of national average	112	128	113	112	109

Western Arizona: Colorado River Retirement

After the wild Colorado River exits from the Grand Canyon, it heads south toward Mexico and the Sea of Cortez. Along the way the Colorado is captured by a series of dams that provide peaceful lakes, contrasting nicely with the desert hills and shaded canyons that enclose the river.

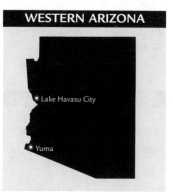

WESTERN ARIZONA

Lake Havasu City

Yuma

Along this stretch of waterway—from the Arizona town of Parker on the south to the Nevada town of Laughlin on the north—growing numbers of retirees and snowbirds settle in every winter. The numbers increase every year, with more and more buying homes and staying year-round. Places such as Lake Havasu have grown from small clusters of trailers and fishing shacks, with catfish and mallards as the only major attractions, into virtual cities with all the facilities needed for comfortable retirement.

Lake Havasu City   When a dam across the Colorado River created a long body of water separating the states of Colorado and California, the lake soon became a best-kept secret among snowbirds. Along the banks of the lake, where Lake Havasu City stands today, a collection of fish camps sprouted. At first they were nothing more than a few rustic RV parks and shacks selling bait and beer—a quiet and inexpensive location to escape the rigors of winter. Snowbirds would arrive by late fall, enjoy the summerlike winter, acquire a deep tan, then pack up their RVs and head north in the spring.

From these unpretentious beginnings Lake Havasu City has boomed to a city of more than 36,000 full-time residents. Houses and condos, trailers and mobile homes, and businesses and services of all descriptions appeared as if by magic. An estimated 6,000 to 8,000 winter residents swell the population and add to the general prosperity.

Lake Havasu City is a very surprising Southwestern retirement destination. When we first visited here, we thought the treeless bank of a desert lake an unlikely place for year-round retirement. Every time we return we're impressed by the area's growth. The community

LAKE HAVASU CITY WEATHER					
In degrees Fahrenheit					
	Jan.	April	July	Oct.	Rain	Snow
Daily highs	68	85	104	90	3"	—
Daily lows	42	55	79	62		

LAKE HAVASU CITY AREA COST OF LIVING					
Percentage of	Overall	Housing	Medical	Groceries	Utilities
national average	99	85	111	104	103

has grown gracefully, not just a quick-and-easy expansion. New residential developments are tastefully done with quality construction. New businesses, shopping facilities, and nice restaurants quickly appear to keep up with the increasing population.

Adding touches of scenic splendor, spectacular erosion sculptures—cliffs, canyons, and ragged peaks—never fail to draw gasps of astonishment as we pass through the region. True, in July and August you'll bake. But not much worse than in Phoenix. And like Phoenix, winter's balminess and gentle warmth makes you forget the rotisserie of summer.

The cost of living here barely reaches the national average. High utilities and medical care costs are offset by exceptionally low home prices (15 percent below average).

Because of the high number of retirees, the Lake Havasu area enjoys a more complete health-care system than ordinarily found in communities of similar size. A 99-bed acute-care hospital staffed with thirty-five physicians and a 120-bed nursing center serve the community. The hospital is in the process of expanding by 50 percent.

Mobile-home and RV parks dot the riverbanks, each with its own boat-loading ramp and nearby bait shop. By the way, boating and fishing aren't the only sports enjoyed in Lake Havasu. Several golf courses and at least one bowling alley will keep you active. A bustling senior center provides a dial-a-ride service in addition to the customary bridge games, arts, and nutrition facilities. A community college offers fee discounts to senior citizens, and some activities are coordinated with Arizona State University, including drama performances, concerts, and lectures.

Yuma   Yuma, the last of the Colorado River towns, anchors Arizona's southwest corner, where the mighty Colorado crosses into Mexico on its way to the Sea of Cortez. At this point the river loses some of its majesty; much of its flow has been siphoned off along the way to irrigate truck farms, supply drinking water to dozens of communities, and make ice cubes for gambling casinos. A sleepy little desert town just a few years ago, Yuma's development can be described as explosive. Since 1980 its population increased from 39,000 to today's 78,000.

Only the center part, or old town, shows evidence of its age and historic past. Everything else looks brand new. Originally described as "the great crossing place of a very wide and treacherous river," this was a trading center for early-day adventurers and settlers.

Because of its low desert altitude (only 138 feet), summers here are exceptionally hot. Throughout the year residents expect just a little more than 3 inches of rain. Make no mistake, this is desert!

Yuma's winter population triples, as snowbirds from all over the country descend upon the area, bringing motor homes, trailers, and campers. But like the Rio Grande Valley area, Yuma convinces many snowbirds to nest for year-round retirement.

Many retirees take advantage of nearby Mexico for inexpensive prescription drugs, dental care, and experimental medications not yet approved in the United States (although most have been in Europe). A Marine Corps base is located in the city limits, sharing its runways with private and commercial aircraft. Residents are treated to an interesting display of Marine fighter jets

YUMA WEATHER

In degrees Fahrenheit

	Jan.	April	July	Oct.	Rain	Snow
Daily highs	69	85	107	91	3"	—
Daily lows	43	56	80	62		

YUMA AREA COST OF LIVING

	Overall	Housing	Medical	Groceries	Utilities
Percentage of national average	104	99	108	102	147

and airliners alternating on takeoffs. This base provides PX, commissary, and medical care for military retirees.

For gaming activity Yuma Greyhound Park presents live dog racing and pari-mutuel betting on horses as well as greyhounds. Then there's the Cocopah Gaming Center, a tribal casino south of Yuma on Highway 95. For the academically inclined a state college, a state university, and two private colleges fill educational needs.

Nevada

Because a high mountain range, the Sierra Nevada, extends along the California–Nevada border cutting off rain-bearing winds from the Pacific Ocean, Nevada is the driest of the Southwestern states. Extensive deserts cover most of the land, with most residents choosing to live in or near one of Nevada's major towns. In fact more than half live in the vicinity of either Las Vegas or Reno. Most rainfall occurs in the spring, at which time barren deserts become a riot of color with the blossoms of cactus, sagebrush, and wild iris.

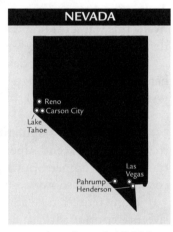

Of all the Western states, Nevada most represents the Old West to me. With new settlers arriving daily, Nevada feels like a frontier, a place of new beginnings. Something about Nevada's wide-open spaces stimulates a spirit of adventure and go-for-broke attitudes. It's a place where string ties, boot-top jeans, and snakeskin boots feel like natural apparel, a place where you might even be tempted to wear a Stetson hat, confident you won't look downright foolish.

Perhaps a hangover from an era of frontier gambling and gold rushes, a definite atmosphere of excitement hovers over Nevada. Gambling casinos are everywhere, and slot machines are strategically located in gasoline stations, drugstores, and supermarkets. Sometimes you'll even find them in rest rooms—the gambling syndicates don't want to miss a bet. This is a state where lucky gamblers made a stake and lucky miners made fortunes. This is evident today: Prospecting for precious metals is a big hobby in Nevada. There's always that chance that the next rock you crack

NEVADA TAX PROFILE

Sales tax: 6.5% to 7%, food and drugs exempt
State income tax: no
Property taxes: approximately 1% of
 appraised value
Intangibles tax: no
Social security taxed: no
Pensions taxed: no
Gasoline tax: 23.5¢ per gallon

open with a hammer will expose a gleaming streak of gold. (I've broken open many a rock myself in Nevada.)

Nevada is the country's fastest-growing state, by the way, with an almost unbelievable population increase of 60 percent over the last decade. Yet there's plenty of room to grow, because 87 percent of the land is public property, owned by the United States Government. Newcomers aren't strangers here, because their neighbors come from all over North America, just as you do. In Nevada casinos you'll notice that blackjack dealers, bartenders, and security guards traditionally wear name tags that tell you where they came from, sometimes without names, just their hometowns.

By the way, Nevada casinos set the odds so they can rake off 10 to 20 percent for overhead and profit. But state lotteries stiff you for 40 to 60 percent—sometimes even more. So, you really can't figure you're gambling when you buy state lottery tickets; you're being robbed.

Should you know that you, or your spouse, has a tendency to go overboard on gambling and succumb to the irresistible fever of chance, then forget Nevada. Go around it, fly over it, or go in the opposite direction. The round-the-clock excitement is just too much for some folks. They end up throwing their household money on the tables in increasing amounts in a desperate attempt to recoup their losses. The sad thing is that if they do hit a lucky streak and win a bundle the fever won't let them quit. They'll play until they are broke again.

On the other hand, many retirees handle gambling quite well, taking advantage of all the freebies and bargains the clubs offer to lure customers inside. Some never put even a nickel in the machines but have a great time anyway. Buffet tables laden with salads, entrees, and desserts offer unlimited visits for three or four dollars.

Prime rib dinners can be as low as $5.50. Lounge entertainment with music, dancers, and comedians is free, although you're encouraged to buy a drink. Some casinos even present free circus acts, complete with animals, high-wire performers, and clowns.

Las Vegas   A few years ago the city of Las Vegas was little more than a glittering curiosity: a flashy carnival of gambling, cabaret shows, and gaudy casinos. This desert oasis was a powerful magnet for Los Angeles high rollers and fun-seekers from all over the world. People came, spent their money, and went home.

Times have changed. Although gambling and showbiz are still important to the economy, Las Vegas's focus is now on population growth. It is an economic and population boomtown, the fastest-growing metropolitan complex in the nation. Approximately 60,000 new residents arrive per year, many of them retirees. The city spreads farther out into the desert every year. To accommodate newcomers new houses quickly sprout up around the city.

Because of this vigorous growth, retirees easily find part-time jobs at more than just minimum wage. Casinos, restaurants, and other tourist businesses need part-time help, but the incoming industries and businesses siphon new residents from the labor pool, offering them full-time jobs. The area consistently leads the nation in employment growth.

As in Reno, casinos give special consideration to hiring senior citizens. The percentage of older employees is impressive. Well, except for the cocktail waitresses, that is, who tend to be young and

LAS VEGAS WEATHER						
In degrees Fahrenheit						
	Jan.	April	July	Oct.	Rain	Snow
Daily highs	56	77	104	82	4"	1"
Daily lows	33	50	76	54		

LAS VEGAS AREA COST OF LIVING					
Percentage of	Overall	Housing	Medical	Groceries	Utilities
national average	105	86	128	114	106

buxom. This is certainly age discrimination, but then, you wouldn't care to run around scantily dressed, delivering drinks to a bunch of gamblers anyway, would you? (Personally I look terrible in one of those frilly tutus with sequins.)

As you might suspect, housing activity has kept up with this influx of newcomers; in fact it has more than kept up. From its inception Las Vegas has tended to overbuild; optimistic developers keep supply ahead of demand, keeping housing costs under control. Apartments are plentiful, with high vacancy rates. In short Las Vegas housing isn't inexpensive, but neither is it prohibitive.

Many people who normally might choose Phoenix for retirement are trying Las Vegas instead. When asked why, they gave various reasons in addition to casino entertainment and gaming excitement: No state income tax and proximity to southern California headed the list. (Las Vegas is a five and one-half hour drive from Los Angeles, compared with Phoenix's seven and one-half hours. Before long a privately financed super-train will link Las Vegas and southern California, moving millions of visitors at a fantastic 250 miles per hour!) Other taxes in the state are low, because about 50 percent of all state tax revenues come from the resort, tourism, and casino industry. Because of this easy income, Nevada doesn't need taxes on corporate or personal income, and its property taxes are among the lowest in the West.

All those questioned about their choice of Las Vegas as a retirement destination included weather in one form or another. Make no mistake, summers in Las Vegas are hot—yet those who retire here maintain that they love it that way.

Because of low humidity and absence of freezing weather, mobile homes are quite practical. Inexpensive evaporative coolers do a fine job during the warm months. Mobile-home parks present a wide choice of options, from inexpensive to super-luxurious. During the winter RV parks fill with fugitives from cold weather, who, as expected, depart for cooler climes come the summer. But unlike in some desert cities, retirees in Las Vegas form a steady year-round population as opposed to the floating second-home group found around Lake Havasu.

Las Vegas has several active senior citizens' groups as well as the usual volunteer organizations like the Retired Senior Volunteer Program (RSVP). Local newspapers run regular features covering news and activities of interest to retirees. Because this is a city instead of a town, senior citizens' centers aren't small and intimate as you might expect in a smaller place, but they certainly offer a wide range of activities to keep active folks busy and happy.

Henderson   The Las Vegas complex is spreading so fast that it will soon meet one of the younger cities of the modern dynamic Southwest, that of Henderson. This popular retirement location sits near the southern tip of Nevada, midway between Boulder City and Las Vegas at an elevation of 1,900 feet. Twenty years ago the population was about 8,900; today it has swollen to approximately 75,000, a large percentage of the newcomers being out-of-state retirees. Henderson is situated on level desert terrain, and several upscale golf communities are in place, including one encompassing 560 acres that features a golf layout designed by Jack Nicklaus. Another gated golf course community is building an ambitious 2,277 residential units on 600 acres. There will be an extensive trail system linking individual neighborhoods to proposed parks and a neighboring 3,000-acre wetlands park.

Reno   Although Las Vegas and Lake Tahoe try to be as formal and glitzy as possible, places like Reno tend to be more informal and relaxed. Except in some of the newer Reno hotel-casinos, neckties and cocktail dresses are rare; Western wear—cowboy hats, ornate boots, and string ties—are seen about as frequently. This is changing in Reno to some extent, because the Las Vegas–Atlantic City gambling corporations are attempting to duplicate their luck in Reno. New elaborate and classy casinos are sprouting up all over, but I suspect this will have little effect upon the Reno of the nontourist.

Reno is an old town in a picturesque setting with a backdrop of snow-fringed peaks looming in the distance. This is a town proud of its rowdy gold- and silver-mining past—demonstrated by its deliberately preserved Old West atmosphere. Originally Reno's major business was supplying the booming mining camps that flourished nearby. About the time the mines played out, a new industry arose in the form of quickie divorces. Reno divorces were once considered the only practical way to go for an uncomplicated marriage dissolution. As other states liberalized their divorce laws, legalized gam-

RENO WEATHER						
In degrees Fahrenheit						
	Jan.	April	July	Oct.	Rain	Snow
Daily highs	45	63	91	70	7"	24"
Daily lows	20	29	48	31		

RENO AREA COST OF LIVING					
Percentage of	Overall	Housing	Medical	Groceries	Utilities
national average	107	104	113	109	117

bling became the leading industry. Ironically today Reno has become a quickie *marriage* center, with wedding chapels scattered around town like fast-food restaurants, and marriages in Reno outnumber divorces by a ten-to-one ratio.

Like Las Vegas, Reno has undergone a building boom, with the city expanding outward at a rapid pace. Including the adjoining city of Sparks, the population has climbed past the 200,000 mark, making Reno a good-sized city. Yet folks here still cling to Reno's self-bestowed title of "The Biggest Little City in the World." Las Vegas construction imitates southern California modern style—stucco, sprawling ranch houses, and tile roofs—whereas Reno prefers houses built of honest red brick. The older neighborhoods are of solidly built, no-nonsense homes—a settled, mature city—but the desert around the city is constantly sprouting subdivisions of modern designs.

Reno also offers twenty-four-hour entertainment and glitter. But there's something hometown about the downtown gaming tables that escapes Lake Tahoe, Las Vegas, and Laughlin. This hometown feeling was deliberately cultivated when gambling was legalized during the Great Depression. Harold Smith, the founder of Harold's Club, decided to go after local money instead of depending upon tourists. He instituted the practice of giving free drinks and double odds on crap tables. He cashed paychecks without charge and tried to make people feel at home. Harold's Club also started the practice of preferential hiring of local people and senior citizens. Retirees work at everything from dealing blackjack to making change.

As a retirement center Reno is one of our favorites. Because of the large number of retirees, the level of services for senior citizens is exceptionally high. Retiree clubs and organizations are unusually active. Thirteen apartment complexes specialize in assisted housing for the elderly, handicapped, and disabled. In addition there are three large, full-service retirement facilities. Private programs such as Meals on Wheels and Care and Share are active, as are several run by the government. There's a senior citizens' employment service, and a senior citizens' law center provides free assistance with wills, Social Security, leases, and things of that nature.

The cost of living is not cheap, but compared with many urban locations, it is reasonable. The Reno area has all the facilities necessary for good retirement: hospitals, colleges, cultural events, and community services.

Some choose Reno retirement for excitement, but everyone likes its extraordinary climate. The 4,440-foot altitude and very low humidity keep the weather pleasant year-round despite its apparent low temperatures. For those who cannot stand hot summer weather, Reno is perfect. Expect to enjoy about 300 sunny days a year here. Even though July and August temperatures usually approach ninety degrees by midafternoon, you will sleep under an electric blanket every night; the thermometer always drops into the forties. Even in the middle of winter, the high temperatures are about the same as summer lows!

Reno is the medical center for the western Nevada-eastern California area. Washoe Medical Center has an important cardiac rehabilitation facility and is the hospital where other hospitals send patients when serious problems arise. St. Mary's and four other hospitals serve the Reno area.

Carson City   Carson City is Nevada's state capital and is the state's fifth-largest city, even though it has a population of less than 50,000. The downtown's old buildings give you a feeling for Carson City's historic past and rich Western heritage. The old State Legislature and the Courthouse probably look much the same as they did back in the days when Mark Twain worked as a printer and newswriter in nearby Virginia City. Even though gambling is big business here, the city's expansion seems to be spreading out into the desert rather than upward with tall casinos. Tourist demand for large, luxurious casinos hasn't hit Carson City as it has Reno and Las Vegas, so the funky old downtown changes little over the years. This is one of the city's charms: a comfortable, slow-paced, and non-tourist atmosphere. Subdivisions fan away from the city with both upscale and moderate construction. All neighborhoods enjoy views of nearby mountains, and the clear air seems to magnify their majestic presence.

Pahrump Las Vegas and Reno are examples of fast-growing cities in the desert, where the emphasis is on entertainment and big-city conveniences. Dozens of other smaller communities throughout the state offer somewhat the same attractions as Las Vegas and Reno, although on a much smaller scale. And some towns, like Pahrump (about 60 miles and a world away from Las Vegas), are popular for desert places to live in. Yes, Pahrump has a tiny casino or so, but you get the feeling gambling isn't the essential part of the scene. (I once hit a quarter jackpot there, and the bartender immediately hung an OUT OF ORDER sign on the machine!)

In a remarkably short time span, Pahrump has grown from little more than a couple of taverns, a handful of stores, and some cotton farms into a small, widely scattered city. Complete with a senior citizen center, a library, a medical facility, a bowling alley, and a community center (with swimming pool), Pahrump has moved from the category of crossroad settlement to a viable retirement community. In fact about 40 percent of the residents are retired. The town has grown at an astounding 15 percent per year for the last several years to its present size of 30,000.

Travelers are often unaware they've entered the town of Pahrump, because its inhabitants are scattered over an area of 25 square miles. A feeling of spaciousness is enhanced by homes sitting on large parcels of land, mostly one acre in size—sometimes ten to twenty acres—and as far off the main highway as possible. Because desert land is inexpensive, folks see no need to crowd themselves next to the neighbors. Pahrump also lacks a compact, traditional downtown center so characteristic of other communities its size. Like residential homes, businesses tend to locate on large pieces of land, spaced apart from competitors. There's never a problem finding a parking space here! Several small shopping centers host a collection of stores grouped about a supermarket, but with plenty of open space between the complex and other businesses. Because everyone drives a car here, sidewalks are absent, adding to the rural feeling of Western desert living.

The major drawing cards in this valley are sunshine, low-cost land, and friendly neighbors. Pahrump ranks just below Yuma, Arizona, as one of the places with the most sunny days in the United States. Its low humidity makes even the hottest days bearable, if not comfortable. Yet water supplies are not a problem because Pahrump sits on the third-largest underground supply of water in the United States.

Lake Tahoe   A short drive from Reno up a wide, four-lane highway is a beautiful, bustling area in a forested lake setting that many consider a prime retirement place. This is South Lake Tahoe, a sprawling community that straddles the line between Nevada and California. Well known for luxurious hotels and gambling casinos, Lake Tahoe is also celebrated for beauty; it sits next to one of the most gorgeous lakes in the world. Mark Twain had this to say about Lake Tahoe in his book *Roughing It*:

> Three months of camp life on Lake Tahoe would restore an Egyptian mummy to his pristine vigor and give him an appetite like an alligator. I do not mean the oldest and driest mummies, of course, but the fresher ones. The air up there in the clouds is very pure and fine, bracing and delicious. And why shouldn't it be? It is the same the angels breathe. Lake Tahoe must surely be the fairest picture the whole earth affords.

Snow is an important part of Tahoe's winter. If there isn't at least a 6-foot pack on the ski slopes, skiers feel cheated. From anywhere in the area it is a matter of minutes to a ski lift, a joy to those who enjoy the sport. The snow typically falls in isolated, heavy storms that dump up to 3 feet in one night; then the weather turns sunny for days or weeks until the next snow. From my perspective, the best thing about Lake Tahoe snow is that it takes only a twenty-minute drive to be out of it. You can be skiing at Incline Village in the morning and wandering through Carson City in shirtsleeves that same evening.

Because the Lake Tahoe economy is basically tourist oriented, many normal cultural and entertainment activities are lacking. For example, to the best of my knowledge, there aren't any traditional senior citizens' centers other than three nutrition programs. But the lack of organized recreation is more than made up for by the top-notch talent presented by the casinos. Hollywood stars and entertainers regularly appear at the gambling emporiums, often at a fraction of the entrance fees you'd expect in a noncompetitive economy. Also the area is served by Lake Tahoe Community College, which offers various courses oriented toward seniors, from computers to exercise classes.

The cost of living here is clearly higher than in nearby Reno or Carson City. With tourist dollars floating around freely, you can expect that prices will float with them. Housing is expensive as well. But for many a higher cost of living is a reasonable tradeoff for the quality of the surroundings and the excitement of the lake area with its outdoor wonderland. For those who aren't ready for a rocking-chair retirement, there are plenty of part-time work opportunities in the casinos.

One major hospital, Tahoe Forest, serves the medical needs of the Lake Tahoe area. The facility is equipped to handle most cases, but when the staff gets in over its head, they have quick transportation to either University of California hospital at Davis, near Sacramento, or to the Washoe Medical Center in Reno.

Why would folks consider retiring here? "Living here is like being on permanent vacation," says a friend of mine who owns a lakefront cottage near North Shore. Like many residents, he bought his home several years ago in anticipation of retirement. He rented out his place by the day or week at premium rates to regular visitors—vacationers, skiers, and gamblers—and by the time he was ready to retire, a good portion of his retirement home had been paid off. The deductions and depreciation as a rental also helped ease his tax burden. Long-term rentals, however, are usually available at rates one would expect to pay in most California urban areas. That can be expensive and worth it only if you cannot consider living anywhere else because you love Lake Tahoe so much. Many people living here feel just that way.

New Mexico

With its inventory of scenic deserts, lush forests, and high mountain ranges, New Mexico clearly lives up to its nickname: Land of Enchantment. The state has a dry to partly dry climate not particularly different from other arid Southwestern regions. A combination of low humidity, high altitude, and abundant sunshine makes this a pleasant and healthy place to live.

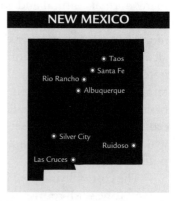

Summer days are hot, but nights in New Mexico are always cool. Many localities commonly find that temperatures may register ninety degrees on a sunny day and then fall to fifty degrees in the evening. Although daytime air-conditioning may be popular in some areas, most of the time you'll sleep under blankets at night. Rainfall varies from 8 inches per year in some places to as much as 24 inches in some mountainous areas. Yearly snowfall ranges from almost nothing to as much as 300 inches near Ruidoso.

About a third of New Mexico's residents consider themselves to be Hispanic and are quite proud of their heritage. Early Spanish explorers and colonists were the first white settlers in this area. The founders were farming and building towns and villages in New Mexico a full generation before the first Pilgrim ever set foot on Plymouth Rock. By the way, don't make the mistake of calling New Mexico Hispanics "Mexican Americans" or you'll run the risk of dirty looks and sarcastic replies. After all, some Hispanic families were living here more than two centuries before there even was a Mexico! People here converse in an archaic form of Spanish, the cultured manner of speaking that was in vogue back in the sixteenth and seventeenth centuries; some words in their vocabulary wouldn't be understood

NEW MEXICO TAX PROFILE

Sales tax: 5% to 6.25%, no exemptions
State income tax: graduated, 1.8% to 8.5% greater than $41,600; can't deduct federal income tax
Property taxes: about 7%
Intangibles tax: no
Social security taxed: no
Pensions taxed: excludes up to $8,000, depending on income level
Gasoline tax: 16¢ per gallon, plus possible local taxes

in Mexico. They've been isolated so long that their customs, cooking, and worldviews are very different from those of Mexico. And although New Mexico shares a border with Mexico, no highways, railroads, or connections with Mexico exist along the desolate southern frontier other than one minor border crossing at Columbus. Historically Mexican immigration (legal and illegal) bypassed New Mexico, moving into California, Arizona, or Texas instead.

Las Cruces   Las Cruces, the largest town in southern New Mexico, is forty-five minutes away from El Paso via Interstate 10. Like some other cities along the Rio Grande, Las Cruces is rapidly attracting retirees. Even though the town is small compared with nearby El Paso (63,000 inhabitants), it offers plenty of amenities for its senior citizens. New Mexico State University is located here. Shopping is more than adequate, with El Paso nearby for anything not available in Las Cruces.

Nestled in the fertile Mesilla Valley, which draws irrigation water from the Rio Grande, the city is in the center of a prosperous farming district, producing cotton, pecans, and chili peppers. Mountains rising to higher than 9,000 feet surround Las Cruces and block some of the northern winter winds to produce a mild, low-humidity winter. Summers are warm, similar to El Paso's, although the large amount of irrigation raises the summer humidity somewhat. Its mild weather permits fishing year-round in nearby Elephant Butte and Caballo reservoirs. Las Cruces has two public golf courses and a private country club. Eighteen lighted tennis courts make for comfortable play on hot summer evenings.

LAS CRUCES WEATHER						
In degrees Fahrenheit						
	Jan.	April	July	Oct.	Rain	Snow
Daily highs	59	79	96	76	9"	3"
Daily lows	27	42	63	44		

LAS CRUCES COST OF LIVING					
Percentage of national average	Overall	Housing	Medical	Groceries	Utilities
	95	95	90	99	93

Las Cruces is an unusually attractive setting with a distinctive, Old West pueblo character. Apparently city planners try to channel architecture toward the pueblo style of Santa Fe, with soft, earthy tones. Yet Las Cruces has avoided a regimented, stiff adherence to this style, permitting pastels and bright colors to break up the muted earth tones. We looked at a display of exceptionally imaginative homes of elegant, Old West style. They were set on landscaped low-maintenance lots that incorporated natural shrubs and cactus. We guessed the price at $100,000 over the asking price.

New Mexico State University brings the community together by inviting the public to join in cultural and entertainment activities, such as drama presentations and a symphony orchestra. Seniors are welcome to take regular courses or take occasional classes at the weekend college, a program just for seniors offering scholarly mini-courses on subjects ranging from local history to opera appreciation.

Medical care here is exceptional, with one of the best-equipped hospitals in the state, the 286-bed Memorial Medical Center. Las Cruces is the medical hub of a five-county region. Even larger medical facilities in nearby El Paso are just a short drive down the interstate.

Albuquerque   High in the desert, sitting on the east bank of the Rio Grande at an altitude of more than 5,000 feet, Albuquerque (pop. 450,000) is a fast-growing retirement area. Its combination of high altitude, dry air, and mild temperatures is exactly what many people look for in a place to live. The thermometer rarely hits one hundred degrees and almost never sees zero. With afternoon hu-

ALBUQUERQUE WEATHER

In degrees Fahrenheit

	Jan.	April	July	Oct.	Rain	Snow
Daily highs	47	71	93	72	8"	11"
Daily lows	22	39	65	43		

ALBUQUERQUE AREA COST OF LIVING

	Overall	Housing	Medical	Groceries	Utilities
Percentage of national average	103	107	110	99	100

midity typcially 30 percent, the weather seems even milder than charts might indicate. July's (the hottest month) average highs of ninety degrees always drop into the sixties at night. A scant 8 inches of rain fall per year, which means lots of brilliant, sunny weather. And the best part is that the winter months of December and January are the sunniest. It's a two-season year, with about 11 inches of snow expected every winter. It doesn't stick around for long, though, because winter days usually hit fifty degrees by noon. Muggy days and long, drizzling spells are just about unknown in Albuquerque. Summers can become quite dry, however, causing the mighty Rio Grande to dwindle to a muddy trickle. Once when Will Rogers was giving a talk in Albuquerque, he cracked, "Why, you folks ought to be out there right now irrigating that river to keep it from blowing away!"

Albuquerque's biggest drawback is that its name is difficult to spell. The problem with spelling started in 1706 when the Spanish Duke of Alburquerque decided that this spot, where the old Camino Real crossed the Rio Grande, would be a great place to have a town named after himself. But when they put up the city limits sign, somebody left an *r* out of his name. And schoolkids have had trouble spelling it ever since. (Shouldn't there be at least one *k* somewhere in Albuquerque?)

The city has taken pains to preserve its historic sector. Preservation was possible partly because the coming of the railroad in 1880 moved the "downtown" away from the original plaza, thus sparing it from development. Today the area, now known as Old Town, offers fine restaurants and shops and maintains the historic flavor of the Old West. Venerable adobe buildings and museums cluster around the Duke of Alburquerque's village.

The downtown section is clean, modern, and prosperous-looking. Everything seems polished and tastefully designed. A pedestrian mall completes the picture of a pleasant city center. The rest of the metropolitan area is also quite pleasant, with many homes designed in an adobe style and lots of huge shade trees in the older areas of town.

The metropolitan hub of New Mexico, Albuquerque is also a high-technology center of the Southwest. As such it attracts people from all over the country to work and live there. The University of New Mexico (enrollment 25,000) accounts for much of the rich cultural offerings of the city. There's a full calendar of lectures, concerts, drama, and sporting events, as well as numerous classes of interest to senior citizens.

Skiing is great, with more than eleven facilities within striking distance. Sandia Peak (15 miles northeast of Albuquerque) has lifts that rise higher than 10,000 feet. Hunting, fishing, prospecting, and rock-hunting are all great outdoor pastimes. But all outdoor activities don't require going into the wilderness. Horse-racing fans will find seven racetracks in New Mexico, with the season starting in January at The Downs at Albuquerque.

Rio Rancho   As an example of Albuquerque retirement away from the city congestion, let's look at Rio Rancho, twenty minutes from downtown Albuquerque and forty-five minutes from Santa Fe. It's a comfortable, safe area of mixed new and older homes. Originally started as a mail-order retirement scheme to sell parcels of worthless desert landscape, Rio Rancho targeted New Yorkers, and as a result, many residents come from that state. Some folks were skeptical about the project, but they were surprised when it actually took off, and it hasn't stopped since. Today about 52,000 people live on ranch land that twenty-five years ago supported less than 200 cows. Rio Rancho is one of the fastest-growing communities in the country. Although many retirees are buying new and older homes here, a recently opened Intel Company facility is bringing high-tech workers from all over the world. It's a great place for retirees, but it's basically a multigenerational community.

With a twenty-seven-hole golf course and a panorama of the Sandia mountains in the distance, Rio Rancho is a blend of Southwest desert and middle-class suburb.

Santa Fe   Fifty-nine miles northeast of Albuquerque, the town of Santa Fe sits like an antique jewel in the picturesque Sangre de Cristo Mountains, perched at an altitude of 7,000 feet. A sense of history pervades the streets and byways of this oldest capital city in the United States. Settled in the year 1610, Santa Fe was a bustling town and commercial center ten years before the Pilgrims set foot on Plymouth Rock! Santa Fe has been a capital city for more than 375 years.

Here you'll find the oldest private house in the United States and the oldest public building in the country, the Palace of the Governors. This building became General Kearney's headquarters in 1846, when his troops captured Santa Fe during the Mexican War. Incidentally, this was the first foreign capital ever captured by U.S. armed forces.

Santa Fe is a town steeped in history and culture, and its residents work hard at keeping it that way. Strict building codes insist that all new construction be of adobe or adobe-looking material; all exteriors must be in earth tones. This preserves the distinctive Spanish pueblo style for which Santa Fe is famous. Occasionally one sees a home that was built in the days before zoning codes, and the blue or white building sticks out like the proverbial sore thumb. At first the shades of sand, brown, and tan can seem a bit somber, but after a while one grows to appreciate the way they complement the setting.

Along with tourism and retirement, artistic endeavors are one of Santa Fe's prime industries. Art affects the everyday lives of Santa Fe residents, with hundreds of painters, artists, and craftspeople doing their thing and almost 200 galleries exhibiting their treasures. The old plaza in the heart of the city is usually lined with street artisans displaying jewelry, paintings, leather goods, and all kinds of quality artwork. Local Native Americans bring intricate silver and turquoise jewelry to sell in the plaza. A highly regarded opera company performs in a unique outdoor theater. Fortunately Santa Fe's weather seldom interferes with the performances, because only about 15 inches of rain falls each year. A year-round calendar of events includes concerts by the Orchestra of Santa Fe, the Chorus of Santa Fe, the Desert Chorale, and the Santa Fe Symphony, as well as Native American festivals

SANTA FE WEATHER

In degrees Fahrenheit

	Jan.	April	July	Oct.	Rain	Snow
Daily highs	40	60	78	62	15"	33"
Daily lows	19	35	57	39		

SANTA FE COST OF LIVING

	Overall	Housing	Medical	Groceries	Utilities
Percentage of national average	113	135	119	104	94

and celebrations. Numerous theater and drama presentations come from the New Mexico Repertory Theatre, the British American Theatre Institute, the Armory for the Arts, the Santuario de Guadalupe, the Community Theatre, and the Greer Garson Theater. There's even a rodeo every summer. Of course the thoroughbreds race at famous Santa Fe Downs from May to Labor Day.

"When I get up in the morning, I know there's going to be sun," said a man who retired in Santa Fe after living most of his life in northern Illinois. "It makes a big difference in my life." Santa Fe is almost tied with Albuquerque for sunshine; almost 300 days a year are guaranteed to be at least partly sunny. Santa Fe gets more rain, though, and there's three times as much snow—about 33 inches annually. This keeps Santa Fe greener. You'll find a true four-season year with very pleasant summers. Be prepared to wear a sweater on summer evenings; the temperature occasionally drops to below fifty degrees at night.

Folks who can afford to buy a second house anywhere they like tend to buy one here. That should tell us something about Santa Fe's quality. The problem is that Santa Fe has such a reputation as a retirement and artist center that outsiders have bid up real estate to an unusual level. "It's getting so we natives can't afford to live here anymore," lamented one hometown resident. Yet housing is curiously mixed in price. Generally it's more expensive than Albuquerque, particularly for nicer housing. But there are also some inexpensive places. Several high-end developments are under way, at least one with its own private golf course. A couple of attractive, full-care retirement residences are located in Santa Fe, one without any endowment or entrance fees; but there could be a waiting list. An active senior citizens program, Open Hands, offers services and an opportunity to volunteer for satisfying and worthwhile community projects.

Taos   Farther up the road from Santa Fe, in the heart of the Sangre de Cristo Mountains, is the delightful town of Taos. A bustling village, quiet retreat, art colony, ski resort—these are but a few of Taos's many faces. Its fifty-five art galleries and numerous art programs hint at the large number of artists in residence. Famous for its picturesque adobes, narrow winding streets, and the ancient Pueblo village on the town's outskirts, Taos provide awesome inspiration for the artistic set.

The population is very small (about 4,100), so resident artists and other residents tend to form a closely integrated group. The successful and well-known mingle with the unsuccessful and rank amateurs much more freely than they would in large-scale Santa Fe. One person told us, "We permanent residents of Taos achieve social equality that you seldom find elsewhere. Some very wealthy, successful people here prefer to drive rusty pickups instead of Mercedes and wear blue jeans and boots instead of city dress. I've attended cocktail parties where starving artists, multimillionaires, and local business people mix as if they were at class reunions."

Bear in mind that Taos is a tourist destination. Skiing at nearby Ski Valley draws snow enthusiasts beginning at Thanksgiving. Ski Valley averages 321 inches of snow each year, so the season lasts into the middle of April. Then, just when ski traffic thins out, camera-toting tourists take up the slack. They come to photograph the ancient adobes in Taos and of course, the very ancient Pueblo Indian village—one of the most-photographed sites in the West. The main complaint you'll hear from permanent residents is tourist traffic and the business community's dependence upon tourism for survival.

Real estate falls into two categories here: the surprisingly expensive (especially for the old adobes) or average to substandard. Because Taos is a popular place and because there are so few properties on the market, buyers can often get their asking prices, especially when selling to seasonal residents. Part-time residents are divided between wealthy folks who can afford a summer home, or perhaps a winter ski home, and those who come to rent a condo for a few months to experience the magic ambience of the area.

Ruidoso   Ruidoso bursts upon travelers as an absolute surprise; it's a setting you don't expect to find in New Mexico. Almost magically the landscape changes from dry desert covered with brush and patches of *carrizo* grass into a gorgeous, winding river canyon graced with majestic evergreens perfuming the breezes. Cool mountain air and lush vegetation make Californians imagine they're at Lake Tahoe. Easterners might recall Maine forests or Canadian mountain vistas.

Of course this isn't news to West Texans; they knew about the Ruidoso Upper Canyon for decades as an excellent place to escape blazing Texas summers. The crystal-clear river cascading through the tree-shaded canyon made for a wonderful escape and family fun. Summer cabins sprang up among the large ponderosa pines and along the small river. By the way, *ruidoso* in Spanish means "noisy," an apt description of the sound of cascading water.

With the opening of the racetrack at Ruidoso Downs in 1947, people started thinking of Ruidoso as a resort instead of merely a summertime mountain getaway. More than thirty years ago, the Mescalero Apache tribe, with the help of a Texas oilman, developed a ski run high up on Apache Peak, a part of the Mescalero reservation. They called it Ski Apache and established Ruidoso's second career as a winter resort. The 12,000-foot ski run immediately attracted the attention of ski buffs from all over the country. This is the southernmost place to ski in the Southwest, and because of its exceptionally high location, skiing lasts long after many other areas have closed down, providing some of the best warm-weather powder skiing in the world. A popular skiing magazine rates Ruidoso as one of the ten best ski towns in which to live.

Skiing did more than simply bring tourists and increase employment opportunities; it brought visitors and allowed them to observe the area under winter conditions as well as summer. Visitors were pleasantly surprised to discover relatively mild winters here and to learn that fall and spring are delightful seasons as well. This launched Ruidoso upon yet another career as a center for year-round residence and retirement.

Summer cabins were enlarged, and larger homes started springing up for both retirees and working families. This continuing growth provides employment for even more new residents and encourages more businesses to open. Today Ruidoso has blossomed into a pleasant town of about 7,500 inhabitants and is still growing, with the county population pushing 13,000. The area supports many more shops, stores, restaurants, and businesses of all kinds than you might expect of a town this size. Because Ruidoso draws visitors and tourists all year long, small businesses flourish, and you'll find an astonishing selection of excellent restaurants serving almost any kind of cuisine imaginable, from French to Chinese, from prime rib to Indian squaw bread. According to local business owners, the only slow time is in April, when they manage to squeeze in their vacation time. April, by the way, is an excellent time of the year to investigate Ruidoso as a retirement destination. You'll not only find less traffic and off-season rates for motels, you'll experience Ruidoso's spring, one of its best seasons.

The tall forest makes a proper setting for Ruidoso real estate, with homes shaded by a thick green canopy casually located in a somewhat hodgepodge way. Elegant homes can sit next door to small cottages, log cabins, and, often, mobile homes. The higher end of the housing scale, at the northern edge of town, is also at the highest elevation. Trees are higher here, as are selling prices.

Silver City   For a thousand years the area around Silver City has been a source of valuable minerals. Early Native Americans mined outcrops of copper to fashion ornaments and spear points. In the 1790s Spanish miners worked the copper deposits, loading the ore on the backs of burros and hauling it south into Chihuahua for smelting. But Silver City itself wasn't established until returning California forty-niners discovered silver ore a few miles north of the present town site. This kicked off a typical mining-boom scenario, with a tent city being replaced by substantial brick buildings and optimistic expansion.

Western-history buffs might be interested that Silver City is where the famous outlaw Billy the Kid grew up, went to school, committed his first crime, was arrested for the first time, and made his first of several escapes from jail. Billy the Kid's first arrest was for robbing clothes from a Chinese laundry when he was fifteen. Had to start somewhere.

Silver City's 6,000-foot altitude provides cool, dry weather and beautiful, forested mountain vistas. With a population of almost 12,000, Silver City is large enough to supply most services but still small enough to escape big-city crowding, crime, and pollution.

The town's architectural style clearly reflects the time of its development. Downtown buildings are influenced by the town's ranching and mining background, rich with Victorian brick buildings

SILVER CITY WEATHER						
In degrees Fahrenheit						
	Jan.	April	July	Oct.	Rain	Snow
Daily highs	47	65	87	69	14"	21"
Daily lows	18	36	60	40		

so popular in Western mining towns during the last century. In fact Silver City's historic district boasts the largest concentration of Victorian homes in southern New Mexico.

The presence of Western New Mexico University takes Silver City out of the category of an ordinary mining town and is responsible in part for inspiring a fast-growing artist colony in Silver City. An astonishing number of galleries, studios, and workshops welcome art lovers, either regularly or by invitation.

Outdoor enthusiasts will find much to do within a short distance from Silver City, which is surrounded by the 3.3-million-acre Gila National Forest. Five fishing lakes offer good catches of bass and crappie, and there are rivers and streams with trout. Five tennis courts and an eighteen-hole golf course augment the ten parks and two swimming pools in Silver City.

Affordable real estate is one of the attractions that draws retirees here. In nearby Tyrone the Phelps–Dodge company decided to move some of its company housing by marketing the workers' homes as retirement locations. Homes were refurbished and sold starting at $40,000. Now that these are gone, executive housing is going on the block at affordable prices.

Colorado

When you think of deserts and mountains, Colorado has to figure big. The state's highways cross the most impressive mountains on the continent, so high that some folks have trouble breathing; several passes climb higher than 10,000 feet. When folks do catch their breath,

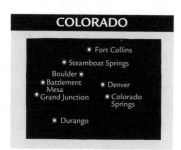

the mountain scenery immediately takes it away again. From legendary old mining towns to ultramodern cities, from farmlands to forests, Colorado has a lot to offer the retiree. Many part-time retirees love the state for its wonderfully refreshing summers, and full-time retirees like the reasonable housing and mild winters of some areas.

Grand Junction   Grand Junction is the largest city in western Colorado, located in a broad valley in the high plateau country west of the Rocky Mountains. Its name came from its location near the junction of the Colorado and Gunnison Rivers (the Colorado was originally called the *Grand* River). Grand Junction is the center of an urban area of some 82,000 people, although the town itself has a comfortable population of 47,000. Shopping malls, a senior citi-

COLORADO TAX PROFILE

Sales tax: 3% to 7.5%, food and drugs exempt

State income tax: 5% of federal taxable income; can't deduct federal income tax

Property taxes: average 1% of purchase price

Intangibles tax: no

Social security taxed: half of benefits are taxable for higher incomes

Pensions taxed: excludes first $20,000; double deduction for taxpayers older than sixty-five

Gasoline tax: 4¢ to 10¢ per gallon

zens' center, and excellent health care are among the attractions. An abundance of sunshine and a mild winter that permits year-round golf and tennis adds to its desirability for retirement.

Earlier we discussed economic disasters that turned out to be bonanzas for retirees. Here's another story. During the late 1970s, encouraged and subsidized by the government, oil companies began experimenting with the enormous shale oil deposits of Colorado and Wyoming. Thousands of workers flocked there to help develop this potentially valuable natural resource.

Grand Junction participated in this welcome economic boom. New houses and apartments went up like mushrooms after a rainstorm. All this new building still wasn't enough, so Exxon, one of the larger companies, was forced to enter the construction business to provide housing for its employees. Among other things Exxon developed a flat mountaintop, a place called Battlement Mesa, into a spiffy housing development. The company constructed 684 residences, complete with a multimillion-dollar recreation center.

Suddenly the bubble collapsed. Slumping oil prices had made it too expensive to squeeze petroleum from the shale. Grand Junction remembers this date as Black Sunday. By the end of a year, almost 8,000 workers lost their jobs. Almost as quickly as they came, they began leaving. Knowing they hadn't even a prayer to make payments, many simply walked away from their homes. They couldn't even *give* the properties away because they owed more money on the mortgages than the current market value of the properties. The few buyers who were in the market waited for foreclosure and then

GRAND JUNCTION WEATHER					
In degrees Fahrenheit					
	Jan.	April	July	Oct.	Rain	Snow
Daily highs	36	65	94	69	8"	25"
Daily lows	15	38	64	41		

GRAND JUNCTION AREA COST OF LIVING					
Percentage of	Overall	Housing	Medical	Groceries	Utilities
national average	102	103	105	105	102

bought from the banks at bargain prices. As in Bisbee and Ajo, the workers who lost their jobs suffered both financially and from their shattered hopes for the future.

The businesspeople who survived realized that the solution to the problem lay in attracting industry with a stable financial base, something not subject to boom and bust like petroleum. Economic incentives such as free land for new and expanding industries were offered. At the same time they began concentrating on a special business, one that's clean, doesn't pollute the air, and brings in an obvious source of steady income: the retirement industry!

Their efforts were successful. Gradually the economy recovered, in large measure as a result of retiree money. Surplus homes were eventually purchased, and the population began rising once more. According to a real estate broker, about 30 percent of today's buyers are retirees from out of state. Although homes are selling at the national averages nowdays, retirees are still coming.

Battlement Mesa   During the Grand Junction petroleum boom era, Exxon found a serene, wooded meadow on a nearby mesa, surrounded by mountains reminiscent of towering battlements, and decided to use it for executive housing. They called it Battlement Mesa and spared no expense in construction, installing a country club–style golf course, swimming pool, and clubhouse. The surrounding homes were high quality. When the boom fizzled the company had little choice but turn the executive housing project into a high-class residential development. Because Battlement Mesa is located some 40 miles from Grand Junction, the long commute makes it more suitable for retired couples than working families. So it became essentially a retirement development.

Today Battlement Mesa is a mixture of single-family homes, townhouses, and manufactured homes priced between $100,000 and $500,000. If the developer's plans work out, there will eventually be 5,000 homes in the development. A medical clinic is located in Battlement Mesa, and an emergency clinic can be found in the town of Rifle, about fifteen minutes away.

Colorado Springs   Towering above Colorado Springs majestic Pikes Peak dominates the view from every corner of the city. The 14,110-foot-high mountain presents an ever-changing picture depending on the angle of the sun, the clouds, and the amount of snow. In 1870 General William Jackson Palmer, founder of Colorado Springs, had this to say about his new home: "Could one live in constant view of these grand mountains without being elevated by them into a lofty plane of thought and purpose?"

Although today's Colorado Springs is booming, with high-tech industries bringing in more residents daily, the town scarcely resembles a boom town. As it grew over the years, Colorado Springs matured gracefully. As a result you'll find a variety of housing and neighborhoods, ranging from older stately homes to modern planned communities to custom homes in outlying wooded areas. Today's population of 359,000 makes Colorado Springs a good-sized city, yet an easy place to drive in, with wide roads and boulevards accommodating traffic and seldom bogging down with gridlock, as often happens in cities this size.

Residential districts near the central part of town are vintage Colorado, with comfortable and affordable residential environs. As you move outward neighborhoods are newer and more expensive. Most neighborhoods are safe, too; Colorado Springs ranks high in personal safety according to FBI statistics. Tri-Lakes area, a few minutes' drive north of Colorado Springs, boasts several

COLORADO SPRINGS AREA WEATHER						
In degrees Fahrenheit						
	Jan.	April	July	Oct.	Rain	Snow
Daily highs	41	60	85	65	15"	43"
Daily lows	16	33	54	37		

newer, upscale communities: the towns of Monument and Palmer Lake, and the luxury developments of Woodmoor and Glen Eagle.

The military plays an important role in Colorado Springs's economy. The North American Air Defense Command (NORAD) is headquartered in nearby Cheyenne Mountain. The Fort Carson Army Base, Peterson Air Force Base, and the U.S. Space Command are all located in or around Colorado Springs. As if this weren't enough, the Air Force Academy is located on the northern side of the city. Many military families choose to retire here because of their experience with the town while stationed at one of the military installations.

Besides Colorado State University you'll find branch campuses of four or five other universities, two junior colleges, and several private colleges. This fertile academic environment exerts a beneficial impact on the community as a college town. Colorado State University, for example, presents plays, lectures, concerts, and book signings to the public, sometimes free, sometimes for a modest admission charge. For continuing education, Pikes Peak Community College offers a program of unlimited courses for $11 for those sixty years of age and older. The University of Colorado gives senior citizens 50 percent off tuition for those auditing classes.

Most retirees who decide to move to Colorado Springs will have some golf clubs tucked away in the moving van. The quality of the courses are famous far and wide. This is where the annual World Senior Tournament is held, as well as the Ladies' and Mens' Invitationals and the Ladies' U.S. Open. Golfers may select from seven public and eleven private courses.

Because of the great skiing available, some sports fanatics golf in the morning and ski that afternoon. Colorado is famous for hunting, fishing, and river rafting. Colorado Springs is in the middle of it all.

Colorado Springs enjoys an abundance of medical facilities. Memorial Hospital has a burn unit and specializes in intensive coronary care and cancer treatment. Other medical facilities are Penrose Community Hospital, St. Francis Hospital, and Cedar Springs Hospital, for a total of 1,000 beds.

Fort Collins This is another city that receives favorable reviews in national publications as a desirable place to live, work, and retire. A scenic place with friendly neighborhoods and 90,000 residents, Fort Collins enjoys a panorama of the nearby Rocky Mountains. The Cache la Poudre River runs along the upper edge of the city, a river famous for white-water rafting, fishing, and just plain scenic enjoyment. The river received its name back in 1836 when a party of French trappers cached an excess cargo of gunpowder on the river in preparation for a trip into the mountains. The French word for gunpowder is *poudre,* thus the name Cache la Poudre.

Skiing at world-class ski resorts is a matter of a few hours' drive from Fort Collins. The runs at Loveland Pass, an hour west of Denver, offer free skiing for those older than seventy. (One lady I interviewed in Colorado Springs moved here when she was seventy-eight to take advantage of the great skiing.) River rafting on the wild and scenic Poudre River can be unlike anything you've ever tried. Although you might get doused with spray and rock and roll as you ride the waves, it's a sport that doesn't require strength or skill—at least not if you go rafting with a guide who will do all the work. If you prefer, you can go with a guide who has the passengers do the work. It's fairly safe, too, because you will be wearing helmets and life jackets.

Hunting and fishing are of course excellent anywhere in Colorado. On the Poudre River, beginning 9 miles northwest of Fort Collins, Colorado's famous "Trout Route" begins. Anglers don't want to miss this. For those who like their outdoor recreation a bit less adventuresome, six public golf courses and plenty of tennis courts provide traditional exercise.

Fort Collins is home to Colorado State, the second-largest university in Colorado with more than 25,000 students, faculty, and staff. Front Range Community College has an additional 3,500 students. The school gives percent discounts off tuition for those older than sixty. You can be sure that the student population

	Jan.	April	July	Oct.	Rain	Snow
FORT COLLINS AREA WEATHER						
In degrees Fahrenheit						
Daily highs	43	61	88	67	15"	60"
Daily lows	16	34	59	37		

makes a difference in the community. One way this manifests itself is in the quality and variety of inexpensive restaurants.

Although Fort Collins was established back in the mid-1800s, more than 65 percent of its homes have been built since 1970. This points to the fast-growing nature of Fort Collins and explains why it's a relatively modern-looking city. The average selling price for a single-family home is somewhat higher than in Denver, reflecting the overall high quality of the city. Although median sales prices range about 10 percent above national averages, several lower-priced neighborhoods are quite affordable. The large college student population places pressures on rentals, so they aren't as plentiful as one might expect.

The Poudre Valley Hospital in Fort Collins acts as the regional medical hub for northern Colorado. The facility boasts 235 beds with an intensive and coronary care unit.

Boulder   A growing retirement trend is movement to college towns. Even if they haven't the slightest interest in continuing education, retirees often find that a university influences a community, serving as an exciting source of entertainment and cultural stimulation. Many of these social and cultural activities wouldn't exist without the school's presence. You don't have to be a registered student to attend lectures and speeches (often free) given by famous scientists, politicians, visiting artists, and other well-known personalities. Concerts ranging from Beethoven to boogie-woogie are presented by guest artists as well as the university's music department. You can attend the school's stage plays, Broadway musicals, and Shakespeare productions with season tickets that cost less than a single performance at a New York theater. Some schools allow senior citizens the use of recreational facilities and access to well-stocked libraries.

Therefore, without hesitation, I highly recommend Boulder as one of the better examples of university retirement locations. In addition to the University of Colorado at Boulder's intensely active college atmosphere, Boulder's immediate surroundings are as beautiful as you could imagine. It's about 27 miles northwest of Denver, with the Flatiron Mountains and snow-covered peaks looming in the background and Rocky Mountain National Park just minutes away. This wonderfully cosmopolitan city of 95,000 inhabitants is the

BOULDER WEATHER						
In degrees Fahrenheit						
	Jan.	April	July	Oct.	Rain	Snow
Daily highs	41	66	88	70	17"	90"
Daily lows	17	45	57	40		

home of the University of Colorado. The university, students, and faculty affect the city's environment in many pleasant ways, carrying the institution's intellectual excitement into the community as a whole.

The school's influence is most obvious in the city center, where you can stroll along the renovated downtown pedestrian mall known as Pearl Street. This vibrant historic preservation district is the focal point of the city, its traditional heart and soul. Mimes, jugglers, and musicians mingle with the crowds, adding a touch of magic to the scene, something you'd expect to find in San Francisco or Paris rather than Colorado. All generations mix here to meet for coffee, read a newspaper or magazine, or perhaps browse a bookstore or a boutique. Pearl Street offers a great selection of good restaurants, art galleries, and specialty shops of a variety and quality seldom seen in downtown areas of today's cities. Pearl Street is the site of continual activities, formal and ad hoc; the site of art festivals, practicing musicians, birthday celebrations; a place for people-watching and relaxing. In short downtown Boulder is a user-friendly, enjoyable place to visit.

The University of Colorado encourages retirees to enroll in classes for credit or as auditors. But for those who don't feel up to total immersion in the university's curriculum, an extraordinary senior center operated by Boulder Housing and Human Services gives classes in everything from papermaking to computers. They even offer sailboat instruction on Boulder Reservoir and day trips to archaeological sites and theaters in Denver. Coupled with an active volunteer program, this is one of the better senior programs we've seen.

Boulder's winter looks bad statistically—that is, if you consider snow bad—because Boulder catches even more snow than Denver! December and February receive the heaviest blankets of the white stuff, but like Denver, it doesn't hang around for long;

daily temperatures climb high enough to get rid of it quickly. Most days of the year can be spent walking, biking, or pursuing outdoors activities. Summer makes amends by providing gloriously sunny and comfortable days.

The cost of living here is about 18 percent above national averages, mostly because of the high cost of housing. The last several years have seen a spectacular increase, with home prices rising steadily.

Durango   Tucked away in a horseshoe of the San Juan Mountains in the southwestern corner of the state, Durango has been the gateway to southwestern Colorado's natural riches for more than one hundred years. Indians and fur traders, miners and prospectors, ranchers and railroad engineers alike passed through Durango on their way to seek their fortunes. Many found that Durango itself was the treasure they sought. Two million acres of national forest surround the city and provide countless places for outdoor recreation, with hunting, fishing, and hiking opportunities galore.

Although the town is relatively young—established little more than a century ago—the Four Corners Region where it's located boasts evidence of ancient glories. Two thousand years ago this was home to a mysterious aboriginal culture known as the Anasazi (the Ancient Ones). For some unknown reason the Anasazi abandoned their sophisticated, several-storied apartment buildings and left the area to the next wave of inhabitants, the Ute tribes, who arrived a couple of centuries later. They were there to welcome the Spanish, who explored the region in the 1500s.

The town of Durango got its start in 1880 as a depot and roundhouse location for the railroad and grew rapidly into a town of 2,000 residents just a year later. Before long the fledgling town boasted twenty saloons and 134 businesses. Today the population is 15,000 and still growing. Retirees make up a good percentage of the inhabitants; almost 30 percent are age sixty-two or older. The business community and residents recognize the treasure of the original buildings constructed by Durango's pioneers that are still in use today. Parts of downtown have been named by the Colorado Historical Society as a national historic district, bestowing Durango with Victorian splendor and elegance.

Residents like the town because it's a pleasant and peaceful

DURANGO WEATHER					
In degrees Fahrenheit					
	Jan.	April	July	Oct.	Rain	Snow
Daily highs	41	62	85	67	19"	71"
Daily lows	10	29	50	31		

community with a below-average crime rate and above-average quality of living. A 6,500-foot elevation ensures a four-season climate with bountiful snowfall in the town, yet not so high an altitude that temperatures don't rise above freezing every winter day. With 85 percent solar exposure, snow removal is seldom a problem. You're also guaranteed cool summer evenings without the need of air-conditioning.

Because Durango sits all by itself near the Four Corners area, by necessity it's become a self-contained little city. As Will Rogers once said, "Durango's out of the way and glad of it." Shopping needs are met by commercial development in and around Durango. Turn-of-the-twentieth-century hotels and commercial buildings abound in the business district, and an unusually high number of good restaurants serve a variety of cuisines. The year-round tourist business encourages upscale establishments to the benefit of year-round residents.

Durango is also gaining recognition as an artist colony. In addition to several well-known painters, half a dozen writers of fiction and nonfiction make this their home, as well as do a number of essayists, freelancers, and poets. Three galleries here are nationally recognized for quality Native American arts, Navajo weavings, jewelry, paintings, and sculpture.

Skiing at Purgatory Ski Resort, 26 miles away, is reputed to be among the best in the country. Nine lifts and 250 inches of snow account for the resort's impressive increase in ski hours. Although the resort has record snowfall, it also has record blue-sky days, which makes for great downhill fun.

The cost of living here is slightly below national averages, and real estate prices possibly slightly higher than in some other Colorado locations. The reason for this is that there are fewer lower-end starter homes than elsewhere. Contractors prefer to build more upscale places because they sell well.

Steamboat Springs   You say you love winter? You can't wait until ski lifts start running? Maybe Steamboat Springs is your town. Snuggled in a high valley at 6,700 feet, the town's alpine climate features low humidity, warm summer days, and cool, crisp nights. It also features winter snow—from 170 to 450 inches! Most of that is on the slopes, thank goodness.

This is a charming, upscale place for those who enjoy delightful summers and abundant outdoor winter sports. Although its winter "champagne powder" skiing brings winter sportsmen from all over the country, Steamboat Springs enjoys wonderful summer weather, just what you might expect from its Rocky Mountain setting. Even in July and August, temperatures rarely climb out of the eighty-degree range, and every evening they drop into the fifties.

The town's name came from a mineral spring that made a chugging noise that sounded like a steamboat to the early fur trappers who passed through the area. More than 150 mineral springs are found nearby, supplying medicinal waters for modern-day residents' hot tubs and baths at the public swimming pool.

Abundant wild game and rivers teeming with fish encouraged settlement, and the development of the town as a ski resort brought Steamboat Springs to its present population of approximately 7,000 inhabitants. Its early development is evident in the well-preserved Victorian homes and substantial brick business buildings that date from the late 1800s. Folks who've moved here recently say they appreciate the change from the hectic, crime-plagued lifestyle of big cities.

Although it sits on U.S. 40, a major east-west highway, Steamboat Springs is somewhat isolated, being 157 miles from the nearest big town (Denver). However, express shuttles to Denver airport plus frequent shuttle flights from the local Yampa Valley Regional Airport keep folks in touch with big-city civilization (if they need that sort of thing).

Of course the major recreational drawing card here is skiing.

STEAMBOAT SPRINGS WEATHER						
In degrees Fahrenheit						
	Jan.	April	July	Oct.	Rain	Snow
Daily highs	30	52	82	60	26"	60"
Daily lows	01	24	41	24		

Steamboat Springs bills itself "Ski Town USA" and has produced more Olympic skiers than any other other U.S. town. With twenty lifts, 108 trails, and a 3,600-foot vertical rise to 10,500 feet, this area is recognized as one of the best in the country. The season runs from Thanksgiving to Easter each year. Snowmobiling, sleigh rides, and backcountry skiing are also enjoyed.

This is not a place to look for bargain real estate; it's an upscale area, and property offerings show this. This higher-priced real estate pulls the overall cost of living up as well. Condos are big here, and practical, because they can be turned into rentals any time you're someplace else.

Utah

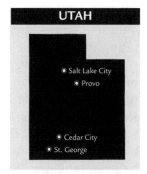

Utah is the fourth-fastest-growing state in the nation, with an increase of almost 30 percent over the 1990 census. Part of this growth can be attributed to Utah's having one of the country's largest concentrations of computer software firms and a growing biomedical industry. As a result the state attracts young working people who come here for jobs. According to the 2000 census, Utah now has the nation's youngest population group as well as the highest birth rate for any state. Retirees, too, account for some of Utah's growth.

Few states can compete with Utah when it comes to sheer beauty of spectacular landscapes. Visitors are overwhelmed by sights of fantastic canyons carved in brilliant red sandstone, lush mountain forests teeming with wildlife, and sapphire lakes brimming with trout. For contrast Utah also displays enormous stretches of uninhabitable desert, sagebrush, and barren alkaline flats. Utah's best-known landmark, of course, is the

UTAH TAX PROFILE
Sales tax: 5% to 6.25%, drugs exempt
State income tax: graduated, 2.25% to 7.2% greater than $3,750; federal income tax partially deductible
Property taxes: average 0.8% of market value
Intangibles tax: no
Social security taxed: half of benefits taxable for higher incomes
Pensions taxed: excludes up to $7,500, depending on income level
Gasoline tax: 19.5¢ per gallon

Great Salt Lake. Actually an inland sea, the water is so salty that few ocean fish could survive in it. In the midst of a desert, hundreds of miles from the Pacific Ocean, it seems strange to see swarms of sea-gulls and pelicans. Most of Utah's gorgeous and scenic panoramas are places that lack drinkable water, so few people choose to dwell there. Other than scattered farms and an occasional village, most people live in areas with more abundant rainfall or near facilities for irrigation.

For that reason about three-quarters of the population is con-centrated around Salt Lake City and other medium- to small-size cities in the north, and around Cedar City and St. George in the south. The rest of the state consists of small towns and villages, where few outsiders settle. These smaller communities would re-quire in-depth research and understanding before considering relo-cating there, because of Utah's unique social structure. In small rural Utah towns, everyday living is greatly influenced by religion—much more so than in Southern Bible Belt communities. In many, if not most, small towns you'll find only one church: the Church of Jesus Christ of Latter-Day Saints (also known as the LDS, or Mor-mons). Occasionally there'll be an alternative, perhaps a Baptist or Catholic denomination in town, but in all cases, non-Mormons will be a tiny minority. Other religious denominations do thrive in the larger cities, which is why most non-Mormons seek out places like Salt Lake City, Cedar City, and St. George—places where the popula-tion is mixed. The larger the town or city, the larger the percentage of residents who are not LDS members. For example, the last time I inquired, there were only two Jewish rabbis in the state, both living in Salt Lake City, and the only synagogue outside Salt Lake City was in Ogden (with no rabbi).

Mormons are known to be warm and loving, showing deep concern for each other's welfare. However, to members of other faiths, Mormons can seem polite but somewhat aloof and distant. Even some converted Mormons complain of discrimination because they were not born into the church. As an indication of how religion permeates Utah life, 90 percent of the state's politicians are active members of the Mormon church.

Having said this, and emphasizing that this is strictly my opinion, I can also say that many non-Mormons tell me that they haven't found religion much of an obstacle. "It's only a problem if you let it be one," said one newcomer to St. George. "We've had no trouble making friends, and our neighbors are quite gracious."

One member of the church I interviewed disputed the existence of discrimination and explained it this way: "What many folks don't understand is that being a member of our church isn't just a 'Sunday' thing. Our everyday lives often involve the church in one way or another. So when Mormon families in a neighborhood all get on a bus to go to a church activity, the uninvited neighbors feel left out. We don't mean to snub our neighbors. It's just that they don't join in our church affairs any more than we participate in their church activities."

This edition highlights three locations—places popular with out-of-state retirees and places where the populations are heterogeneous.

Salt Lake City   In 1847 Brigham Young led a band of Mormons westward across the plains and mountains in search of freedom from religious persecution. When the travelers looked down from mountains overlooking the valley of the Great Salt Lake, Brigham Young announced that this was the Promised Land where they would live. They set to work tilling the soil that same day and began transforming the dry and desolate land into beautiful, well-planned Salt Lake City.

The capital of Utah and one of the largest cities in the Rocky Mountain region (pop. 173,000), Salt Lake City is also the world capital of the Church of Jesus Christ of Latter-Day Saints. It sits in a valley bordered to the north and east by mountains, near the southeastern shore of the Great Salt Lake.

SALT LAKE CITY WEATHER						
In degrees Fahrenheit						
	Jan.	April	July	Oct.	Rain	Snow
Daily highs	37	61	93	67	15"	58"
Daily lows	20	37	62	39		

SALT LAKE CITY AREA COST OF LIVING					
Percentage of	Overall	Housing	Medical	Groceries	Utilities
national average	96	88	91	104	90

At first the city's growth depended on the inflow of Mormon converts from Europe and America. Later industrial and business expansion attracted many gentiles, or non-Mormons, who now make up almost half the population. This makes for a more cosmopolitan community than is found in most areas of Utah.

In the center of the city, surrounded by beautiful grounds, are the chief buildings of the Mormon Church. Other buildings of note in the city are those of the University of Utah, the state capitol, the city and county building, the museum, the exposition buildings, and two former residences of Brigham Young. In Temple Square is the Sea Gull Monument; at this point the altitude is 4,400 feet. Most neighborhoods are clean and well kept, with reasonably safe conditions.

Recreation and cultural opportunities abound here. The region's low humidity and abundance of sunshine makes golf a year-round sport, with eight courses open for play. Hiking and bicycling in the nearby mountains are popular recreational activities. Salt Lake City is the home base of the Utah (formerly New Orleans) Jazz professional NBA basketball team. Skiing in nearby Park City, home of the U.S. Ski and Snowboard Team and other winter sports, draws snow enthusiasts in the winter. Utah's snow is unusually dry powder—it receives as many as 400 inches a year—and it is considered by many skiers to be the world's best. Seven ski resorts are less than an hour's drive from Salt Lake City.

Part of Salt Lake City's rich quality of life derives from its enthusiastic support of the arts. A haven for creative expression, residents have daily choices of performances, exhibits, and events for entertainment or enrichment. A world-class symphony orchestra, the Utah Opera Company, and one of the country's largest ballet companies attract professionals from around the world. Five major universities are within an hour's drive from Salt Lake City, as are several community colleges.

The overall cost of living in Salt Lake City is slightly above average, helped in part by exceptionally low utility costs. A robust, diverse economy attracts newcomers and has created an increase in real estate prices over the past few years. Despite this increase, Salt Lake continues to be an affordable place to live, ranking sixteenth among seventy-five major U.S. cities.

Seven major medical facilities serve this area, making it one of the premier places for health care in the West. Altogether Salt Lake City has thirteen hospitals and Provo, about 40 miles south of Salt Lake City, is currently served by two excellent hospitals.

St. George   The largest city in southern Utah, St. George works hard to attract retirees and has acquired a strong reputation as a retirement community. It consistently receives top recommendations from national magazines and retirement guides as a place to retire, often ranking number one in the West.

Because of St. George's relatively mild winters, boosters like to refer to the area as Utah's "Dixie." The truth is the designation "Dixie" derived partly from the town's southernmost location in the state, but more from the early-day cotton fields that brought prosperity to the pioneer community. However, it is true that a lower elevation—only 2,840 feet—blesses St. George with warmer winters than its nearby retirement counterpart, Cedar City. The tradeoff is warmer summer temperatures, but evenings are always cool enough to sleep under blankets.

Conveniently located on Interstate 15, a little more than two hours' drive from Las Vegas, St. George isn't as isolated as it might seem. The city's population of about 30,000 is large enough to provide adequate services, and the community stands on its own commercially.

St. George's picturesque surroundings are some of the more dramatic of any retirement destination described in this book. Stark red cliffs loom over the town, sometimes rising vertically from residents' backyards. You get the feeling that you're living on the set of

ST. GEORGE WEATHER
In degrees Fahrenheit

	Jan.	April	July	Oct.	Rain	Snow
Daily highs	54	76	101	80	11"	5"
Daily lows	26	44	66	45		

ST. GEORGE AREA COST OF LIVING

Percentage of	Overall	Housing	Medical	Groceries	Utilities
national average	95	83	93	112	83

a Western movie. In its own way St. George is as spectacular as Sedona, Arizona, although on a smaller scale.

According to locals, St. George has more golf course facilities per capita than any place this side of Palm Springs. I'm not sure that's true, but golfers do enjoy eight golf courses, open year-round and within a fifteen-minute drive from town. There's even an 1,800-square-foot indoor golf facility to help you find out why your slice is so messed up.

This combination of beauty, relatively mild winters, and great golfing draws more retirees from outside Utah than do other Utah communities. This is important for non-Mormons, because outsiders dilute the religious majority, and newcomers won't be so likely to feel like outsiders. In fact St. George has twenty-four community churches besides those of the Mormon faith. These range from Roman Catholic to Jehovah's Witness, as well as Baptist, Episcopal, Lutheran, Presbyterian, Methodist, and several I've never heard of. Of course the majority of the residents are Mormons, but it looks as if there's plenty of room for others.

Settled in 1861 by 309 Mormon families, St. George was transformed from a forbidding alkali flat into a livable town in the space of a decade. Some of the original homes survive and are treated with reverence by local residents. Included is the house where Brigham Young spent a few of his last years. Streets are wide and tree-lined, and homes are as neat and orderly as Brigham Young would have wished.

As the health-care center for the surrounding area, St. George is noted for providing quality care, with top facilities and at lower costs than the national average. The 130-bed Dixie Medical Center is a progressive, regional referral facility that serves the health-care needs of nearly 100,000 in a tristate area of southern Utah, southern Nevada, and northeastern Arizona.

Cedar City   Many communities we've visited in the state of Utah present a pleasant, old-fashioned look—neat as a starched shirt, as the saying goes. Mormon Church members claim that the religious commitments of church followers are responsible for this, as well as the state's exceptionally low crime rate. This could be the subject of debate, but the fact remains that tranquillity and safety are the norm in most Utah communities. Cedar City is typical of

CEDAR CITY WEATHER					
In degrees Fahrenheit					
	Jan.	April	July	Oct.	Rain	Snow
Daily highs	54	76	101	80	11"	5"
Daily lows	26	44	66	45		

CEDAR CITY COST OF LIVING					
Percentage of national average	Overall	Housing	Medical	Groceries	Utilities
	92	72	92	111	84

Utah's small cities and always ranks low in crime according to FBI statistics.

This small university town of 21,000 offers many advantages for retirement living. Sheltered in the foothills just a few miles from some of the most spectacular landscapes in the world, Cedar City combines the cultural atmosphere of an active university with some of the best skiing and outdoor sports to be found anywhere. The 5,800-foot altitude guarantees a vigorous, four-season climate. According to residents there are usually four good snowfalls every winter, but warm afternoons and plenty of sunshine make quick work of melting them away.

Cedar City is located on Interstate 15, which gives it easy access to St. George, 52 miles south, and to Salt Lake City, 270 miles north. Las Vegas is little more than three hours away. You might expect a small city like Cedar City to be safe, and it is, exceptionally so. According to our calculations, only a few cities in the United States have lower crime rates than Cedar City.

Even though a huge majority of Cedar City residents are members of the Latter-Day Saints church, Cedar City also has a respectable percentage of non-Mormons as well (there are thirteen other traditional Christian churches in town). This is partly due to workers moving into the community with manufacturing companies that have relocated here. Cedar City has a low cost of living, usually about 10 percent below its sister city of St. George. Housing costs are dramatically lower as well. Valley View Medical Center is a forty-eight-bed, full-service facility with some secondary-level services. It has an intensive care/cardiac care unit.

Because of an exciting variety of cultural presentations, Cedar City calls itself the "Festival City." Now in its twenty-sixth season, the Shakespeare Festival is famous throughout the West and draws fans from far and wide. Running from the last week in June through Labor Day, each year Southern Utah University presents four Shakespeare plays plus another stage play and a musical. Another interesting festival is the yearly Jedediah Smith High Mountain Rendezvous. This follows an old-time Western theme, assembling trappers, traders, and mountain men for a nostalgic festival of frontier contests and camaraderie. Southern Utah University's campus is the focus of many other community events such as music festivals, ballet, and the Utah Summer Games.

California

THERE ARE DEFINITE DIFFERENCES BETWEEN FOLKS who live in the extreme western part of the nation and those who live in the East, Midwest, and South. The reasons for the differences are partly historical and partly environmental. Personalities and worldviews vary with each section, and sometimes the differences are not so subtle.

Folks who live in the southern portions of the United States are, by tradition, rural and outdoor-oriented. Midwesterners share much of the Southern tradition, yet their larger cities, larger farms, and industrially developed environments, plus a history of Eastern immigration and Eastern ideas, distinguish them from Southerners.

On the other hand, the Eastern mindset is shaped by closely packed cities, little open space, and an orientation toward business and industry. In heavily populated areas the friendliness and hospitality of the South and Midwest just aren't possible.

The West Coast has a comparatively short history, and with the exception of a few Native Americans, it is composed principally of newcomers from every part of the country and the world. The population is mixed and so are their personalities. Southern hospitality mixes with Northeastern reserve, and the love of open spaces mixes with a love of the city. The result is a multifaceted, laid-back lifestyle.

Yes, the West Coast has earned a reputation for being laid-back. So what's wrong with kicking back and enjoying life? I'm convinced you'll live longer and enjoy life more. We have friends in Connecticut who think nothing of commuting an hour and a half each way to work. That's almost two extra working days a week, or ninety working days a year, spent staring out a train window! On the other hand, most Californians complain bitterly if their commutes are longer than twenty minutes (except for Los Angeles, where businesspeople spend their spare time parked on the freeways).

One factor for this difference in attitude is the environmental circumstance of so much open land. Much of it actually does belong to everyone. A huge percentage of Western lands is in nationally owned forests, deserts, and mountain slopes. Unlike the East Coast, where just about every acre is fenced and posted as private property, most Western land is public and open for anyone to enjoy. Almost 50 percent of California and Oregon belongs to the U.S. government. Nevada is 85 percent federally owned and Arizona, 44 percent. Compare this with only 3.8 percent in New England, the Eastern seaboard, and the Midwestern states.

Openness means more than forests and deserts. The ocean also belongs to the people. Unlike the Atlantic and Gulf shores, where property owners own the beach in front of their homes and can post no-trespassing signs, Pacific beaches belong to everyone. By law property owners must provide public access to their beachfront properties; their ownership extends only to a certain distance above the high-tide line. You can stroll along any beach you please, secure in the knowledge that it is as much your property as anyone's.

West Coast Weather

Because West Coast weather is mild and generally pleasant year-round, people tend to find outdoor things to do. Most live within a few hours' drive of excellent ski country or uncrowded beaches. They can enjoy snow sports in the afternoon, then drive down the mountain to swim in a pool or relax in a hot tub the same evening. Outdoor living is the hallmark of Westerners.

The West Coast offers the most amazing smorgasbord of retirement choices imaginable. Choose from mountain communities with Alpine winters, deserts that look more like the Sahara than the Sahara, farmlands that remind one of Iowa, rugged coasts as pretty as the Spanish Mediterranean, and beaches as smooth as Hawaii's (albeit with colder waters). Within an hour or so of most retirement locations you can be hunting deer, fishing for trout, or trolling for salmon. From a rustic cabin deeply isolated within a redwood forest you can drive for thirty minutes to an art museum, the theater, or an ocean beach. From a city home you can drive twenty minutes to a wild and scenic wilderness. Almost any ecological, environmental, or climatic feature can be found on the West Coast.

Along the ocean temperatures vary little between winter and summer. It is pleasant year-round from San Diego to Vancouver. Granted, the farther north, the cooler the temperatures, but they remain remarkably stable regardless of the season. This is due to the chain of low, coastal mountains that runs along the entire West Coast, from Washington's Puget Sound to San Diego. This ridge separates the coast from the inland valleys and prevents the cool Pacific air from sweeping eastward.

A natural "air-conditioning" system occurs when the sun heats up the inland valley air. This warm air rises, creating low pressure that then draws air from the ocean across the coast and over the mountains to cool things off. If it weren't for this occurrence, the coast would be as hot as the interior valleys. In the winter the air currents are stable and the cooler air stays offshore, allowing both beaches and inland to bask in the sunshine. Often the "heat waves" of the coastal lands occur in November, with eighty degrees common, as opposed to the seventy-degree days of August.

Therefore, the coastal towns are for those who don't like air-conditioning and also hate freezing weather. Los Angeles is a bit different, because the mountains are farther from the coast and the sun heats the entire coastal plain. However, the ocean breeze performs somewhat the same natural air-conditioning function. That's why Los Angeles has such pleasant weather: warm in the winter but rarely extremely hot in the summer. This climate is exactly why so many people live there.

California for Retirement

Are there really affordable places in California, without smog and without horrendous traffic? Places with hunting and fishing and quality living? A four-season climate? The unqualified answer: Yes!

Contrary to popular stereotype California is not all palm trees, movie stars, and surfers. Much of the state, particularly the northern part, is almost Midwestern in character. Small towns set in national forests or in the wine country are pretty much like small towns everywhere when it comes to cost of living and lifestyles. The northern California coast is as different from southern California resort and surfing areas as New England towns are from Florida beaches.

CALIFORNIA TAX PROFILE

Sales tax: 7.2% to 8.5%, food and drugs exempt
State income tax: graduated, 1% to 11% greater than $207,200 ($25,000 at 8%); can't deduct federal income tax
Property taxes: vary widely, depending on when home was purchased and locality; typically from 1.5% to 1.75%
Intangibles tax: no
Social security taxed: no
Pensions taxed: all
Gasoline tax: 18¢ per gallon, plus possible local taxes and state sales tax

California's glamorous cities are well known—places such as Santa Barbara, San Diego, and San Francisco. We'll discuss them later, of course; it would be neglectful of our duty to do otherwise. But let's first start with some retirement possibilities generally unfamiliar to folks from other states.

The California Desert

Although many commonly think of California as surfing beaches, Hollywood, and redwood forests, the majority of California is desert or semidesert. After all, that most famous of all U.S. deserts, Death Valley, is in California. The great Mojave Desert covers a good portion of southern California and continues up the eastern portion of the state.

Traditionally California deserts are divided into two classifications: high desert and low desert. As you would expect, the higher country has colder winters and more pleasant summers. However, "colder" winters doesn't mean continual freezing weather; it means that when cold winds blow from the north, it gets cool enough to freeze the hair off a bald mouse. But most of the time, whenever it's sunny, daytime temperatures climb to either shirtsleeve or light sweater weather.

CALIFORNIA DESERT

Desert
Hot Springs
Palm Springs

Imperial Valley

Victorville and Apple Valley are examples of high-desert locations that draw retirees. They mostly come from the Los Angeles area, attracted here by the low crime rates, cheap land, and wide open spaces. Because few folks outside of California actually retire in high-desert country, the discussion here covers mostly low-desert towns, although Yucaipa almost falls into the high-desert category.

Overall California desert living may not be as affordable as living in other Western desert states, but for some folks money is less of an issue than locale. And for many retirees California remains the land of their retirement dreams, no matter the cost.

Palm Springs   When people speak of Palm Springs they could mean any of a half-dozen towns scattered along Interstate 10 from Palm Springs to Indian Wells. Playground of millionaires, movie stars, and other rich and famous types, Palm Springs is synonymous with class. Well-known personalities—such as Bob Hope, Bing Crosby, Gerald Ford, and a host of others—have made golf fans aware of the great, year-round golf courses. When people with enough money to live anywhere in the world choose the Palm Springs area for their homes, there must be something special going on!

Sheltered in the lee of the rugged San Jacinto Mountains, with abundant water, Palm Springs is verdant and livable year-round. Green landscaping, huge palm trees, and manicured golf courses convert the desert into a botanical wonderland. The area supports more golf courses than most cities have supermarkets, ninety-three in all, although many are private, belonging to residents of the surrounding developments.

Winters are as delightful here as summers are hot. As one real estate salesperson put it, "Which is worse, a low-humidity, hot summer—or an icy, freezing winter?" (As I work on my notes, it's the middle of January here in Palm Springs. I am outdoors—barefoot, wearing shorts and no shirt—listening to radio reports of 18-below-zero storms savaging the Midwest and Eastern states, with snowdrifts deeper than my pool!)

Instead of snowstorms Southern California deserts have windstorms. One reason for Palm Springs's popularity is that nearby mountains block most of this wind. The farther south from the interstate, the more protection.

A drive through expensive neighborhoods can be overwhelming: one street after another competing for the title of the fanciest and most opulent. Shopping centers that look as if they were built for sultans or nobility offer any kind of luxury item you

PALM SPRINGS AREA COST OF LIVING					
Percentage of national average	Overall 116	Housing 104	Medical 154	Groceries 120	Utilities 125

can afford (and many that you can't). Clean desert air and a rugged mountain backdrop give Palm Springs an aura of pristine beauty combined with regal affluence.

The curious thing is, although this is one of the more expensive retirement areas in the country, it's not necessarily out of reach for folks with moderate incomes. Most residents are *not* rich; they work for wages and can't afford a super-expensive lifestyle. The main industry is support services: restaurants, stores, hotels, or gardening for wealthy families, and other jobs of that nature. Wages for grocery clerks or waiters are seldom so high that they drive up the housing market. Palm Springs real estate is an either-or thing: either you can't afford high payments, or you're rich and you don't give a damn!

The fanciest homes are found in adjoining towns, places such as Rancho Mirage, Palm Desert, or Indian Wells. Yet interspersed with these exclusive enclaves are affordable neighborhoods for ordinary wage-earners and retirees, often just a few blocks away. Mobile-home and RV parks also provide moderate-cost alternatives. Some are elegant, complete with golf privileges; others are more plain, with competitive rates.

At times real estate prices in Palm Springs can fluctuate wildly. A condo priced at $150,000 at one point in time might sell for only $90,000 two years later. Why would that be? Because home prices here fluctuate according to the health of the national economy and particularly in response to California's business ups and downs. It turns out that the Palm Springs real estate market crashes every time there's an abrupt downturn in Los Angeles's economy. When defense industry jobs dry up, when lucrative businesses go bankrupt, when high-paid executives go on unemployment, one of the first things to be sacrificed is that second home in Palm Springs. None of this affects people who maintain their main residences here; nothing much changes except home prices. The trick is to buy in at one of the low cycles, because you can be sure they will return to the top eventually.

During a research trip to Palm Springs a few years ago—during one of those defense-industry slumps—we noticed an unusual number of foreclosure sales and HUD offerings. To our surprise prices of homes, condos, and country-club residences had dropped drastically since our previous visit. We looked at three-bedroom homes in a gated development with a pool, tennis courts, and adjacent golf course priced at what an ordinary tract home would sell for in many California locations. We almost bought a small, two-bedroom condo within walking distance of downtown Palm Springs for $44,000! (Unfortunately we passed on it.)

We were so impressed that I immediately wrote a magazine article encouraging retirees to look at Palm Springs and also included the recommendation in one of my books on retirement. Unfortunately by the time the book came off the press, these wonderful bargains were history. The market recovered when Los Angeles achieved yet another of its dramatic recoveries. Second homes in Palm Springs became popular again.

Desert Hot Springs   If the posh atmosphere of Palm Springs is a little intimidating, you'll find a "Poor Man's Palm Springs" just across Interstate 10 about fifteen minutes' drive away. This is the town of Desert Hot Springs (pop. 17,000). Its name comes from the hot water that seeps beneath the town from nearby mountain slopes. Homeowners commonly tap the steaming water and enjoy it in their backyard swimming pools and hot tubs. Much smaller than Palm Springs or any of the ritzy sections on the other side of Interstate 10, Desert Hot Springs has a lot to offer in pleasant, economical desert retirement.

Desert Hot Springs bestows many of Palm Springs's advantages without the higher prices. The fabled restaurants, golf courses, shopping, and social life of Palm Springs are just a few minutes away. With an elevation about a thousand feet higher than Palm Springs, Desert Hot Springs enjoys summer temperatures a smidgen lower than communities on the valley floor. Winter days are often warmer because of the mountains, which block north winds that occasionally bring cold down from Alaska. The most common weather complaint concerns annoying westerly winds that hit Desert Hot Springs but circumvent Palm Springs.

Like Palm Springs a large percentage of the residents live here year-round. Many are retired, but there's also a large balance of younger people who work in Palm Springs but can't afford its prices. The downtown area is low key, as is the rest of the town.

Imperial Valley   The Imperial Valley's desert stretches southeast from the Palm Springs area, past the Salton Sea, to the Mexican border, and west to Yuma. The land is flat and broken by rolling hills, sometimes dipping below sea level. For those who enjoy desert living without the formality and expense of a place like Palm Springs, several other desert locations here are worth investigating. Property is quite inexpensive throughout the region (occasionally trending toward being somewhat tawdry). The emphasis is on the word affordable.

This is truly desert country. With less than 2 inches of rain a year, the region probably soaks up more sunshine than anywhere in the United States. Were it not for irrigation from the Colorado River and from deep wells, this countryside would look as barren as Death Valley. The towns of Brawley, El Centro, and Calexico sit in a straight 25-mile line north from the Mexican border. Spanish is often the first language here, especially in the border town of Calexico, because 95.3 percent of the population is of Hispanic descent!

Some people live in or near Calexico because of the availability of alternate medical treatment and low-cost medical care across the U.S.–Mexican border. Many patients swear by Mexican arthritis medications, acupuncture treatments, or laetrile injections, despite the fact that most medical authorities disagree vigorously with this kind of medication. All swear that dental work—such as crowns, bridges, and dentures—is of top quality in Mexicali and at prices long forgotten on the U.S. side of the line. For some illogical reason prescription drugs cost significantly less than in the United States, even brands manufactured by the same company.

Gold Country

In 1847 in a part of Mexico called Alta California, a group of workers labored to construct a sawmill on a rushing stream that flowed down from the Sierra Nevada range. This was in the north-central part of what was to become California, near what is now Sacramento. As they dug into the river's bank, one man noticed something curious in his shovel's blade. Sparkling metal pebbles mixed with the gravel. Gold!

This event touched off one of the most exciting chapters in United States history. News of the discovery spread; the rush was on.

People came by covered wagon and horseback; some sailed around Cape Horn to join in a frenzy of prospecting. Eager miners attacked streams with gold pans and sluice boxes to fill their pockets with gold nuggets. Gold deposits were so rich that miners called the area the Mother Lode.

CALIFORNIA GOLD COUNTRY

Yreka
Dunsmuir
Chico

Mount Shasta
Fall River Mills/
Burney
Paradise
Grass Valley/
Nevada City
Amador
County

Within a short span of time, rude mining camps became towns and then small cities. Paved streets, brick buildings, theaters, and businesses flourished, creating replicas in miniature of Midwestern and Eastern towns of that era.

When gold claims finally played out, gold miners drifted on to other enterprises. Some moved to fertile California valleys to seek fortunes as growers. Others settled in the growing coastal cities. When miners moved away, Mother Lode towns became virtual ghost towns. Luckily this abandonment preserved many old mining towns in time-capsule form, fascinating pictures of life as it was during California's romantic past. Because of low-cost housing and pleasant environments, these are now great places for retirement.

Gold Country is about as far from the usual California image as you can get. Its collection of old mining towns, with narrow streets and buildings of native stone and brick, harmonize perfectly with the green-clad mountain backdrops. The state jealously preserves the sites as a charming part of California's past—the country of Brett Harte, Mark Twain, and John Fremont.

From rolling hills studded with black oaks and manzanita to the majestic peaks of the Sierra Nevada, the Mother Lode encompasses a unique scenic wonderland. Here you find not only a true four-season climate, but variation on the seasons, depending on the altitude you choose. From mild winters and warm summers in Jackson and Angels Camp to deep snowpack and cool summers in Lake Tahoe, you have a complete selection of climates and seasonal colors. Trout streams are well stocked, with rare golden trout waiting to be hooked in higher lakes.

GOLD COUNTRY AREA COST OF LIVING

Percentage of national average	Overall	Housing	Medical	Groceries	Utilities
	105	93	110	111	139

The Mother Lode encompasses a 300-mile stretch of rolling-to-rugged country that runs from Downieville in the north down to Coarsegold in the south. It takes in nine counties: Madera, Mariposa, Tuolumne, Calaveras, El Dorado, Placer, Nevada, Sierra, and Amador. Then 100 miles to the northwest, another area of historic gold-mining towns spreads across several more counties: Butte, Siskiyou, Tehama, Shasta, Trinity, and Lassen.

By the way, the forty-niners didn't get *all* the gold. They left enough to keep hundreds of weekend prospectors and amateur miners working at their dredges and sluice boxes. With most of the countryside designated public land and national forest, you'll have ample opportunity to try your luck if you wish. A favorite family outing is to take a picnic lunch and a couple of gold pans and spend the afternoon working one of the many creeks and streams that traverse hills covered with oak, pine, and cedar. Some people do quite well, but you can expect them to be very close-mouthed about where they found their private bonanzas. Others are ashamed that they can't locate much gold, and they lie about how much they find. That's what I do.

Amador County   As an example of the Gold Country, let's look in detail at one location in the center of the Mother Lode. Amador County straddles historic Highway 49, which runs along the route of the trail that once connected the busiest of the mining towns from north to south. One of the richest gold-mining districts, Amador County accounted for more than half of all the gold harvested from the Mother Lode. Here are found such fascinating towns as Jackson, Sutter Creek, Volcano, Fiddletown, and Plymouth.

In more mountainous western locations, climate varies with altitude, and the altitude varies widely in Amador County. Lower elevations start at 200 feet and climb all the way to more than 9,000 feet. Magnificent views of snow-covered peaks, mountain lakes, and meadows are everywhere. With low summer humidity even the warmest days are comfortable. Winters are short and mild (January highs average fifty-six degrees), and the area enjoys a true spring and colorful fall season.

Jackson is the largest town in Amador County with a population of 3,900. Founded as a Gold Rush camp in 1848, the town was destroyed by fire in 1862. It was rebuilt, and many existing historic Main Street buildings date from that reconstruction era. Jackson works hard at maintaining the historic atmosphere and is the shopping center for nearby gold-country retirement communities. All is not historic architecture here; modern ranch-style homes and subdivisions are plentiful on the outskirts of the city.

Amador County contains several suitable places for retirement: not only towns and villages, but also small farms or wooded acreage. Amador City has a population of less than 250 inhabitants, making it one of California's smallest incorporated "cities." Located on Highway 49, the community was named for Jose María Amador, who mined the creek in town in 1848–49. Just a mile or so from Jackson, the town has little in the way of a business district; residents depend on Jackson for shopping.

Plymouth straddles Highway 49 on the northern edge of the county and is the site of the Amador County Fairgrounds. The annual county fair each July is considered by many to be one of the best county fairs in California. Plymouth's present-day population is 832, and it has several old buildings dating from the forty-niner mining days.

Sutter Creek was named for famed gold discoverer Captain John Sutter, who arrived here in 1844 to establish a lumber mill with whipsawing pits. The community became a supply center for quartz mines in the 1850s. Today's population is a little more than 2,000. It is a favorite with tourists because of its original mining-era buildings, antiques stores, and bed-and-breakfast inns. It looks like a movie set for a gold-rush movie.

Historians believe that Drytown may have been the first gold camp established in the area after the discovery of gold in 1848. Despite the presence of some twenty saloons, the town derived its name from the creek where water flowed only in winter. Most housing is scattered among the woods on both sides of the road that runs through the small business district.

Two other old mining communities that attract retirees are Fiddletown and Pine Grove, both settled in 1849. During the height of the Gold Rush, Fiddletown had the largest Chinese settlement outside of San Francisco. Historic sites include the Chew Kee store, where Chinese artifacts and relics are displayed.

A growing population created the need for better medical facilities in Amador County. The Sutter Amador Hospital has been undergoing major enlargement and now offers a new 93,000-square-foot hospital, an eighty-nine bed facility with twenty-four-hour emergency services.

Grass Valley/Nevada City   Other popular retirement towns are found to the north of Jackson, places like Grass Valley and Nevada City, which are a bit more sophisticated and offer a more cosmopolitan charm than Jackson. The area teems with a sense of history and abundant natural beauty. Gold rush architecture with white church steeples and Victorian buildings is shaded by century-old sugar maples and liquidambars that early settlers brought with them from the New England states. Thousands of miners came here in the 1800s—this was one of California's richest gold-producing regions—and today retirees are finding their personal bonanzas in quality living.

The towns of Grass Valley and Nevada City sit in the foothills of the Sierra Nevada Mountains at an average elevation of 2,500 feet. The surroundings vary from rolling hills to rugged peaks, with plentiful forests of oak, pine, cedar, and fir. Residents enjoy four gentle seasons, with homes perched above the fog line yet below the heavy snow line.

Grass Valley is the larger town, with almost 10,000 residents, and nearby Nevada City adds another 3,000. Conveniently close to Interstate 80, trips to Reno (ninety minutes), Sacramento (one hour), or San Francisco (three hours) are a piece of cake for those who crave action from time to time. Many dynamic cultural activities are available right here, however, including classical music festivals, concerts, and theater productions. Several theater companies entertain with productions almost year-round. A community college is the latest addition to the cultural scene.

Gold-mining technology, for which Nevada County was famous, today has been replaced by twenty-first century computer technology. Earning the nickname "Silicon Valley of the Sierras," more than thirty high-tech companies have relocated here. These facilities design and build digital video, multimedia, control, and ro-

AMADOR–GRASS VALLEY WEATHER						
In degrees Fahrenheit						
	Jan.	April	July	Oct.	Rain	Snow
Daily highs	54	62	85	71	40"	5"
Daily lows	35	38	54	44		

botics equipment, as well as perform medical data processing. More than 1,000 hardware and software development professionals call Nevada County home. It isn't surprising that many high-tech residents here use the Internet to telecommute for distant employers, and many operate their own high-tech companies without ever leaving their homes.

For outdoor recreation the region is filled with lakes, streams, parks, campgrounds, and hiking trails. Winter skiing is only an hour away at half a dozen resorts, and the short drive makes returning home after a hard afternoon's skiing less of a chore. Summers see very little rainfall, so you'll have plenty of sunshine to accompany you on fishing trips and picnics. There are four golf courses—one public and three private.

Nevada City, by the way, has an exceptionally active senior center, with activities and volunteer opportunities galore. The Gold Country Telecare network keeps folks in touch by phone for problem solving, assistance, and counseling. Telecare volunteers are available for seniors who can't afford to hire someone to fix a leaky faucet or to repair porch steps. Legal and tax questions are covered by other volunteers, and still others make sure seniors don't miss shopping, recreational activities, or an appointment with the dentist. Medical care is excellent, with a nonprofit hospital with a 124-bed acute-care facility offering state-of-the-art diagnostic, surgical, and therapeutic equipment.

Scattered around the countryside are any number of smaller communities—historic places such as Rough and Ready, Gold Run, or Colfax—away from town but only a few miles from shopping. Before you settle on a gold-mining location, you must see 'em all!

Paradise   About 100 miles to the north of Amador County, the Feather River yielded another rich harvest of shining metal. Scattered above the canyon on a place called Nimshew Ridge, a collection of little villages and mining camps sprang up, with vivid names such as Dogtown, Toadtown, Poverty Ridge, and Whiskey Flats. At

Dogtown (now Magalia) a prospector uncovered a fifty-nine-pound gold nugget back in 1859. Several nuggets weighing up to nine pounds each turned up later, but after the Dogtown nugget, everything else seemed anticlimactic.

Apparently folks grew tired of explaining why they lived in Whiskey Flats or on Poverty Ridge, so they agreed to form one town and call it something more romantic: Paradise. Thousands of modern-day retirees believe they've found their paradise here. Forty-nine percent of the residents are older than fifty-five.

Paradise and nearby Magalia share a particularly scenic location. Heavily forested, sitting at an altitude of 2,000 feet, the area is below the snow belt yet above the Sacramento Valley's smog level. (There isn't really that much smog in the valley except when farmers burn the rice fields every fall.) This higher altitude also means summer temperatures ten degrees lower than the valley floor below.

Being below the snow belt doesn't mean that Paradise is snow-free. Around these parts higher elevations (more than 4,000 feet) are generally covered with snow most of the winter. When winter rains fall on Paradise, it's a good bet that it'll be snowing in Stirling City, some 20 miles away and a thousand feet higher. But when conditions are right, Paradise's rain turns to snow. At this altitude snow doesn't come down in small flakes and particles—it forms large puffs the size of golf balls. Very soft and fluffy, it piles up incredibly fast. What might be a 4-inch snow in Stirling City becomes 12 inches in Paradise or Magalia. Old-timers tell of 3 feet of snow falling overnight. This type of snow melts quickly, however, as soon as the sun warms things up. Even in the coldest months, afternoons are usually warm enough for a light sweater to feel comfortable, and golf courses are open year-round.

Contractors take care to build homes without disturbing the trees any more than necessary. Building lots are large, usually a quarter to half an acre, sometimes several acres, and houses are scattered so that it's hard to believe there could be 40,000 people

PARADISE WEATHER					
In degrees Fahrenheit					
	Jan.	April	July	Oct.	Rain	Snow
Daily highs	52	71	92	85	45"	18"
Daily lows	32	45	61	48		

living in the area. With low housing density and lots of forest, Paradise is a sanctuary for wild animals, because hunting is prohibited in town. Deer and raccoons saunter about town insolently, as if they were taxpayers.

As a normal response to a large retiree population, health care is unusually good. There's a 109-bed hospital, two convalescent hospitals, three medical care centers, and several residential-care and guest homes. This large population of retirees means lots of organized activities and clubs. In addition to the usual AARP organization, there is a Golden Fifties Club, a Retired Teachers Association, a senior singles club, and a couple of senior citizens' political action coalitions.

Paradise–Magalia is a peaceful and safe place, ranking seventh highest in our safety research. Many of the local cops, like the retirees, are from Los Angeles. When Paradise organized its own police force, the city recruited in Southern California. One ex-LAPD officer said, "What a difference! Here I spend my time helping people instead of dealing with criminals. In Los Angeles it was always 'them against us.'"

Paradise has been a retirement tradition in California for decades, so the retiree population is high, with one-third of the residents older than sixty (almost 16 percent are older than seventy-five). Because such a large group of residents is living on fixed incomes, housing costs and rents haven't been pushed to the ridiculous highs of some other parts of California. Because of a large number of absentee owners, rents are reasonable. Mobile homes on large, forested lots make great retirement homes, and landscaping makes them indistinguishable from conventional housing.

Chico   In contrast, only a twenty-minute drive from the mountain city of Paradise is the flatland city of Chico, another excellent retirement location. Although its population is about the same as Paradise's, the two places are a world apart. Chico is a typical Sacramento Valley town, with live oak and huge ash trees shading quiet streets on topography as flat as a table.

The thing that lifts Chico above most small, agriculturally centered valley towns is its university and vibrant academic timbre. Precisely because of the town's laid-back atmosphere, away from the distraction of big-city life or surfing beaches, Chico State University

CHICO WEATHER					
In degrees Fahrenheit					
	Jan.	April	July	Oct.	Rain	Snow
Daily highs	54	73	98	79	22"	1"
Daily lows	36	44	59	47		

is preferred by many California parents when helping their kids select a school. Like all California state universities, Chico State encourages senior citizen participation with free and reduced tuition rates. Cultural events—such as concerts, plays, lectures, and foreign films—are plentiful and, more often than not, free.

Many good home buys in Chico are found in older neighborhoods and in some more recent developments on the edge of town. Typical construction is frame with stucco finish, favored because of its resilience in earthquakes. (A brick building tends to crack and suffer damage; a frame house simply twists and rolls with the shaking.) Because of the university, housing prices are higher than in ordinary Sacramento Valley cities, and inexpensive rentals are either snatched up by students or are located in student neighborhoods where stereo music is commonly played at a volume that blisters wallpaper.

Retirees living in Chico point out the advantage of being close to the mountains: good fishing, hunting, and camping. A short drive takes you to the natural beauty and the recreational opportunities of the Feather River Canyon wilderness. Skiing is enjoyed at Inskip, about forty minutes away, and some of the best striped bass in the West are caught in the nearby Sacramento River. Incidentally, fishermen haul monster sturgeon from this river, many fish tipping the scale at more than 200 pounds! Because sturgeon is a game fish and not sold commercially, few people have ever tasted a succulent steak from one of these large creatures. It's like no other fish you've ever tasted—as firm as lobster and as juicy as a filet mignon, yet with a flavor closer to frogs' legs than fish.

Chico weather, as in all Central Valley towns, is both a blessing and a drawback, depending on your opinion of how hot summers should be. You can find days on end with temperatures approaching one hundred degrees. Balance that against the warm, seldom-frosty winter days, and I believe Chico's weather comes out a winner. After all, when the summer gets going, that's the time for you to get going to the nearby mountains for a picnic beside a cool stream or a day's prospecting and panning for gold in the Feather River.

Dunsmuir   The Sacramento River, which passes through Chico on its way to San Francisco Bay, has its origins farther north, past Redding and beautiful Lake Shasta, in the mountains not far from the town of Dunsmuir. Dunsmuir sits in a canyon, overlooked by ridges covered with Christmas-tree pines and segmented by streets that climb steeply from river bottom to the interstate highway above town. The town enjoys a spectacular year-round view of snow-covered Mt. Shasta in the distance. This ancient volcano is one of the highest peaks on the continent and offers some pretty fair skiing at a place called Snowman's Hill.

Dunsmuir is an old town, with many homes older than fifty years. A sense of history permeates the old-fashioned downtown section and its one main street. Here the bus station is still called the "stage stop" by older residents, and the Greyhound bus is called the "stage." Although some mining went on in the area, Dunsmuir originated as a roundhouse and repair service for passing trains, providing fuel and water for the locomotives and food for the dining cars.

With the decline of steam engines, the original purpose of the town faded. Some railroaders moved away when they lost their jobs; others retired and stayed there. Thus began a continuing tradition of Dunsmuir as a retirement location. When the railroaders left, the bottom dropped out of the real estate market, which didn't have far to drop, because property was always quite reasonable. Retirees found this an ideal location, with great fishing, economical living, a gorgeous view from the front porch every morning, and unforgettable sunsets.

Lurking trout, sometimes large native ones, tempt the fisherman to the shores of the Sacramento River. Wild blackberry bushes on the banks yield delicious makings for cobblers, should the fish not be biting that day. The river has recovered nicely from a

DUNSMUIR WEATHER

In degrees Fahrenheit

	Jan.	April	July	Oct.	Rain	Snow
Daily highs	50	53	90	68	30"	18"
Daily lows	30	36	58	39		

horrendous pesticide spill a couple of years past. Once again the odor of rainbow trout frying for breakfast fills the morning air.

Because Interstate 5 bypasses the town by a quarter-mile, the pace along the town's main street is leisurely and unhurried. Dunsmuir's northern location and 2,300-foot elevation ensure at least a couple of good winter snowstorms. Because I spent one winter here working on the old *Dunsmuir News,* I can attest that snow here is of a special sort—soft, fluffy, and pretty (as long as you don't have to shovel the blasted stuff). But it does pile up quickly. The canyon turns into a billowy white winter fantasyland for a day or two until a warm rain clears it all away.

Mount Shasta   Dunsmuir's close cousin is reached by a short drive up the Sacramento River Canyon, where the landscape changes into a plateau of gently rolling hills. Mount Shasta is larger than Dunsmuir, with a population of 3,700, and sits at an elevation of 3,500 feet, literally at the foot of the majestic mountain peak of Mount Shasta. This ancient, snow-covered volcano is one of the highest peaks on the continent at 14,110 feet. The stark cinder cone of Black Butte presents another ever-present landmark to the north. Because of the increased altitude, Mount Shasta receives much more snow than Dunsmuir; 96 inches of the stuff falls every winter, compared with Dunsmuir's 38 inches. And it stays on the ground longer here.

Mount Shasta sits on a wide expanse of more-or-less-level land instead of a narrow canyon like Dunsmuir. Room for expansion means you'll find more contemporary housing and upscale residences here. The commercial district is also much larger. This is where Dunsmuir residents come for serious shopping purchases.

College of the Siskiyous brings performing arts and musical presentations, making Mount Shasta the cultural center of Siskiyou County. Included are drama, music, and art productions staged by the college as well as by internationally renowned performing

MOUNT SHASTA WEATHER						
In degrees Fahrenheit						
	Jan.	April	July	Oct.	Rain	Snow
Daily highs	42	58	85	65	37"	96"
Daily lows	26	33	51	37		

troupes. The school's learning resources center is geared toward continuing education for older students.

Four golf courses are within driving distance: one in Mount Shasta, one in McCloud, and two in Weed. On the southern slope of Mount Shasta, between the town and McCloud, Mount Shasta Ski Park is a full-service winter resort featuring Alpine and Nordic skiing as well as snowboarding in one convenient nearby location.

Mount Shasta's Mercy Medical Center is an eighty-bed hospital with twenty doctors on staff and a twenty-four-hour emergency care center. The hospital covers a wide range of services. At the time of writing, Dunsmuir has two family doctors and three dentists.

Yreka   Located 22 miles south of the California–Oregon border, Yreka is a quiet little city of 7,150 nestled in the northernmost corner of the majestic Shasta Valley. The name Yreka (pronounced *why-REE-ka*) is said to be a Shasta Indian word meaning "north mountain." The community often ranks high in where-to-retire surveys conducted by major U.S. magazines, usually placing in the top fifty small towns in the United States. This is the largest full-service community on Interstate 5 between Ashland, Oregon, and Redding, 120 miles south. The population base provides support for professional services, medical facilities, and a full range of retail businesses, making Yreka the trade center for the county. The town supports several retail shopping areas, many antiques stores, thirty-two restaurants, auto service stores, thirteen motels, two bed-and-breakfast inns, and the Yreka Western Railroad/Blue Goose Steam Train.

Downtown Yreka's fascinating historic district reflects its gold-mining past. The town's genesis came in 1851, when one of the drivers of a mule train from Oregon discovered glittering metal near a ravine called Black Gulch. Within six weeks of the discovery, 2,000 miners had created a gold rush boomtown of tents, shanties, and rustic cabins. Before long the substantial brick and gingerbread buildings you see today were under construction. In 1853 Joaquin Miller described Yreka as "a bustling place with a tide of people up and down and across other streets, as strong as if in New York." More than seventy-five homes built in the 1800s have been preserved, as well as many more of those constructed after the turn of the twentieth century. The residential district of Third Street is on the National Register of Historic Places.

Although Yreka sits at an altitude of 2,625 feet, it receives much less rain and snow than some of its neighbors. The town catches about 6 inches of snow, compared with 98 inches in Mount Shasta (at an altitude of 3,500 feet) and 38 inches in Dunsmuir (at 2,300 feet). Yreka typically gets no more than one or two snowstorms per year.

Close at hand are recreational opportunities featuring four golf courses within easy driving distance, tennis courts, great fishing, white-water rafting, hiking, backpacking, camping, hunting, water-skiing, bowling, snowmobiling, snow skiing (at two nearby ski parks), racquetball, and bicycling.

The College of the Siskiyous in Yreka sponsors a senior college to meet the needs of the senior community. A number of classes are tailored to continuing education, such as those in woodcarving, beginning computers, and memoir writing. Some courses are offered during the day, but most are held in the evening. The facility includes a state-of-the-art computer lab and a fitness center. The school recently combined its performing arts series with the Yreka Community Theatre to produce an extensive series of performances.

Yreka is the health-care center for the region, boasting two hospitals. The largest is Siskiyou General Hospital, a full-service facility with fifty-seven beds. Fairchild Medical Center is an acute-care hospital with twenty-eight doctors representing a wide spectrum of medical specialties.

Fall River Mills/Burney   One last example of Gold Country retirement is called the Intermountain Area. It nestles between the Sierra Nevada and the Cascade mountain ranges in the northeast corner of California. This is just one of many such picturesque and unspoiled areas of the state with inexpensive living. The highway east from Redding winds past several abandoned mines as it makes its way to the towns of Burney and Fall River Mills. Today gold mining is no longer an economic force, having been pushed aside by wild-rice farming in Fall River Mills and lumber mills in Burney.

Tall Douglas firs shade Burney's streets and homes. A recent forest fire devastated large tracts of forest, but firefighters heroically stopped it before it could damage the town. Twenty miles away, in a sharply different terrain, are Burney's sister towns of Fall River Mills and McArthur. The panorama in these towns is a wide, grassy valley

FALL RIVER MILLS–BURNEY WEATHER						
In degrees Fahrenheit						
	Jan.	April	July	Oct.	Rain	Snow
Daily highs	40	74	91	69	40"	25"
Daily lows	28	47	68	46		

circled by tree-clad mountains. A remarkably clear stream (the Fall River) wells up from the depths of a volcanic formation a few miles away and collects the waters of a dozen sparkling trout streams as it meanders through the valley. The views are enhanced by Mount Lassen (10,466 feet) to the southeast and by majestic, snowcapped Mount Shasta (14,162 feet) to the northwest.

"Fall River Mills," I hear you saying. "Never heard of it. Why would anyone want to live there?" Well, you've heard of one of Fall River Mills's earlier residents: Bing Crosby. With all of the country to choose from, Bing bought a ranch there as a place to raise his boys. (Another Hollywood personality owns the ranch now; I won't say who, because local people don't like to bring attention to the area that way.)

Bing's favorite sports were golf and fly fishing. The superb trout streams throughout the Intermountain Area satisfied the latter interest, but Bing could not survive without golf. This explains the existence of a beautiful eighteen-hole championship golf course located just west of Fall River Mills on the main highway. It's reputed to rank among the top fifty courses in the United States. The unique layout of the course poses a challenge to professionals and amateurs alike. Amenities include a restaurant, a clubhouse, and a pro shop, with other facilities planned for the future.

Between these two towns you'll find most of the services available in a city, yet the towns cling to an away-from-it-all atmosphere. Burney has a bustling "downtown," complete with shopping district; Fall River Mills is scattered over several miles of highway and ends at an even smaller town, McArthur. Even though the nearest city of any size, Redding, is an hour's drive away, the Intermountain Area is self-sufficient, with shopping centers, banks, restaurants, and a hospital.

Those seeking low-cost retirement living will find housing bargains in Burney, with large three-bedroom homes selling for a third of the cost of many California tract homes. Land is inexpensive, so large building lots are the norm. Fall River Mills property is priced a bit higher because of a recent real estate land rush. In smaller communities like this, just a few people moving at once can create a scarcity.

The Mountain Senior Center, located in Burney, is a complex consisting of single-family homes and one-bedroom apartments situated within easy walking distance of shopping and medical facilities. It also features a park, community center, and RV storage, all designed for use by people age fifty-five or older. Free bus transportation is also available to seniors throughout the Intermountain area for special needs.

The waterways of the Intermountain Area offer many varieties of fishing. Choose from deep, cold lakes or mountain streams for bass and trout; try the warmer waters for catfish and crappie. Lakes Britton, Eastman, Fall River, Baum Crystal, and Iron Canyon are a lure to all types of anglers. With a short drive to the northwest, anglers will find other hot spots on Bear Creek, Medicine Lake, McCloud River, and others. Two wild trout streams—Hat Creek and Fall River—offer trophy trout to the dedicated fly fishers or those fishing with artificial lures. (Live bait is prohibited.)

Northern California Coast

The northern California coast is highlighted by the urbanity and sophistication of the San Francisco Bay area. But the City by the Bay shouldn't be your only stop on a tour of this area's retirement possibilities. After you cross the Golden Gate Bridge going north,

Highway 1 winds through some of the most peaceful and rural landscapes to be found anywhere. The towns are small, neighborly, and uncrowded. The only large town on the California stretch of coast is Eureka, the next "metropolitan" area being the Coos Bay–North Bend area in Oregon. Several picturesque villages sit along the coast, interspersed with forest and grazing land, sleepy and laid-back, just as they should be. Small, family-owned wineries and their tasting rooms make for interesting visits. If you are looking for discos, beach parties, and tourist traps, you are much too far north.

Along this coast the traditional industry has always been lumbering, which appears to be in a permanent state of depression all over the West. The second industry is fishing, much of which is done by amateurs or people just out for fun. Because neither industry is hiring workers, jobs are scarce, and younger people are leaving for the cities. That means housing is affordable. The moral of this story is, if you need to work part-time to make ends meet, forget about the northwest coast. If you can satisfy your need for work through meaningful volunteer jobs, you will do just fine.

If you are members of that class that hates hot summers and cold winters, you've come to the right place. Frost is all but unheard-of, with forty degrees just about as cold as it ever gets in January. Highs in January in Eureka, for example, average fifty-three degrees; but the July and August highs rarely top seventy degrees! Compare that with *your* town's average July temperatures. Every night of the year you will sleep under blankets; an air conditioner would be a waste of money. On the other hand, because lows are never sub-freezing, many homes don't have central heating systems, depending upon a wall furnace or fireplace for comfort.

California's Napa Valley wine-producing country and its delightful little towns and villages are great for retirement. People choose places like Calistoga, Healdsburg, or St. Helena, just to name a few. For quality living at moderate costs, the Napa–Sonoma region merits closer investigation. But there's a lesser-known wine country—just as pretty, less crowded, and not far away—on the Mendocino Coast, with the Pacific Ocean on one side and the low coastal mountains on the other.

Mendocino/Fort Bragg   The Mendocino Coast is accessed only by a slow, two-lane coastal highway; most casual tourists and hurried travelers choose to travel inland, along multilane, high-speed Highway 101. This leaves the towns along the coast untouched by those who aren't specifically interested in enjoying the special ambience of this area.

Founded in 1852 as a mill town, Mendocino started with a Cape Cod flavor that has been carefully preserved. This Cape Cod look didn't come about by accident. The Mendocino Coast's history dates back to California gold rush days when fishermen and

MENDOCINO–FORT BRAGG WEATHER					
In degrees Fahrenheit					
	Jan.	April	July	Oct.	Rain	Snow
Daily highs	53	54	64	63	39"	1"
Daily lows	41	44	52	49		

loggers from New England found the region very much to their liking. They brought New England–style architecture with them. In fact so many homes were shipped around the tip of South America and reassembled here that the region is referred to as "Cape Cod Shipped 'Round the Horn." Logging and fishing were early industries and continue to play a part in today's economy.

This is a community of artisans, which accounts for the many art galleries and boutiques in the town. It's a small place, unincorporated, with approximately 1,100 residents, although more than 8,000 live in the surrounding area. The village sits high on a bluff, surrounded on three sides by the Pacific Ocean. Hollywood filmed several motion pictures here, taking full advantage of Mendocino's picturesque setting.

Popular with tourists and those looking for beautiful seascapes, the basic business here deals with art in one form or another. Mendocino is popular with those looking for quality living in a rural, cool (but not cold) climate. Housing prices are not as inexpensive as you might expect; well-off San Franciscans like their weekend homes here. Real estate can be pricey in the village, but when you leave the immediate vicinity of the town center, prices drop considerably. For more inexpensive real estate, look toward Fort Bragg.

Ten miles north of Mendocino on Highway 1 is the working community of Fort Bragg, a lumbering and fishing community of more than 6,000 residents. A no-nonsense business section makes Fort Bragg the place where people come for necessary services and shopping. It's an exceptionally clean and attractive place, more modern in appearance than Mendocino. Several local performing-arts companies produce concerts, stage plays, musicals, and revues. San Francisco Symphony musicians join local musicians for the Mendocino Music Festival in July.

Housing costs are in line with local wages, thus less expensive than Mendocino. Both communities are attracting retirees as well as artisans, many coming from the San Francisco and Los Angeles areas.

The Mendocino Coast District Hospital in Fort Bragg is a fully licensed, fifty-four-bed, acute-care, nonprofit community hospital. The hospital has more than thirty physicians on staff representing many medical specialties. The hospital operates an ambulance service with air service for emergency transfer.

Eureka/Arcata   This is another area that owes its origins to the gold rush. In 1850 its location on Humboldt Bay made it ideal as a port to supply mines east in Trinity County. Eureka flourished overnight as gold seekers poured into the port fresh from San Francisco. Arcata, on the north side of Humboldt Bay, was also founded in 1850. Brett Harte put in a brief stint as editor at a newspaper here until some local toughs took exception to his writing. He hopped a steamboat for San Francisco, where he achieved fame for his tales of life in the mining camps.

After the gold fields played out, prospectors stayed and looked for steadier work as fishermen, farmers, and lumberjacks. The stately redwoods became the backbone of the economy in the late 1800s. Victorian homes built of almost indestructible redwood lumber grace the landscape of Eureka and the surrounding communities. These old homes are showcases for now-forgotten arts of carpentry. Because many early settlers were lumber barons, you can imagine the care and attention to detail with which the artisans constructed the homes. For this reason the town has been declared a State Historical Landmark.

Humboldt Bay fishing highlights Eureka's economy nowadays. More than 300 fishing vessels call this port home and land more rockfish, crab, oysters, and shrimp than any other place in California. Strolling along Eureka's quaint Old Town waterfront is a favorite activity, breathing in the fresh sea air, watching boats returning with catches of salmon and tasty Dungeness crab.

Although its population is less than 30,000, Eureka is the center, culturally and commercially, of another 45,000 residents in the immediate urban area. Approximately 86 percent of Humboldt County's 117,000 population lives within a 20-mile radius of Eureka. The famous Redwood Empire forests begin near the edge of town and climb the mountains beyond and into the

EUREKA–ARCATA WEATHER

In degrees Fahrenheit

	Jan.	April	July	Oct.	Rain	Snow
Daily highs	53	55	61	60	39"	—
Daily lows	42	44	52	48		

Trinity Alps, with backdrops as high as 6,000 feet. Although this is primarily a mountainous region encompassing six wild and scenic river systems and stands of majestic redwood groves, Eureka itself is located on a level coastal plain. Eighty percent of the county is forested public lands.

The weather here, typical of beach towns along the coast north to Washington, makes this a place for retirees who hate the thought of hot, steamy summers or icy, frigid winters. Except for more rain in the winter months, there's little difference in the weather year-round. A sweater feels comfortable almost every evening of the year, and noonday weather is seldom, if ever, hot enough to make you sweat. Air-conditioning is something people here read about. Winters are mild enough that many homes heat with fireplaces or wood-stoves. Many older houses have fireplaces in every room. Annual rainfall here is around 38 inches, a lot for California but much less than most Midwestern and Eastern cities. Snow shovels are as unnecessary as air-conditioning.

Located on Highway 101, a main north-south artery, the Eureka area also has an airport with regional carriers for short flights to San Francisco and other important local cities. The airport is located a few miles north of Arcata, about 15 miles from Eureka, and is served by a shuttle bus.

Three excellent hospitals serve the area, one each for Eureka and the neighboring communities of Arcata and Fortuna. Arcata's hospital can boast that its staff makes house calls, because they operate a home-care service for those who need ongoing treatment outside the hospital. The service is carried out by registered nurses, home health aides, and physical therapists under the direction of a physician.

The Eureka Senior Center, housed in an old grammar school building, is one of the most extensive and comprehensive we've seen. From classes such as arts and crafts to an Alzheimer's day-care center, the services are superb. The Retired Senior Volunteer Program counts on more than 700 retirees who contribute their skills and interests in service to the community.

Fishing, of course, is a favorite sport here, with salmon, albacore, and Dungeness crab to catch. With generally benign weather, some kind of fishing, crabbing, or clamming is possible all year. For those who get seasick, the country immediately behind the town, continuing 100 miles or so, is full of great trout streams. Deer, river otters, herons, and other wildlife are plentiful, for much of the Coast Range and inland Klamath Mountains are jealously preserved as wildlife areas.

Nearby Arcata (pop. 17,000) is the home of Humboldt State University, one of the area's economic mainstays. With a good reputation as a serious school, the university is also the source of many cultural and intellectual events open to the public. In addition there is the College of the Redwoods, a two-year school, and Eureka Adult School, with many community locations. The academic atmosphere complements the old-fashioned, Victorian atmosphere of the area, a place where mountains, forest, and blue Pacific all come together.

Along this northern coast, all the way to Washington state, low wages and living costs are the rule. As a result housing is quite reasonable—probably as low as you might expect to find anywhere on the West Coast. We looked at several Victorians. Our favorite, going for what a garage would cost in San Francisco, had high ceilings, a claw-foot bathtub, an antique wood cookstove, and three bedrooms. Mobile homes are located away from the city's residential sections and seem to be in abundant supply, because they sell at very reasonable prices. In the countryside, many place mobile homes on spacious wooded lots. Except for Arcata, where students compete for housing, rentals are readily available.

A place famous for Victorians is Ferndale, a short drive south of Eureka. Started in the late 1800s as a prosperous dairy center, the early settlers built some splendidly ornate homes that became known as Butterfat Palaces. Even though the town is a tourist attraction, it's mostly a "stop-for-lunch, look around, and get-going-again" sort of tourism. Retirees find it a place to stay. Ferndale, like the other towns around Eureka, preserves a small-town atmosphere of neighborliness. Bed-and-breakfast places are popular.

The Southern California Dream

When most folks think about California, they conjure images of Hollywood, surfboards, swimming pools, and convertibles. They picture southern California towns like Santa Barbara, Beverly Hills, or San Diego with broad, palm-lined boulevards, pastel-colored mansions, and ultramodern apartment buildings. Easterners imagine southern California as a place to fantasize over, not a practical place to live.

Although some of these images are indeed true, hundreds of thousands of retired folks will tell you they wouldn't consider living anywhere else. Don't misunderstand: This is not a place to look for bargain living; most southern California locations are not cheap places to live. In many neighborhoods Los Angeles home prices are 55 percent higher than national averages! Yet there are some excellent southern California communities where housing is comparable to many parts of the country—not next door to movie stars, but certainly in pleasant, safe neighborhoods.

Southern California living costs aren't out of line; after all, groceries, clothing, automobiles, and such cost about the same no matter where you live. Competition for consumer business keeps prices competitive in the Southland (as folks here like to refer to their home). You'll find the Los Angeles area always has among the lowest gasoline prices in the state. And because the climate is mild to warm, neither air-conditioning nor heating costs make drastic dents in the budget.

Why do people keep coming to southern California? Primarily because of the weather, but also because of the wide variety of things to do and sights to see. Places like Los Angeles and Santa Barbara owe much of their early growth to retirees coming to visit and to stay. Land promoters used to run cross-country passenger trains with free tickets just so retirees could investigate southern California as a retirement haven. When the unsuspecting retirees were hooked on the lovely orange-grove dreamland, the slick promoters would sell them building lots for as much as $175 per parcel and then a house for an additional $3,000—places that wouldn't sell for much more than $375,000 today. Unscrupulous!

San Diego   San Diego, with a population of more than a million, is an excellent example of a city in transition from old to new. The downtown section, once rather ordinary and deteriorating—as most U.S. cities are lately—has been transformed into an exciting, welcoming city center. Trees, landscaping, and careful planning are doing the trick.

The attraction here is the superb weather—statistically San Diego has the best climate in the continental United States. It never freezes or snows, and it rains a scant 11 inches a year, just enough to keep shrubbery and flowers fresh. A constant breeze from the Pacific pushes heat into the desert and nullifies cold snaps. There is no smog or air pollution, and little need for air-conditioning. This results in less use of utilities and lower bills.

The San Diego area has an unusually large percentage of retirees. There are more than 100 senior citizens' organizations, with membership totaling more than 100,000. Numerous life-care centers and seniors-only apartments and housing complexes are scattered around the region.

The big drawback with San Diego is expensive housing, some of the costliest in the nation. The median price of a single-family home is more than 60 percent above national averages. Selling prices of homes are inflated, rents are costly, and mobile-home parks are scarce and ridiculously expensive; many have been converted to commercial use, with tenants forced to look for other nonexistent

SAN DIEGO AREA WEATHER						
In degrees Fahrenheit						
	Jan.	April	July	Oct.	Rain	Snow
Daily highs	65	68	76	75	9"	—
Daily lows	48	55	65	60		

SAN DIEGO AREA COST OF LIVING					
Percentage of	Overall	Housing	Medical	Groceries	Utilities
national average	130	167	133	124	97

parks. The inflated cost of keeping a roof over your head drags the overall cost of living index up as well.

Like Los Angeles, however, it isn't necessary to live in the city itself to enjoy the weather and ambience. At the eastern edge of San Diego the country turns into desert hills, with dramatic boulders and rock formations garnished with cactus and desert brush. Within easy shopping distance from San Diego are the towns of El Cajon, Alpine, Lakeside, and several other smaller communities. Land is far less expensive, and lots tend to be spacious, sometimes large enough to keep horses. Riding trails take off in all directions to wander through the empty mountain country. Although housing is less expensive, the tradeoff is warmer summers and cooler winters.

From your suburban home you can run into San Diego to enjoy professional sports: the San Diego Chargers, the Padres, the Hawks, or the Andy Williams PGA Open. San Diego State brings collegiate football as well as the usual artistic presentations, and the San Diego Opera, Theater, and Symphony are nationally renowned.

As an example of a nearby retirement location, El Cajon (pop. 95,000) maintains a separate identity, self-contained as far as retirement living is concerned, yet only 15 miles via interstate to downtown San Diego. Senior citizens account for about 19 percent of El Cajon's population and enjoy numerous services provided by the East County Council on Aging and Grossmont Hospital. Two other hospitals are there, including a Kaiser Foundation facility.

For those who like dry, warm weather, El Cajon is a good prospect for retirement. It isn't all that hot, either. According to the U.S. Weather Bureau, the maximum temperatures for July average eighty-eight degrees (at only 28 percent humidity), and January high temperatures average sixty-seven degrees. How does that compare with your summer weather?

Northeast of San Diego about 30 miles is the town of Escondido (pop. 134,000). The climate is similar to El Cajon's—dry and pleasant—but it is situated in rolling, grassy country. Low mountains loom in the background, and ranches and homes on acreage lots dominate the outlying areas here. Many homes have horse stables. Houses and condos rent for considerably less here than in San Diego, and homes sell for 25 to 50 percent less than similar homes in the city. Escondido offers most amenities retirees demand: a hospital, an excellent senior service center, a community college, and adult education programs that are free to those older than sixty.

Los Angeles   This is where the southern California dream started. Retirement became big business back in the 1880s when promoters began capitalizing on its ideal climate. From that time on retirement remained big as the town grew larger and larger. But Los Angeles didn't simply grow larger, as most cities do; it grew quite unpredictably, spreading out in this direction and that, until the result is a city that looks different and is different from any other major city in the world.

Recently an Argentinian couple came to visit us. We met them at the Los Angeles airport and treated them to a sight-seeing tour. They were excited at the opportunity of finally seeing fabulous Los Angeles. But after an hour of driving around, they became puzzled. "But where is the city?" they asked. "We were expecting tall buildings. Everything here is small!" We drove through Hollywood, Beverly Hills, and all the other obligatory areas, and they found few places that matched their image of what Los Angeles should be. To them a real city should resemble Buenos Aires, Paris, or New York. There should be tall, elegant apartment buildings, graceful skyscrapers, fancy restaurants with sidewalk cafes, and all the metropolitan delights that combine to make a real city. Instead they found single-family homes and one- and two-story commercial buildings. The occasional tall building seemed lonely and out of place.

In most large cities of the world land is at a premium, far too valuable to waste on lawns and landscaping. Buildings start at the sidewalk and rise as high as possible. When room is left over for a lawn, it is placed *behind* the house and jealously guarded for the family's personal use. To be sure the Los Angeles city center does have a group of high-rises, but they are for commerce, not for people to live in. They stand out like lost visions, mistaken attempts to create something impossible: a real city.

There is, of course, a downtown section, but it isn't the same as in other big cities. People don't go downtown for Christmas shopping or to seek out those special restaurants as they do in New York, San Francisco, or Buenos Aires. People avoid the central downtown and go to the nearest shopping mall instead. Like satellites, a garland of smaller cities surrounds Los Angeles. Each features its own "downtown" focus, which could be a giant shopping mall, and in turn each is surrounded by even smaller shopping centers and neighborhoods.

LOS ANGELES WEATHER						
In degrees Fahrenheit						
	Jan.	April	July	Oct.	Rain	Snow
Daily highs	65	67	75	74	12"	—
Daily lows	47	52	63	59		

LOS ANGELES AREA COST OF LIVING					
Percentage of	Overall	Housing	Medical	Groceries	Utilities
national average	138	209	113	112	105

This ring of small towns is where retirement is best considered, not in Los Angeles proper. The FBI crime charts show that some of the towns circling Los Angeles are quite safe. Hermosa Beach, Agoura Hills, and Redondo Beach, for example, rank in the top levels of personal safety. People who live here seldom if ever venture into less safe zones; they have no reason to do so.

There are so many delightful communities here that it's impossible to list them. If the weather here is a strong enough magnet, it's worth spending time driving and looking from Capistrano in the south to the San Gabriel Mountains to the north or out to the desertlike settings in the east as far as San Bernardino. By the way, the smog problem disappears as you leave the Los Angeles Basin, as does the population density. Nice mobile-home parks are increasingly plentiful the farther you travel from Los Angeles.

The area's superb year-round climate makes outdoor recreation practical, with golf, tennis, and swimming available in most every neighborhood. Wilderness areas are but one or two hours' drive from city hall. Gold panning in the San Gabriel Mountains, skiing and trout fishing at Lake Arrowhead and Big Bear, or rockhounding in the desert—all these and more are available. Fishing off the piers, jogging, walking, or loafing on the beaches add another facet of outdoor recreation: The ocean can be enjoyed to the limit. Sailboats and fishing craft can be berthed at numerous places along the coast.

Those who locate away from the city will find that Los Angeles itself offers cultural advantages found only in big cities. World-famous art galleries, museums, and symphonies are easily accessible, as are theaters, universities, and all types of senior activities. It's a great place for short visits. Most satellite towns have community colleges, and none are very far from a state university branch.

The Los Angeles area is not an inexpensive place to retire, yet it doesn't have to be prohibitive. Everybody here isn't rich; it takes some shopping to find a comfortable niche, a place where housing prices aren't off the wall. Nothing here is cheap, but compared with San Diego or Santa Barbara, real estate can be reasonable. But it's important to look beyond housing prices here; the quality of a neighborhood is far more important than affordability. The bottom line around Los Angeles is: If you can't afford to live in a safe neighborhood, forget it.

Pismo Beach/Five Cities Area   Once the butt of many Jack Benny jokes, Pismo Beach is today having the last laugh. People are discovering that it's a very pleasant place to spend a vacation, plus it's a great place to retire. Located about 200 miles north of Los Angeles, Pismo Beach has a population of approximately 6,000. It's just one of five adjoining towns spread along the beach and near-inland areas that gives the Five Cities its name. (By the way, the word *pismo* comes from the famous pismo clams that at one time seemed to almost pave the long stretches of sandy shoreline.) Pismo Beach is a typical example of smaller beach-retirement towns on the California coast.

Until recently the favorite sport here was digging into sand at low tide in search of the large, succulent clams. Both locals and tourists still do, but today's clam diggers aren't like the crowds of a few years ago. Too many clam forks and voracious sea otters have thinned the mollusk population considerably. But clams are still there for the persistent, and fishing is still great from the long pier that juts out past the surf (no license required). Bottom fish such as ling cod, red snapper, and sand dabs are favorite catches. Fishing and clamming are year-round sports. Boat-launching facilities are available at nearby Avila Beach, just north of the Five Cities.

Pismo Beach is one of the few places along the California coast where it is permissible to drive a motor vehicle onto the sand, and there are several ramps that give access to the beach. Huge, undulating sand dunes are meccas for four-wheel-drive vehicles and dune buggies. Converted Volkswagens, Jeeps, and other souped-up contraptions zip up and down the dunes like motorized roller coasters (away from the more quiet beach crowd, of course). Another favorite

PISMO BEACH–FIVE CITIES AREA WEATHER

In degrees Fahrenheit

	Jan.	April	July	Oct.	Rain	Snow
Daily highs	64	68	72	74	13"	—
Daily lows	43	48	53	51		

beach activity is horseback riding. A couple of stables rent horses for leisurely rides along the surf line. Golf is popular, with several courses in the area.

The loosely connected communities that together comprise the sprawling, lightly populated Five Cities area are Shell Beach, Oceano, Grover City, Arroyo Grande, and Pismo Beach itself. Arroyo Grande is away from the beach, but it is the largest (pop. 11,000) of the Five Cities and is considered part of the metropolitan area (pop. 30,000). Housing is naturally more expensive along the cliffs or anywhere an ocean view fills your picture window.

Until recently the Five Cities area was considered one of the best real estate buys on California's Central Coast. One reason for this was the exodus of workers who labored on the nearby Diablo Canyon nuclear-power project when the facility was completed. Real estate was a glut on the market for a while. But a wave of popularity and economic growth soon boosted prices to the level of similar California locations. New developments with upscale housing have been competing with large, luxury homes. This isn't to say this is now an expensive area, just that prices are back to "normal" for California. A nearby place where real estate is a bargain, at the moment, is Avila Beach. This is due to an environmental disaster, when it was discovered that an oil-pumping facility had polluted the land under the beach. The government is in the process of completely removing the oil-soaked sand and replacing it with clean material. In the meantime the downtown area—where tourists and residents used to enjoy a beautiful beach—is fenced off and nonfunctional. Real estate is at a rock bottom. However, within a year or so the restoration work will be complete, and presumably property prices will once again rise to normal.

As you might expect, where there are large numbers of retired folks, you will find active senior citizens' organizations. Pismo Beach supports several organizations, ranging from grandmothers' clubs to a singles' club for people older than sixty. You'll find an active

RSVP chapter, Meals on Wheels, and a senior citizens' ride program—plus plenty of opportunities to get involved in volunteer projects.

San Luis Obispo   The university town of San Luis Obispo (pop. 43,000) lies just a fifteen-minute drive north of the Five Cities area. This is a real charmer and from our perspective perhaps one of the best places for retirement in the entire state.

A city beautification program, started some twenty-five years ago, has paid off handsomely, making the downtown a treat for the eyes. Large, leafy trees arch over commercial avenues lined with prosperous businesses and stores with tastefully designed exteriors. Nationally known outlets you would expect to find only in shopping malls—fashionable clothing stores, large drugstores, and boutiques of all description—are located right in the center of town, not a ten-minute drive away. San Luis Obispo was recently awarded the distinction of having "the best downtown in the Western U.S." by *Sunset Magazine*.

Like most university towns San Luis Obispo enjoys a vibrant combination of services and facilities that satisfy tastes and requirements of students and retirees alike. Interesting yet affordable restaurants, bookstores that stock more than just best-sellers, foreign and award-winning movies that other towns would never think to present are just a few items that retirees say they like about San Luis Obispo living. Another downtown tradition is the Thursday night Farmer's Market, a delightful hubbub of flowers, organically grown local greens and flowers, street musicians, and barbecued ribs. There's also a burgeoning wine-growing area on the outskirts of town, with tours and tasting rooms galore.

Residential neighborhoods present enticing retirement scenarios, with nicely landscaped properties and views of mountains in the distance. Although property values never were cheap and have increased considerably—as have many California communities—homes and condos appear to be bargains when compared with other quality central coast locations, such as Monterey or Santa Barbara. Prices of some homes we looked at in the $300,000 range would cost twice as much in those more high-price towns. For less expensive real estate, take a look at the nearby communities of Arroyo Grande, Grover Beach, and Nipomo in the Five Cities area and Atascadero, Templeton, and Paso Robles to the north and inland.

The university sponsors a multitude of cultural events, such as plays, lectures, and concerts, many free to senior citizens. The Performing Arts Center on the Cal Poly campus attracts Broadway shows and big-name performers like Bob Dylan, Judy Collins, Joan Baez, and Bobby McFerrin. The Mission Plaza, once just a street in front of the Mission, is now the cultural heart of the city—a place for craft fairs, promotional events, and special events such as the Mozart Festival, wine festivals, and free Friday evening concerts in the plaza.

All of the above make San Luis Obispo a pleasant retirement location for those who don't feel that they have to be able to walk to the beach (although the ocean is only a fifteen-minute drive from town). The advantages of living close to but not right on the ocean include abundant sunshine and comfortable evenings, with shirtsleeve weather rather than the typically cool, sweaters-required sundowns by the ocean.

As the health-care center for the region, San Luis Obispo has several medical facilities: Sierra Vista Regional Medical Center, French Hospital (with an outstanding cardiac unit), and the county-operated General Hospital, as well as several outpatient clinics, including a recently introduced VA clinic. Because the area is a draw for professionals from all walks of life, there is a full range of medical practitioners to ensure good care.

The Pacific Northwest

OREGON AND WASHINGTON OFFER a dramatic collection of varied landscapes providing a broad range of choices for retirement living; there's something here for everyone. Rugged seascapes and coastal mountains contrast nicely with inland valleys and fertile plains. High mountain passes of the Oregon Cascades resolve into the lava beds and the ponderosa pines of the high desert, then into the magnificent waterfalls and cliffs of the Columbia Gorge. You can test your luck with salmon, steelhead, sturgeon, or bottom fishing—from the banks of a river, an ocean boat, or in a sunny forest glade. The nice thing is that the overwhelming majority of acreage in the Pacific Northwest is publicly owned, with national forests and deserts open to everybody for hiking, camping, and general outdoor enjoyment.

The conventional image of Oregon and Washington is that of a place of continual rain, where long-term residents develop duck feet and where ducks wear galoshes. I admit that I once believed this myself. Years ago, when I accepted a job by telephone on a newspaper in Pasco, Washington, my expectations were of green, verdant mountains towering over lush river valleys with misty waterfalls and leaping trout. There are, of course, scenes in the Northwest exactly like that. But when I arrived in Pasco, I discovered that particular part of Washington is practically treeless! As far as the eye can see, it's rolling hills of wheat, scrub grasses, and an occasional, thirsty-looking sagebrush.

An interesting thing about Washington and Oregon weather is that places 50 miles apart can have climates and topography so different it's hard to believe you're in the same state. The extreme eastern parts are high-mountain country, with tall evergreen trees, harsh winters, snow-covered peaks, and great skiing. The central portions have scanty rainfall—about half that of Kansas—with a mild four-season climate and light snowfalls. The Pacific coast catches enough rain to keep everything perpetually green—even though it may snow occasionally. The ocean moderates temperatures far inland, because the warm Japan Current flows by the coast, sending temperate breezes inland and keeping freezing weather to a minimum. With a steady, year-round mildness, the climate approaches perfection for those who detest hot, sweltering summers. All but the higher elevations escape the Montana-like winters you might expect at this latitude. There's even a conifer and fern rain forest on the Olympic Peninsula, the only one in the northern hemisphere. Annual rainfall here is as much as 140 inches!

Despite Washington and Oregon's reputation for rain, statistics show that Olympia, Washington, has about the same yearly rainfall as Orlando, Florida (51 inches), and Portland, Oregon, averages 37 inches of rain each year, about the same as Buffalo, New York (except that Buffalo also receives 92 inches of snow). Rainfall in places like Ashland or Grants Pass is approximately 30 inches a year or less—about the same as San Antonio, Texas, and only half as much as most parts of Florida.

Having defended Oregon's weather so strongly, I must admit that sometimes it feels like Oregon gets much more rain than statistics indicate. This is because rain tends to fall gently upon the landscape here, slowly, mostly in the winter, and over long periods of time while it builds up the accumulated totals. And along the coast low clouds can hang around for days upon end, even when it isn't raining, giving the impression of dampness.

Just a few years ago, some of the best housing bargains in the country were to be found in Washington and Oregon. The economy was staggered by the near-collapse of fishing and lumbering, and already reasonable prices tumbled. The states were losing population as families moved away to find employment.

This has changed dramatically, with local economies booming and real estate prices on the rise. The more popular towns have seen housing costs rise far beyond the national norm. A great deal of this increase is due to the immigration of people looking for pleasant places for retirement.

Oregon

When it comes to taxes in Oregon, I must rely on the old cliché of "good news and bad news." The good news is Oregon has no state sales tax. But the bad news is property taxes are high to make up the deficit. The good news: A state referendum sent outraged property owners to the polls to vote a reduction in property taxes to a maximum of $15 per $1,000 valuation, with a prohibition against raising assessed values to make up for lost revenue. The bad news: Voters didn't notice that the prohibition applied only to commercial property; private homes could be (and were) reappraised. It turns out that the tax reduction proposition was the brainstorm of business property owners. Eventually the good news should be that the reassessment loophole will be closed, because property owners are really outraged now!

OREGON TAX PROFILE
Sales tax: no
State income tax: graduated, 5% to 9% greater than $5,000; federal income tax deductible to 7% on $25,000 and greater
Property taxes: because of a ballot "reform" measure, property tax rates go down every year while assessments go up; there's no way to predict future rates; current rate may be about 1.6%
Intangibles tax: no
Social security taxed: no
Pensions taxed: $5,000 exemption for government pensions or low income; private fully taxable
Gasoline tax: 24¢ per gallon, plus possible local taxes

Oregon's Inland Valleys

As it traverses the state north to south, Interstate 5 travels through a string of exceptionally desirable retirement locations, from Ashland near the California border to Portland on the Columbia River at Oregon's northern edge. From our point of view, this entire region offers more of what retirees say they want than any other part of the nation. Yet few people outside the West Coast ever hear much about this part of the country. Californians, of course, have heard of it—much to Oregonians' chagrin—and they come here with open checkbooks, snapping up bargain retirement homes like alligators on a chicken ranch. Of course this pushes up prices.

The landscape changes quickly as you cross into Oregon from California. Suddenly everything looks green, even in the middle of summer when most of California turns golden tan. Tall pines cloak the hills, and meadows are lush with grass; there are cows standing knee-deep in clover. It's easy to imagine the early pioneers' amaze-

OREGON'S INLAND VALLEYS

Portland

The Dalles/Hood River

Salem

Eugene/Springfield

Cave Junction
Grants Pass/Rogue River
Ashland/Medford
Jacksonville

ment as their covered wagons rumbled along the Oregon Trail to California. We understand why so many of them stayed right here! Although rainfall in most inland valley locations averages only 25 to 37 inches, enough moisture falls in the summer to keep things fresh. Without heavy frost in winter to kill the grass, fields are greenest in December through March, because that's when more rain falls.

The operative climate word here is "mild." Although an occasional light snow may fall, it seldom stays around more than a few hours because of warm afternoon temperatures. January lows are typically around thirty to forty degrees, with highs of fifty to sixty degrees. Bacause it rarely freezes, few homeowners bother to insulate their water pipes. A recent cold snap caught them by surprise, however, giving plumbers scads of overtime work.

Outdoor recreation is accessible year-round. Golf courses never close; fishing is possible in all seasons; bicycling and walking will lure you outdoors to do healthy things instead of watching television. Summers are mild, with average highs in the eighties, although July and August do have their share of hundred-plus-degree days in the inland valleys. These are tempered by a low, 38 percent relative humidity.

Ashland/Medford   These two cities are about fifteen minutes apart along Interstate 5. They share a pleasant countryside of gently rolling hills, with sporadic remnants of the thick forests that once covered the area. Rich farmland and dairy farms spread out beginning at the edges of the towns. Off in the distance, about 30 miles to the east, the forest-covered mountains of the Cascade Range are sometimes covered with snow in the winter, with Mount McLaughlin rising majestically in white-frosted splendor. To the south, another 30 miles distant, is Mount Ashland, which dominates the Siskiyou Mountain Range. Skiing is available there from Thanksgiving through April, with up to twenty-two runs operating (snow permitting). Elk, deer, and other wildlife abound in the area. With thirteen lakes only a short drive in any direction from Ashland and Medford, recreational activities are abundant.

Medford (pop. 63,000) and Ashland (pop. 19,000) are traditional retirement choices not only for Californians but for folks from all over the country who appreciate a blend of culture, year-round outdoor activities, and affordable housing costs. Medford is the commercial center, Ashland its academic counterpart. This area enjoys a very low crime rate, with Ashland ranking in the top 25 percent of towns nationally in personal safety. Here you'll find small-town living combined with city conveniences.

Ashland is one of our all-time-favorite college retirement towns. Set in a pleasant countryside of gently rolling hills at an elevation of 1,800 feet, the town enjoys a very mild climate, with low rainfall and very little to no snow. Much of the town is beautifully landscaped and graced with lovingly restored turn-of-the-twentieth-century homes. Victorians that would look at home in San Francisco command view sites on the hills overlooking the valley and mountain peaks in the distance.

As usual, when you combine a large number of students, professors, and support staff with an array of young retired couples, you create a demand for quality shopping, restaurants, and services at reasonable costs. The result is Ashland's charming downtown area. Residents from Oregon towns near and far journey here to dine in restaurants serving French country cooking, wood-fired pizza, or Thai cuisine; to browse in used-book stores; or try on tweed fashions imported from Scotland.

Part of the rich cultural atmosphere of Southern Oregon State College and the school's outreach into the community is Ashland's nationally acclaimed Shakespeare Festival. This is a year-round production in three theater facilities, with contemporary theater and other popular entertainment in addition to classic presentations. Local residents enjoy volunteering in theater production, costuming, ushering, or even acting as part of their social activities. Tourists are delighted to encounter costumed actors wandering about town, having a snack in a restaurant, and discussing their roles in the current theater production.

A bonus for Ashland retirement is the city's unusually low crime rate, with violent crimes at 50 percent of normal. At one time Ashland was one of the country's "undiscovered" real estate bargain

ASHLAND–MEDFORD WEATHER					
In degrees Fahrenheit					
	Jan.	April	July	Oct.	Rain	Snow
Daily highs	45	64	91	69	20"	8"
Daily lows	30	37	54	40		

places. Today prices have risen along with the number of retirees moving into town. Even though the average sales price of real estate is higher than in similar-sized Oregon towns, the overall cost of living is several points below national averages.

The wonderful, mild climate here makes outdoor sports possible year-round. Fishing in nearby rivers with crystal-clear waters produces catches of salmon and steelhead trout, and five lakes within a half-hour drive of Ashland are favorites for swimming, waterskiing, and picnics. Golf at six public courses in Ashland and Medford is played throughout the four seasons.

Jacksonville   A few miles west of Medford is the historic town of Jacksonville, site of another famous festival. The ongoing Britt Festivals are the oldest outdoor music and performing-arts festivals in the Northwest. Five events featuring world-class artists are presented each summer. Concertgoers combine theater with picnics, sipping wine and sampling cheeses while they relax to classical music, jazz, bluegrass, ballet, or light opera.

Once the site of a major gold strike, Jacksonville lost its chance to become the largest town in southern Oregon back in 1883 when the Oregon & California Railroad pushed its tracks northward. When the railroad requested a $25,000 "bonus" to place a station in Jacksonville, the city fathers unwisely refused to pay. Instead the station was built at a crossroads called Middle Ford. Middle Ford shortened its name to Medford and grew while Jacksonville languished. In some ways this was fortunate, because "progress" passed the town by, saving its historic old buildings from the bulldozer.

Jacksonville's shady, tree-lined streets, 130-year-old brick hotels, commercial buildings, and restored Victorian homes assured its designation as a National Historic Landmark Town in 1966. Antiques stores, boutiques, and interesting restaurants line the main street, and quiet residential neighborhoods are set back from the commerce. Except for during the festivals, Jacksonville is basically quiet, a place many folks have selected for retirement. The sur-

rounding countryside and north toward the community of G
Hill are perfect for horses, with pastures and breeding ranch ⌐
spaced at frequent intervals.

Grants Pass/Rogue River Downriver toward Grants Pass,
the scenic Rogue River flows through several small towns and communities where retirement is a pervasive theme. Mobile-home parks
and cozy-looking houses sit in close proximity to the river, allowing
anglers to enjoy record steelhead and salmon fishing just a few yards
from their back doors.

Eight miles to the south of Grants Pass is the city of Rogue
River (pop. 6,000), a delightful little community sitting where Interstate 5 and the Rogue River intersect. Quiet streets, shaded by mature
trees, provide inexpensive homes, condos, and small apartments for
those who prefer to be within walking distance of stores and the library. To the east a vast countryside of small farms and forested
homesites captivates the get-away-from-it-all crowd.

The river wends its way downstream to Grants Pass, a traditional
retirement area for Southern Californians. With about 17,000 people
living within the city limits, Grants Pass supports enough commerce
to take it out of the realm of a small town. Yet it is surprising how often
residents drive forty-five minutes to Medford for heavy-duty shopping.

Houses in town are predominantly older frame buildings,
mostly single family, neat, well cared for, and affordable. Newer
houses tend to be away from downtown, built on an acre or so, with
trees and natural shrubbery planted as low-maintenance landscaping devices. As in the case in the Rogue River area, a great
number of retirees choose to retire out in the more rustic places.
Oregon becomes mountainous at this point, with forests and
rugged hills covering much of the landscape. A fifteen-minute drive
from Grants Pass's downtown takes you to wonderfully secluded
and wild-looking properties where you will be plagued by deer
eating your flowers and black bears raiding your garbage cans.

GRANTS PASS–ROGUE RIVER WEATHER						
In degrees Fahrenheit						
	Jan.	April	July	Oct.	Rain	Snow
Daily highs	47	69	96	69	28"	4"
Daily lows	32	40	56	42		

After the river leaves Grants Pass on its way to the ocean, the going gets rough. White-water enthusiasts who have braved rapids all over the world will tell you that rafting Oregon's Rogue River is the ultimate white-water experience because of its incredible beauty. Congress designated it as the first of the nation's protected rivers under the Wild and Scenic Rivers Act of 1968. Here is where Zane Grey chose to build his home and to write many of his famous Western novels. Many scenic descriptions in his books were inspired by the picturesque Rogue River country. Moviemakers have found inspiration as well, with Hollywood crews making the trek to Grants Pass to take advantage of the scenery.

Cave Junction   Some folks love small towns and rural life and can't stand the thought of living in a city, even a small one. These folks might direct their attention toward any number of small settlements tucked away in the hills and low mountains surrounding Grants Pass. (My wife and I used to live in one delightful little community on the Rogue River, not far from Grants Pass.) While doing research in this part of Oregon's interior valley, we made a minor discovery in Cave Junction, a crossroads town of 1,235 inhabitants with the distinction of being one of the most affordable places in the state.

Cave Junction is just one of several similar communities scattered along the scenic highway that winds its way across the mountains toward the ocean at Crescent City. This area is known as the Illinois Valley, named after the Illinois River that runs through here. You'll find several "wide-spot-in-the-road" communities, such as O'Brien, Kirby, and Selma. Because there is neither industry nor jobs, most residents seem to be retired. Their younger neighbors have to commute to Grants Pass for work. Most homes hereabouts are placed on generous plots of land. They are mostly homes of modest construction, often built by the owners themselves. Manufactured homes are zoned okay, so you may buy acreage and place a large mobile home on it.

Cave Junction sits in the heart of Illinois Valley and the center of one of Oregon's famous wine-producing regions. Three small, family-owned wineries operate in the Cave Junction area, places where you have to beep your horn to alert someone that you want to visit the tasting room. The town calls itself the gateway to the

Oregon Caves, a fascinating complex of nearby limestone caverns.

People living here forfeit the benefits of city life, accepting instead the solitude and charm of country living. However, realize that in order to fit into this rustic world, you have to bring a certain amount of country mentality with you. You'll not find Greyhound buses zipping through here, and the nearest airport is 58 miles away (Medford). You'll have to adapt to local norms, and you cannot expect your neighbors to change to your way of thinking. But that's part of living in the country.

But it isn't so rustic that civilized amenities are absent. The Illinois Valley Golf Club is an eighteen-hole, par-seventy-two layout. Hunting and fishing are big here. Bird hunters go after pheasant, quail, pigeon, geese, and ducks. The Illinois, Rogue, and Applegate Rivers provide salmon, steelhead, and trout, and Selma's 160-acre, man-made Lake Selmac is the state's premier trophy bass lake. A 55-mile drive to the coast affords surf casting, rock fishing, and deep-sea adventures.

For medical emergencies it isn't necessary to travel to Grants Pass; Cave Junction now has its own medical clinic and an excellent ambulance service. But it's comforting to know that top-quality medical care isn't far away.

Eugene/Springfield   Located halfway up the state at an elevation of 426 feet above sea level, the twin cities of Eugene and Springfield are separated by the Willamette River as it runs through the heart of the metropolitan area. Enjoying a typically mild Oregon climate, the Eugene area catches about 40 inches of rainfall a year—about what you would expect in most East Coast towns—but very

EUGENE–SPRINGFIELD WEATHER						
In degrees Fahrenheit						
	Jan.	April	July	Oct.	Rain	Snow
Daily highs	46	60	82	65	40"	6"
Daily lows	33	34	50	41		

EUGENE-SPRINGFIELD AREA COST OF LIVING					
Percentage of national average	Overall	Housing	Medical	Groceries	Utilities
	107	120	120	102	75

little snow. Summers are gloriously sunny, with only fifteen days a year reaching temperatures of ninety degrees or higher. The city of Eugene counts about 120,000 inhabitants, whereas Springfield has less than 50,000.

The biggest "industry" here is the University of Oregon, with an enrollment of nearly 18,000 students. Like Ashland, university life and the excitement of learning and culture spill over into the community. Ongoing schedules of lectures, concerts, plays, and sports offerings, many of which are free, provide a constant source of interest for the retirement community. The Hult Center for the Performing Arts houses two theaters: a concert hall and a playhouse, which feature plays, concerts, and performances by local, regional, and national talent.

Eugene's business center features a large pedestrian mall for a pleasant shopping experience. Popular with students and residents alike, the center is well stocked with excellent restaurants and upscale shops. A large old building known as the Fifth Street Market houses a family of unique crafts and specialty retailers, bookstores, and restaurants, all of which make shopping downtown Eugene a treat. Toward the outskirts, two large shopping malls—one enclosed, the other open-air—offer shoppers a vast array of goods, food, and services. Eugene's open-air Saturday market is a popular, ongoing event from April to Christmas. Housing prices in Eugene are usually higher than in similar-size Oregon towns.

Across the river in Springfield, housing costs are usually about 10 percent lower, and its downtown makes up for lack of size with extra charm. By the way, Springfield supports one of the best senior centers we've encountered in Oregon or anywhere, for that matter. Facilities are excellent, the staff dedicated, and retirees unanimously pleased with their center.

Much outdoor activity centers on the Willamette River, which runs through Eugene and Springfield, providing trout fishing, picnicking, miles of bicycle trails, and river walks. For ocean fishing, clamming, and beachcombing for driftwood or Japanese glass fishing floats, Pacific beaches are just a ninety-minute drive west through beautiful low-mountain country and the Siuslaw National Forest. A short drive in the opposite direction is the Deschutes National Forest, crowned by the Mount Washington and Three Sisters wilderness areas. To the north similar towns suitable for retirement await your investigation, places such as Corvallis, Albany, and Salem (Oregon's capital). Some of the state's best trout fishing can be enjoyed toward the east after a scenic drive to the Diamond Lake area.

Salem   Sometimes called the "Cherry City," Salem is known for flowering orchards in the surrounding countryside. Fertile soil brings bountiful crops of strawberries, raspberries, pears, filberts, and walnuts. The region is becoming known for wine, especially pinot noir, riesling, and chardonnay.

Salem is the third-largest city in Oregon, with a population of 120,000, and its appearance gets a double boost from being both the site of Oregon's state capital and the home of Willamette University. These institutions help keep the downtown alive and thriving. A great deal of commerce and business is generated by both entities. The city has one of the best libraries we've ever seen, not only for its book collection, but also for the public conference rooms available for residents to use for meetings, classes, lectures, and social events. The library is one of the focal points of the community for many retirees, a place to meet people and make friends.

As you might expect of a state capital, the downtown center is vibrant, with nice restaurants, shopping, and excitement in the air, yet with an informality not expected in a capital city. During our last research trip to Salem, a retired couple invited us to one of the local microbreweries for a snack. The place is famous for good hamburgers in addition to its homemade beer. While we were ordering our hamburgers, a couple walked in and sat at the table next to us. They turned out to be Oregon's governor, John Kitzhaber, and his wife, Sharon. Both were dressed casually; he wore his "trademark" blue jeans, sport coat, and tie. Our friends exchanged pleasantries with the governor, and we returned to our conversation. By the way, Governor Kitzhaber is a good friend to retirees. He is a medical doctor and the architect of Oregon's unique health-care program, which is often mentioned as a possible health-care model for the nation.

SALEM WEATHER						
In degrees Fahrenheit						
	Jan.	April	July	Oct.	Rain	Snow
Daily highs	46	62	84	65	40"	6"
Daily lows	34	38	51	42		

For a fairly large city, Salem manages to retain a vestige of small-town atmosphere. Some friends of ours, who retired here from Los Angeles, said, "We thought we'd have a difficult time making friends and keeping busy here. First thing we did was join a church group and register for senior classes at the university. Before long, we had too much to do and more friends than we had before we retired."

Willamette University's contribution to senior learning is another example of why college town retirement is such a good idea. Called the Institute for Continued Learning, this program costs $80 per person for the entire year and includes summer sessions; participation in all twice-weekly seminars; use of the gym, swimming pool and exercise equipment; free tickets to Willamette athletic events; and the use of the copy and learning resource centers. Seminars and lectures are given by noted scholars on a wide variety of subjects, such as literature, music, art, history, philosophy, and current events. Taking classes in a university environment is an excellent way for newcomers to meet friends with common interests and ideas.

Salem is the major care center for many surrounding communities. The largest hospital is a 419-bed facility with a large skilled-care center. The hospital is augmented by a large rehab center.

Portland   Reno, Nevada, bills itself as "The Biggest Little City in the West"; Portland turns this around, claiming the title of "The Biggest Small Town in the West." And it is big, with a million people living in its urban area; the city limits alone include about half a million in population. Portland's influence spreads from the foothills of Mount Hood to the plains of the Coast Range, covering a four-county area.

As an important West Coast seaport, Portland has always supported industry—everything from lumber to light manufacturing. But over the past decade, the city has evolved into a major high-tech center. More than 1,200 technology companies have located here. In addition to many software firms, electronic companies such as Hewlett-Packard, Epson, and NEC have plants in the Portland area. Intel, the high-tech giant, employs 11,000 workers. This makes Portland especially popular with aging computer and Internet specialists who are looking at retirement before long with possible part-time jobs.

PORTLAND WEATHER						
In degrees Fahrenheit						
	Jan.	April	July	Oct.	Rain	Snow
Daily highs	44	60	80	64	37"	6"
Daily lows	34	41	56	45		

PORTLAND AREA COST OF LIVING					
Percentage of	Overall	Housing	Medical	Groceries	Utilities
national average	104	95	115	109	97

Portland works hard to maintain its small-town atmosphere and its second motto, "City of Roses." Fortunately the city's founding fathers incorporated a large number of parks, some quite large, which contribute to a feeling of uncrowded spaciousness. Rolling hills and lots of shade trees extend this feeling into Portland's neighborhoods.

Unlike many American cities, where shopping malls have destroyed downtowns by luring consumers into the suburbs, Portland has managed to keep its central core alive and well, a pleasant place to visit or shop. During the 1970s the city built a transit system and instituted a system of free public transportation in a 340-block downtown area known as Fareless Square. A combination of pedestrian-only streets and free buses makes shopping downtown Portland a pleasure. Well-preserved buildings, upscale shops and restaurants, and good law enforcement complete the picture of a "small-town big city."

Because Portland's cool climate, sophisticated setting, and hilly picturesqueness are reminiscent of San Francisco, Portland draws many retirees from that area. Coming here from one of the most expensive parts of the country is a pleasant surprise for ex–San Franciscans. Lovely Victorian homes, which would cost a fortune where they came from, can be purchased for California tract-home prices. (You realize, of course, that some California tract homes can be expensive.) At least one San Francisco publisher and several authors we know of have made the switch to Portland from "Baghdad by the Bay."

Portland has a reputation for rainy weather, but truthfully, the region gets much less than most places in the Eastern United States, less than 40 inches (compared with Miami's 60 inches). North-western Oregon just seems to have more rain because it mostly falls in the winter months in a long, lazy drizzle rather in vigorous showers. Winter rains can sometimes drag on for several days on end. But glorious spring, summer, and fall weather makes amends for wet winters.

Retirees who live in the Portland area love the convenience of their location. A short drive in one direction takes you to beautiful Pacific beaches. Go the other way and you are in Oregon's famous wine country. Mountains are nearby, with lush forests and rushing trout streams. Not much farther west you'll find yourself in desert country and rugged lava beds.

According to FBI reports on Oregon cities, Portland ranks just below Grants Pass, Oregon, for personal safety. Nationally it ranks about average for cities of similar size. That's not to suggest that Portland is crime-free by any means; like all large cities, its suburbs are generally tranquil, with more crime found on the fringes of downtown.

And although many people prefer living in the various neigh-borhoods near central Portland—again reminiscent of San Fran-cisco's charming neighborhood settings—more retirees like the sections on the fringe of the city. There are too many charming sub-urbs and adjoining towns to begin to mention here, but a couple of the most popular are listed below.

On the west side of the river, and bordered on one side by Forest Park, Portland's Northwest District is an area densely popu-lated by 1920s-era apartments, renovated Victorian homes, and older bungalows. The Northwest District's commercial area is en-dowed with upscale retail shops, restaurants, coffeehouses, theaters, microbreweries, and bookshops. Housing may be a bit on the ex-pensive side, but rentals are plentiful and not outrageous. The Northwest District is a neighborhood for those who like to be in the middle of lots of activity.

The area known as Southwest Hills is a scenic neighborhood that embraces some of the most expensive property in the area. Thirty percent of the residents earn more than $100,000 per year, and housing costs reflect this affluence. Although Portland's city center is just a short drive from Southwest Hills, the district's quiet streets and almost crime-free atmosphere make downtown seem leagues away. Prices of homes drop as you move south from the hillier parts.

The Dalles/Hood River   The drive up the Oregon side of the Columbia River from Portland is another scenic marvel. A half-dozen historic little towns space themselves along the way, with the huge river flowing past, carrying fishing boats, cargo barges, and windsurfers. Two places in particular make wonderful retirement locations: Hood River (pop. 20,000) and The Dalles (pop. 12,000).

The Dalles received its name from French Canadian voyagers who used to "shoot the rapids" here instead of tediously unloading their boats and dragging them around the narrow rapids (which are now buried beneath the dam). The French used the word *dalle* to refer to a place where waters were constrained between high rock walls. They called this exciting stretch of river la *grande dalle de la Columbia,* "the great rapid of the Columbia." Those traveling the Oregon Trail who floated downriver to this point had to portage around the rapids for the final leg of the trip. Others arrived with their wagons and either had to build rafts and float their belongings downriver from this point or detour inland around Mount Hood. Some weary travelers decided to give it up and settle in The Dalles, making it one of the earliest towns in the state. Later on steamboats made their way up the Columbia as far as The Dalles—the trip taking twelve hours and the fare $1.00 round-trip.

Today The Dalles is the center of a thriving agricultural region, with wheat fields and orchards fringing the town limits. It's definitely dry here, with less than half the rainfall of Portland just 100 miles downriver. The Dalles catches about 14 inches of rain (about the same as Los Angeles) and a couple of inches of snow two or three times each year. Summers are warm, often in the nineties, but it's a dry heat, with lots of breeze off the river and almost no rain during July and August.

In the historic downtown shopping district, streets run parallel with the river, full of substantial brick buildings of late 1800s vintage. The town center seems to be active and spared from traffic by

THE DALLES–HOOD RIVER WEATHER						
In degrees Fahrenheit						
	Jan.	April	July	Oct.	Rain	Snow
Daily highs	42	60	90	63	37"	5"
Daily lows	31	38	52	41		

the interstate that bypasses The Dalles. Most major shopping retailers are represented on the edge of town. Residential neighborhoods climb the rather steep hillside behind the town, each street enjoying panoramic views of the Columbia River Gorge and Dallesport Peninsula. At the very top the Columbia Gorge Community College and the large Sorosis Park command the final view across the river into the state of Washington.

Residential neighborhoods are almost sitting on streets that stairstep up the steep hillside. Most homes, therefore, enjoy great views of the river and of the state of Washington in the distance. Residential neighborhoods vary from elegant to economical, something for every pocketbook.

When it was settled in 1854, early residents of Hood River called the community Dog River, but under pressure by housewives the name was changed. This was one of the first places along the Oregon Trail where pioneers found enough rain to grow some of the same kinds of crops they were used to back East. Some of the first things planted were apple trees and strawberries. Today the region is famous for pear and apple orchards.

It's interesting how just a little distance between The Dalles and Hood River (22 miles) makes a real difference in the climate. Hood River gets 30 inches of rain and lots more snow than The Dalles. This extra precipitation makes a big difference in the vegetation as well. Everything is green, even through the summer, and more lush. Still, Hood River gets less precipitation than Portland, or about the same as Des Moines or Detroit.

The downtown business center, varying from 1 to 3 blocks wide, follows along the river. It seems to be holding up well against the heavy shopping competition on the highway leading out of town. Several interesting restaurants and historic buildings with specialty stores draw downtown shoppers. Residential neighborhoods close to the town center vary from comfortable to not-quite-elegant, and most older homes are shaded by large trees. The newer homes away from downtown can be quite upscale and command great views of the Columbia River. Many places, either up or down the river, combine views and acreage. Behind Hood River, ascending the mountain slopes toward Mount Hood, a series of small communities and towns adds to Hood River's regional population—such places as Odell, Dee, and Parkdale.

Oregon Coast

A wonderful, often overlooked, retirement area is found along Washington and Oregon's Pacific coast. North along Highway 101, an inviting string of small towns dot the shore, starting with Brookings, just across the California state line, to Astoria, on Oregon's northern border and on up to Washington's Grays Harbor.

Ask people who retire along this picturesque stretch of coast, and they'll most likely give "wonderful year-round climate" as a major reason for their decision. Forget about air-conditioning and snow shovels. Because it seldom freezes, sweaters or windbreakers are the heaviest winter clothing required. Because midday temperatures rarely top seventy-five degrees, folks here sleep under electric blankets year-round.

However, it's this stretch of Pacific Coast that earns Oregon and Washington a reputation for being rainy. Gold Beach is perhaps the wettest of all, with almost 80 inches per year. Most of it falls in the winter; it would fall as snow somewhere else. The summers are often sunny and dry, although low clouds are also common. This is a great place for part-time retirees, those seeking to escape Arizona's scorching July and August or Florida's muggy summers.

Overcrowding? Coast residents have plenty of elbow room. Along Washington and Oregon's 500-mile stretch of Pacific coastline you'll only find about twenty towns plus a scattering of villages. Most have between 1,000 and 5,000 friendly residents. The only cities are Coos Bay, Astoria, and Aberdeen, and they are just barely large enough to be called cities. Most beaches are deserted, with unrestricted public access guaranteed by state law. Five or ten minutes' drive inland takes you to a low mountain range, the Cascades, with

OREGON COAST WEATHER						
In degrees Fahrenheit						
	Jan.	April	July	Oct.	Rain	Snow
Daily highs	53	54	62	58	65"	1"
Daily lows	41	44	51	48		

thousands of square miles of wilderness—almost all publicly owned or in national forest.

Good fishing, both ocean and river, is another plus. Steelhead, chinook salmon, and rainbow trout lurk in streams flowing from nearby mountains. Clamming, crabbing, and whale-watching are popular activities. The open countryside is perfect for camping, picnicking, or beachcombing as well as golf and horseback riding. White-tailed deer are plentiful, and you might see an occasional black bear or cougar. A large proportion of beachfront is dedicated to public parks and campgrounds, in the midst of the most beautiful seascapes to be found anywhere in the world.

Brookings/Harbor   Just across the California line are the twin towns of Brookings and Harbor. An estimated 30 percent of the population here are retirees. That seems like a low estimate, because retirement is big business along this coast.

Residents love their unusually mild climate, optimistically referring to the area as Oregon's "banana belt." There's some justification, because flowers bloom all year; about 90 percent of the country's Easter lilies are grown here. Rhododendrons and azaleas bloom wildly in the late spring, and an Azalea Festival is held every Memorial Day. Let's face it, bananas don't grow well at all in this banana belt.

When we asked one man why he chose the Brookings–Harbor area for retirement, he invited us into his small travel trailer for coffee. "This is my home," he said proudly. "It's only 25 feet long, but it's all I need as a bachelor and fisherman. My rent is $100 a month, and this trailer cost me $2,800. Paid more than that for my boat. So here I am, gettin' by on my government money and goin' fishin' anytime I care to, which is almost every day."

Like all Oregon coastal towns, Brookings and Harbor have plenty of things for retired folks to do, both organized and do-it-yourself. The main problem, as far as I am concerned, with these smaller towns is the distance from large shopping centers. People who live here insist there's an adequate supply of hardware stores, grocery markets, and the like, but I suppose some of us are spoiled and want huge selections of everything.

Gold Beach   The mighty Rogue River empties into the ocean at Gold Beach. A road follows its course for a few miles inland, passing many retirement places favored by anglers who prize the steelhead and salmon that pass their doors every day. Some folks just can't choose between ocean or river fishing. They have to have both. Behind the town stretches mile after mile of forested wilderness, with trout, steelhead, and salmon streams and deer hunting.

Gold Beach has an interesting history. It derived its name from an incident that started a frantic gold rush back in the forty-niner days. A prospector passing through the area discovered a small quantity of gold mixed in with beach sand. He panned a tiny bit of color and casually mentioned the fact to some other miners. As the word spread the story expanded until gold-mining camps all over California and Oregon fluttered with news of a place where the ocean's waves deposited nuggets of gold in the sand, the beach strewn with riches, there for the gathering. Mining camps in California's Mother Lode all but emptied as miners frantically rushed to the "gold" beach.

Actually gold is rather common on Oregon and California beaches, usually found in black streaks of magnetite sand mixed in with beach terraces. The problem is that it is very fine and difficult to separate from the coarser sand. Back during the Great Depression, when many people had nothing else to do, a lot of gold was gleaned from the beaches, but it was tedious work.

The gold stampede in Gold Beach was short-lived, but some miners, tired of jumping from place to place in search of riches, decided to retire from gold panning and settle down. They started the first retirement community on the Oregon coast. The tradition continues today, with retirement becoming a significant industry.

Single-family homes, cottages, and mobile homes are the general rule, with people living in multigenerational communities rather than strictly adult developments. A small hospital with an emergency room takes care of Gold Beach's medical needs.

As you drive north along the Oregon coast and catch a glimpse of the coast at Port Orford, you will see the ultimate picture-postcard scene. Dramatic rock formations jut from the sea, catching the force of waves, sending spray flying, and then the swells continue on to become gentle breakers on the sandy beach. Beaches here are known for semiprecious stones such as agates, jasper, and jade, as well as being places to look for redwood burls.

Newport The entire Oregon coast, from the California border to the Columbia River, is sprinkled with small towns and villages that make great retirement choices. We can heartily recommend towns such as Port Orford and Bandon as places with great potential for a coastal retirement. Other choices are Florence, Seaside, and Astoria. Some places have retiree populations equal to or greater than those still working. The requirements for living here are a distaste for extreme hot or frigid weather and a love of ocean beaches. An affordable cost of living is the bonus.

Of all these Oregon coast towns, the little city of Newport is our own personal favorite. One reason we like it here is the town's rich diversity of cultural interests and local arts that make it a stimulating place to explore your own creativity. The Newport Performing Arts Center is a vibrant arts community of working artists, talented young people and senior citizens, exuberant volunteers, and dedicated audiences who have developed a year-round season of theater, music, dance, exhibitions, readings, and lectures.

With 9,500 inhabitants Newport strikes a balance between being a village beach community and being large enough to provide all services. The larger city of Corvallis is a 52-mile drive, not too far to go shopping for the day, and Portland is 119 miles away.

Yaquina Bay and the ocean beaches offer an endless array of recreational activities to revitalize and recharge your batteries. Fishing, crabbing, clamming, boating, canoeing, bike riding, kite flying, tidepooling, or taking long walks on the beach are favorite activities, and there's a public golf course at Agate Beach (nine holes, par thirty-six).

Newport's homes are a curious mixture, from older cottage styles in the historic Nye Beach District to beautiful custom-built homes with views. You'll also find condominiums, manufactured homes, retirement villages, and homes on wooded parcels hidden away in the quiet rural countryside. An especially interesting part of Newport is the old port area, "below the bridge," where interesting restaurants, seafood markets, and old buildings remind you of Newport's marine history. Every now and then a filmmaker uses the many colorful spots in and around Newport as a shooting location.

Because the economy here is booming, prices have risen in recent years, yet real estate prices still average below the national median. Many outstanding values can be found in Newport and the surrounding areas of Lincoln County. Newport living alternatives offer unique ocean, bay, and river properties with dramatic sandy beaches, breathtaking rocky shorelines, and hillsides with colorful landscapes and magnificent views.

Oregon High Country

On the sunny side of Oregon's spectacular Cascade Mountains, the high-desert country basks in a moderate climate boasting 263 days of sunshine a year. Rainfall is low enough to call this region a desert, but the sun doesn't get so hot that it discourages vegetation growth, as happens in many desert regions. The high-desert country is not only a place of four seasons, it's a place where winter makes its presence known.

Most moisture falls in the winter, much of that in the form of snow. Because it only takes an average of 1 inch of rain to make 1 foot of snow, the white stuff can really pile up here in the cold season! Snowfall averages 38 inches, with occasional heavy overnight buildups. Unlike most of Oregon, snow tends to stick around here in the high desert. Summers are quite pleasant, almost always sunny, with an average of only fifteen days a year with temperatures higher than ninety degrees. Rarely is one hundred degrees reached.

Bend   A passion for outdoor recreation lures uncounted tourists to Oregon's high-desert city of Bend. Shielded by the nearby Cascade Mountain range, Bend enjoys four distinct seasons, including a livable winter. Tourists enjoy fantastic trout and steelhead fishing, downhill skiing, and rafting through the exciting triple waterfalls of the Deschutes River. They love golfing at one of twenty-six nearby courses, as well as hiking, camping, and exploring the weird lava fields in the region. As might be expected, regular vacationers eventually become retirees, choosing retirement homes in or near the city of Bend. They join the influx of younger newcomers who are attracted by area's booming job market. According to local boosters only Las Vegas, Nevada, is growing at a faster rate than Bend, Oregon.

SUNRIVER–BEND WEATHER					
In degrees Fahrenheit					
	Jan.	April	July	Oct.	Rain	Snow
Daily highs	37	56	84	62	10"	46"
Daily lows	18	30	54	34		

Bend's population is now pegged at 58,000 (up from 25,000 twenty years ago), a very livable town with lovely residential areas and inexpensive country properties just a few minutes from the city center. True, the town suffers from main-artery traffic congestion, especially at the height of the tourist season, but a parkway and a traffic bypass promise to alleviate the problem. All in all, Bend manages to blend high growth and urban sophistication with a relaxed quality of life. It's interesting that the largest growth in newcomers are those in the fifty- to sixty-year-old age group—many work, at least part-time, as consultants or telecommute via their Internet connections. Most newcomers admit that they come here to work or retire primarily because of the nearness of outdoor recreation and the beautiful mountain and forest surroundings.

Although tourism and retirement revenues nourish Bend's expanding economy, local planners work diligently at enticing "living-wage" industries to relocate here, further enhancing the affluence of the region. The city has also done wonders with its old city center. All but abandoned a few years ago as businesses moved to the strip malls, Bend's riverside downtown has become transformed into a pleasant place for shopping, with boutiques, restaurants, and specialty shops of all descriptions. An old-fashioned horse-drawn coach offers to show you the turn-of-the-twentieth century buildings and other highlights of downtown Bend. Wide stretches of green grass along the Deschutes River bestow a restful counterpoint to the old brick and masonry buildings that compose Bend's once-dying business area.

Continuing education, important for today's retirees, is provided by Central Oregon Community College, a popular school that has more noncredit students enrolled than regular students. A large percentage of students are older and take classes for personal growth rather than to achieve occupational goals. The college library is open free of charge to district residents.

The Bend area has a total of four hospitals, all accommodated by an emergency air-ambulance service. The hospital serving Bend is St. Charles Medical Center—a comprehensive facility with 181 beds and 188 physicians on call. The facility maintains a trauma center and an upgraded intensive care unit.

Although economical housing is available, prices have been edging up over the past few years. The average price for a home in late 2002 had risen to almost $160,000. This marks a significant increase over past years, reflecting the pressure of a growing population and making Bend one of Eastern Oregon's more costly communities. The average price for a place on rural acreage was approximately $180,000. Property values outside the city of Bend are determined to a large extent by the availability and quality of water.

Sunriver   Sunriver, a resort retirement community, is an upscale alternative to living in Bend and is a twenty-minute drive away. A self-contained community on 3,300 acres, Sunriver's 1,300 homes range from relatively inexpensive condos to ultradeluxe homes with airstrip access for the family Cessna. A shopping mall, an emergency medical center, and a full complement of services makes Sunriver nearly self-sufficient.

The interesting thing about the layout of the resort is that each house has plenty of land separating it from the next, so even condos don't seem crowded. Hiking paths and 80 miles of paved bike trails pass by each living unit. Two eighteen-hole golf courses, twenty-six tennis courts, two swimming pools, hot tubs, stables, and a racquet club provide summer sports for active retirees. Winter sports are skiing at nearby Mount Bachelor and cross-country skiing over the hiking trails and golf courses.

Of the 1,500 full-time residents, better than half are retired, most from other states. Retired couples are even more strongly represented among the many part-time owners. They spend part of the year there—whichever is their favorite season—and rent their property for other seasons. A close family friend owns a house there, but spends most of her time in Monterey, California. "One of the advantages of owning," she says, "is that if my kids don't want to use the place in the winter ski season or for summer golf, I just call the management company and they generally find tourists who are happy to pay $120 a day for my place." The winter ski tourists and the summer fishing and golf enthusiasts just about cover our friend's payments. This is done through one of several management companies that advertise the rentals, collect the rent, and clean after each tenant leaves.

Something that needs to be stressed about places like Sunriver: They aren't full-service retirement communities. Sunriver isn't a place where you can expect assisted-living or round-the-clock home-care workers to look after you. Instead this is a place for active and alert people—the kind who won't mind an average of 2 feet of snow during winter or who might like to try cross-country skiing. Why is this any different from places in Idaho and Montana? Because, despite the snow, the Oregon High Country doesn't get the severe low temperatures, and spring comes earlier and fall stays longer.

Several smaller towns within easy shopping distance of Bend attract retirees who are looking for lower-cost housing with full access to the recreational and cultural amenities Bend offers. One is Redmond, situated just a half-hour drive from the Cascade Mountains and just minutes from several good fishing lakes and streams full of trout. Just 14 miles north of Bend, residents participate in all that city offers, yet still enjoy a small-town ambience.

The land around Redmond is flat and agricultural, but just a short distance away, the dramatic rock spires and craggy palisades of Smith Rock Park provide a scenic backdrop for the town. In the distance two of Oregon's highest mountains, Mount Hood and Mount Jefferson, are visible.

The mountain town of Sisters sits in the lower Cascades, about a 20-mile drive from either Bend or Redmond. Named for the snow-capped Three Sisters mountain peaks, the town has towering pines and an unusually attractive setting with a rejuvenated, inviting downtown area of quaint Western-looking storefronts, restaurants, and buildings. It's a small town, to be sure, with less than a thousand full-time residents, but tourism is on the rise, and before long Sisters could be much larger. Despite its high-sierra mountain setting, you might be surprised to learn that Sisters is actually 500 feet *lower* in elevation than Bend, with even less winter impact. When we asked the chamber of commerce about average snowfall, the director replied, "That's hard to say. Last year we had no snow that stayed on the ground for more than a few hours. But two years ago we had 8 feet total snow!"

Klamath Falls   An overlooked retirement area, but not overlooked by bargain-hunting California retirees, is Klamath Falls.

KLAMATH FALLS WEATHER						
In degrees Fahrenheit						
	Jan.	April	July	Oct.	Rain	Snow
Daily highs	38	59	85	64	14"	12"
Daily lows	22	33	54	36		

About 18 miles from the California border, Klamath Falls offers a high-desert climate similar to Bend, some 137 miles to the north. Fishing and hunting are great, with camping, nature trails, and sailing on the huge Klamath Lake providing a full range of outdoor activities. Landlocked salmon and steelhead grow to outstanding sizes. Local anglers claim that the average trout taken from the water measures 21 inches. (Would local anglers lie?)

Sitting at an altitude of 4,100 feet, Klamath Falls enjoys a dry climate with 280 days of sunshine and crisp, cold winters. This region experiences much less snow than Bend. In fact the nearest ski resort is about a two-hour drive from here because of this low snowfall. The countryside is definitely a desert environment, with fewer trees (and those you do see are more stunted) until you get into the nearby mountains. The City of Klamath Falls has a population of approximately 19,000, with an additional 25,000 population in the surrounding county. The town looks much larger than that because it spreads far out into the countryside from its old-fashioned, low-key downtown city center. Shopping centers on the southern edge of town have lured away most businesses.

One of Klamath Falls's unique features is an natural underground supply of hot, geothermal water used to heat homes and businesses. This heating source is completely sustainable, nonpolluting, and inexpensive. It warms downtown sidewalks and bridges to keep them frost-free in the winter.

The big drawing card for most retirees (besides excellent trout fishing) is affordable real estate. Housing prices are as low as anywhere we've investigated, and considering the quality of the area, it's perhaps one of the best buys in the country. Another economic benefit here is an unusually low cost of utilities, more than 25 percent below national averages. This helps offset higher heating bills in the winter.

Klamath Falls's Merle West Medical Center serves the Klamath Basin's health-care needs with 176 beds, more than eighty-five physicians, and 1,039 employees. It has cancer and heart centers, and a family practice residency program. There are also a number of smaller clinics, home health-care operations, and several emergency services.

Washington

Oregon has traditionally attracted more West Coast retirees than Washington; however, this is changing. More and more retirees are traveling just a little farther to investigate Washington. The state's electronics and aerospace industries are bringing skilled workers from all parts of the country to join the steady stream of Californians who have been jumping over Oregon to land in Washington. They are pleased to find pleasant living conditions, a mild climate, and moderate housing costs.

Worthy of special mention is Washington's philosophy on state income taxes: It's one of the few states in the country that does not collect them! Furthermore, it's one of those states with laws prohibiting other states from placing liens to collect taxes owed to that other state. Another good idea here is property-tax breaks for the elderly. Under state law, retirees age sixty-one and older with incomes less than $28,000 are entitled to a full exemption from special assessments, and those earning less than $18,000 can be exempt from 30 to 50 percent of regular property taxes. Widows and widowers at least fifty-seven years old whose spouses qualified for exemption at the time of death, and those who are disabled at any age, are also eligible for the property-tax exemption. Retired persons older than age sixty-one with less than $34,000 total income, as well as those who are disabled at any age, can defer their entire property tax indefinitely. When the tax liability reaches 80 percent of the home's equity value, the liability becomes a lien on the property, payable when it is sold or probated.

WASHINGTON TAX PROFILE

Sales tax: 6.5% to 8.2%, food, drugs exempt
State income tax: no
Property taxes: average 1.8% of assessed value; exemptions for those sixty-two and older.
Intangibles tax: no
Social security taxed: no
Pensions taxed: no
Gasoline tax: 23¢ per gallon, plus possible local taxes

The other side of Washington state's no-income tax policy is that money has to come from somewhere, and that somewhere is property and sales tax. Sales taxes start at approximately 8 percent, and property is taxed at 1 percent of its appraised value. Because property values have been increasing at a rapid rate over the last ten years, the burden is growing.

The most popular retirement locations in the state are found in high-quality towns near Seattle and on Puget Sound's network of bays, coves, straits, and inlets. Because so much of Washington's coastline is in Puget Sound, the total land fronting the sea is almost twice as long as Oregon's. This large mass of water moderates temperatures, which rarely drop below freezing or rise above eighty degrees.

Places like Shelton, Sequim, and Port Townsend share Seattle's climate and scenic beauty but also offer the benefits of small-town living. Equally charming are the communities set on islands, large and small, in and around the sound, among them Whidbey Island, Fidalgo Island, and the San Juan Islands. These quaint coastal towns nestled in forests of Douglas fir remind us of New England fishing villages. One drawback is that both Olympic National Park and the San Juan Islands attract tourists by the thousands, which can mean waiting in line for several hours to board a ferry during the summer and on weekends year-round.

All around Puget Sound, however, the cost of living is relatively high. In some places, especially the San Juan Islands, it can be extremely high. More affordable living can be found farther south in seaside communities such as Grayland and Long Beach on the Pacific coast.

Seattle Area

Seattle offers all the advantages of a large city, as well as all the disadvantages. Its setting—between Puget Sound and Lake Washington, with magnificent mountain views in all directions—helps make it one of the more beautiful cities in America. Lofty evergreens shade its parks and suburbs, which blend into the surrounding forest. Its location—on the water and sheltered from Pacific storms by the mountains of the Olympic Peninsula—keeps winters mercifully mild and summers pleasantly cool. There is an all-pervasive community spirit such as is found in few other major cities. As you

might expect from a big city, crime rates are a little higher than in surrounding communities, but for an urban area the safety factor here is reassuring. Most local neighborhoods in Seattle are as safe as you can find anywhere.

It's the high-quality towns near Seattle or on Puget Sound's network of bays, coves, straits, and inlets that makes this such a great retirement choice. Places like Bellingham, Burlington, or Olympia—to name just a few—share in Seattle's climate and scenic beauty, but also offer the benefits of small-town living. Anacortes, for example, located on a peninsula jutting out into the bay, enjoys one of the lowest crime rates in the country. Edmonds is another attractive area, sitting between Seattle and Everett; its downtown is right on the water, with a beach and ferry terminal at the end of the main shopping street.

The San Juan Islands must also be accessed by ferryboat and are among the more popular, albeit expensive, retirement places of the Puget Sound. Real estate prices are a bit high compared with some of the other island complexes nearby, but the quality lifestyle possible here makes it worthwhile. Whidbey Island, another favorite retirement area, has the advantage of being accessible by highway bridges rather than ferry boats.

SEATTLE AREA WEATHER

In degrees Fahrenheit

	Jan.	April	July	Oct.	Rain	Snow
Daily highs	44	57	75	60	39"	7"
Daily lows	35	41	55	46		

SEATTLE AREA COST OF LIVING

	Overall	Housing	Medical	Groceries	Utilities
Percentage of national average	104	105	112	111	91

Bainbridge Island   One of Seattle's most exclusive suburban neighborhoods, Bainbridge Island is linked to the peninsula by a highway bridge and to Seattle by a ferry route. Here you'll find many gracious homes secluded on large estates hidden from casual view by stands of evergreens. The 48-square-mile island is home to 20,000 people, of whom nearly half commute to Seattle on a daily basis. Another island connected to the peninsula, Vashon Island, has a part bucolic, part artsy population of 10,000 and is linked by ferry to Tacoma.

The most intriguing communities on the peninsula are those farthest from the ferries that carry commuters to the urban side of the sound. Poulsbo, a waterfront community 16 miles north of Bremerton, got its start in the 1880s as a fishing village of Norwegian immigrants. The Scandinavian heritage lives on along the town's main street, now filled with art and craft galleries, antiques shops, and waterfront cafes, as well as in annual events ranging from the Viking Fest in May and the Midsommarfest in August to a traditional lutefisk dinner in October and the Christmastime Yule Fest. Hartstene Island, connected by bridge to the southeastern corner of the Kitsap Peninsula, has forests, beaches, and meandering roads that provide access to hundreds of residences concealed deep in second-growth forest.

Olympia   When the town of Olympia was established back in 1846, it was the first settlement in the region. The founding fathers had a vision that Olympia someday would become the capital of the future state, so they provided a hilltop site for the future capitol building. The vision became reality seven years later when Olympia became the capital of the newly formed Washington Territory. The town was modeled after the New England towns where the pioneers came from, with the obligatory central town square and wide, tree-lined streets. Over the years the city has maintained the kind of dignified, not-too-big atmosphere that every state capital should have.

Recent population growth in Washington has resulted in a rapidly expanding state government and a resulting job boom in this region. In the process Olympia has grown to a comfortable-size city of 43,000. It's the commercial center for the neighboring towns of Tumwater and Lacey, which have expanded until they've become almost contiguous. More than half of the area's almost

200,000 residents live in outlying rural areas, which are full of small ranches, vegetable farms, and homes on large acreage.

As the seat of Washington's government, Olympia serves as a proving ground for social programs, including several new intergenerational programs designed to bring together elders and young people. The Grandfolks Brigade places seniors from area retirement communities as mentors in elementary schools, and the Synergy Intergenerational Arts Program fosters creative collaborations between older adults and schoolchildren. One experimental program brings local third-grade students to adult day-care centers as companions to elderly and fragile seniors.

Retired military personnel who discovered the area while stationed at nearby Fort Lewis or McChord Air Force Base account for a sizeable segment of Olympia's active senior community. It's an especially good place for military retirees because it's convenient to commissaries and base hospitals. Another medical facility that serves the Olympia area is St. Peter Hospital, with 314 beds and 450 physicians. The facility can perform all major procedures except heart transplants.

The weather here is typically Pacific Coast mild, although Olympia receives a bit more rain and fog than Seattle and other Puget Sound communities farther to the north. It usually doesn't rain hard, but it rains often, with an average of 230 cloudy days a year. There is more than a trace of rain on 147 of those days and fog on 75 of them.

Shelton   An easy drive from Seattle, the town of Shelton (pop. 8,500 people) is the county seat and only incorporated town in rural Mason County. Traditionally a bedroom community of Olympia, commuters enjoy the county's only stretch of four-lane highway to the city. The area is known as the South Sound. As a place to stay home and enjoy the quiet, peaceful little Shelton and Mason County have a character that is completely different from the Olympia area.

Shelton sits on the edge of Oakland Bay, a saltwater inlet not much wider than a river. Its town center dates from the 1850s when it was a logging camp, but today it boasts dozens of historic buildings dating back to the era between World War I and the Great Depression. (In Washington that's historic; in Boston, that would be recent history.) Then, as now, it provided shopping, banking, schooling, and other services for many smaller logging camps, farms, and fishing villages scattered throughout the area. Even today, two-thirds of Mason County residents live in rural areas away from Shelton. An interesting aspect of the population here: Two Indian tribes, the Skokomish and Squaxin Island people, live on separate reservations within a few miles of Shelton.

Bremerton/Kitsap Peninsula   Bremerton, the site of the Puget Sound Naval Shipyards, is directly across Puget Sound from Seattle. The 37,000 population here is predominantly military personnel and their dependents, being the site of western Washington's largest military base. Bremerton itself clearly lacks the Pacific Northwest charm that lures retirees to the Puget Sound region. However, within a few minutes' drive of the dock where ferries arrive from Seattle, you'll find custom-built homes and vacation cabins hidden along rustic unpaved country lanes that wind through the forests of the Kitsap Peninsula.

In fact nowhere else in the region will you find so many secluded woodland homes and homesites so close to a major urban area. Many retirees on the Kitsap Peninsula first discovered the unique area while stationed here in the military. A large number of houses here are used as weekend getaways by Seattle residents. Eventually they plan to use their places as retirement homes, either on a full-time or part-time basis. The marvelously scenic ferry ride from Bremerton to downtown Seattle takes about fifty minutes—not bad when you consider that it takes just as long to get downtown from many Seattle suburbs such as Edmonds, Lynnwood, or Bellevue.

Port Townsend   Port Townsend, with its carefully preserved Victorian architecture and magnificent vistas of sea and glacier-clad peaks, may well be Washington's prettiest town. As the original shipping port on Puget Sound, it prospered from the 1860s to the 1890s. Because the architecture of this epoch has been carefully preserved, the entire town of Port Townsend has been designated a National Historic Landmark. Sitting on the northwesternmost tip of the Olympic Peninsula at the mouth of Puget Sound, Port Townsend is just remote enough from the Seattle metropolitan area to be out of the question for commuting to the city.

Because of brisk tourist trade in season, Port Townsend has become home to many artists, crafters, and bed-and-breakfast

PORT TOWNSEND WEATHER					
In degrees Fahrenheit					
	Jan.	April	July	Oct.	Rain	Snow
Daily highs	44	59	76	61	49"	4"
Daily lows	33	41	53	45		

innkeepers. In the off-season, the town slows down so much that many locals migrate south to sunnier, livelier climes until spring.

Port Townsend has been described a split-level town. A neighborhood of stately Victorian homes and churches surrounds the ornate courthouse, overlooking the water from atop limestone cliffs as much as a hundred feet high. At the foot of the cliffs, red-brick buildings preserve the memory of bygone days when Port Townsend was reputed to be the roughest seaport on the West Coast. Then the commercial district around the docks was filled with saloons and bordellos; today they have been replaced by restaurants and art galleries.

The oceangoing ships of former times are gone. Some of the old docks have decayed away to leave only stubs of pilings standing in rows far out into the water, ideal perches for seagulls and pelicans. At the center of the old waterfront is the modern Washington State Ferries dock. There is no direct service from Port Townsend to Seattle; car ferries run frequently to Whidbey Island, where an 18-mile drive takes motorists to another ferry that carries them to the mainland at Mukilteo, an Everett suburb about an hour by interstate north of Seattle. In other words a trip to the city can take all day. In the summer a private ferry company offers daily passenger service to the San Juan Islands from the same docks.

Living and housing costs in Port Townsend are similar to those in most other communities on the Olympic Peninsula.

Sequim   Sequim (pronounced "Skwim") has a reputation as Washington's top retirement haven. Hundreds of older newcomers move to Sequim each season, contributing to phenomenal growth: The area population has risen from 4,000 residents a decade ago to 25,000 today. Less than 15 percent of the populace lives in Sequim's small town center; the rest live in suburban and semi-rural areas of the surrounding Dungeness Valley. The town of Sequim itself has about 4,500 inhabitants.

The main factor accounting for Sequim's rise to retirement mecca status is the weather, which has earned the area its nickname, the "Banana Belt." More than any other western Washington community, Sequim is protected from foul weather by the rain shadow of Mount Olympus, the massive peak 30 miles to the southwest. The town receives approximately the same annual rainfall as Los Angeles, and the sun shines 306 days a year. Average annual rainfall increases 1 inch per mile going west from Sequim, and almost as much going east.

Although Sequim lacks the architectural charm of other nearby towns, notably Port Townsend, the downtown area has a growing number of antiques shops, as well as galleries that show the work of artists and crafters who make their homes in the area.

Seafood gourmands prize the local Dungeness crabs. The sunshine factor makes Sequim a great place for gardening. Flowers, vegetables, and fruits thrive and sometimes reach prodigious size. Several raspberry and strawberry farms in the area let you pick your own baskets of berries in season for a small charge. Area growers sell their produce at the Sequim Farmer's Market every Saturday during the summer months.

San Juan Islands   The San Juan Islands, in the northern portion of Puget Sound, are one of the scenic wonders of the entire country. The islands, with rocky shorelines, coves, and bays, are covered with tall evergreens and are often separated from their neighbors by sometimes narrow channels. More than 400 islands comprise this group, but only sixty are inhabited and only four have ferry service. These four islands—San Juan, Orcas, Lopez, and Shaw—have about 10,000 residents altogether, an estimated half of them retired.

The San Juan Islands are not for everyone; they appeal to a special type who values scenery over conveniences. Because ferry service is very slow, often involving long waits, commuting to a job is hardly practical. The islands are basically residential, with almost no available jobs for newcomers, other than those that can be done by Internet connections. Residents tend to be either retired, writers or artists, or else those wealthy enough to afford a place here as a second home. Those who choose to settle here must enjoy cool weather, because the average July high temperatures are only seventy

SAN JUAN ISLANDS WEATHER					
In degrees Fahrenheit					
	Jan.	April	July	Oct.	Rain	Snow
Daily highs	44	57	70	58	29"	1"
Daily lows	34	40	49	44		

degrees. Finally, because island property is becoming more expensive as time goes by, those who retire here must be able to afford to the housing costs. Those who do fit this profile clearly feel that the high-quality lifestyle, tranquillity, and beautiful surroundings make it all worthwhile.

One possible drawback about living here is health care. At the time of writing there is neither a hospital nor an around-the-clock medical facility. For emergencies you'll have to rely on a doctor who lives on San Juan Island who is on call twenty-four hours a day; for more serious problems, you'll have to take a helicopter to a mainland hospital. For routine health care there are medical centers on San Juan, Lopez, and Orcas Islands.

Real estate is among the most costly in the Northwest. Property is priced in three categories, depending upon location. The most expensive category is waterfront, where you have can have a dock and a boat. Next is view property, with prices depending on how gorgeous the view of the water and nearby islands (these can be spectacular). And the third category is "inland, no view." But even these can be expensive. Rentals and condos are almost nonexistent.

Port Angeles   The largest town on the Olympic Peninsula, Port Angeles (pop. 18,500) is the main gateway to Olympic National Park. This fact alone makes it an appealing choice for nature lovers. Besides limitless hiking trails and unparalleled wildlife watching, the park has special programs that provide volunteer opportunities for senior citizens.

Port Angeles itself is a busy town that stretches along the waterfront. Its two parallel main streets and the downtown area, small enough for walking, are complete with turn-of-the-twentieth-century architecture in need of a fresh coat of paint. A long waterfront park has paved hiking trails and well-groomed woodlands. Growth has been slow and steady, so residential areas contain a mix of older and contemporary homes.

PORT ANGELES WEATHER						
In degrees Fahrenheit						
	Jan.	April	July	Oct.	Rain	Snow
Daily highs	44	54	67	57	49"	—
Daily lows	36	40	51	44		

Homesteaders came to the mountain valleys around Port Angeles long before the creation of the national forest and national park, so the fringe areas around the park are a patchwork quilt of federal and private land. You'll find houses of every description, from rustic log cabins to contemporary custom-built homes, many of them secluded miles in on unpaved forest roads. The area's rural residents actually outnumber the population of Port Angeles itself.

Recreation and hiking enthusiasts will find hundreds of miles of trails of every length and difficulty in Olympic National Park. The park is also one of the best places in Washington for wildlife viewing. The Port Angeles area is a great place for saltwater and freshwater fishing, with four public boat launches inside the city limits. Favorite catches are black-mouth salmon and halibut. Clams, crabs, and shrimp are also abundant in offshore waters. Anglers cast in dozens of nearby rivers and lakes for steelhead, cutthroat, and rainbow trout. Fishing charters and river float trips are available in season.

Whidbey Island Whidbey Island was known as a retirement area long before the first senior citizen thought of moving to Sequim. Langley, a residential community on the southwest shore of the island, is nicknamed "Port of the Sea Captains" because it has been a favorite retirement spot for mariners for more than a century.

Measuring 55 miles from north to south, Whidbey Island is the longest island in the United States—a distinction it gained in 1985 when the U.S. Supreme Court ruled that Long Island, New York, was actually a peninsula. It has the advantage of being accessible by highway bridge, but only from the north. Frequent ferries carry vehicles and passengers from terminals on the island to both Mukilteo, north of Seattle, and Port Townsend on the Olympic Peninsula.

Whidbey Island is predominantly rural in character, with three towns and a scattering of tiny villages along the protected coast that faces the mainland across Skagit Bay and the Saratoga Passage. The biggest town on the island is Oak Harbor, with a population of

20,000, including many personnel from nearby Whidbey Naval Air Station; however, the county seat of Island County (Whidbey Island, that is), is little Coupeville, an old-fashioned, Victorian-era port town of 1,800. For the most part Whidbey Island residents live on small dairy and truck-produce farms nestled in the fir trees that line a seemingly endless labyrinth of nameless little paved roads.

Whidbey Island is the place to go if the ultimate in peace and quiet is your goal. Any kind of excitement is highly unlikely here; in fact retirees we've talked to in such laid-back places as Sequim, Port Townsend, and Anacortes dismiss the prospect of life on Whidbey Island as "too boring." Boredom gives way to congestion on sunny weekends and during the summer months, when day-trippers from the Seattle area arrive as fast as the ferries can carry them and clog the island's only highway with bumper-to-bumper traffic bound for Deception Pass State Park and other popular recreation areas.

Beyond Seattle

Bellingham   If any area of the northwestern Washington coast can claim to be "undiscovered," it is Whatcom County, which stretches along the Canadian border from the Straits of Georgia shoreline to the crest of the North Cascades.

The population center of Whatcom County is Bellingham, a city of 68,000 people located 18 miles south of the Canadian border. The setting, on a series of hills along Bellingham Bay, is as spectacular as the most romantic of Pacific Northwest daydreams. Many neighborhoods and parks have beautiful views of the San Juan Islands across the water to the west, and just a few miles to the east rises 10,775-foot Mount Baker in all its glacier-clad majesty. Although Bellingham is situated just off Interstate 5, a mere ninety-minute drive north of Seattle, it's historic charm has never been overwhelmed by the growth boom that has transformed other cities to the south.

Over the years Bellingham has developed an intriguing cultural mix. Through much of the twentieth century, the town's economy depended mainly on Canadians from Victoria and Vancouver,

British Columbia, who came south to buy U.S.-made goods duty-free. Though the North American Free Trade Agreement is gradually eliminating import tariffs between Canada and the United States, you still see about as many British Columbia license plates as Washington ones in shopping mall parking lots. As the site of Western Washington University, Bellingham has a college student population of nearly 11,000. It is also one of the favorite communities in Washington among aging hippies and enlightenment seekers. Smaller neighboring villages retain distinctive Dutch and Scottish influences from early settlement days. In addition approximately 5,000 Lummi and Nooksack Indians make their homes on two nearby reservations.

Senior residents find that it's hard to get bored in Bellingham. The exceptionally active senior center offers more than sixty classes, health programs, and social events each week. Additional activities are offered by AARP and the Older Women's League (OWLS). Whatcom County Senior Services sponsors low-cost boat, train, and bus trips to destinations throughout Washington, Oregon, and even Alaska. Independent-living apartments including dinner, transportation, and social activities are available at the Willows Retirement Community near St. Joseph's Hospital.

Pasco/Kennewick   Earlier in this chapter I poked fun at Pasco because of its dry, desertlike surroundings. Actually it's a highly productive wheat-producing area and has grown immensely over the years since I worked there. Most neighborhoods are new here, a consequence of fast growth during the past two decades, and an overall prosperity is evident.

PASCO AREA WEATHER						
In degrees Fahrenheit						
	Jan.	April	July	Oct.	Rain	Snow
Daily highs	37	64	89	65	16"	6"
Daily lows	20	35	53	35		

PASCO–KENNEWICK COST OF LIVING					
Percentage of	Overall	Housing	Medical	Groceries	Utilities
national average	100	98	122	99	90

Although Pasco may not live up to the damp and green expectations most folks have of Washington, there are certain advantages to living in the eastern part of the state. Besides being a place that actively seeks retirees, the Pasco–Kennewick–Richland area offers great real estate prices and an interesting climate. Even in the coldest part of winter, when the temperature dropped to twenty degrees in the morning, I could be fishing that same afternoon on the Columbia River bank in my shirtsleeves. Like rain, snowfall here is slight; it didn't snow at all the winter we lived in Pasco. Sunshine was plentiful, and being outdoors was a pleasure year-round. A low-humidity summer rounds out the weather picture.

Fishing for salmon and sturgeon are favorite outdoor sports.

Vancouver   Sitting on the north bank of the magnificent Columbia River, the city of Vancouver is but a short commute across a scenic bridge to metropolitan city of Portland, Oregon. Some might consider Vancouver to be one of Portland's numerous bedroom communities, but with a population of 144,000, that designation is somewhat misleading. Vancouver's city center is lively, dynamic, and self-contained. Vancouver high-tech manufacturing, traditional industry, and small businesses provide ample employment opportunities that do not entail commuting.

One difference between Vancouver and Portland is that Vancouver's residential neighborhoods tend to have larger lots for homes, yet smaller price tags. More than 40 miles of river frontage set the tone for a community that offers recreation and leisure as well as a vibrant, well-balanced economy. Always within view, the startling beauty of Mount St. Helens and the challenging ski slopes of Mount Hood are just a short drive away.

Like neighboring Portland, wet, mild winters and moderately dry summers are typical of Southwest Washington. With year-round golf and fishing galore, the region offers year-round enjoyment of the beauty that is the Pacific Northwest.

VANCOUVER WEATHER						
In degrees Fahrenheit						
	Jan.	April	July	Oct.	Rain	Snow
Daily highs	44	60	80	64	16"	6"
Daily lows	34	41	56	35		

A most significant difference between Vancouver and Portland is the matter of taxes. As mentioned earlier, the state of Washington does not impose a state income tax, whereas the state of Oregon does not collect a state sales tax. As you can imagine, both states make up for the loss of tax revenue by collecting it through property taxes. (Can't win, can we?) But residents of Vancouver have it both ways. They pay no taxes on income, yet by crossing over the Columbia River bridge, they can make major purchases in Oregon and avoid sales tax! Property taxes? Well, we can't have everything, can we?

The Vancouver Parks and Recreation Department presents an awesome array of services and programs for seniors. Its Marshall Luepke Center offers a series of tours that would put a travel agency to shame.

Upriver on the Washington side of the Columbia are several delightful little towns strung along a winding, scenic road. Camas, Washougal, and Skamania are close enough to the city for convenience but not so close as to feel overwhelmed by it. The river's bank rises from the waterline, with streets forming tiers that provide scenic views for the towns' homes. There's an exceptionally peaceful air about this stretch of river, a combination of woods, meadows, and steep hills that invites retirement.

Index

About the Author

John Howells and his wife, Sherry, spent many months of travel by automobile, motor home, and airplane gathering information to produce this book. They interviewed retired folks in all sections of the country, collecting experiences, advice, and valuable insights into successful retirement lifestyles.

John has written and coauthored several other books about retirement locations. Among them are *Choose the South, Choose Mexico,* and *Choose Costa Rica.* He also writes about retirement and travel for mature Americans in magazines such as *Consumers Digest* and *Where to Retire Magazine.* He was a member of the board of directors of the American Association of Retirement Communities. John and his wife live in California and Costa Rica.